First and Second Chronicles

Westminster Bible Companion

Series Editors

Patrick D. Miller
David L. Bartlett

First and Second Chronicles

PAUL K. HOOKER

Westminster John Knox Press
LOUISVILLE
LONDON·LEIDEN

Book design by Publishers' WorkGroup
Cover design by Drew Stevens

First edition

Published by Westminster John Knox Press
Louisville, Kentucky

This book is printed on acid-free paper that meets the American National Standards Institute Z39.48 standard. ∞

PRINTED IN THE UNITED STATES OF AMERICA

01 02 03 04 05 06 07 08 09 10 — 10 9 8 7 6 5 4 3 2 1

Library of Congress Cataloging-in-Publication Data
Hooker, Paul K.
   First and Second Chronicles / Paul K. Hooker.—1st ed.
      p. cm. — (Westminster Bible companion)
   Includes bibliographical references.
   ISBN 0-664-25591-4 (pbk.)
   1. Bible. O.T. Chronicles—Commentaries. I. Series.

BS1345.53 .H66 2001
222'.6077—dc21   2001035516

H46884293

Contents

Series Foreword

This series of study guides to the Bible is offered to the church and more specifically to the laity. In daily devotions, in church school classes, and in listening to the preached word, individual Christians turn to the Bible for a sustaining word, a challenging word, and a sense of direction. The word that scripture brings may be highly personal as one deals with the demands and surprises, the joys and sorrows, of daily life. It also may have broader dimensions as people wrestle with moral and theological issues that involve us all. In every congregation and denomination, controversies arise that send ministry and laity alike back to the Word of God to find direction for dealing with difficult matters that confront us.

A significant number of lay women and men in the church also find themselves called to the service of teaching. Most of the time they will be teaching the Bible. In many churches, the primary sustained attention to the Bible and the discovery of its riches for our lives have come from the ongoing teaching of the Bible by persons who have not engaged in formal theological education. They have been willing, and often eager, to study the Bible in order to help others drink from its living water.

This volume is part of a series of books, the Westminster Bible Companion, intended to help the laity of the church read the Bible more clearly and intelligently. Whether such reading is for personal direction or for the teaching of others, the reader cannot avoid the difficulties of trying to understand these words from long ago. The scriptures are clear and clearly available to everyone as they call us to faith in the God who is revealed in Jesus Christ and as they offer to every human being the word of salvation. No companion volumes are necessary in order to hear such words truly. Yet every reader of scripture who pauses to ponder and think further about any text has questions that are not immediately answerable simply by reading the text of scripture. Such questions may be about historical and geographical details or about words that are obscure or so loaded with meaning that one cannot tell at a glance what is at stake. They may be about the fundamental meaning of a passage or about what connection a particular text might have to our contemporary world. Or a teacher preparing for a church school class may simply want to know: What should I say about this biblical passage when I have to teach it next Sunday? It is our hope that these volumes, written by teachers and pastors with long experience studying and teaching Bible in the church, will help members of the church who want and need to study the Bible with their questions.

The New Revised Standard Version of the Bible is the basis for the interpretive comments that each author provides. The NRSV text is presented at the beginning of the discussion so that the reader may have at hand in a single volume both the scripture passage and the exposition of its meaning. In some instances, where inclusion of the entire passage is not necessary for understanding either the text or the interpreter's discussion, the presentation of the NRSV text may be abbreviated. Usually, the whole of the biblical text is given.

We hope this series will serve the community of faith, opening the Word of God to all the people, so that they may be sustained and guided by it.

Introduction

Sensitive readers often find that reading the Bible generates more questions than answers. Certainly that experience is not foreign to readers of 1 and 2 Chronicles. Who is the writer of Chronicles? When was it written? Why was it written? What is the relationship of 1 and 2 Chronicles to other biblical history? Why does the Old Testament contain this work, which seems on its surface to duplicate much of what is written in the books of 1 and 2 Samuel and 1 and 2 Kings? We will try to answer some of these questions in this introduction.

1. What is a "Chronicle," and why is this book part of the Old Testament? We are most familiar with the title "Chronicle" from the realm of the press; "Chronicle" is a frequent title for a newspaper. That is not a bad way to start defining the meaning of the term in the ancient world. A chronicle is a time-oriented record of events. Ancient Near Eastern cultures from Egypt to Persia kept chronistic—that is, time-oriented—accounts of events in the kingdom or the royal court. The Assyrian Royal Inscriptions and the Babylonian Chronicles are fairly well-known examples of such royal chronicles, recorded at the behest of the king or temple leadership and preserving official accounts of major events for the preceding year.

"Chronicles" is not the earliest title for the work. The actual Hebrew title of the work we now have as 1 and 2 Chronicles is "the books of days." This title presents the work as a record (although certainly not a daily one) of the events of the Israelite monarchy. As such, it would seem to offer an alternative to the account of the same time in 1 and 2 Kings. In fact, 1 and 2 Chronicles have both great similarities to and great differences with the Kings account. Emphasis on the differences between the two accounts undoubtedly led to the title of the work in the Septuagint (the Greek translation of the Old Testament): "the things left out." The title "Chronicles" was first applied by the Christian scholar Jerome in the fourth century A.D.

1

Its place in the canon has also not been constant. In the Hebrew canon, it is found at the end of the third and last great section, commonly called "the Writings." Its position there may be intended to imply that the canon covers the entire story of Israel from the beginnings of creation in Genesis to the restoration of Israel from the Babylonian exile at the end of 2 Chronicles. When the Hebrew scriptures were translated into Greek, 1 and 2 Chronicles were repositioned after 1 and 2 Kings; both works were understood as historical writings, an assessment early Jewish scholars may not have shared. Modern translations have retained the positioning of the Greek and therefore also the perception that 1 and 2 Chronicles offers an alternative history to that presented in the Samuel-Kings complex.

But one cannot avoid the question raised by the apparent duplication of the two accounts: Why is it necessary to include Chronicles at all? The answer may be the same as the logic for including four Gospels in the New Testament: that they arise from different contexts and articulate different theological emphases. The Samuel-Kings narrative came to its final form at a point during the Babylonian exile, when exiled Judahites were seeking to come to terms with the reasons for the disastrous fall of Judah and Jerusalem and the destruction of the Temple in 587 B.C. The judgment of the Deuteronomistic History (the name most scholars apply to the Samuel-Kings account) is that the disaster of 587 B.C. was the result of the faithlessness of Israel and Judah, especially on the part of the monarchy (see 2 Kings 25). The Chronicles account, on the other hand, dates from the Persian period (see below, question 2) during a time of relative stability for Israel. The central issues of the time are no longer the explanation for the past catastrophe but the exploration of the future. The issues before Chronicles are thus questions about structure and self-awareness: the establishment (or reestablishment) of religious and cultural institutions and national identity. By including Chronicles alongside the Samuel-Kings account, the Old Testament offers us a vision of the community of faith reflecting on its own past and drawing from the experience new insights appropriate to its changing circumstances. Nothing less than this ongoing reflective process lies at the heart of continued study of and preaching on the biblical story by both Jewish and Christian communities even today.

2. What is the historical background of Chronicles? This commentary takes the position that Chronicles dates from the Persian period (see below, question 3). A word about the history of this period (538–333 B.C.) is appropriate.

After the Persian conquest of Babylon in 538 B.C., many of the peoples removed from their homelands by Babylonian kings and resettled in other parts of the empire were allowed by their new Persian overlords to return to their homes and rebuild their national identities. One such people were the Jews who had been exiled by the Babylonians following the destruction of Jerusalem in 587 and resettled not far from Babylon. Sometime after the Persian conquest of Babylon in 538, Cyrus permitted groups of Jews to return to Jerusalem to rebuild the city and its Temple, and he organized the old kingdom of Judah as the province of Judea in the Persian imperial government.

Not all the exiles leaped at the chance to return. Instead, it seems that groups of Jews left Babylon and headed for Jerusalem in rather a piecemeal fashion, and that some Jews never returned at all, choosing instead to remain in Babylon or other foreign lands. For those who did choose to return, the Persian king provided some assistance, principally in the form of authorized leadership. Early in the Persian period, some Jews returned under the leadership of Joshua and Zerubbabel, the latter of which seems to have borne the title "governor," and was presumably a Persian appointee. Under Zerubbabel's leadership, the rebuilding of the Temple was begun about 520 (Ezra 3:3) and was apparently completed around 515 (Ezra 6:15). Later on, probably about 458, another group of Jews returned to Jerusalem, this time under the leadership of the priest Ezra (Ezra 8). Ezra's work focused on the promulgation of a new Torah, or Law, to govern the life of the city; that law is probably the books of Genesis through Deuteronomy, or something very like them in content (Nehemiah 8). Ezra was also responsible for seeking to regulate the function of the Temple (Ezra 7). In 445, a third group arrived in Jerusalem under the leadership of Nehemiah, a Jewish official in the Persian court. Nehemiah was, like Zerubbabel, the governor of the province that included Jerusalem, and he had as a specific responsibility the rebuilding and strengthening of the city walls (Nehemiah 2—6).

Life in Persian Judea continued relatively peacefully through the fifth and much of the fourth centuries B.C. Toward the middle of the fourth century, however, Persian authority and strength began to show clear signs of decay. Persia lost its influence in the Greek-speaking cities along the Aegean coast of Asia Minor, and in Egypt a revolt successfully threw off Persian overlordship. Then in 336, Alexander claimed the throne in Macedonia and began organizing resistance to the Persians throughout Asia Minor in preparation for a great campaign into the Middle East. The result of that campaign was the Greek victory at Issus in 333, followed later by the death of the last Persian king. In the year after Issus, Alexander extended his control over Palestine and Egypt, and then set out to push the frontiers of Greek authority all the way to the Indus River in modern India. In the process, wherever Greek soldiers went, they left

behind Hellenism—the Greek culture, values, and way of life. The coming of Hellenism dramatically changed the theological, political, social,
and economic landscape of Judea, opening the doorways toward the
world of the New Testament.

Chronicles belongs to the Persian period. It was written in an era of
peace and stability in Judea and Jerusalem, during which there was time
to reflect on what it means to be the people of God. The great issues
before Chronicles are the struggles to reestablish .the operation of the
Temple and redefine the very identity of the people of Israel. Even
though its subject matter is the story of an Israel that ceased to exist as a
political entity in 587 with the destruction of Jerusalem and the Temple,
it nonetheless reflects through that story on lessons for its own time.

3. *When was Chronicles written, and who wrote it?* A conclusive
answer to the question of authorship will almost certainly elude us. I have
suggested above that the work comes from the Persian period, and this
conclusion is supported by details within the text. In 1 Chronicles 29:7,
the text mentions a "daric," a Persian coin not minted before 515 B.C., so
the date of the work can be no earlier than the end of the sixth century
B.C. In 2 Chronicles 16:9, there appears a quotation of Zechariah 4:10,
implying that the words of Zechariah were sufficiently well-known by the
time of the composition of Chronicles as to be cited without reference.
Since Zechariah was at work in Jerusalem in the years immediately following the initial return of Israelites from exile (about 520–515 B.C.), the
composition of Chronicles must postdate this period. The text of
Chronicles shows no evidence of influence by Greek or Hellenistic
thought, and so it is reasonable to assume that it came to form before the
Greek conquest of Palestine by Alexander in the years following 333 B.C.
Clearly, Chronicles dates from the Persian era (ca. 515–ca 330).

Within this range, we can take note of several clues, although they are
more speculative in nature. First, the system of Temple operation that the
Chronicler details (albeit anachronistically ascribed to David) appears
stable and extensive; one might imply from this that some time has passed
between the reconstruction of the Temple (completed about 515) and the
writing of Chronicles. Tradition associates the writer of Ezra and
Nehemiah with the writer of Chronicles, largely because the last verses
of 2 Chronicles 36 and the first verses of Ezra 1 are nearly identical. If
the same writers composed both pairs of works (but this is questionable;
see next paragraph), we might place his work in the second half of the
fifth century B.C., or after 450. More precise dating appears to be impossible on the basis of available information.

Who wrote Chronicles? Once again, the answer proves elusive. Jewish
tradition preserved in the Talmud credits Ezra as the author of not only

the book that bears his name but Nehemiah and Chronicles as well. That position was the consensus of most scholars until recent decades, with minor variations. Perhaps the most significant such variation is the proposal that there were a series of editions of Chronicles, one appearing soon after the return of the exiles to Jerusalem (about 520–515), a second completed after the arrival of Ezra in Jerusalem from Persia (458), and a final version including the genealogies in 1 Chronicles 1—9, completed about 400. Even in this proposal, however, the assumption is that the final version or versions derive from the hand of Ezra.

The claim that the author of Ezra-Nehemiah is also responsible for Chronicles has rested on three main observations. First, Ezra 1:1–3a is identical to 2 Chronicles 36:22–23, leading to the conclusion by many that the two works, although inscribed on different scrolls, were intended to be read continuously. Indeed, the apocryphal book 1 Esdras describes events from 2 Chronicles 35—36 and Ezra 1 in consecutive narratives, perhaps implying that there was no interruption in the account. Second, several scholars have pointed to a number of similarities in the language and style of Chronicles and Ezra-Nehemiah, which they cite as evidence of common authorship. Third, scholars have argued that the two works share certain theological concerns and emphases, most notably their common fondness for genealogy, their concentration on the Temple and religious ritual, and their enhancement of the position of Levites.

Recent scholarship, however, has begun to challenge the assumption that Ezra-Nehemiah and 1 and 2 Chronicles come from the same author. It has been argued that the list of stylistic and linguistic similarities used to support the case for common authorship is actually much smaller than previously thought and that significant differences are also manifest between the two. Further, there are important theological differences between the two works. In Ezra-Nehemiah, more attention is paid to traditions about the northern kingdom, Israel, than in Chronicles. In Chronicles, the doctrine of moral responsibility plays an important role (see below, question 4); in Ezra-Nehemiah, on the other hand, it plays no role at all. For Chronicles, the figure of the prophet as the spokesman for God is a prominent feature of the narrative; in Ezra-Nehemiah, prophecy makes no appearance.

While none of these reasons can fairly be regarded as conclusive in overturning the case for common authorship in Chronicles and Ezra-Nehemiah, the accumulation of such evidence means that we cannot simply assume common authorship either. Perhaps the best that can be said, then, is that the two works are the products of the same general school of theological thought, if not from the same hand. Throughout this commentary, we will refer to the author of 1 and 2 Chronicles as "the

Chronicler"; this is the practice of the majority of scholars. We shall refer to him as male, simply because the likelihood is small that a woman would have been writing so large a work at the time; we are, of course, unable to be sure about the author's gender.

What else can be said of the Chronicler beyond the uncertainty about his identity with Ezra? Unfortunately, very little else is known. However, from a careful reading of the text, one can imply at least a few characteristics. His fascination with and attention to details about the Temple operations, especially the large role he gives to the Levites, has led many to suspect that he may have been a Levite. While this cannot be ascertained, it is at least clear that he knew the Temple and its systems of staffing and operation intimately. He also was clearly well read in the literature of Israel. He makes extensive use of a wide variety of biblical sources, especially the Samuel-Kings narrative (see below, question 5). But his use of older literature is not confined to direct quotation; instead, the Chronicler edits and/or augments his source material in the service of his own theological interests. He displays thereby some skill as an editor and exegete, and as a theologian. The fact that Jerusalem is regarded as the center of the events described in Chronicles leads to the impression that the Chronicler was an inhabitant of the city.

4. What is Chronicles all about? The Chronicler had reasons for undertaking this great retelling of the history of Israel, and those reasons emerge as themes within the work itself.

God is active in human history, and especially in the history of Israel. For the Chronicler, history is the stage on which is acted out the drama of divine grace and command. Both the grace and the command have their roots in the very beginnings of humankind and are traceable through the long genealogy of the people of Israel and Judah. But they flower most fully in the dynasty of David in the southern kingdom of Judah.

From the Chronicler's vantage, there is a direct relationship between the acts of the king and the good or evil that God brings upon him. Throughout this commentary we will refer to this relationship as the doctrine of moral responsibility (other commentaries use the term "retribution"; unfortunately, this term carries principally negative connotations in our era that do a disservice to the Chronicler's theology). It implies that acts of good or evil are rewarded or punished within the lifetime of the one who commits them. Unlike the theology of 1 and 2 Kings, which argues that the faithlessness of past kings, especially Manasseh, was so great that later generations had to bear the punishment for it in the form of the Babylonian exile, 1 and 2 Chronicles works carefully to insure that the life of each king reflects behavior that justifies the events which befall him. For this reason, the Chronicler must rehabilitate the reputation of those kings who seem rewarded with blessings such as long life or military success (see the story of Manasseh in 2 Chron. 33:10–17) and explain the sufferings of otherwise good kings whose behavior seems not to warrant their situation (see the story of Uzziah's leprosy in 2 Chron. 26:16–21).

We must be clear, however, that the Chronicler's doctrine of moral responsibility is not a mechanistic quid pro quo arrangement. Rather, its purpose is always reconciliatory. Throughout the story of Israel and Judah, the God who holds human beings accountable for their behavior also consistently warns and forgives. Solomon's great prayer at the dedication of the Temple echoes one theme over and over as it rehearses the various ill fates that befall Israel: the call to God to "hear and forgive" (2 Chron. 6:21). God matches the prayer with the divine commitment, "I will hear from heaven, and will forgive their sin" (2 Chron. 7:14). The Chronicler is theologically realistic in that he knows that evil deeds engender evil consequences that cannot be avoided in life. But he is also theologically hopeful, and he holds out continually the possibility that a sinful people may yet "seek the LORD" and be reconciled.

God calls a particular people, Israel, into special relationship. From the beginning of his work, the Chronicler argues that the call of Israel into relationship with God lies at the heart of God's intention for creation. The genealogies of 1 Chronicles 1–9 make the point by their gradual narrowing of focus, beginning with the origins of humankind and proceeding to the selection of a single family, the descendants of Jacob, through whom the story will proceed. The sense conveyed here is that the emergence of Israel onto the world scene is the result of the divine plan for the human race and the center of human history.

Within the Chronicler's narrative, "Israel" includes all the descendants of Jacob. This is somewhat problematic historically because, after the death of Solomon, the descendants of Jacob were gathered into separate kingdoms: the Northern Kingdom (also called Israel), with its capital at Samaria, and the Southern Kingdom (Judah), with its capital at Jerusalem, the home of the Davidic dynasty. Unlike the narrative of 1 and 2 Kings, 1 and 2 Chronicles virtually ignores the political events that compose the story of the Northern Kingdom. For the purposes of the Chronicler, the Northern Kingdom is an aberration of the true Israel whose history can be ignored except in a few places where the history of the Davidic dynasty requires mention of it. That is not to say, however, that no one from outside the Southern Kingdom is worthy of mention in the Chronicler's narrative. In point of fact, several northerners are favorably treated by the Chronicler (see 2 Chron. 11:13–15; 15:9–15; and 30:11, 25–26). The Chronicler gives the impression that the Northern

Kingdom represents a group of people who were unfaithful to God, largely because they established houses of worship at places other than the Temple in Jerusalem. Their unfaithfulness has separated them from the true Israel (all those who continue to worship God at the Temple in Jerusalem). Still, there is hope even for these apostates; if they repent and return to Jerusalem, they may be included in the community of Israel. For the Chronicler, faith, and not political or national boundaries, determines the content of the true Israel.

The issue of who comprises the people of God is an important one not only for the purposes of history but for the Chronicler's own day. By the time Chronicles was written, the national boundaries and monarchical institutions that had defined Israel were gone. People who worshiped the God of Israel lived not only in Palestine but in Babylon, Persia, Syria, Egypt, and elsewhere. Moreover, some who lived in the midst of Judea and Jerusalem were not worshipers of Israel's God. Precisely how, then, were the people of God to be defined? The Chronicler's dual fascination with the faith and the genealogy of Israel are his answer to this question. Israel was that body of people descended from the sons of Jacob who were faithful to the God of Jacob.

God chooses a particular person (David) and through him a family (the house of David) as the agents of the divine will. Just as the genealogies focus the action of God from the large scope of the whole human race down to the descendants of Jacob, so the rest of the Chronicler's narrative focuses the weal and woe of Israel onto the affairs of the family of David. As goes the house of David, so goes Israel. Although the kingship of Saul is recognized briefly in 1 Chronicles 10, it is obvious from the Chronicler's dramatic presentation that the story of the kingdom of Israel begins in truth when God "turned the kingdom over to David" (1 Chron. 10:14).

For the Chronicler, David's role is not merely king but also founder of both a faith and a dynasty. Once settled on the throne, David has the central role in three great events, as the Chronicler describes his reign. The first is the movement of the ark of the covenant, the ancient symbol of Israel's faith, into Jerusalem and under his personal protection (1 Chron. 13:1–16:43), thus uniting the traditions of Moses and the tribes with his own destiny as king. The second great event is the founding of a dynasty (1 Chron. 17:1–27), insuring that a scion of the house of David will sit on the throne of Israel in perpetuity. The third and most important event is the preparation for the construction of the Temple (1 Chron. 22:2–29:29). Although it is Solomon and not David who actually builds the Temple, David's hand is ever active in the assembling of material and the organization of the clergy and administrative structure around the Temple.

Commentators routinely note that the Chronicler omits any mention of David's affair with Bathsheba, wife of Uriah the Hittite, of the murder of Uriah (2 Samuel 11—12), or of the revolts against David led by his son Absalom or Sheba the son of Bichri (2 Samuel 15—18 and 20). For some, this is clear evidence of the glorification of the figure of David to the point of incredibility. Indeed, it is not unfair to say that the Chronicler has idealized the figure of David, especially in regard to David's role as the author of Israel's faith and worship tradition. But this idealization of David should not be understood as blindness to any fault of David. In fact, the Chronicler does mention David's census of Israel (1 Chronicles 21), which he took at the displeasure of God and for which he brought punishment down on himself and the nation. Moreover, it is clear from the manner in which the Chronicler edits his source that he is fully aware of the Bathsheba narrative and expects no less of his readers. It appears, therefore, that the Chronicler is simply not interested in the private life of David but only in the public David and his role in founding both a kingdom and a faith. Becoming entangled in the details of David's life and reign that do not serve that larger story of the founding of Israel's faith is, in the end, an unwarranted distraction to the Chronicler; such details can be read in the "records of the seer Samuel" (1 Chron. 29:29), but they need not detain the forward motion of the Chronicler's story.

God chooses a particular place in which to be worshiped: the Temple in Jerusalem. A central piece of the Chronicler's presentation of Israel's story is his careful attention to the Temple. More time and space are lavished upon the details of the Temple construction and the practice of worship within it than on any other subject. The discussion of the reign of David includes several chapters enumerating the various members of the clergy and staff of the Temple: Levites (1 Chronicles 23; 24:20–31), priests (24:1–19), musicians (chap. 25), gatekeepers (26:1–19), and other officials (26:20–32). Most of the space devoted to Solomon's reign is given over to the construction and dedication of the Temple (2 Chronicles 2—7). In addition, the central features of the descriptions of Hezekiah and Josiah are the reorganization of the Temple operation and the reestablishment of the great Passover celebration (2 Chronicles 29—31; 34—35). So much attention is paid to the subject of the Temple and the worship of God within it that Sara Japhet has referred to the Chronicles as "a systematic history of Israel's worship" (Japhet, 45).

The Chronicler's focus on a Temple now destroyed (the Temple was sacked and burned by the Babylonians in 587 B.C.) may seem arcane at first. But when we remember that the Chronicler is writing to a Jewish community living in the Persian period under the shadow of a newly reconstructed Temple, the concern begins to make sense. The Chronicler's history of Israel's worship also lays before his audience a vision of the proper place of the (new) Temple in their own lives. Part celebration of the Temple and part polemic against those who might consider the new Temple less important in the religious life of postexilic Israel, Chronicles is an attempt to restore to the Temple a glory not found there since the days of the kings. By showing his audience the central role played by the Temple throughout Israel's history, the Chronicler seeks to rehabilitate that role for the newly rebuilt Temple in the Israel of his own day.

God is still active in the story of Israel: Chronicles as bridge between past and present. Chronicles tells the story of the kingdoms of Israel and Judah from the perspective of a later era, but the principal thrust of the work is not merely historical. Rather, the Chronicler provides a continuity between the storied past of his nation and the present predicament of his people. The institutions and theology of the past are used to legitimate and give foundation to those of the present, and the practices of the present are seen as having their origins in the past. This continuity can be seen clearest in the material associated with the Temple. The careful attention to the details of the Temple envisioned by David and built by Solomon reflects the attempt to legitimate the practice of the present by showing its foundations in the past. This connection between sacred past and present can also be seen in the interest the Chronicler shows in genealogy and lineages: By tracing the descendants of the heroic characters of Israel's history, the Chronicler connects the members of his own generation to that history and makes the claim that the present is continuous with the past.

An important theological point is made by this sense of continuity between present and past. If past and present are continuous, then the God who guided the story of Israel's past still guides the present. Contemporary life for the Chronicler and his generation is therefore no less meaningful and important than was the past because it is still the arena for the activity of God. Jewish and Christian theology ever since has continued to make this claim: God is Lord of the past, but God is never confined to or contained within it.

5. What are the sources for Chronicles? Every work of history is based on sources, and Chronicles is no exception. Indeed, throughout the work, the Chronicler refers the reader to other literature where further details about the reigns of kings or the acts of the prophets are preserved. But the question of what sources the Chronicler employs and whether all the citations of sources that appear in Chronicles are traceable to some existing work is a complex one. At its simplest level, the question can be divided into two parts: (a) what sources does Chronicles cite or quote that are known to us, and (b) what can be said of the documents Chronicles mentions that are unknown to us?

What known sources does Chronicles cite, quote, or allude to? The Chronicler is clearly familiar with the traditions of Israel as represented in the books of the Old Testament. Quotations, excerpts, or allusions to the books of the Pentateuch (Genesis–Deuteronomy), the Deuteronomistic History (Joshua, Judges, 1 and 2 Samuel, and 1 and 2 Kings), and to Ezra-Nehemiah are common throughout Chronicles. The selection of source material reflects the themes and theological commitments of the Chronicler. From Genesis through Deuteronomy, the Chronicler has chosen two kinds of material: genealogical tables that provide the connection between Adam and the descendants of Jacob, and traditions associated with the tabernacle and the worship of early Israel. As is clear from the previous section, these themes are important to the Chronicler's theology. The Chronicler also uses some genealogical material from Joshua but virtually ignores any material descriptive of the period before the rise of David to the throne. Such omissions are completely consistent with the Chronicler's view that the meaningful history of God's people begins with David.

With the Samuel-Kings narrative, the Chronicler's treatment becomes more nuanced. The Chronicler's presentation of the reign of David relies heavily upon the material in 1 and 2 Samuel for narratives about David's career, but not without frequent and even drastic editorial intervention. Throughout 2 Chronicles 10—36, the stories of the kings drawn from 1 and 2 Kings are used as the narrative framework onto which the Chronicler then places narratives of his own creation. The additions serve, as the commentary shows, to advance the Chronicler's theological agenda. The Chronicler also omits a great deal of 1 and 2 Kings, especially extended discussions of affairs in the Northern Kingdom.

What can be said of the references to unknown sources in Chronicles? Throughout the Chronicler's narrative, he refers to works otherwise unknown to us, at least by the titles the Chronicler provides. In all, there are eighteen sources of various titles, including, "The Book/s of the Kings of Israel," "The Book/s of the Kings of Judah," "The Books of the Kings of Israel and Judah/Judah and Israel," "The Chronicles of the Kings of Israel," "The Book of the Chronicles of the Kings of Israel and Judah," and the "chronicles," "records," and "visions" of various prophets. The similarity of many of these titles has led some scholars to suggest that they are all slightly variant ways of referring to the same principle work, presumably a comprehensive history of Israel and Judah. But what work? At least three possibilities exist. First, all references are to a noncanonical history of Israel and Judah, now lost to us, but still widely known in the Chronicler's time. That such a work is now lost means that all arguments concerning it are essentially arguments from silence, but this is not impossible. Second, all references are in fact to the canonical works Joshua, Judges, 1 and 2 Samuel, and 1 and 2 Kings. The Chronicler's use of various titles for these works would then reflect the fact that no consistent titles had emerged by the Chronicler's day by which the earlier works were known. Third, all references to otherwise unknown books are "mere show," as C. C. Torrey has put it—that is, they are essentially false footnotes, intended to convey authority and authenticity to the narrative (Japhet, 23). This is a rather cynical view but also not outside the realm of possibility. Each of these positions has both support and criticism, and the debate is not settled. At the very least, however, it is clear that the Chronicler has relied on sources in the writing of his history, by whatever names those sources were known. Chronicles must therefore be understood as a descendant of earlier Israelite history-writing, conversant with past interpretations of that history and also creative of new interpretations to serve the needs of the Chronicler's own time.

For the purposes of this commentary, it seems clearest and most convenient to assume that the principal source used by the Chronicler is the great narrative of Samuel and Kings. That other sources are used is obvious; where those sources are identifiable we will identify them. In the main, however, we will make the assumption that material diverging from the principal source of the Samuel-Kings tradition is either the creation of the Chronicler or preserved by him in an effort to advance his theological agenda.

6. Can Chronicles be regarded as historically reliable? Probably the most hotly debated question in the last fifty years of research on Chronicles is the question of the historical reliability of the narrative. Until the late nineteenth century, most scholars assumed Chronicles to be as reliable a source for historical reconstruction as Samuel-Kings. However, scholarship in this century has cast increasing doubt on the reliability of Chronicles, and many now understand it as little more than a theological commentary on the Samuel-Kings account.

It may be of the greatest value for our present purpose to pose the question in two parts. First, does Chronicles satisfy the standards of modern history-writing? When phrased in this manner, the answer is almost certainly negative. Chronicles relies on divine intervention and involvement, assuming that God's activity is determinative for the course of history; this fact alone would render it suspect in modern discussions of history. Perhaps more important to the issue, the Chronicler often assumes a kind of divine perspective and authority on the events he relates, claiming that particular events took place because God sought to fulfill a divine word from a prophet (2 Chron. 10:15, for example) or because God intervened in some way (2 Chron. 22:16, where "the LORD aroused against Jehoram the anger of the Philistines"). Judged by the canons of modern history-writing, Chronicles is less a reliable history than it is a theological document.

We may also ask this question in a second way, however: Did the Chronicler understand his work as history-writing? Viewed from the perspective of the Chronicler's own day, the answer should probably be affirmative. To put the matter more carefully, the sharp separation between history and theology imposed by modern history-writing would have been foreign to the Chronicler's world. Writers of what we call the "historical books" in the scriptures assume routinely that divine intervention, accomplished either directly or through intermediaries such as prophets, is part of the story of human life. Moreover, that the Chronicler's presentation of, for example, the rehabilitation of Manasseh (2 Chron. 33:10–17) differs sharply from that of 2 Kings would have been of small concern; ancient writers were free to rearrange or even augment the details of a story in the service of the theology being advanced (as the Gospel writers do, for instance, with the story of Jesus clearing the Temple; the story comes during the last week of Jesus' life in Matthew, Mark, and Luke, but is near the beginning of Jesus' ministry in John). The difference between ancient and modern history-writing stems from different assumptions about the purpose of such writing. While each seeks to preserve and interpret the events of the past, modern history-writing is more concerned with recreating those events, while ancient history-writing is more committed to teaching a theological lesson.

Even though Chronicles is not completely reliable as a source for modern reconstructions of the history of ancient Israel, we should not conclude that it has no historical value at all. To do so would be to forget that Chronicles provides us a window on the theological, political, and social concerns of the postexilic community in and around Jerusalem. By viewing Israel's past through the lens of the Persian era, we can glean important information about the issues before Persian-era Judaism, such as the reestablishment of the Temple and its religious practice, and the definition of "Israel." In addition, we can come to understand something of the way the ancient community used the resources of its own past to address the crises of its present. This knowledge may finally be of greater value than the Chronicles story itself, especially if it teaches us something about how we might mine the treasures of our biblical heritage for guidance in facing our own crises of faith and practice. In the end, Chronicles may well serve us better in teaching method than in teaching history.

Part I: Genealogies

1 Chronicles 1—9

From the perspective of the modern reader, one could hardly pick a worse way to begin a book than with a genealogical table of the sort we meet in the opening pages of 1 Chronicles. For the first nine chapters of 1 Chronicles, we encounter one list of daunting names after another, some of them familiar but most of them unknown. There is neither accompanying narrative to set the names in context nor introductory remarks to explain the importance of the genealogy as a whole. The presentation of the beginning of the Chronicles story thus begs the question: why genealogies?

Perhaps the way to begin answering such a question is to understand what a genealogy is and does. Genealogies are lists of the names of ancestors. They preserve for the present and future the names of people who gave birth to those who gave birth to us. Genealogies are ways of connecting one's present with one's past, especially with a past that occurred before one's birth and that one may be in danger of losing because of lack of knowledge and memory.

This is also true for the genealogies of the Chronicles narrative, except that it is true for a people rather than for an individual. The Chronicles genealogies serve the purpose of connecting Jews of the Persian period (538–333 B.C.) with a past they were in danger of losing. In the wake of the conquest of Jerusalem by the Babylonians in 587 B.C., much that identified the people of Israel and Judah was jeopardized, if not lost. Worship in the Temple was disrupted by its destruction, the political structure of the nation was dismantled, and the economic and social patterns of daily life disintegrated. The exile of many Jews to Babylon for the next half-century introduced an even more pronounced discontinuity between the Israel and Judah of the past and the Jewish province of the Persian empire. Those who returned from exile to Jerusalem with Nehemiah and Ezra were, in large measure, not those who had been carried away by the Babylonians but rather their children, grandchildren, or even great-grandchildren. They had little or no connection with the lives of those Jews who had remained in Jerusalem and its environs, and no memories of the traditions of ritual and worship that had once bound the nation together. The Babylonian exile and its aftermath thus posed a kind of identity crisis for Jews both in the land and in the Dispersion. The Chronicles genealogies are intended to speak to that crisis by reminding the Jews of the Persian era that they were the product of a lineage that stretched all the way back to the beginning, to Adam. They were not, as the circumstances of the times seemed to imply, rootless or homeless; rather, they were rooted in a great lineage that bore the very fingerprints of God.

The genealogies also claim that the election of Israel as the chosen people of God is rooted in the very beginning of the human story. The genealogical work of Chronicles begins with Adam and proceeds from him through Abraham and on to David, where the great story of the nation begins. Such a lineage is the Chronicler's way of claiming that the path of divine intent runs from the creation of human life to the flowering of that creation in the people of ancient Israel under the reign of David. Moreover, as the genealogy moves from generation to generation, the reader notices that it narrows and restricts the field of discussion, highlighting only one family among several possibilities. By narrowing the genealogical line in this way, Chronicles implies that what was begun in the creation of human life is brought to fulfillment in the descendants of Abraham, and especially in the kingdom of David.

Readers of the Christian Gospels are familiar with this theological use of genealogy. Matthew's genealogy traces Jesus' lineage from Abraham, making the point that the election by God of the descendants of Abraham is focused and fulfilled in Jesus. Luke traces Jesus' heritage to Adam, making the case that the life of Jesus has universal significance for the deliverance of humankind. In each case, the implication of the genealogy forms a theme then replayed in the narrative of the Gospel itself. Understanding the genealogy as a kind of theological introduction to the narrative enhances the narrative as a whole.

1. From Adam to Israel (Jacob)
1 Chronicles 1:1–54

The first block of genealogical material carries the reader from Adam to Jacob, renamed "Israel" in Genesis 32. In so doing, it gathers into a single list the entire prehistory from creation to the stories of Abraham. Readers familiar with the Genesis narrative will immediately notice that the genealogies here bear a close resemblance to the lists of Genesis 5, 10—11, 25, and 35—36. In fact, most scholars are convinced that the Chronicler has simply borrowed the Genesis genealogies, making only minor changes in them.

Structurally, 1 Chronicles 1:1–54 falls into three sections: from Adam to Abraham (vv. 1–27), descendants of Abraham (vv. 28–34), and descendants of Esau, including the leaders of the Edomites (vv. 35–54). The twelve sons of Isaac and their descendants who form the traditional twelve tribes of Israel are reserved for the next chapter in order to give them special emphasis.

The genealogy of 1 Chronicles 1 consistently lists the names of those persons through whom the story of Israel is not carried before listing those through whom it is to be told. For instance, in verse 4 the sons of Noah are listed in the traditional order: Shem, Ham, and Japheth. The genealogy then lists the descendants of the sons in reverse order: those of Japheth (vv. 5–7), followed by those of Ham (vv. 8–16), and concluding with those of Shem (vv. 17–26). It is, of course, through Shem that Abraham's lineage is traced (vv. 24–26). By reversing the traditional order of the sons of Noah, the Chronicler makes the presentation of the genealogy smoother and furthers the sense that the lineage of humankind is narrowing to focus exclusively on Israel. The same practice is visible in the order of the sons of Abraham: Ishmael and his descendants are listed first (along with the children born to Keturah), then Isaac and his sons.

Readers familiar with the geography of the ancient Near East may recognize in the descendants of Noah's sons the names of various countries and kingdoms of the Mediterranean world. The practice of associating a place or group of people with a mythic ancestor who bears the same name is called *eponymy*, and the name of the ancestor in this practice is an *eponym*. By employing an eponym, the Chronicler locates both historically and geographically the various nations with which he was familiar, providing a kind of map for the world of his day. This section of the genealogy is based on Genesis 10—11, the "Table of Nations." In general, it is organized so that the three sons of Noah are the progenitors of the inhabitants of different parts of the world. The descendants of Japheth (vv. 5–7) are eponymous ancestors for inhabitants of Europe and Asia known to the Chronicler: The Madai are the Medes, neighbors of the Persians east of the Tigris River; the Kittim are generally regarded as the inhabitants of Cyprus and Greece; the Rodanim are the inhabitants of Rhodes. Ham's sons (vv. 8–16) bear eponyms associated with kingdoms and populations in Africa and Syria-Palestine: Cush is the name for the ancient kingdom now known as Ethiopia; Egypt is readily recognizable as the great ancient kingdom of the Lower Nile; and Canaan is the collective name given to a number of small population groups in the coastal plains, hills, and valleys of Palestine. Canaan's descendants include Sidon, the eponym of the great Phoenician city of the northeast Mediterranean, and Heth, the eponym for the great Hittite kingdom of what is now eastern Turkey. The Hethite list also includes the list of smaller groups who lived in Canaan—"the Jebusites, the Amorites, the Girgashites, the Hivites, the Arkites, the Sinites, the Arvadites, the Zemarites, and the Hamathites"—many of whom are listed as the inhabitants of the land to be driven out by the Israelites (cf. Gen. 15:19–21; Ex. 3:8; 23:23; Deut. 7:1). Shem's descendants are the eponymous patriarchs of peoples of Mesopotamia and Arabia: Elam is a country east of the Tigris-Euphrates Valley well-known from Assyrian records; Asshur is the eponym for Assyria, the great Mesopotamian power of the ninth through seventh centuries B.C.; Aram is the eponym for groups of people in northern Syria who will eventually form a regional power with its capital at Damascus. While many of the names here remain unknown, enough is clear to indicate that the Chronicler understood Israel's position in the great international drama on the world stage.

2. The Descendants of Jacob
1 Chronicles 2:1–9:44

THE SONS OF JACOB (ISRAEL)
1 Chronicles 2:1–2

> 2:1 **These are the sons of Israel: Reuben, Simeon, Levi, Judah, Issachar, Zebulun,** 2 **Dan, Joseph, Benjamin, Naphtali, Gad, and Asher.**

The Chronicler now turns to the characters that form the cast for the drama of Israelite and Judahite history. Once again, the names of Jacob/Israel's sons are eponyms, this time for the traditional twelve tribal groups of early Israel. The names of the sons are the same ones given in Genesis 29:31–30:24 and 35:16–18, although the order of their appearance in the list here does not match the order of their births as described in Genesis. It is also not the order in which the various genealogies of the twelve will be presented in this and subsequent chapters. In addition, no relationship is discernable between their appearance in the list and the geographical location of the tribes they represent. Even as a list of Jacob's known descendants the list is incomplete: Dinah, Jacob's daughter who was raped and kidnapped by the Hivite Shechem (Genesis 34), is not mentioned.

THE DESCENDANTS OF JUDAH
1 Chronicles 2:3–4:23

The first and largest block of the Israelite genealogies details the descendants of Judah. The Judahite genealogy can be divided into three main sections: the descendants of Judah (2:3–55), the house of David (3:1–24), and miscellaneous genealogies related to Judah (4:1–23). Some of the material contained within these sections has direct antecedents in other biblical lists, while other material is not known outside of Chronicles. In addition, there appears within these sections a variety of styles. Some portions of the lists are in the form, "The sons of X: . . . these were the sons of X" (e.g., the sons of Jerahmeel, [2:25–33], the sons of Caleb, [2:42–50a], and the sons of Hur [2:50b–55; 4:2–4]). Other portions display the style, "X became father of Y" (e.g., the genealogy of David [2:10–12] and the descendants of Sheshan [2:36–42]). Still other material is more narrative (e.g., the reference to the death of Judah's son Er [2:3–4], the relationship between Caleb and Ephrath [2:18–19, 21–24], and the information about Jabez [4:9–10]). Such stylistic variety in adjacent lists leads to the conclusion that the Chronicler drew on several different sources in compiling the Judahite genealogy.

1. *The descendants of Judah, 2:3–55.* There are several aspects of the list of Judah's descendants that require consideration. First is the way in which the description of Judah's own children (2:3–4) is written.

> 2:3 **The sons of Judah: Er, Onan, and Shelah; these three the Canaanite woman Bath-shua bore to him. Now Er, Judah's firstborn, was wicked in the sight of the LORD, and he put him to death. 4 His daughter-in-law Tamar also bore him Perez and Zerah. Judah had five sons in all.**

The reader notices immediately the two striking elements of this paragraph: (1) the notation that Er was wicked and put to death by the Lord, and (2) that Judah's fourth and fifth children were the products of his union with his own daughter-in-law, Tamar. The full story of Judah and Tamar is found in Genesis 38; here a summary must serve us. Tamar, wife of Judah's eldest son, Er, was left widowed by Er's unexplained death (the Chronicler quotes exactly the description of Er's death in Genesis 38:7; no explanation of his "wickedness" is offered there either). According to the custom of levirate marriage, Judah was responsible to provide for Tamar another of his sons to father children with her. Onan, second of Judah's sons, was chosen, but refused to complete the act. For this refusal, Onan too was slain by the Lord. Judah was now reluctant to provide a third son to Tamar and instead sent her away. But rather than go back to her father's house for the rest of her life, Tamar set herself up as a prostitute in the region where Judah lived. At a subsequent time, Judah fathered children with Tamar, unaware of her identity. When she revealed herself to be his daughter-in-law, Judah recognized his failure to live up to his responsibility to provide her with a husband from among his sons and also her righteousness in forcing him to do so. He then claimed as his own the children she bore, Perez and Zerah. The story is hardly a flattering one to Judah, and the Chronicler might easily have glossed over it by ignoring Tamar and listing all five of Judah's sons at once. Instead, he focuses attention on it by mentioning both Er's wickedness and Tamar's motherhood of Perez and Zerah. The presence of this story here, albeit in abbreviated form, serves both to explain how the lineage of Judah continued beyond the generation of his original three sons and to point out the importance of repentance and obedience on the part of Judah, since he does finally admit and rectify his error. Having then recognized Perez and Zerah as his sons, Judah's lineage continues through Perez, eventuating in the family of David.

A second part of the Judahite list that deserves comment is the small section on the descendants of Perez and Zerah, (2:5–8):

> 2:5 **The sons of Perez: Hezron and Hamul.** [6] **The sons of Zerah: Zimri, Ethan, Heman, Calcol, and Dara, five in all.** [7] **The sons of Carmi: Achar, the troubler of Israel, who transgressed in the matter of the devoted thing;** [8] **and Ethan's son was Azariah.**

Two questions emerge immediately: (1) Who is Carmi in verse 7, and (2) what is this "devoted thing" in reference to which Achar has transgressed? Both questions can be answered by referring to Joshua 7, to which these verses allude. Again, a summary of the narrative will have to suffice. Following the destruction of Jericho in Joshua 6, God commanded that all items of gold, silver, bronze, and iron be brought to the treasury of the house of the Lord (in this text, the tabernacle). But one of the Israelites, Achan (=Achar in 1 Chron. 2:7), kept back for himself some of the gold and silver and a piece of clothing from the booty captured and devoted to the Lord (Josh. 7:21). On account of this sin, the Joshua narrative implies, the initial assault against Israel's next target, Ai, failed. Only by determining that Achan/Achar was the culprit and stoning him to death was the guilt expunged and the capture of Ai accomplished. Achan is identified in Joshua 7:1 as "son of Carmi son of Zabdi [an alternate spelling of Zimri] son of Zerah, of the tribe of Judah." In the reference in 1 Chronicles 2:7 to this incident, the Chronicler has omitted the connection between Zimri and Carmi, probably because he has no other need to list the sons of Zimri. Once again, the Chronicler preserves a less-than-complimentary story about the lineage of Judah, and once again, the point seems to be that through obedience and rectification of the transgression, the story of the people of God is continued.

Perez's son, Hezron, provides the familial connection for the remainder of the Judahite genealogy in 2:3-55. From Hezron come three sons: Jerahmeel, Ram, and Caleb; each is taken up in turn. The descendants of Ram (2:10–12) have importance as the family of David. The lineage between Ram and David is precisely that given in Ruth 4:19b–22, except that the Chronicler supplements it with the names of David's brothers and sisters. Some of those names, the three eldest brothers of David, are listed in 1 Samuel 17:12–14; the younger three are otherwise unknown. It is interesting to note that the Samuel narrative understands David to be the youngest of eight sons of Jesse (see 1 Sam. 16:11), while the Chronicler understands David as the youngest of seven.

Of further interest is the inclusion in this list of the two sisters of David and their sons in verses 16–17. Zeruiah's sons Abishai, Joab, and Asahel, and Abigail's son Amasa, form the core of David's military leadership in the narratives of 1 and 2 Samuel. Joab and Abishai are among the commanders who remain loyal to David during the Absalom revolt (2 Sam. 18:2); Amasa defects to Absalom but is received back into David's command structure after the revolt is put down (2 Sam. 19:14). The Chronicler includes none of this in his description of the reign of David. The absence of reference to the narrative is not due to ignorance on the Chronicler's part but rather to the fact that the violence and intrigue within David's court are not germane to the image of David as founder of Israel's faith.

The genealogy of Hezron is continued in 2:18–24 with the descendants of Hezron's son Caleb, called "Chelubai" in 2:9 (the two names have the same consonantal spelling in Hebrew). Problems in the Hebrew text of verse 24 make the translation of this verse an issue worthy of note:

After the death of Hezron, in Caleb-ephrathah, Abijah wife of Hezron bore him Ashhur, father of Tekoa.

The implication of the text is that the child of Hezron is born after Hezron's death; admittedly, this is not impossible, but it seems somewhat curious. Also curious is the place name, "Caleb-ephrathah," especially since it is composed of the names of Hezron's son Caleb and his wife Ephrath. An alternate reading based on ancient Latin and Greek manuscripts may solve the problems and provide a simpler reading. These texts read "Caleb went in to Ephrathah" (an alternate spelling of "Ephrath") instead of "in Caleb-ephrathah." In addition, they also read the name "Abijah" as "his father" by changing the final consonant of the Hebrew. If these two changes are adopted, verse 24 would then read:

After the death of Hezron, Caleb went in to Ephrathah, the wife of Hezron his father, and she bore to him Ashhur, the father of Tekoa.

This reading makes clear that after the death of his father, Caleb took Ephrathah, one of his father's wives (but presumably not his mother) as his own wife, and had with her a son, Ashhur. But while it resolves some difficulties, it may pose another. Verse 19 records the birth of a son to Caleb and Ephrath, named Hur; verse 24 names another son of this union (if our proposal is adopted), Ashhur. Clearly a similarity exists between these two names of the children of Caleb and Ephrath. One may resolve this difficulty either by assuming that the names are correct as they stand, or by treating Hur as an abbreviated form of Ashhur and seeing the two as the same person. The former may be implied from 2:50b and 4:4, where Hur is called "the firstborn of Ephrathah," indicating that there were other children from the marriage.

The Chronicler places more emphasis on the descendants of Hur than on those of Ashhur, and it is from Hur that the final section of the Calebite genealogy is traced (vv. 50b–55). But this short list seems again to be discontinuous with the brief enumeration of Hur's descendants in verse 20. No mention is made in verses 50b–51 of either Uri or Bezalel from verse 20, but a new group of sons is given: Shobal, Salma, and Hareph. Each of the three is then given at least one son, and in the cases of Shobal and Salma, more. The reader notes that this second generation from Hur are eponyms for cities and towns known from the biblical narrative: Kiriath-jearim, Bethlehem, and Beth-gader, thereby identifying a locale with an ethnic group.

2. The house of David, 3:1–24. The development of the lineage of David from 2:10–12 is taken up again in chapter 3, with David as the progenitor. The chapter has two sections: the immediate family of David (vv. 1–9) and the list of the house of David from Solomon to the postexilic period (vv. 10–24).

The list of the sons and one daughter of David in verses 1–9 is divided in verse 4 by the distinction between those born in Hebron and those born in Jerusalem. Verses 1–4 are taken directly from 2 Samuel 3:2–5, except that David's second son is here named Daniel while in 2 Samuel 3:3 the name is Chileab.

Verses 5–8, the list of sons born to David in Jerusalem, are clearly related to 2 Samuel 5:13–16, but the correspondence between the two texts is less close than between 1 Chronicles 3:1–4 and 2 Samuel 3:2–5. There are differences in the spelling of names: "Shammua" in 2 Samuel 5:13 is "Shimea" in 1 Chronicles 3:5; "Elishua" in 2 Samuel 5:15 is "Elishama" in 1 Chronicles 3:6. Also, we are given the information that the first four names on the list in 1 Chronicles 3:5 are sons of David "by Bath-shua [=Bathsheba], daughter of Ammiel"; in the Samuel narratives, only Solomon is named as a surviving son of Bathsheba. In 1 Chronicles 3:7, the name Nogah appears; it is unknown in 2 Samuel 5. Finally, in verses 6 and 8 the names Elishama and Eliphelet appear twice. While various attempts have been made to reconcile the differences between the two lists, in the end it may be best to regard the version in 1 Chronicles 3:5–8 as reflective of a tradition available to the Chronicler that differed somewhat from that known to the writers of 2 Samuel.

The list of the descendants of Solomon in 3:10–16 is a straightforward list of the kings of Judah, already well-known in 1 and 2 Kings. No deviation from this list is likely, and none occurs from Solomon to Josiah. However, in 3:17, the matter becomes more complex in the presentation of the descendants of Josiah. From the Kings account of the last days of Judah, we know of three sons of Josiah: Jehoahaz (2 Kings 23:31), Eliakim (whose name is changed to Jehoiakim when he becomes king [2 Kings 23:34]), and Mattaniah (whose name is changed to Zedekiah when the Babylonians make him a puppet king [2 Kings 24:17]). Eliakim/Jehoiakim is credited by the Kings account with one son, Jeconiah, who adopts the throne name Jehoiachin in 2 Kings 24. The Chronicler makes two changes in this lineage, however. First, he adds a fourth and otherwise unknown son of Josiah, Johanan; second, he names a second son of Eliakim/Jehoiakim: Zedekiah. Which is correct? At this remove we can only speculate. Perhaps the nod of preference ought to be given to the Kings account, however, on the grounds that it is much closer to the events themselves than is Chronicles. The line of Judahite succession after the death of Josiah would thus be

1. Jehoahaz, son of Josiah
2. Eliakim, renamed Jehoiakim, son of Josiah
3. Jeconiah, called Jehoichin in 2 Kings 24, son of Eliakim/Jehoiakim
4. Mattaniah, renamed Zedekiah, son of Josiah and uncle of Jeconiah/Jehoiachin

One might easily understand how, over the centuries intervening between the fall of Jerusalem and the writing of Chronicles, confusion might have arisen between Mattaniah/Zedekiah, son of Josiah who succeeded Jehoiachin as king, and a later Zedekiah, child of Jehoiachin, who never reigned in Jerusalem.

Verses 17–24 preserve a list of the Davidic house into the exile and beyond. Its presence is a testimony to the continuing importance to the Chronicler of the lineage of David, even long after the throne of David is defunct. There are few connections between the names mentioned here and other postexilic narratives available in the Old Testament, but one name merits at least some comment. Zerubbabel was the governor appointed by the Persian king to organize the rebuilding of the city of Jerusalem after the Babylonian exile. He is called "son of Shealtiel" in

Ezra 3:2, 3:8, and Haggai 1:1; here he is listed as the son of Pedaiah, who was the brother of Shealtiel.

3. Miscellaneous genealogies related to Judah, 4:1–23. The Judahite genealogy resumes with a series of small and apparently independent lists, all generally subsumed under the general category of derivation from Judah, but having little or no direct connection with each other. 1 Chronicles 4:1 briefly recapitulates the genealogy of Judah in chapter 2, leading up to Shobal (cf. 2:53). The structure of the chapter then seems to be provided by these independent lists: the sons Etam (vv. 3–4), the sons of Ashhur (vv. 5–8), the sons of Chelub (vv. 11–12), the sons of Kenaz (vv. 13–14), the sons of Caleb (v. 15), the sons of Jehalelel (v. 16), the sons of Ezrah (vv. 17–18), the sons of Hodiah (v. 19), the sons of Shimon (v. 20), and the sons of Shelah (v. 21). As we have seen before, the names of various descendants appear to be eponyms for cities and towns known elsewhere in the Old Testament: Etam (v. 3), Jezreel (v. 3), Penuel (v. 4), Bethlehem (v. 4), Tekoa (v. 5), Ziph (v. 16), Eshtemoa (v. 17), Gedor (v. 18), and Soco (v. 18).

Interspersed among the genealogical lists are two bits of narrative that deserve some attention. The first is the story of Jabez in verses 9–10. The story is essentially an explanation of the origin of the name of the main character but with an interesting twist:

> 4:9 **Jabez was honored more than his brothers; and his mother named him Jabez, saying, "Because I bore him in pain."** [10]**Jabez called on the God of Israel, saying, "Oh that you would bless me and enlarge my border, and that your hand might be with me, and that you would keep me from hurt and harm!" And God granted what he asked.**

The text intends for us to understand that the name Jabez (*yabeṣ* in Hebrew) is derived from the verb *'aṣab*, to have pain. But the spelling of Jabez reverses the final two consonants of the verb, *b* and *ṣ*, so that the etiology is not clean and direct. They do, however, seem to anticipate the reversal of circumstance related by the story. The mother's words are a sort of curse, reminiscent of Genesis 3:16, the curse upon Eve that she will bear children in pain. The words of the prayer of Jabez work to reverse the curse: Instead of incurring hurt and harm, Jabez asks for and is granted protection from them. Perhaps even more striking is the mention of God here; God has made no appearance in the narrative to this point. The mention of God's involvement in this minor sidelight may serve to point up the Chronicler's belief that God's presence and imprint may be found throughout the history of Israel, in the small no less than in the great.

Recent devotional literature has featured this prayer of Jabez as a sort of formula for obtaining personal blessing. The theme of much of this thinking seems to be that there are untold stores of blessing, spiritual and material, in the heavenly larders. God, according to this line of reasoning, is simply waiting for people to pray with the directness and audacity of Jabez in order to grant those blessings. While there is certainly nothing in the traditions of Judaism and Christianity that would discourage believers from seeking blessing from God, there are at least two respects in which this use of Jabez's prayer as a means of access to divine favor runs counter to the Chronicler's theology. First, such use is dangerously close to magical thinking: we ask and God responds. The theology of the Chronicler affirms that blessing is the divine prerogative; God is not obligated to deliver it as a *quid pro quo* in response to human requests. The Chronicler's theology of moral responsibility holds that faithfulness is the context for divine favor, but it never assumes that favor will be automatically granted in response to the utterance of a magical prayer. Second, such use is self-referential: I pray for my own blessings. Prayer in the Chronicler's narrative is finally focused on the good of the whole community of God's people, not merely on individual well-being. Solomon's prayer at Gibeon (2 Chron. 1:7–13) comes closest to a prayer for individual blessing; even here, however, Solomon asks not for material favors but for the "wisdom and knowledge to go out and come in before this people, for who can rule this great people of yours?" That Solomon receives material blessing is, in the Chronicler's eyes, a by-product of Solomon's faithful selflessness in seeking God for the good of the kingdom; it is not the point of the episode.

The other bit of narrative information comes at the end of this section, in verses 21–23. In these verses we are given some striking information about the descendants of Shelah, namely, that among their number were members of a guild of linen workers and potters who lived in Netaim and Gederah "with the king in his service." Among all the names given in the genealogies thus far, only here and in the reference to scribes in 2:55 have we seen into the sociological structures of the society of ancient Israel.

Verse 22 contains an interesting textual problem:

> . . . and Jokim, and the men of Cozeba, and Joash, and Saraph, who married into Moab but returned to Lehem (now the records are ancient).

In Hebrew, the verb translated by the NRSV "married into" can also be translated "ruled over" or "was master over"; indeed, this is how the RSV translated the phrase ("ruled in Moab and returned"). The matter is made more mysterious by the succeeding remark that "now the records are ancient," which may be intended to mean that, even by the Chronicler's day, the matter was obscured by the mists of time. At any rate, the question of translation here is at best a guess, since the meaning is obscure.

THE DESCENDANTS OF SIMEON
1 Chronicles 4:24–43

Of the nineteen verses associated with the Simeonite genealogy, only four (vv. 24–27) are the sort of genealogy we have come to expect thus far in Chronicles. The remainder of the information the Chronicler provides about the Simeonites comes in narrative form. Indeed, one notices that, in comparison to the rather extensive genealogy of the various Judahite groups, the lists for Simeon, Reuben (5:1–10), Gad (5:11–22), Manasseh (5:23–26 and 7:14–18), Issachar (7:1–5), Naphtali (7:13), and Asher (7:30–40) are all brief and, in several cases, more narrative than geneaological. We may account for this by remembering that the Chronicler understands the great story of Israel to be told through the lineage of Judah. It is only logical therefore that the Judahite lists would be more detailed.

The Simeonite section of the Chronicler's genealogy falls into three parts: the sons of Simeon (vv. 24–27), the original towns and villages of Simeonite settlement (vv. 28–33), and the conquests of the Simeonites (vv. 34–43). The third part can be conveniently subdivided into three parts as well: the leaders of the Simeonites during the days of Hezekiah who were responsible for the expeditions (vv. 34–38), the story of the settlement of the entrance to Gedor by Simeonite elements (vv. 39–41), and the settlement of the region of Mount Seir (vv. 42–43).

1. The Simeonite genealogy, 4:24–27. Five sons of Simeon are listed in verse 24: Nemuel, Jamin, Jarib, Zerah, and Shaul. The Chronicler's list corresponds most closely to the list of Simeonite clans in Numbers 26:12–14, with some variations explained largely by differences in spelling. Two other lists of the sons of Simeon appear in Genesis 46:10 and Exodus 6:15; each of these lists contains six names rather than the five known here and in Numbers. The likelihood is that the Numbers and Chronicles lists derive from a different source than the Genesis and Exodus lists.

The subsequent generations of Simeonites (vv. 25–26) are not specifically connected with any of the original five sons of Simeon, but it is most reasonable to assume that we are intended to understand Shallum as the son of Shaul. Thus, in keeping with the previously established practice of the Chronicler, the Simeonite genealogy is narrowed and traced through only one of Simeon's sons, the final one mentioned. Whether the names presented in verse 25 are intended to be read as one per generation (Shallum is the father of Mibsam who is the father of Mishma) or as sons of Shaul (Shallum, Mibsam, and Mishma are brothers) is unclear. In either case, the thrust of the section seems clearly expressed in the final sentence of verse 27: that the Simeonites were not as numerous as the Judahites. The Chronicler accounts for the dominance of Judah over the Simeonites (who inhabit a portion of the territory that is historically Judahite) by referring to the paucity of Simeon's descendants.

2. *Towns and villages of Simeonite settlement, 4:28–33.* The list of towns and villages settled by Simeonites is largely dependent on the list that appears in Joshua 19:1–9 describing the inheritance of Simeon. The same thirteen towns appear in both lists. Few of these place names can be identified with modern locations, and only Beersheba and Ziklag play significant roles in other biblical narratives. It is clear, however, that these towns and villages were located in the extreme southwest of Judahite territory, on the northern edge of the Negeb (the great desert area in the south of Palestine). Simeonite territory was as impoverished and unproductive as were the Simeonites themselves.

It is worthy of note that many of the towns and villages listed here as part of Simeonite possessions are listed as Judahite in Joshua 15:21–32 and also appear in Nehemiah 11:25–36 in the list of towns outside Jerusalem where Judahites lived in the postexilic period. Their presence in Judahite lists indicates that Simeonite territory came to be regarded as Judahite by the end of the monarchy and continued to be so understood after the exile. The Chronicler's inclusion of the note in 1 Chronicles 4:31b, "These were their towns until David became king," may be intended to indicate that the Simeonites were subsumed under Judah at the accession of David.

3. *The conquests of Simeon, 4:34–43.* Of particular interest is the inclusion of the narrative section concerning Simeonite military and settlement activity later in the period of the monarchy. The section begins with a list of names, subsequently identified in verse 38 as leaders in their families. The names are unconnected to the genealogical list of verses 24–27. For some of the leaders, no new genealogical information is provided; for others, lineage for two to five generations is given. The statement at the end of the list in verse 38, that "these were mentioned by name," leads to the conclusion that the Chronicler is relying on a source distinct from the sources used to compile the earlier genealogy.

Verses 39–41 describe the Simeonite conquest of an area near Gedor. The location of Gedor is uncertain. It is clear, however, that the Chronicler regards its vicinity as desirable land; the narrative goes to some length to describe its beauty, tranquility, and utility for grazing. The movement of the Simeonites took place during the reign of Hezekiah of Judah (727–698 B.C.). This gives an air of historical precision that is unusual in the genealogies so far. There are, however, good reasons for regarding this historical datum as reliable. The material in verses

38–41 has no parallel in 1 and 2 Kings, so it is not obviously borrowed from another source. It does not obviously serve to support any of the Chronicler's theological biases, thereby avoiding suspicion that it is influenced by theological concerns. And it does not obviously reflect circumstances known to exist in the Chronicler's own time but not earlier. There is, therefore, no reason to suppose that the Chronicler is anachronistically reading a later social or political reality back into the time of Hezekiah.

The text indicates that the former inhabitants of Gedor were Hamites (i.e., Canaanites) and that when the Simeonites arrived they attacked both the Hamites and the "Meunites who were found there." While the designation "Hamite" can refer to Canaanites in general, the name "Meunite" is more helpful in locating this text both geographically and historically. The Assyrian king Tiglath-pileser III, during the course of his campaign deep into Syria-Palestine in 734 B.C., recorded contact with a group of people called "Meunim" in the vicinity of Gaza. Assuming that the two names describe the same population, we can with relative certainty assume that the area conquered and settled by Simeonites was indeed the northwestern Negeb near Gaza, and that the action took place during the same era that the Chronicler claims—the reign of Hezekiah in the last decades of the eighth century B.C.

THE DESCENDANTS OF REUBEN, GAD, AND MANASSEH
1 Chronicles 5:1–26

The Chronicler clearly intended for the tribal groups of Reuben, Gad, and the half-tribe of Manasseh to be understood as a unit. One reason is their geographic proximity: All three are located east of the Jordan. Another is the narrative in verses 18–22, which describes the military exploits of the three groups together, implying that they acted as one. The chapter has four parts: the Reubenite genealogy (vv. 1–10), the Gadite genealogy (vv. 11–17), a narrative about a war with the Hagrites (vv. 18–22), and the Manassite genealogy (vv. 23–26).

1. The Reubenite genealogy, 5:1–10. The Reubenite genealogy is interesting for its inclusion of the explanation of Reuben's loss of Jacob's birthright. The Chronicler's text represents a theological development of a tradition articulated in Genesis. Genesis 35:22 indicates that Reuben "went and lay with Bilhah," his father's concubine, but concludes only that "Israel [i.e., Jacob] heard of it." Genesis 49:4 judges this act as Reuben's having "defiled" Jacob's bed and applies to Reuben the curse that Reuben "will no longer excel." The Chronicler picks up the theme of the curse in 5:1 and interprets it as justification for his claim that Joseph, rather than the firstborn Reuben, inherited the birthright of Jacob. The claim of the primacy of Joseph might, however, be understood as contradictory to the clear prominence given Judah in the Chronicler's genealogy so far, and so verse 2 is added to explain the discrepancy. Again, the Chronicler appears to be drawing on Jacob's speech in Genesis: Genesis 49:8–10 affirms the preeminence of Judah among the tribes and explicitly states that "the scepter shall not depart from Judah," precisely the two affirmations made about Judah in 1 Chronicles 5:2.

The Reubenite genealogy presented in 5:4–8 descends from a previously unknown ancestor, Joel. The section has two genealogical trees, each proceeding from Joel's son Shemaiah. The first details the lineage of Beerah, who is described as a chieftain and is given a fairly precise historical location by the mention of his exile by the Assyrian king Tiglath-pileser III (in Chronicles, always rendered "Tilgath-pilneser"). Since Tiglath-pileser III carried on campaigns in Syria-Palestine in 734, 733–732, and 727 B.C., it is impossible to say with precision which date the Chronicler intends. Of the three, the 734–732 date is the most likely because it was the most thorough and destructive of the three to Israel. The second genealogical tree is that of Bela, who is described as "son of Azaz, son of Shema, son of Joel" In all probability, Shema is a shortened form of Shemaiah. Reubenites descended from Bela are credited with raising cattle in the region north of the Arnon River, an eastern tributary of the Jordan north of the Dead Sea. The place names Aroer, Nebo, and Baal-meon are all mentioned in the Mesha inscription, a ninth-century B.C. stele erected by the Moabite king Mesha in celebration of his liberation of this region from Israelite control and its reclamation as the Moabite homeland.

The final verse of this section makes reference to a war with the Hagrites during the days of Saul, or during the first half of the tenth century B.C. The Hagrite war is mentioned in slightly greater detail in verses 19–22. As a population group, the Hagrites play a relatively minor role in the Old Testament; they appear only here and in Psalm 83:6, where they are associated with the Moabites. Presumably, the name derives from the eponym Hagar, the concubine of Abraham who is driven out into the wilderness after the birth of Isaac (Gen. 21:8–21)

2. The Gadite genealogy, 5:11–17. The tribe of Gad is located by the Chronicler in Bashan, just to the north of Reuben, in the Transjordan. Four main families are listed first: those of Joel, Shapham, Jannai, and Shaphat. The next seven names may be intended as an extended family rather than as immediate descendants, hence the use of the term "kindred" in describing them. A third group of families is listed in verses

14–15, the descendants of Abihail. Ahi is listed as chief in the family of Abihail. The Chronicler indicates in verse 17 the approximate date of his genealogical source for the descendants in the reigns of Jotham of Judah (759–744) and Jereboam II of Israel (788–748), implying that the chronology would have been recorded in the decade of 759–749.

3. The war with the Hagrites, 5:18–22. This section returns to the theme of verse 10 in the Reubenite genealogy: war against Arab tribes in the Transjordan. In this case, however, it is clear that not only the Reubenites but Gadites and Manassites participate in the campaign. The description of the battle in verses 20–22 is significant for its note that the Israelites "cried to God." Throughout his narrative, the Chronicler will provide examples of military victories won not because of the strength or tactical superiority of the Israelites or Judahites, but because of their faithful reliance on God in the moment of crisis (see 2 Chron. 13:14–15; 14:9–15; 18:31). The phrase in verse 22, "the war was of God," formally claims the Hagrite campaign as a holy war. For the Chronicler, the only proper foundation for military action was holy war, because in his theological scheme, war is the province of God.

4. The Manassite genealogy, 5:23–26. The third tribal group described in this section is that of the half-tribe of Manasseh, son of Joseph. The term "half-tribe" is a reference to the fact that Manasseh and Ephraim are the sons of Joseph rather than of Isaac and cannot therefore be accorded full tribal status along with the remaining sons of Isaac. The need for two tribal groups is created by the removal of the Levites from the list of tribes so that they might serve priestly functions. Less a genealogy than a narrative, this section identifies the location of the Manassites as the area from Bashan north to Mount Hermon, in the northern Transjordan, and lists seven family heads within the Manassite tribe.

Verses 25–27 should be taken as a comment not merely on the Manassites alone but, as verse 26 makes clear, on all three Transjordanian groups. According to verse 25, the three tribes abandoned the worship of the God of Israel in favor of that of local deities. For their apostasy, the tribes were punished with defeat and exile by Tiglath-pileser III. This is the third time in this chapter the Chronicler has made reference to the loss of the Transjordan to the Assyrian king. We noted above the initial reference in verse 6; the exile mentioned in verse 22 is almost certainly not that of the Babylonian period but rather the same captivity imposed by the Assyrians in the wake of their campaigns into Syria-Palestine in 734–732 B.C. For the Chronicler, however, the central point to be made here is that if trust in God results in success and long life in the land, apostasy and abandonment of God results in exile and the loss of the land.

THE DESCENDANTS OF LEVI
1 Chronicles 6:1–81

This chapter, which deals with the various lineages of Levitical priests and musicians, is the most carefully developed in the genealogical material of chapters 1–9. This should not be surprising, given the Chronicler's great interest in the Temple and matters of religious practice. The care exhibited here in presenting the Levitical genealogy reflects the Chronicler's concern with establishing a solid theological foundation for the function of the Temple in his own day. The Chronicler returns to the subject of the Levitical priests, musicians, and other officials in 1 Chronicles 15—16 and 23—26, where he describes their place and function in the religious practice established by David in Jerusalem.

The chapter is easily divided into five segments. The Levitical genealogies, verses 1–49, comprise the first four: the genealogy of the Levitical priests, traced through Aaron, the grandson of Levi (vv. 1–15), a list of Levitical families or clans, identified by the name of the clan head and traced from each of the three sons of Levi (vv. 16–30), the genealogical trees of three families of musicians in the Temple, each traced from one of the three sons of Levi (vv. 31–47), and a summary of the functions of the two Levitical groups, the musicians and the Aaronide priests (vv. 48–49).The final section is a list of the cities and towns dispersed among the other tribes in which the Levites settled (vv. 50–81).

1. The genealogy of the Levitical priests, 6:1–15. Prominence among the Levites is given to the priestly family descended from Aaron. The Aaronide genealogy begins both of the major sections of the chapter, here and in verses 50–53. In both places, the list is founded on the lineage of Aaron ("the sons of Aaron," vv. 3, 50), rather than on Levi. The Chronicler's concern here is clear: to establish the legitimacy of the Aaronide priesthood and to ground it in the very earliest experiences of Israel with its God. The genealogy moves forward from Aaron to the "exile by the hand of Nebuchadnezzar" (v. 15), providing an unbroken line of Aaronide priests from the exodus and wilderness wanderings to the destruction of the Temple in 587 B.C. This is surely what makes this list so important to the Chronicler, for it provides a direct link between the priests of his time and the origins of the sacred story of Israel.

2. The Levitical clans, 6:16–30. While the list of Aaronide priests is traced through one son of Levi, Kohath, the lists of both Levitical clans and musicians are traced from all three sons. In developing this section, the Chronicler is dependent on two other biblical lists of Levites, Exodus 6:16–19 and Numbers 3:17–20. While neither of these lists is as long as the Chronicler's (the Numbers list goes only to the third generation and the Exodus list to the fifth in selected families), it is clear that the Chronicler has inherited the structure of his list from them. In all three lists the form is the same: The sons of Levi are listed (Gershom, Kohath, and Merari), and then each son's sons are named. In 1 Chronicles 6:19b–30, though, the Chronicler moves well beyond the names of descendants from each son available in either Exodus or Numbers, providing eight generations of Gershomites, ten Kohathites, and seven Merarites. In the case of the Kohathites, the Chronicler also provides two additional genealogical lists, one descended from Elkanah that ends in a second Elkanah (vv. 26–27) and one of the "sons of Samuel" (v. 28). Although the Chronicles list is not specific about the relationship between Elkanah and Samuel, the fact that Samuel was the child of Elkanah by Hannah would have been well-known from the story of Samuel's birth in 1 Samuel 1. The effect of these additional lists in verses 26–28 is to make Samuel a Levite, despite the fact that his ancestry is identified as Ephraimite in 1 Samuel 1:1.

Samuel plays a very minor role in the Chronicles narrative. Unlike the prominent positions of king-maker and king-breaker he holds in the Samuel-Kings story, Samuel of the Chronicles narrative is confined to a name in Levitical genealogies in this chapter, a reference to the anointment of David "according to the word of the LORD by Samuel" in 1 Chronicles 11:3, and a citation of the "records of the seer Samuel" in 1 Chronicles 29:29. This difference in the importance of Samuel is reflective of the Chronicler's view of David as the ideal and divinely ordained king of Israel. In the Samuel-Kings story, David might be understood as a usurper of the throne that is legitimately Saul's. Samuel plays a great role in the struggle between David and Saul, denouncing Saul (1 Sam. 13:1–15) and anointing David even while Saul is still alive (1 Sam. 16:1–13). Samuel serves as the divine spokesman, legitimizing David's claim to power. In Chronicles, however, there is no need to legitimize David's claim to rule; rather, it is assumed and unquestioned from the outset that David is God's choice to rule Israel. None of the stories about the struggle between David and Saul, David's flight from Saul, or the challenges to David's reign after his assumption of the throne appear in the Chronicles narrative. Samuel is thus reduced from king-maker to Levitical leader, whose only role in David's accession to power is a second-hand reference to his approval of David's reign.

3. The Levitical musicians, 6:31–47. The Chronicler prefaces his list of the Levitical musicians with a remark about their function (vv. 31–32):

6:31 **These are the men whom David put in charge of the service of song in the house of the LORD, after the ark came to rest there.** 32 **They ministered**

with song before the tabernacle of the tent of meeting, until Solomon had
built the house of the LORD in Jerusalem; and they performed their service
in due order.

Several things are worthy of note in this comment. First, this is the initial reference to the ark of the covenant in Chronicles. The ark, according to Exodus 25:10–22, was a large box made of acacia wood and covered
with gold ornamentation, the lid of which featured carved angelic figures
supporting the "mercy seat," a symbolic divine throne. Within the ark
were kept the tablets of stone on which God had written the law at
Mount Sinai (see the Chronicler's description in 2 Chron. 5:7–10). The
ark had come to represent the presence of God to Israel in the pre-
monarchic era, perhaps even serving as something of a talisman.
According to 1 Samuel 4:1–7:2, the ark was lost to the Philistines in the
battle at Aphek but subsequently returned to Israel. After its return, the
ark was housed at Kiriath-jearim, a small village to the west of Jerusalem,
until David brought it into his capital (see 2 Sam. 6:1–23; and 1 Chron.
13:1–14; 15:1–29; and 16:1–43).

Second, this text marks the Chronicler's definition of the roles and
responsibilities of the Levites with regard to worship around the ark.
Elsewhere in the Bible, Levites are responsible for carrying the ark when
it is moved from place to place (cf. Lev. 3:5–8) and for assisting the priest
and performing duties in worship at his instruction (Num. 3:5–10). Here,
the Chronicler specifies that the Levites have responsibility for the "service of song," that is, the music that accompanies worship. Only a few
chapters later, in the discussion of the establishment of worship in
Jerusalem, 1 Chronicles 15:16 is more detailed: Levites are appointed as
"singers to play on musical instruments, on harps and lyres and cymbals,
to raise loud sounds of joy." The effect of this redefinition is to give the
Levites a permanent role in the established religious practice of Israel,
even before the construction of the Temple. The Chronicler will feature
the role of the Levitical musicians prominently throughout the narrative,
enhancing their position in the story of Israel.

Finally, the text here is clear that this responsibility of the Levites for
worship is to be executed "before the tabernacle of the tent of meeting."
The language here is deliberately reminiscent of Numbers 3:7:

[The Levites] shall perform duties for [the priest] and for the whole congregation in front of the tent of meeting, doing service at the tabernacle.

The "tabernacle" and the "tent of meeting" refer to the moveable structure used to house the ark of the covenant and the worship activities

around it during the period prior to the settlement of Israel in Canaan. The Chronicler's choice of words here is significant. He invokes the language of the older tradition about the ark as a way of connecting the worship ritual established by David with that of Moses while Israel wandered in the wilderness.

The Levitical singers are divided into three lineages, as are the priests earlier. Each lineage is traced to one of the three sons of Levi: Gershom, Kohath, and Merari. But where the priestly genealogy is traced through the eldest son of Gershom, Kohath, or Merari, the musicians' genealogy is traced through the second son. In addition, the musicians' genealogy is in reverse order, that is, it begins with the musicians appointed to their position in the time of David—Heman, Asaph, and Ethan (cf. 1 Chron. 15:17)—and develops the genealogy back to the sons of Levi.

4. *The summary of Levitical functions, 6:48–49.* This brief two-verse section brings the genealogical section of the chapter to a conclusion by reviewing the function of Levitical musicians and priests. Verse 48 indicates broadly that the Levites were appointed for "all the service of the tabernacle of the house of God." Verse 49 provides somewhat more information about the role of the priests than does the priestly genealogy in verses 1–15. The priests are responsible for the offering on each of two altars, one for whole burnt offerings and the other for incense. The presence of two altars, each with its own specialized function, reflects a well-developed and stable sense of religious activity, probably from the Chronicler's own day. In addition, the priests are responsible for doing service in the "most holy place," the inner sanctuary where the ark was kept. Theologically, the Chronicler conceives of the work of the priests as "making atonement for Israel," or seeking reconciliation between God and the people, principally by means of the conduct of the sacrificial ritual.

It is difficult to overstate the importance of the Levites for the theology of the Chronicler. Together, the priests and Levitical servants, musicians, and other officers not only lead worship (in the tent of meeting during David's day and the Temple during the Chronicler's), but are the link between the practice of Israel's faith in the postexilic era and that of the sacred past of Moses. They are the caretakers for the great arc of tradition of the worship of God, an arc with one end in the very earliest beginnings of Israel's life as the people of God and the other in the era to which the Chronicler addresses his writing. That the Chronicler's readers could look at the institutions of their own day and see through his efforts the foundations of those institutions in the origins of sacred memory is surely the Chronicler's aim, both here in this genealogy and throughout much of the work that follows. The need for such connections between the present and the sacred past has never been lost on the community of faith, and for that reason those connections still flourish in the liturgy and language of church and synagogue. At least part of the function of pastor, priest, or rabbi is captured in the notion that he or she is one who does "the work of the most holy place" in accord with the traditions and instructions of the past.

5. *The list of Levitical settlements, 6:50–81.* The Chronicler turns from the provision of genealogy to a discussion of geography in the final section of this chapter, providing a list of the places where the Levites settled. The list is organized geographically, that is, Levitical settlements are listed according to their location in various tribal territories. Unlike other geographical entries for the tribes of Israel that demark territory by means of boundary descriptions (e.g., 4:34–41; 5:9, 23), this list provides the names of cities and villages interspersed throughout the tribal lands where Levites were settled. The reason is that the Levites as a tribe are devoted to the service of God in the tabernacle and Temple and are therefore not given a portion of the land from which to draw sustenance (Josh. 14:4). Instead, as the Chronicler understands it, their support is the responsibility of the whole community of Israel (see 2 Chron. 31:1–19), and so they are dispersed to live among the people in the land.

One of the Chronicler's purposes in writing was to enhance the role of the Levites in the religious and social culture of postexilic Israel. The Levites are given a place—many places, in fact—throughout Israel, and are thereby accorded status and importance in the reconfiguration of the people in the years following the exile and its disruption. Moreover, the figure of the Levite is set alongside the priest as central to Israel's religious and social life. Finally, the Chronicler's attachment of the Levites to David emphasizes again the importance of David as the "founder of the faith" of the Temple.

THE TRIBES OF THE CENTRAL HILL COUNTRY: ISSACHAR, BENJAMIN, NAPHTALI, MANASSEH, EPHRAIM, AND ASHER
1 Chronicles 7:1–40

Chapter 7 of 1 Chronicles deals with the genealogies of all the tribal groups as yet unmentioned in the Chronicler's list. They share a common geographic area: the hill country north of Jerusalem and west of the Jordan, including the Galilee. They also share a common political heritage: They are all Israelite groups, or peoples outside the boundaries of Judah. Since Judah and Judahite history is the clear center of gravity for the Chronicler's presentation, it is not at all surprising that these groups should receive more summary treatment than those more integrally involved in the Chronicler's story. Beyond these two commonalities, however, there is not much to unite the genealogical units of the chapter. They differ significantly in content and style, leading the reader to conclude that the Chronicler's sources were themselves not of a similar style. Moreover, as we shall see below, the tribe of Naphtali receives only cursory attention, and Dan and Zebulun are omitted altogether (although a remnant of a Danite genealogy may be present in fragmentary form). The chapter is composed of six units: the descendants of Issachar (vv. 1–5), the descendants of Benjamin (vv. 6–11), the descendants of Bilhah: [Dan and] Naphtali (vv. 12–13), the descendants of Manasseh (vv. 14–19), the descendants of Ephraim (vv. 20–29), and the descendants of Asher (vv. 30–40).

1. The descendants of Issachar (7:1–5), Benjamin (7:6–11), and Asher (7:30–40). Some formal similarities are shared by the genealogical material for Issachar, Benjamin, and Asher genealogies: (1) the use of the formula "the sons of X: . . . ," followed by a listing of the names of heads of clans, (2) the use of military terminology in registering the descendants of the tribe ("warriors," v. 6; "ready for service in war," v. 11; "mighty warriors . . . for service in war," v. 40), (3) the use of large, perhaps even exaggerated, numbers in describing the size of each tribe's fighting force (cf. vv. 5, 11, and 40), and (4) the absence of the sort of narrative material found in both the Manassite and Ephraimite genealogies (vv. 14–19 and 20–29). From the prominence of military language and the clear organization of the generations into groups listed as fighting forces, it seems likely that the Chronicler has composed these sections using military registration lists.

2. The descendants of Bilhah: [Dan and] Naphtali, 7:12–13. Perhaps the most significant problem posed by this section of the genealogies is to be found in verses 12–13:

7:12 **And Shuppim and Huppim were the sons of Ir, Hushim the son of Aher.** [13] **The descendants of Naphtali: Jahziel, Guni, Jezer, and Shallum, the descendants of Bilhah.**

This section evokes several questions. Why does the Chronicler refer to the "descendants of Bilhah" rather than of Naphtali, and why is the genealogy for Naphtali so abbreviated? Further, where are the genealogies for Dan and Zebulun, the only sons of Jacob not given lineages in 1 Chronicles 1—9?

In developing the genealogies in this chapter, the Chronicler appears to have relied on two sources, the list of the descendants of Jacob in Genesis 46:1–27 and Moses' census list in Numbers 26:4–65. If we look through these sources for the names Shuppim and Huppim, we note the consonantally similar names "Shephupham" and "Hupham" among the Benjaminites listed in Numbers 26:39. In addition, the name of the father of Shuppim and Huppim, "Ir," is very similar to that of Iri, son of Bela and grandson of Benjamin in 1 Chronicles 7:7. It seems likely, therefore, that Shuppim and Huppim are sons of Iri, grandsons of Bela, and great-grandsons of Benjamin, and that they belong to the Benjaminite genealogy. Hushim (v. 12b), on the other hand, seems to be part of a different lineage. The Benjaminite lists in both Genesis 46:21 and Numbers 26:38–41 contain no similar name. However, both lists provide only a single son for Dan. In Genesis 46:23, the name Hashum is given as the son of Dan; in Numbers 26:42, the name of the son of Dan is Shuham, which is Husham with the first two consonants inverted. It is quite likely, therefore, that Hushim ought to be understood as the Chronicler's genealogy of the tribe of Dan rather than a descendant of Aher, a Benjaminite, as verse 12b indicates. Somehow, in the transmission of Chronicles through the generations, the phrase "the sons [or descendants] of Dan" has dropped from its original position before the name Hushim. Such an omission would also explain the odd reference at the end of verse 13 to "the descendants of Bilhah." Bilhah was the concubine of Jacob, servant woman of Jacob's wife Rachel; Bilhah bore two sons to Jacob: Dan and Naphtali (Gen. 30:1–8). If the genealogy here originally contained a section for Dan as well as for Naphtali, the final reference to "the descendants of Bilhah" would make sense as a summary comment.

The brevity of the Naphtali (and Dan?) genealogies and the absence altogether of a genealogy for Zebulun might imply that some portion of the Chronicler's source or of 1 Chronicles itself has been lost. Indeed, Genesis 46:14 and Numbers 26:26–27 both provide Zebulunite lists, and it seems unlikely that the Chronicler would have simply ignored them or chosen to omit them. The most reasonable explanation, therefore, would be that some portion of this chapter containing at least the Zebulunite genealogy and perhaps more of Danite and Naphtalite lineages has been lost. Certainly such a lacuna could have prompted subsequent copyists of 1 Chronicles 7 to attempt to make sense of what remained, creating the current arrangement of verses 12–13.

3. The descendants of Manasseh, 7:14–19. Of particular interest in this section is the mention of Zelophehad in verse 15. The allusion here is to the story in Numbers 27:1–11 and 37:1–12 of the daughters of Zelophehad, who petition Moses to be allowed to inherit their father's portion of the land when Israel enters Canaan. Under normal circumstances, the eldest son received the inheritance, the sacred possession of the land given by God to each family descended from Jacob. In Zelophehad's case, however, there is no son but five daughters. Rather than lose the association of their father's name with the land, they seek and receive permission to inherit the land and divide it among themselves, so long as they marry within the tribe of Manasseh. The story is something of a landmark in Numbers, showing how the ancient tradition is at once flexibly interpreted and still maintained. The Chronicler includes Zelophehad here not only because his name is prominent among the biblical accounts associated with Manasseh but also because the incident provoked by his daughters marks an early stage in the task of updating the commandments and instructions of Moses to the changing circumstances of subsequent eras.

4. The descendants of Ephraim, 7:20–29. This section is composed of three parts: a genealogy descended from Ephraim (vv. 20–21a), a narrative concerning the birth of Beriah and the genealogy associated with him resulting in the birth of Joshua (vv. 21b–27), and a description of the territory settled by the Ephraimites (vv. 28–29).

The list of Ephraim's descendants appears straightforward, presenting a list of nine sons of Ephraim. Of the names of Ephraim's sons present in these two verses, only one, Shuthelah, appears in the genealogy of Numbers 26:34–37. The other two names of Ephraimites in Numbers, Becher and Tahan, are somewhat similar, although by no means identical, to Bered and Tahath of 1 Chronicles 7:20. The rest of the names listed by the Chronicler are unknown elsewhere as descendants of Ephraim.

The genealogy is interrupted in verse 21b by a narrative that recounts the death of certain of the Ephraimites, presumably Ezer and Elead, at the hands of the people of Gath. As the story has it, the Ephraimites had come down out of the hill country and raided cattle in the environs of the city of Gath, for which crime the Gittites killed them. Ephraim thereafter fathers another son, whose name is Beriah. The purpose of this narrative appears to be threefold. First, it explains the name of the son, Beriah, by connecting it to the Hebrew phrase *bera'ah*, "in disaster." Attention is thus drawn to this particular son of Ephraim, and through this one alone come all the other named descendants of Ephraim. Clearly, Beriah is for the Chronicler the only significant son from among the ten born to Ephraim. Second, the Beriah genealogy offers a unique vision of the important role played by a daughter, Sheerah. Sheerah is credited with building three towns, Uzzen-sheerah and both Upper and Lower Beth-horon; these latter two are important sites in that they guard one of the passages from the seacoast leading up to Jerusalem from the west. For the third time in this chapter, then, the

Chronicler has lifted up women in the genealogy as important participants in the progress of Israel (the other two occasions are Hammolecheth and Maacah and the daughters of Zelophehad in the Manassite genealogy, vv. 14–19). Third, and clearly most importantly, the genealogy that begins in Beriah results in the naming of Joshua, great leader of the conquest of the land and successor to Moses (v. 27). Since the Chronicler begins the story of Israel with the rise of David, Joshua has no other role in the narrative. The Chronicler includes him (and presumably those who subsequently trace their lineage to him) in the story as the last and greatest of the Ephraimite lineage.

The final section of the Ephraimite genealogy is not genealogy at all but rather a list of the towns and villages occupied by the Ephraimites. The practice of listing these settlements with the formula, "X and its towns," reflects the fact that each of the larger towns or cities would have had a small number of insignificant and probably impermanent villages in its environ. The area described by the town list includes cities in the central hills of Israel north of Jerusalem as far north as the great Jezreel Valley that runs northwest to southeast across Israel from Mount Carmel to the Jordan River. Megiddo, Gezer, Taanach, Beth-shean, and Dor are in or near the Jezreel Valley, and all play important roles in the subsequent history of the land.

THE DESCENDANTS OF BENJAMIN
1 Chronicles 8:1–40

The Chronicler returns to the Benjaminite genealogy in 1 Chronicles 8. After a reprise of the original Benjaminite family (vv. 1–2), the chapter is structured in two large sections: a list of Benjaminite ancestral houses in various locations (vv. 3–32) and a genealogy of the family of Saul (vv. 33–40). Within the former section, several different lists of clans or ancestral houses may be identified.

1. *The sons of Benjamin, 8:1–2.* The list of the sons of Benjamin provided here differs from both the list in 1 Chronicles 7:6 and that presented in Numbers 26:38–39. Only the name of Bela occurs in all three, implying that of the descendants of Benjamin, the family of Bela was clearly most important. In this case and in the case of Numbers 26:39, the only genealogical material subsequent to the first generation given in the text is traced through Bela.

2. *The descendants of Bela, 8:3–7.* The text of this section is sufficiently confusing to merit closer attention:

8:3 And Bela had sons: Addar, Gera, Abihud, ⁴Abishua, Naaman, Ahoah, ⁵Gera, Shephuphan, and Huram. ⁶These are the sons of Ehud (they were heads of the ancestral houses of the inhabitants of Geba, and they were carried into exile at Manahath): ⁷Naaman, Ahijah, and Gera, that is, Heglam, who became the father of Uzza and Ahihud.

We should probably make four changes that would make this text more understandable. The first is to replace the name "Abihud" with the words "the father of Ehud" (the two are identical in spelling). This would make Abishua through Huram sons of Ehud rather than Bela. The second change is to read the phrase "These are the sons of Ehud," as referring to Abishua through Huram. The third change is to delete the names "Ahijah" and "Gera" from verse 7; they are probably inadvertent duplications of the names "Ahoah" and "Gera" that follow Naaman in verses 4 and 5. Finally we should read "Heglam" in verse 7 not as a proper name but as the verbal phrase, "carried them into exile." With these changes, the section would read:

> ³And Bela had sons: Addar and Gera, ⁴the father of Ehud. ⁵These are the sons of Ehud: Abishua, Naaman, Ahoah, ⁶Gera, Shephuphan, and Huram. They were the heads of ancestral houses of the inhabitants of Geba, and they were carried into exile at Manahath. ⁷Naaman carried them into exile; he became the father of Uzza and Ahihud.

If such a reading is correct, we would then have a genealogy of Benjaminites consisting of five generations: Benjamin—Bela—Ehud—Naaman—Uzza and Ahihud. In addition, the section provides the information that in the fourth generation, Naaman's clan was removed from the central hill country around Geba (just north of Jerusalem) into exile.

3. The descendants of Shaharaim, 8:8–14. The list of the descendants of Shaharaim is unconnected to other Benjaminite lists and constitutes a separate genealogy within the larger tribe of Benjamin. Verses 22–25 and 26–28 comprise two more apparently unconnected lists of Benjaminites, so it is probable that the Shaharaim list here is independent as well.

The Shaharaim genealogy is interesting in at least two respects. First, it gives us the names of the wives with whom Shaharaim had sons. While this is not unique in the Chronicles genealogies, it does serve to call attention to the fact that there seem to have been different branches of the family. Second, the branches seem rather cleanly divided not only by the names of the mothers but also by geographical setting. One group, born of the wife Hodesh, is born in Moab, the plateau on the east side of the Dead Sea (vv. 8–10). The other, born of Hushim, whom Shaharaim is said to have divorced, seems centered in the area of Aijalon, located in the hill country west and slightly north of Jerusalem. We might reasonably see this division in the lineage of Shaharaim as reflective of attempts on the part of Benjaminite elements to expand out of the hills immediately north of Jerusalem in both easterly and westerly directions. Indeed, some support for each may be visible in other places. The Moabite Stone, a stele erected by the Moabite king Mesha in the mid–ninth century, B.C., indicates that Israelite elements controlled the central Moabite plateau for some time prior to his arrival on the throne. And our reconstruction of 1 Chronicles 7:12 would credit the name Hushim to the lineage of Dan, originally centered in the area west of Benjamin around Aijalon. While Hushim is clearly female in this text, it is not impossible to see the presence of the Danite name in the western Benjaminite family tree as an indication of mixture between the two tribal groups.

4. Benjaminite ancestral houses, 8:15–28. The next section of the Benjaminite list contains five short lists of clan or ancestral houses. The first three, Beriah (vv. 15–16), Elpaal (vv. 17–18), and Shimei/Shema (vv. 19–21) are all mentioned in the western genealogy of Shaharaim as children of Hushim. The final two, Shashak (vv. 22–25) and Jehoram (vv. 26–28) are not otherwise connected to the Benjaminite structure. The section concludes with the summary comment, "These lived in Jerusalem." While it cannot be established with certainty, it would seem likely that only the latter two clans are intended to be included in this comment; the others seem more closely associated with Aijalon and the western hill country. However, the distance between Jerusalem and Aijalon is not great, and it is not at all difficult to argue that all five families came to be associated with the environs of Jerusalem. The significance of this reference ought not to be missed. For the Chronicler, the story of the tribes of Israel that did not remain part of the kingdom of David is relatively inconsequential, and little reference is made to them. However, the Benjaminites who were neighbors of Jerusalem and were intimately involved with the story of David's kingdom are more important to him, and they are accorded a share in the reorganized people of God whom the Chronicler is seeking to define.

5. Benjaminites in Gibeon, 8:29–32. The Chronicler sets apart the next group of Benjaminites as being "in Gibeon." Gibeon is a city located about five miles north of Jerusalem but well within the country typically associated with Benjamin. It is the Gibeonite clans from which Saul comes, as is clear from the next section of the chapter.

6. The family of Saul, 8:33–40. The final section of the chapter consists of the genealogy of Saul. The placement of this section can hardly be accidental; it brings to a conclusion the genealogies of the various tribal groups and in so doing paves the way for the Chronicler's presentation of the rise of the monarchy in Israel. Chronicles contains no full discussion of the period of the Judges; instead, the genealogies take the place of that discussion, presenting a panoramic view of the distribution of Israelites in the land. The Chronicler draws that view into focus with this presentation of the genealogy of Saul, whose monarchy should be viewed as the transition between the tribal period on the one hand and the great story of the rise and reign of David on the other.

The list presents a problem in the parentage of Saul. According to verse 33, the name of Saul's grandfather is Ner, but in 1 Samuel 9:1, the name of Saul's grandfather is Abiel. In 1 Samuel 14:50–51, on the other hand, both names are present: Abiel is father of two sons, Kish and Ner, who are then fathers of Saul and Abner, respectively. The genealogy of Saul here can be made to conform to the information of 1 Samuel by replacing the first "Kish" of verse 33 with "Abner." The resulting text would then read:

Ner became father of Abner, Kish of Saul, ...

The problem created by this solution is that the name of Ner is not grounded in the genealogy of verses 29–32. It may be the case, however, that "Zur," which does appear in verse 30 as a brother of Kish, is a misreading of the name Ner (the initial consonants of both names are formed in similar ways and might easily be mistaken for each other).

An interesting element of the Benjaminite genealogy in verses 29–40 is the prominence of the theophoric element "Baal" in a number of names (Baal, Eshbaal, Meribaal). Baal is, of course, the name of the Canaanite deity worshiped by the inhabitants of the land before and during the Israelite period. Names that include this element do homage to the deity (e.g.,"Esh-baal" = "man of Baal"). Apparently, the Chronicler is not particularly concerned with the remnants of Baal worship evidenced in the clan names. The same cannot be said of the Samuel and Kings version of the story, which alters the name Esh-baal to Ish-bosheth, "man of shame."

The Saulide genealogy presented here and repeated in 9:35–44 follows the family of Saul down some ten generations, or well into the eighth century B.C. The fact that such an extensive list of descendants of Saul, one that carries the family tree down two centuries beyond the era of Saul, indicates the importance of the family, even among Judahite circles. Despite the loss of the monarchy by Saul to David, the Saulides continued to play a role in the lore of Israel.

THE INHABITANTS OF JERUSALEM
1 Chronicles 9:1–44

After concluding the genealogical registry of the descendants of Jacob (1 Chronicles 1–8), the Chronicler adds one final section listing the inhabitants of Jerusalem, and especially the priests (vv. 10–13), Levites (vv. 14–16), and gatekeepers (vv. 17–33). Following a summary comment (v. 34), the Chronicler appends to this list a repetition of the Saulide genealogy of 1 Chronicles 8:29–40. The primary source for the material in verses 1–34 is Nehemiah 11:3–24, although the Chronicler has altered his source for use in this context. Nehemiah 11:3–24 is clearly a list of the inhabitants of the postexilic city of Jerusalem. That the Chronicler intended his version of the list to be read in that way is somewhat less clear.

   1. The introduction to the Jerusalem list, 9:1–2. At the beginning of the list of the inhabitants of Jerusalem, the Chronicler provides the following introduction:

> 9:1 **So all Israel was enrolled by genealogies; and these are written in the Book of the Kings of Israel. And Judah was taken into exile in Babylon because of their unfaithfulness. ² Now the first to live again in their possessions in their towns were Israelites, priests, Levites, and temple servants.**

The parallel material in Nehemiah 11:3 is obviously similar, although with important differences as well:

> These are the leaders of the province who lived in Jerusalem; but in the towns of Judah all lived on their property in their towns: Israel, the priests, the Levites, the temple servants, and the descendants of Solomon's servants.

Both statements make clear that Israelites were living in or on their possessions or property, and both subdivide the inhabitants into categories: Israel, Levites, and temple servants. The initial difference between the two statements is the Chronicler's addition of 9:1, indicating that the genealogies of Israel—presumably those found in the previous eight chapters—are recorded in "the Book of the Kings of Israel." Since no such list occurs in the books of Samuel and Kings, it is clear that some other (and now presumably lost) source is cited here. In fact, the Chronicler refers at least once more to such a book in 2 Chronicles 20:34 and probably to the same work again in 2 Chronicles 33:18, where he cites the "Annals of the Kings of Israel." The identity and content of this book are unknown (see the introduction).

Some scholars have proposed that the phrase, "they were taken into exile because of their unfaithfulness," is a gloss or a later addition to the text by a subsequent editor or copyist and should be deleted. The text would then read:

> So all Israel was enrolled by genealogies, and these are written in the Book of the Kings of Israel and Judah. Now the first to live . . .

The deletion of this phrase (only three words in Hebrew) would also remove the only specific reference in this chapter to the exile, thus opening the possibility that the Chronicler intended this chapter not as a list of *postexilic* inhabitants of Jerusalem at all but as a list of Jerusalemites at a previous time, such as at the start of the reign of David. This suggestion finds support in the fact that the word "again" is not directly translated from the Hebrew of verse 2 but is rather an inclusion in the NRSV (and the RSV before it). The inclusion of "again" implies that the Israelites, Levites, and Temple servants had lived in the land once before and were now returning, a description appropriate to the situation of the return from exile. Its absence implies that the "Israelites, Levites, and Temple servants" of verse 2 were the first to live in their possessions in the towns.

If the deletion of "they were taken into exile because of their unfaithfulness" is correct, the nature of the chapter is transformed. What stands now as a list of the postexilic inhabitants of Jerusalem—somewhat out of place in a genealogical structure that seems to culminate with the arrival of David—might become instead a description of the population of Jerusalem as David comes to the throne. The focus of the list is on the personnel of the Temple: priests, Levites, singers, gatekeepers, and others. It is these offices to which the Chronicler devotes considerable space and attention in the account of the reign of David (cf. 1 Chronicles 23—26). In the end, of course, such reasoning is confined to the realm of speculation, and the presence of the phrase in the final version of verse 1 requires that we construe the whole list as postexilic. Under such a view, we would then see the Chronicler as having completed his genealogical view of Israel with a list of the Jerusalemites of his own day, implying that they are the descendants of the great lineage of God's will.

2. Non-Levitical inhabitants of Jerusalem, 9:3–9. The first division of the inhabitants of Jerusalem is the Chronicler's list of non-Levitical clans living in the city. Nehemiah 11:4–9 provides lists of Judahites and Benjaminites living in the city, but the Chronicler differs from his source in two ways. Most importantly, he adds Ephraim and Manasseh to the list (v. 3), where Nehemiah 11:4 and 7 know only the two bordering tribes,

Judah and Benjamin. The Chronicler has already demonstrated special interest in these tribal groups, principally because of their proximity to Jerusalem. That he would include people from outside Judah among the inhabitants of Jerusalem might be taken as a sign of his wish to include a larger portion of the people of David's kingdom in his vision of the reconstituted Israel. The Chronicler also differs from Nehemiah in the content of his genealogical material. Verses 4–6 are a list of Judahites descended from the three great Judahite clans of Numbers 26:20: Perez (v. 4), Shelah (v. 5), and Zerah (v. 6). Nehemiah 11:4–6 lists only descendants of Shelah and Perez and provides different names in each case. The correspondence between the Benjaminite list in verses 7–9 and in Nehemiah 11:7–9 is initially closer, but they too soon diverge, and beyond the third generation there is no correspondence at all. It seems clear that, while he follows the structure of the Nehemiah list, the Chronicler is working with a different genealogical source in constructing this section.

3. Priestly families in Jerusalem, 9:10–13. The Chronicler's list of priestly families in Jerusalem falls into three groups. The first is a genealogy tracing the lineage of Jedaiah back to Ahitub; the second traces Adaiah back to Pashhur, son of Malchijah (v. 12); the third provides the genealogy of Maasai from Immer. All three of these priestly families are identified in Nehemiah 11:1–14; the same three are listed in Ezra 2:36–39, but Ezra adds a fourth family, Harim, otherwise unknown.

The first of the priests, Jedaiah, is the only one given a title beyond the general designation "priest"; he is specifically called "chief officer in the house of God." The precise meaning of this phrase is uncertain. The Hebrew word, *nagid*, is translated "officer" in other places in Chronicles but does not always seem to imply priestly function. Later in this chapter, we hear that Phinehas was "chief" over the gatekeepers (9:20), and later we learn that Shebuel, grandson of Moses, was "chief officer in charge of the treasuries" (1 Chron. 26:24). On those occasions when it is clear that a priest is described by the term, however, that priest is otherwise known as a high priest: Azariah, in 2 Chronicles 31:10 and 13, and Hilkiah in 2 Chronicles 35:8b. It therefore appears that at least Jedaiah and possibly also Adaiah and Maasai may have been high priestly figures in the Chronicler's sources; at the very least, we must accord to them a certain importance by virtue of their stature as priests in Jerusalem.

4. Levitical families in Jerusalem, 9:14–16. A comparison between this list and the list of Levites in Nehemiah 11:3 shows a strong similarity in the names registered in both. However, the Nehemiah list is much clearer about the difference in function between groups of Levites than is the list here. In Nehemiah, the first group of Levites (Shemaiah,

Shabbethai, and Jozabad; Neh. 11:15–16) are "over the outside work of the house of God," while the second group (Mattaniah, Bakbukiah, and Abda; Neh. 11:17) were "to begin the thanksgiving" (i.e., they were singers and song leaders). The Chronicler does not draw such functional distinctions between Levitical groups listed here; Shemaiah, Bakbakkar (=Bakbukiah of Neh. 11:17), and Mattaniah—along with Obadiah and Berechiah (two names not found in the Nehemiah list)—are simply categorized as Levites without further definition.

   5. The gatekeepers, 9:17–32. We meet in this section a Levitical function not previously described in Chronicles, the gatekeeper (see 1 Chron. 26:1–20). The names of the gatekeepers listed here and in the parallel in Nehemiah 11:19–21 are mostly similar. The most significant difference is the Chronicler's emphasis on Shallum, who is identified as the "chief" among the gatekeepers (v. 18), a role played in earlier times by Phinehas, son of Aaron (v .20). In distinction from the material in Nehemiah, however, the Chronicler makes two important changes. First, he provides the gatekeepers with a two-part pedigree: a genealogy that links them to Korah, son of Levi (v. 19a; see also 1 Chron. 26:1) and a description of the foundations of their order in the practices of the tabernacle and their establishment in office by David and Samuel (vv. 20–22). Second, the Chronicler provides a lengthy discussion of the responsibilities of the gatekeeper, to clarify those responsibilities to a readership that might be unaware or underappreciative of them (vv. 23–32). Principally, the gatekeepers were guardians of the house, stationed at entrances on the four sides of the house (v. 24) and relieved weekly by other members of the Levitical groups charged with the same responsibility. Some of the gatekeepers were also charged with guarding important inner chambers, especially the treasury (v. 26). Other responsibilities seem to have included protection of the sacred utensils used in the sacrificial rites of the Temple, various pieces of cultic furniture, and supplies and foodstuffs within the Temple (vv. 28–29). The Chronicler makes clear, however, that their responsibilities did not include the actual preparation of spices or the making of flat cakes (the "baked pieces" associated with the grain offering; cf. Lev. 6:14–23) and showbread (Lev. 24:5–9). These latter are reserved to other Levitical and priestly figures. The final verse of the section (v. 33) also removes the singers from work associated with the preparation of ritual foods so that they might be free to lead worship "day and night" in the Temple.

   6. Summary conclusion, 9:34. The Chronicler completes his presentation of the Jerusalem clergy with a summary statement that provides a brief insight into the operation of the Temple in his own day. Members of the Levitical clans—priests, Temple servants, singers, and gatekeepers—were "living in the chambers of the temple free from other service, for they were on duty day and night" (v. 33). From this short comment we learn three things about the Chronicler's view of the Temple. First, the Temple contained a residential section where the Levites and priests "on duty" were housed during their period of service. Second, that service in the Temple meant that other work—farming, military service, commercial activity—was set aside in order to free the clergy for undistracted focus on Temple service. Third, the Chronicler conceives of a Temple that never sleeps but is open to and for the prayers of Israel "day and night."

7. The Saulide genealogy, 9:35–44. This section is virtually identical to the genealogy of the family of Saul in 8:29–40; little more needs to be said by way of explanation than has already been said. However, the question of why the material is repeated here so soon after its earlier presentation deserves comment. With the completion of the Jerusalem lists in verse 34, the Chronicler has accomplished his presentation of the composition of the people of God. He must now turn his attention to the great narrative of the reign of David and the further story of the Israelite monarchy. As a connecting link between the presentation of all Israel distributed across the land and that larger story, he offers again the genealogy of Saul. Saul is uniquely suited for the purpose; his family arises out of the Benjaminite tribal heritage but in Saul that tribal way of life is superceded by the monarchy. However short-lived and vexed the monarchy of Saul was, it was nonetheless the doorway to the great future of the people of God held in the hands of David. The Chronicler has no wish to recount the story of Saul or to get bogged down in the morally questionable nature of David's relationship with and final replacement of Saul; those stories distract him from his greater purpose, which is to present David as the author and founder of the religious hopes and traditions of Israel. So the Chronicler merely presents again the names of the lineage of Saul, both those that root Saul in the past and those that link him to the future in the story of David and the kingdom.

The genealogies of 1 Chronicles 1—9 largely accomplish the first great theological task of the Chronicler's work: that of defining the community of Israel, both as it existed in the days of David and as that existence is echoed in the Chronicler's own day. In addition, they point the way toward the second and third tasks of the book: to depict the Temple and its associated religious traditions established by David as the embodiment of God's will for the worship of Israel and to present David himself as the ideal king whose reign was the model for faithful government as the Chronicler envisioned it.

Part II: The Rise and Reign of David

1 Chronicles 10—29

The Chronicler devotes the greatest portion of his work to the story of David; no other king is given so much space in the narrative. In creating his account of David's career, the Chronicler uses his source narrative in 2 Samuel carefully, augmenting it frequently with additional material. In the main, this additional material is focused on David's role as founder of Israel's faith and organizer of its religious practice. There is much less focus here than in the 2 Samuel material on David as warrior, and none on the internal upheavals that characterized David's family and court. From the outset, the Chronicler's theological agenda is clear: He seeks to present David as the agent of the divine will in the establishment of Israel as God's people.

3. David's Rise to Israel's Throne
1 Chronicles 10:1–12:41

First Chronicles 10 is a turning point in the narrative of Chronicles in at least two ways, one obvious and the other perhaps more subtle. At an obvious level, the chapter presents us with a shift in the type of information we read: We move from genealogical lists to narrative. At a more subtle level, we have moved from timelessness to history, from the vague to the concrete. Behind us are the lists of eponymous ancestors whose lives reach back into the unremembered past; the text now speaks of characters and events we know from the great historical narratives of 1 and 2 Samuel and 1 and 2 Kings. The Chronicler thereby conveys to us a sense of having arrived at the moment toward which all the prehistory of Israel was moving: the story of David.

THE DEATH OF SAUL
1 Chronicles 10:1–14

> 10:1 Now the Philistines fought against Israel; and the men of Israel fled before the Philistines, and fell slain on Mount Gilboa. 2 The Philistines overtook Saul and his sons; and the Philistines killed Jonathan and Abinadab and Malchishua, sons of Saul. 3 The battle pressed hard on Saul; and the archers found him, and he was wounded by the archers. 4 Then Saul said to his armor-bearer, "Draw your sword, and thrust me through with it, so that these uncircumcised may not come and make sport of me." But his armor-bearer was unwilling, for he was terrified. So Saul took his own sword and fell on it. 5 When his armor-bearer saw that Saul was dead, he also fell on his sword and died. 6 Thus Saul died; he and his three sons and all his house died together. 7 When all the men of Israel who were in the valley saw that the army had fled and that Saul and his sons were dead, they abandoned their towns and fled; and the Philistines came and occupied them.

⁸ The next day when the Philistines came to strip the dead, they found Saul and his sons fallen on Mount Gilboa. ⁹ They stripped him and took his head and his armor, and sent messengers throughout the land of the Philistines to carry the good news to their idols and to the people. ¹⁰ They put his armor in the temple of their gods, and fastened his head in the temple of Dagon. ¹¹ But when all Jabesh-gilead heard everything that the Philistines had done to Saul, ¹² all the valiant warriors got up and took away the body of Saul and the bodies of his sons, and brought them to Jabesh. Then they buried their bones under the oak in Jabesh, and fasted seven days.

¹³ So Saul died for his unfaithfulness; he was unfaithful to the LORD in that he did not keep the command of the LORD; moreover, he had consulted a medium, seeking guidance, ¹⁴ and did not seek guidance from the LORD. Therefore the LORD put him to death and turned the kingdom over to David son of Jesse.

First Chronicles 10 is the only narrative about Saul included by the Chronicler. None of the stories known to us from 1 Samuel of Saul's early heroism in battle against the Philistines are included, as are none of the stories about the ill-fated triangle of Saul, his son Jonathan, and David or any of the tales of David on the run from Saul (although they are alluded to in the next chapter). Their absence should not be understood as an indication of the Chronicler's ignorance of them but rather his assessment that including them would distract from the purpose of presenting the story of David as founder of both the kingdom and faith of Israel. We need only to know that Saul is dead and that David is the divinely chosen successor to the throne.

The chapter is structured in two parts: the account of Saul's death (vv. 1–12) and the summary of Saul's reign (vv. 13–14).

1. The account of Saul's death, 10:1–12. Saul dies in battle against the Philistines. The Philistines were a loosely organized group of people, probably Greek in origin, who had settled along the coast of Palestine during the Late Bronze Age. Having established cities along the coastal plain, they began to press inland into the western slopes of the Judahite hill country in search of arable land. At the same time, Israelite settlements in the hill country both north and south of Jerusalem began to push eastward into this same country for the same reasons. Conflict between the two groups was inevitable and seems to have started long before the reign of Saul (cf. the story of Samson in Judges 16—19). By the end of Saul's reign, periodic skirmishes between the two had given way to warfare on a larger scale. The location of the final battle of Saul's career is Mount Gilboa, north of Jerusalem; the location indicates how successful the Philistines had been at pushing Israel back toward the Jordan.

The source of this story is 1 Samuel 31:1–13, but the Chronicler has altered the Samuel account in two important ways. First, the Chronicler notes that Saul, his sons, and "all his house" died together on Mount Gilboa (10:6); the parallel statement in 1 Samuel 31 is that "Saul and his three sons and his armor-bearer and all his men" died in battle (1 Sam. 31:6). By this change, the Chronicler removes any claimants to the throne from the family of Saul, leaving David's claim unopposed. Second, the 1 Samuel 31 account of the disposal of Saul's body makes clear that the Philistines displayed Saul's headless corpse from the walls of the town of Beth-shan, to the north of Mount Gilboa, and that having heard of this dishonor, the men of Jabesh-gilead traveled all night and took Saul's body away to provide a more honorable burial. The Chronicler omits the detail of the display of Saul's body on the town wall, implying that all the soldiers of Jabesh-gilead had to do was to retrieve the body from the battlefield, a far less risky enterprise. Thus, the homage done to Saul is less impressive, and the story becomes little more than an account of Saul's burial place.

2. The summary of Saul's reign, 10:13–14. At the end of the account of each king's reign, the Chronicler provides a summary of that king's life. Drawn largely from similar summaries in 1 and 2 Kings, these short notices provide information about each king's length of reign and his age at accession to the throne, and often make reference to other documents containing accounts of the king's activities (see introduction). The Chronicler also augments these summaries with additional comments, usually of an evaluative character.

The summary of Saul's reign is unique among the Chronicler's regnal summaries in that it provides none of the standard information about the length of Saul's reign or his age at coming to the throne, nor does it refer the reader to any other source for accounts of Saul's activity. Instead, the Chronicler provides in verses 13–14 a theological assessment of Saul's reign and death that is consistent with his theological program. The death of Saul, according to the Chronicler, is the direct result of Saul's own faithlessness, which is demonstrated in two charges: that he "did not keep the command of the LORD" and that he "consulted a medium." The former charge is unspecific but may refer to Saul's decision to allow Agag, the Amalekite king captured in battle, to live, despite Samuel's instructions to the contrary (1 Sam. 15:10–35). The latter almost certainly refers to Saul's consultation with the "witch of Endor," a spiritualist or medium, in order to seek guidance from the spirit of Samuel (1 Sam. 28:8–25), despite the specific prohibition of such practices in Israel (Lev. 19:31; 20:6, 27). More significant in the second charge is the fact that Saul "did not seek guidance from the LORD" (v. 14). Throughout Chronicles, the mark of a faithful king or nation is that he or they "seek the LORD." Initially, the term means what it implies here, that one asks God for guidance in making decisions. Gradually, however, the Chronicler imbues this term with greater meaning, until it comes to describe a religious lifestyle characterized by obedience and reliance upon God (see 2 Chronicles 15 and commentary). The Chronicler judges Saul for seeking guidance from the wrong spiritual authority in both this specific incident and in his life as a whole.

For this unfaithfulness, "the LORD put [Saul] to death." The Chronicler is not ignoring his own account of Saul's suicide but rather affirming that his suicide was the working out of God's intent. As noted in the introduction, the Chronicler arranges his account to make clear the direct connection between the fate of a character and his or her moral and spiritual behavior. Saul's death is the first example of this principle of moral responsibility but by no means the last. Throughout Chronicles, the fate of an individual rests in the hands of that individual rather than with large forces behind the scene. For the Chronicler, then, the death of Saul is not a historical accident, nor is it merely the result of complex internal emotional forces or external political pressures; it is the direct result of his faithlessness.

The death of Saul does accomplish one thing beyond itself, however; it clears the way for the accession of David. "The LORD . . . turned the kingdom over to David son of Jesse" (v. 14) is a direct statement of the divinely ordained nature of David's kingship. This does not mean that the Chronicler is either unaware of or in disagreement with the longer, more involved narrative of David's rise to power in 1 Samuel. Rather, what is intended here is a theological summary of that process. The Chronicler hereby leaves no doubt that the story of David's reign is the story of God's will for the people.

DAVID'S ACCESSION TO THE THRONE OF ISRAEL
1 Chronicles 11:1–12:41

Chapters 11 and 12 of 1 Chronicles should be treated as a single unit. That this is true may be seen in the fact that the same scene brackets the two chapters: Both 11:1–3 and 12:38–40 depict people of Israel gathered at Hebron for the celebration of David's accession to the throne of Israel. In between these two passages are various lists and short narratives that provide information about those who were "with David," that is, who were numbered among his supporters as he began his rise to the throne. The Chronicler wants to be very clear that as David begins his reign, "all

Israel" is represented among those who accompany him into power. In distinction from 2 Samuel 5:5, in which David is first king of Judah for seven years before claiming the Israelite throne, David is made king over a united Israel from the beginning. To make this point, the Chronicler uses the phrase "all Israel" twice, once as "all Israel" gathers at Hebron (1 Chron. 11:1) and again in the note that "all the rest of Israel were of a single mind to make David king" (12:38).

The story of David's accession to the throne may be divided into five sections: the anointing of David at Hebron (11:1–3), the capture of Jerusalem (11:4–9), David's "mighty men" (11:10–47), the list of David's followers in the wilderness (12:1–22), and the list of David's army at Hebron (12:23–41).

1. The anointing of David at Hebron, 11:1–3. The description of David's anointing as king in Hebron is taken almost verbatim from the source narrative in 2 Samuel 5:1–3. The elders of Israel come to David while he is at Hebron, a Judahite city south of Jerusalem. Recognizing his leadership even while Saul was alive, they now turn to him as the logical choice to be Saul's successor. They make a covenant "before the LORD" and anoint David as "king over Israel." The Chronicler makes only one significant change to his source: the addition of the phrase, "according to the word of the LORD by Samuel," at the end of the announcement that the elders and people anointed David king (1 Chron. 11:3; cf. 2 Sam. 5:3). By adding this phrase, the Chronicler reminds his readers that David's kingship is neither the result of political machinations nor the accident of historical events but the specific expression of the divine will as articulated by Samuel.

2. The capture of Jerusalem, 11:4–9.

11:4 David and all Israel marched to Jerusalem, that is Jebus, where the Jebusites were, the inhabitants of the land. 5 The inhabitants of Jebus said to David, "You will not come in here." Nevertheless David took the stronghold of Zion, now the city of David. 6 David had said, "Whoever attacks the Jebusites shall be chief and commander." And Joab son of Zeruiah went up first, so he became chief. 7 David resided in the stronghold; therefore it was called the city of David. 8 He built the city all around, from the Millo in complete circuit; and Joab repaired the rest of the city. 9 And David became greater and greater, for the LORD of hosts was with him.

The account of the capture of Jerusalem is somewhat enigmatic and requires a word of explanation. Jebus was the ancient name of Jerusalem, and the Jebusites were, as the text indicates, the inhabitants not only of the city but of the surrounding region as well. Most scholars believe that the city was given the name Jerusalem after David's conquest, although there is some evidence to suggest that both names were in use well before the arrival of David and that Jebus and Jerusalem may originally have been separate cities. By the Chronicler's day, however, any distinction between them had been lost, and he assumes that Jebus is Jerusalem. The reference to "the Millo" is not clear; it is variously interpreted to refer to supporting terraces on the hillsides below the Temple and palace structures in the heart of the old city of Jerusalem or to a gap between the Temple mound and the rest of the city.

It is particularly helpful in understanding the Chronicler's theological agenda to look at the difference between his version of the capture of Jerusalem and that of his source, 2 Samuel 5:6–10. The Chronicler has altered his source in at least three significant ways. First, he replaces "his men" in 2 Samuel 5:6 with "all Israel" in 1 Chronicles 11:4, thereby making it clear that the capture of Jerusalem is not a feat accomplished by a select corps of David's personal troops but a pan-Israelite achievement. Jerusalem is therefore not only the city of David but also the capital of all Israel. By implication, no other capital—especially one established at Samaria by later Israelites—can be so regarded.

Second, the Chronicler omits the strange and difficult references to "the blind and the lame" in 2 Samuel 5:6b and 8a. On the lips of the Jebusites, it was probably meant to extol the strength of the city's defenses: Even the blind and the lame could keep out an invader. In David's command, it was probably sarcastic in tone: Do they think the defenses are so strong? Let us get inside and we will take care of "the blind and the lame." The origin of the phrase may be glimpsed in its third use in 2 Samuel 5:8b, the saying regarding the prohibition of blind and lame (and otherwise physically deformed persons) from entering the Temple (see Lev. 21:18). By the Chronicler's time, the phrase had almost certainly become obscure, and the reference to David hating the blind and the lame presented a less than positive picture of the king. By omitting any reference to it, the Chronicler simultaneously clears up an obscurity in the text and removes a potential blemish on the character of David.

Third, the Chronicler alters the command of David regarding the invasion of Jerusalem in verse 6. In 2 Samuel 5:8, David commands his soldiers to "get up the water shaft to attack." The water shaft was a large vertical tunnel inside the city walls that led down to a pool of water. The pool was created by digging a second, nearly horizontal tunnel from the bottom of the water shaft to a spring located outside the walls at the base of the hill on which the city sat. Water then ran downhill through the near-horizontal tunnel and back inside the city instead of outside the walls, providing a safe water supply during times of siege.

As long as the exterior opening of the spring was well hidden, the city and the water supply were secure. But if an invader discovered the outside opening, it might provide a passage for a small commando-type force to enter the city and undermine its defenses. In 2 Samuel 5:8, this is precisely the sort of attack David orders. The Chronicler removes this reference, along with the military stratagem it depicts, leaving the impression that "all Israel," under the leadership of Joab, captures the city by main force. Rather than a stealth attack accomplished by a few elite troops, the capture of Jerusalem is done openly and by all the people with David.

3. David's "mighty men," 11:10–47. The lists and stories in 1 Chronicles 11:10–12:38 are intended to document the names of those who came to power alongside David and in his service. The first of these is the list of David's "mighty men" in 11:10–47. The list here is closely dependent on the parallel material of 2 Samuel 23:8–39; the Chronicler preserves the distinction of 2 Samuel between the "Three" and the "Thirty," two categories of elite warriors and officers under David's personal command. The list of the Three in 2 Samuel 23 includes Josheb-basshebeth (Jashobeam in 1 Chron. 11:11), Eleazar, and Shammah. The Chronicler has collapsed the separate but similar accounts of Eleazar and Shammah in 2 Samuel 23:9–10 and 11–12, respectively, into a single account in 1 Chronicles 11:12–14. In so doing, he omits the name of Shammah altogether, leaving the curious situation of references to the Three in verses 11, 12, 18, and 19, while only two names are mentioned. Some of the names of the Thirty, presumably a second echelon among David's elite corps, are familiar from the accounts of David's struggles both before and after his accession to the throne: Abishai (v. 20; see 2 Sam. 18:1–5), Benaiah (v. 22; see 2 Sam. 8:18; 20:23; and 1 Kings 1—2), Asahel (v. 26; see 2 Sam. 2:18–23), and Uriah the Hittite, first husband of Bathsheba (v. 41; see 2 Samuel 11). However, the Chronicler does not relate any of the stories associated with their names; the focus is on David and his role as founder of kingdom and cult, not on the exploits of his chiefs and soldiers.

The one exception is the inclusion of the story of the Three who bring to David water from the well at Beersheba (vv. 15–19, see 2 Sam. 23:13–17). The story relates the heroism of the Three in breaking through enemy lines to bring water from a specific well for which David had expressed a desire. Upon seeing the water and knowing the risk involved in obtaining it, David pours it out as an oblation, or offering, to God, explaining that it is far too precious for him to drink. The story serves two purposes here. At its simplest level, it is a story about the respect David and his chiefs have for one another: they, that they are willing to risk their lives to fulfill his desires, and he, that he considers the results of their efforts too precious to consume as he might other, less sacred water. At a more subtle level, however, the Chronicler enhances the image of David by having David see himself modestly. Rather than drink what he has proclaimed precious, David announces that such a great gift can only be received by God and not by any mortal, including himself. David thus emerges as humble and pious, even in this moment of legendary greatness.

4. David's followers in the wilderness, 12:1–22. The first half of chapter 12 offers several names of warriors who joined David while he was at Ziklag, the town given to him by the Philistine king Achish of Gath while he was in the service of the Philistines shortly before the death of Saul (see 1 Sam. 27:5–12). Of particular interest in this section is verse 1:

> 12:1 **The following are those who came to David at Ziklag, while he could not move about freely because of Saul son of Kish; they were among the mighty warriors who helped him in war.**

The Hebrew verb translated by the English phrase, "could not move about freely," might more properly be rendered "restrained," or "kept back." In a literal sense, of course, David is restrained by Saul in that he is unable to move about the countryside freely for fear of capture. But one scholar has noted that a more theological sense attaches to this phrase; David is "kept back" from becoming the king he is intended to be by divine will as long as Saul is alive. If we assume this interpretation, it casts a somewhat different light not only on David but also on those who have come to join him at this stage. In 1 Samuel 22:2, those who join David in the wilderness are characterized as distressed persons, debtors, and "discontents" (the latter phrase might better be translated "hotheads"); here in 1 Chronicles 12:1, on the other hand, they are "mighty warriors." If we understand David as the Chronicler does, not as a rebellious servant on the run from his legitimate master but as the true king prevented from his rightful throne by a usurper, then those who have come to join him are not malcontents but mighty warriors and patriots.

Verses 16–18 contain a conversation that takes place between David and various Benjaminites and Judahites who come to join him. It is impossible to miss David's concern and wariness in the speech; he is cautious about receiving the Benjaminites—the people from whom Saul comes—because of the potential for betrayal they represent. The idea that not everyone in Israel was eager to have David as king is clear in the narratives of 1 and 2 Samuel (see, for example, 1 Sam. 23:1–14 and 19–29), but it survives in 1 Chronicles only in the echo of concern in

David's voice here as he greets the arrival of these Benjaminites and Judahites.

The response of Amasai, apparently one of the Benjaminites, who is identified as "a chief of the Thirty," is important. The text is careful to note that "the spirit came upon Amasai," indicating that what he says must be understood as a prophetic utterance. Prophetic statements play an important role in Chronicles, not as predictive speeches to reveal the course of the story ahead but as divine confirmation (or, on occasion, rejection) of actions or plans at the moment. The function of Amasai's prophetic speech here is to confirm David's movement toward the throne. But the speech serves another purpose as well, one that is not clear until we reach the speech of the people of Israel to Rehoboam, son of Solomon, at the point of the dissolution of the kingdom after the death of Solomon (2 Chron. 10:16). The relationship between the two speeches is immediately clear when they are placed side by side:

1 Chronicles 12:18	2 Chronicles 10:16
We are yours, O David,	What share do we have in David?
and with you, O son of Jesse!	We have no inheritance in the son of Jesse.
Peace, peace to you	Each of you to your tents, O Israel!
and peace to the one who helps you!	Look now to your own house, O David.
For your God is the one who helps you.	

Amasai's speech emphasizes the unity of the people of Benjamin and Judah with David ("We are yours"), a unity that is dissolved after the death of David's son Solomon ("What share do we have?"). Amasai's speech prominently employs the term "peace" (*shalom* in Hebrew), which implies not only the absence of conflict but also wholeness, completeness, and integrity. Opposed to that term in the Israelite speech of 2 Chronicles 10:16 is the exhortation, "Each of you to your tents, O Israel!" which points to dissolution, division, and conflict. Where Amasai's speech promises to David the help he seeks in verse 17, the Israelite speech explicitly shrugs off any notion of cooperation ("Look now to your own house, O David"). Noticeably absent from the Israelite speech is any parallel to the final affirmation of Amasai's speech, "For your God is the one who helps you," implying perhaps that the Israelite speech has no word to say that interprets the word and will of God. The Chronicler's theology is clear here. David's accession to the throne of Israel is the will of God, and the continued reign of the Davidic dynasty is God's intent. The division of the kingdom of David into Judah and Israel by Israelites acting after the death of Solomon is a direct reversal of that intent and therefore a rebellion against God's will. For this reason, Amasai's speech binding Benjamin and Judah to David is spoken in the prophetic spirit, while no such claim is made for the Israelite speech.

Verses 19–22 recount the arrival of some of the Manassites to David "when he came with the Philistines for the battle against Saul." Their arrival at this late juncture in the period before David's accession to the throne provides the Chronicler the opportunity to make reference to the fact that David, although nominally a Philistine vassal, did not participate in the battle that ended Saul's life. Citing the Philistines' distrust of David's loyalty (v. 19), the Chronicler is careful to note that David was sent away from the battlefield. In this manner, David is exonerated of any complicity in Saul's death.

The summary comment in verse 22 returns again to the request of David to Amasai in verse 17 ("If you have come . . . to help me"), assuring us that David is indeed receiving the help he needs, not only from the people who gather to him but, by extension as well, from the God who "is the one who helps you" (v. 18). Small wonder then that in the Chronicler's eyes, the gathered host associated with David as he stands on the verge of claiming the throne intended for him looks "like an army of God."

5. David's army at Hebron, 12:23–41. Much of the second half of 1 Chronicles 12 is a list of the tribes who come to David at Hebron after the death of Saul for the official acclamation of David's kingship over Israel. All the tribes of Israel are represented in this list, including those already mentioned earlier in this chapter. In the main, the Chronicler names the tribe and notes the number of warriors who have come to join David, occasionally also citing the name of a leader among them. In a few cases, comments that seem unusual are added as well. The Benjaminites, for example, are noted in verse 29; some three thousand have come to David, even though "the majority had continued to keep their allegiance to the house of Saul." In all likelihood, the purpose of this comment is to make clear that not all of Benjamin had abandoned Saul and allied with David when Amasai did (vv. 16–18) but that those who had remained loyal to Saul did not come to David until Saul and his family were dead. Perhaps more unusual is the comment given concerning the troops of Issachar, who in the Chronicler's words, "had an understanding of the times, to know what Israel ought to do" (v. 32). The precise intent of this phrase is lost, but it probably implies that Issacharites were perhaps more ready than others to come to David's side or that they were instrumental in persuading others that the moment was right to join with David.

Chapters 11 and 12 conclude where they began, with "all Israel" gathered at Hebron "with full intent to make David king" (v. 38). As if to emphasize the point, the Chronicler adds that "likewise all the rest of Israel were of a single mind to make David king." From the Chronicler's perspective, the choice of David is not only the divine choice but also the unanimous choice of the people. The confluence of divine and human will is therefore an occasion for celebration, and from one end of Israel to the other, people and abundance flow into Hebron for the party (v. 40).

4. David Transfers the Ark of God to Jerusalem
1 Chronicles 13:1–16:43

First Chronicles 13—16 are crucial chapters for the Chronicler's story, for in them he seeks to establish his theme of David's central role in founding the religion of Israel. We have seen hints and references to this theme in the work so far, played in one key or another, but now the Chronicler gives it full voice. Once again, in developing this theme, he relies on material taken from other sources, especially 2 Samuel 5—6; once again, however, he gives that material his own theological spin, requiring his readers to understand even old stories in a new light.

The ark of God, or ark of the covenant as it is more often called, is first described in Exodus 25:10–22, in which Moses is commanded to have Israel make a box of acacia wood in which to store the documents of the covenant made between God and Israel (see Ex. 25:16, 21). The ark was to have been just under four feet long and slightly more than two feet wide and deep (2½ cubits x 1½ cubits x 1½ cubits, where a cubit is about 18 inches), overlaid with gold. It was to have been supported by two gold-covered poles that were set through rings attached to the sides of the ark. Atop the ark was the mercy seat (Ex. 25:17–22), a throne-like structure made of pure gold and fashioned in the shape of cherubim, or heavenly beings. The ark accompanied Israel throughout the years in the wilderness, and after the land of Canaan was settled, it came to rest at the shrine at Shiloh.

It is important to understand that as much as ancient Israel treasured the ark and mercy seat, it did not understand the ark as an idol or a representation of God but rather as a sort of locus at which God and the people might meet so that God might "deliver to you all my commands" (Ex. 25:22). The ark was a powerful symbol of the presence of God in the midst of the people, and because it was rooted deep in the traditional past of the nation, it also represented contact with the earliest layers of Israelite religion. To be in the presence of the ark might be, if God so

62

chose, to be in the presence of God. Even though the theology of later years would have forbidden such thinking, it is quite probable that early Israel looked upon the ark as something of a talisman or good luck charm.

This explains Israel's decision to carry the ark into battle against the Philistines, where it is captured when the Israelites are defeated (1 Sam. 4:1–11). After a series of disasters overtakes the Philistines who try to keep and display the ark as captured booty, the ark is sent back to Israel and comes to rest at the town of Kiriath-jearim, west of Jerusalem. There the ark remains throughout the story of David's rise to power in 1 Samuel, until in 2 Samuel 6:1–23, David accomplishes the transfer of the ark from Kiriath-jearim to Jerusalem.

The Chronicler picks up the story at this point, presuming that his readers already know the significance of the ark as a religious symbol and also something of its history. For his purposes, the importance of the ark is its symbolic value: It represents the potential presence of God. The one who lives with the ark near him or within his dwelling is blessed by God (see 1 Chron. 13:14), and for the Chronicler, that blessing must rest first and foremost on David. In addition, for David to bring the ark into Jerusalem is to marry the ancient past with the dawning future and to invite God's blessing on that future. The religion that David establishes around the ark in 1 Chronicles 15—16 is therefore the religious life and tradition blessed by God and, by extension into the Chronicler's own time, the tradition to be kept and observed in the latter days, even if the ark itself is no longer present.

The Chronicler does not present the story of David's transfer of the ark in the same order as 2 Samuel. Instead of presenting the entire story in a single narrative, the Chronicler divides the story into four sections: the initial failure to move the ark into the city (13:1–14), David's personal success as king (14:1–17), the succesful transfer of the ark into Jerusalem (15:1–29), and the installation ceremony for the ark (16:1–43).

THE FIRST ATTEMPT TO MOVE THE ARK
1 Chronicles 13:1–14

13:1 **David consulted with the commanders of the thousands and of the hundreds, with every leader.** 2 **David said to the whole assembly of Israel, "If it seems good to you, and if it is the will of the LORD our God, let us send abroad to our kindred who remain in all the land of Israel, including the priests and Levites in the cities that have pasture lands, that they may come together to us.** 3 **Then let us bring again the ark of our God to us; for we did** not turn to it in the days of Saul." ⁴ The whole assembly agreed to do so, for the thing pleased all the people.

⁵ So David assembled all Israel from the Shihor of Egypt to Lebo-hamath, to bring the ark of God from Kiriath-jearim. ⁶ And David and all Israel went up to Baalah, that is, to Kiriath-jearim, which belongs to Judah, to bring up from there the ark of God, the LORD, who is enthroned on the cherubim, which is called by his name. ⁷ They carried the ark of God on a new cart, from the house of Abinadab, and Uzzah and Ahio were driving the cart. ⁸ David and all Israel were dancing before God with all their might, with song and lyres and harps and tambourines and cymbals and trumpets.

⁹ When they came to the threshing floor of Chidon, Uzzah put out his hand to hold the ark, for the oxen shook it. ¹⁰ The anger of the LORD was kindled against Uzzah; he struck him down because he put out his hand to the ark; and he died there before God. ¹¹ David was angry because the LORD had burst out against Uzzah; so that place is called Perez-uzzah to this day. ¹² David was afraid of God that day; he said, "How can I bring the ark of God into my care?" ¹³ So David did not take the ark of God into his care into the city of David; he took it instead to the house of Obed-edom the Gittite. ¹⁴ The ark of God remained with the household of Obed-edom in his house three months, and the LORD blessed the household of Obed-edom and all that he had.

The Chronicler sets the stage for the movement of the ark into Jerusalem with a four-verse introduction unique to this account. One notices immediately the lengths to which David has gone to secure approval and participation in the decision from others. He consults with "commanders of the thousands and of the hundreds, with every leader" (v. 1), and he ultimately addresses "the whole assembly of Israel." The language is persuasive rather than imperative: "If it seems good to you, and if it is the will of the LORD our God, let us send abroad. . . . Then let us bring the ark." The sense is that David seeks a consensus decision so that the responsibility of moving the ark rests not on his shoulders only but on those of the whole nation. And indeed, "the whole assembly agreed to do so, for the thing pleased all the people" (v. 4).

The remainder of the chapter is built closely on the source narrative in 2 Samuel 6:1–11, but with a minor change at the outset. The account in 2 Samuel 6:1 has David assembling thirty thousand "chosen men" for the task; 1 Chronicles 13:5 makes clear that David assembled "all Israel from the Shihor of Egypt to Lebo-hamath." This phrase is a description of the geographical extent of Israel, at least as it was claimed to be at the height of the nation's life. The Shihor of Egypt is one of the western courses of the Nile River through its vast delta in Egypt. Lebo-hamath (literally, "the gate of Hamath") was the lower end of the great Bekaa, the valley between the Lebanon and Anti-Lebanon mountains far to the north. By employing this description, the Chronicler includes everyone who lived in land Israel claimed as its own at any point in its history. The movement of the ark is undertaken, therefore, by "all Israel" in the most expansive sense of the term.

The story of the movement of the ark from Kiriath-jearim toward Jerusalem is fascinating and disturbing. The ark is placed on a cart for the journey and escorted by Uzzah and Ahio, while David and the rest of his entourage dance in the procession. At one point along the way, the oxen drawing the cart cause the cart to shake, and Uzzah reaches out—perhaps instinctively—to steady it. The reaction of God to Uzzah's action is swift and decisive: "He struck him down . . . and he died there before God" (v. 10). The abrupt death of Uzzah raises unsettling questions. The first and most obvious is: Why did it happen? The second, perhaps less obvious but no less important, is: What does this disaster say about God's relationship to David?

In the case of the first question, the text is not explicit either here or in 2 Samuel 6:1–11, and the reader is left to speculate as to the reason for God's outburst. One is tempted to suggest, for instance, that Uzzah's instinctive steadying of the ark implies an assumption on his part that the presence of God requires human assistance in order to keep from falling. Following this line of reasoning, Uzzah is punished for his arrogance. At this point, of course, the text provides only the explanation that the incident is remembered because it gave a name to the place of its occurrence: Perez-uzzah, which means "bursting out [against] Uzzah." The matter will be resolved by the Chronicler but not until chapter 15, as David and Israel try again to bring the ark into the city. For now, all is chaos and confusion on the road from Kiriath-jearim to Jerusalem.

The fact that David is at least temporarily confused by Uzzah's death leads directly to the second question about the relationship between God and David. According to 1 Chronicles 13:12, David was "afraid of God that day." In the context of the Chronicler's treatment of David, this is a powerful statement. Heretofore, God has been David's ally and strength, giving the kingdom into his hands, enabling the capture of Jerusalem, and uniting all Israel under David's banner. But suddenly, in the midst of David's attempt to secure the symbols of the ancient religion of Israel under his own roof, God seems to have turned against him. Small wonder, then, that David should exclaim, "How can I bring the ark of God into my care?" In the Chronicler's theological system, every disaster is the result of some sinfulness on the part of those who suffer the calamity. The Chronicler's David must wonder now what sin he has committed suddenly to deserve such a divine outburst against him. Where has God's blessing gone? Has the relationship between God and David, until now so sweet, suddenly turned sour?

DAVID'S SUCCESS AS KING
1 Chronicles 14:1-17

Chapter 14 provides the answer to the question raised in the previous chapter, but in an indirect way. The Chronicler relocates to this point material found prior to the movement of the ark in 2 Samuel (2 Sam. 5:11-25). In this portion of the story, David is blessed by God in three specific ways: in international prestige (vv. 1-2), in progeny (vv. 3-7), and in military accomplishments (vv. 8-17). By presenting this material here rather than prior to the Uzzah episode, the Chronicler seeks to make clear that God's displeasure is not directed at David.

1. David's international prestige, 14:1-2. Verses 1-2 describe for us a David whose international prestige is such that neighboring kings offer significant presents to him. Hiram is king of Tyre, an ancient Phoenician maritime center on the northeast coast of the Mediterranean. He figures prominently in the story of Solomon, lending material and craftsmen for the construction of the Temple (1 Kings 5; 2 Chron. 2:3-16). His gift of cedar trees, masons, and carpenters to David indicates recognition of David as king of Israel and a potential ally in international affairs. The narrative makes clear that David takes Hiram's gift as a signal that "the LORD had established him king over Israel" (v. 2).

2. David's progeny, 14:3-7. David is described as becoming father to several more sons and daughters (vv. 3-7). The thirteen sons named here correspond closely to those listed in the Davidic genealogy in 1 Chronicles 3:5-9; there are minor variations in spelling of some names, but they are similar enough to presume that they derive from a common source. Only eleven names are mentioned in the parallel material in 2 Samuel 5:13-16; that list omits Elpelet and Nogah. However, the names of David's sons are not so important as the fact that David has them. In the ancient world, as in many modern cultures, one of the measures of wealth, prestige, and blessing is the number of one's children. That David is father to more sons after the Uzzah incident is seen by the Chronicler as evidence that God continues to bless David.

3. David's military successes, 14:8-17. Finally, the Chronicler repeats here material found in 2 Samuel 5:17-25 concerning David's military exploits. Two engagements against the Philistines receive attention here, both taking place in the valley of Rephaim, a valley floor located to the southwest of Jerusalem. The first battle takes place near Baal-perazim; the tradition associates the name with David's remark that "God has burst out" against his enemies (v. 11; the name, literally translated from Hebrew, is "Baal [or "the lord"] bursts out"). But it is surely important that the Chronicler situates the name and its explanation here, after the "bursting out" of God against Uzzah in the previous chapter. There, God seems to have burst out against David and his servants for reasons that are so far ambiguous. Now, however, God has burst out against David's enemies and in favor of David himself. This is an unambiguous sign of God's favor toward David.

David responds to God's favor with piety and obedience. Twice in these two stories (v. 10 and v. 14), David explicitly seeks the will of God, asking whether or not to join the battle. In one case, the divine command is to attack; in the other, it is to wait in ambush. But the point in both is that David takes no action without consulting God, and therefore his actions represent obedience to God's command. The point is strengthened by the reference to the burning of the abandoned gods of the Philistines in verse 12. In the account of this battle in 2 Samuel 5:21, David and his men "carried [the gods] away"; the Chronicler alters the account to specify that David commanded the incineration of the gods. This change brings David's action into accord with the provisions of Deuteronomy 7:5 regarding the treatment of idols captured in battle; he thus reiterates the point of David's obedience to the command of God.

The final sentence, 1 Chronicles 14:17, is unique to the Chronicler and is a summary comment intended to reflect on the chapter as a whole:

The fame of David went out into all lands, and the LORD brought the fear of him on all nations.

At one level, the statement is an appropriate response to David's military exploits. Beyond this, however, the prestige, wealth, and power of David are, in the view of the Chronicler, becoming internationally significant. Most importantly, though, the statement serves as an objective verification of David's internal awareness in verse 2, where David "perceived that the LORD had established him as king." No longer is the perception confined to David's spirituality; it is now an objective fact for the narrative. The Chronicler means for us to know that God has not abandoned David and that God is not angry with him for reasons associated with the movement of the ark. The dark questions about David's relationship to God have received bright answers, and we take up again the initial question raised by the Uzzah narrative: Why did it happen?

DAVID BRINGS THE ARK INTO JERUSALEM
1 Chronicles 15:1–29

15:1 David built houses for himself in the city of David, and he prepared a place for the ark of God and pitched a tent for it. 2 Then David commanded that no one but the Levites were to carry the ark of God, for the LORD had chosen them to carry the ark of the LORD and to minister to him forever. [3] David assembled all Israel in Jerusalem to bring up the ark of the LORD to its place, which he had prepared for it. [4] Then David gathered together the descendants of Aaron and the Levites: [5] of the sons of Kohath, Uriel the chief, with one hundred twenty of his kindred; [6] of the sons of Merari, Asaiah the chief, with two hundred twenty of his kindred; [7] of the sons of Gershom, Joel the chief, with one hundred thirty of his kindred; of the sons of [8] Elizaphan, Shemaiah the chief, with two hundred of his kindred; [9] of the sons of Hebron, Eliel the chief, with eighty of his kindred; [10] of the sons of Uzziel, Amminadab the chief, with one hundred twelve of his kindred.

[11] David summoned the priests Zadok and Abiathar, and the Levites Uriel, Asaiah, Joel, Shemaiah, Eliel, and Amminadab. [12] He said to them, "You are the heads of the families of the Levites; sanctify yourselves, you and your kindred, so that you may bring up the ark of the LORD, the God of Israel, to the place that I have prepared for it. [13] Because you did not carry it the first time, the LORD our God burst out against us, because we did not give it proper care." [14] So the priests and the Levites sanctified themselves to bring up the ark of the LORD, the God of Israel. [15] And the Levites carried the ark of God on their shoulders with the poles, as Moses had commanded according to the word of the LORD.

[16] David also commanded the chiefs of the Levites to appoint their kindred as singers to play on musical instruments, on harps and lyres and cymbals, to raise loud sounds of joy.

(Verses 17–24 then list the members of the Levitical families designated as lyre players, trumpeters, and gatekeepers.)

15:25 So David and the elders of Israel, and the commanders of the thousands, went to bring the ark of the covenant of the LORD from the house of Obed-edom with rejoicing. [26] And because God helped the Levites who were carrying the ark of covenant of the LORD, they sacrificed seven bulls and seven rams. [27] David was clothed with a robe of fine linen, as also were all the Levites who were carrying the ark, and the singers, and Chenaniah the leader of the music of the singers; and David wore a linen ephod. [28] So all Israel brought up the ark of the covenant of the LORD with shouting, to the sound of the horn, trumpets, and cymbals, and made loud music on harps and lyres.

[29] As the ark of the covenant of the LORD came to the city of David, Michal daughter of Saul looked out of the window, and saw King David leaping and dancing; and she despised him in her heart.

After resolving the question of whether God has withdrawn divine blessing from David, the Chronicler proceeds to resolve the matter of the reason for God's outburst against Uzzah. Once again, however, the Chronicler's interest here is not merely the retelling of the ancient story. Just as he has used material from 2 Samuel in the previous chapter to advance the theme of David's special relationship to God, now he uses other material in chapters 15 and 16 to develop the theme of David as founder of the faith of Israel. The present chapter is composed of three sections: David's instructions to the priests and Levites (vv. 1–16), the list of Levitical singers who accompany the ark (vv. 17–24), and the procession of the ark into the city (vv. 25–29).

1. David's instructions to the priests and Levites, 15:1–16. The obvious focus of 1 Chronicles 15:1–24 is the preparation David makes for the reception of the ark into Jerusalem. The Chronicler signals a theme that will become more prominent throughout the remainder of 1 Chronicles: that David does everything to establish the religion of Israel except physically construct the Temple. We are told that David "prepared a place for the ark of God and pitched a tent for it" (v. 1), that David gathers the Levites and descendants of Aaron to serve as ministers and priests for the ark (v. 4), and that he commands them specifically regarding their duties to it (vv. 11–15). Finally, we learn that David organizes the Levitical singers to accompany the ark on its journey and to sing before the Lord after the ark is established in its new home (vv. 16–24).

Alongside the theme of David as founder of the faith is also the resolution to the Uzzah incident. The Chronicler hints at its explanation in verse 2 in saying that "no one but the Levites were to carry the ark of God." The reason for God's outburst is finally explicit in David's comments to the Levites in verses 11–13. There, after commanding them to sanctify themselves in preparation for bringing up the ark of the LORD, David at last explains the disaster that befell Uzzah: "Because you [Levites] did not carry it the first time, the LORD our God burst out against us, because we did not give it proper care." The obedience of the Levites in verses 14–15 then makes clear why Levitical care of the ark is important: because Moses had commanded it. The reference is to Deuteronomy 10:8:

> At that time the LORD set apart the tribe of Levi to carry the ark of the covenant of the LORD, and to stand before the LORD to minister to him, and to bless his name, to this day.

By adding this material to the story, the Chronicler presents David as carefully obedient to God, having learned the lesson of casual disobedience on the road outside Kiriath-jearim. At the same time, however, the Chronicler shows us a David whose obedience extends even beyond that of Moses. Where Moses commands the Levites to carry the ark, David not only does this but also brings the ark to the place prepared for it. David establishes the ark in a permanent home, Jerusalem, where it remains under his personal aegis.

2. The list of Levitical singers, 15:17–24. The Chronicler makes clear that music is the responsibility of the Levites, and he understands it to be at least as important as carrying the ark. The Levites who are selected as musicians include the three mentioned in the list of Levitical singers in 1 Chronicles 6:31–48: Heman, Asaph, and Ethan, descendants of the great Levitical families of Kohath, Gershom, and Merari, respectively. The Chronicler then adds names of "kindred of the second order"; most of these are new in this context. The one exception is Obed-edom, whose house is chosen to shelter the ark during its stay in Kiriath-jearim. The prominence given to the Levitical singers is reflective of their importance in the operation of the Temple during the Chronicler's own day, and indicates that the Chronicler regarded the musical life of the Temple as a vital element of the ministry to God. Like the handling of the ark, the musical atmosphere around it must be prepared with precision and care.

3. The procession of the ark into the city, 15:25–29. At last, the ark makes its way into the city in verses 25–29. While the account here is closely parallel to that of 2 Samuel 6:12b–16, there are several changes worthy of note. First, David is explicitly accompanied by "the elders of Israel and the commanders of the thousands" (v .25) as he goes down to Kiriath-jearim; as noted in the discussion of chapter 13, the Chronicler uses this detail to indicate that this is not David's act alone but the expression of the will of all Israel. Second, the Chronicler gives a specific reason for the sacrifices offered along the route: God is present to help the Levites who were carrying the ark, and sacrifice is appropriate whenever one is in the presence of the divine. The animals sacrificed are of greater worth: seven bulls and seven rams here, as opposed to oxen and fatlings in 2 Samuel 6:13. In all, the emphasis in the Chronicles account is shifted toward the liturgical significance of the occasion. Third, the Chronicler gives David more clothing to wear. In 2 Samuel 6:14, David wears only an ephod (a kind of loincloth), and his near nakedness becomes the issue of an argument between David and his wife Michal in 2 Samuel 6:20–23. The Chronicler removes the issue here by clothing David in a "robe of fine linen," as well as the ephod. The detail is not accidental; Exodus 39:22 and 27 refer to the linen robe as a priestly garment. The additional item of David's apparel thus serves not only to limit his self-exposure but also to cast him in the role of high priest over this crucial liturgical occasion.

We should also note the Chronicler's presentation of the encounter between David and Michal or, more precisely, the lack of it. In 2 Samuel 6:20–23, Michal, daughter of Saul and wife of David, despises David because, in his wild dancing while wearing only the ephod, he has exposed himself; Michal clearly considers such behavior beneath the royal dignity to which she aspires. The Chronicler, however, has removed any reference to David's lewdness and made such a charge impossible. Yet he preserves the tradition of Michal's disdain for her husband, while identifying her only as "daughter of Saul." The conclusion left to be drawn is that Michal's disdain for David is political rather than personal. She is more a member of the house of Saul than of the house of David, and she shares the antipathy of her father toward his successor.

The importance of this chapter is hard to overstate. Not only does it provide the explanation for the problem of Uzzah's death while serving David's will, thereby exonerating David of any blame in the affair, but it also makes some basic claims about Israel's worship and, by extension, about our own. The Chronicler claims that David is the organizer and guiding spirit behind Israel's faith and worship. In his speech to the Levites, David teaches that Uzzah died because he handled the ark improperly. Such an explanation seems strange to us, in an age when we no longer regard sacred objects with mystical or magical awe. But we should not allow the strangeness of the explanation to blind us to the underlying truths. For the Chronicler, worship—life in the presence of God—is not a casual affair; it cannot be treated casually or haphazardly. Failure to attend to the divinely ordered traditions and procedures is equal to disrespect and sacrilege. In the ongoing conversation in our time about ordering worship, when ideas about casual dress and contemporary patterns of speech and music command so much of our attention, such truths are well worth bearing in mind.

THE INSTALLATION CEREMONY OF THE ARK
1 Chronicles 16:1–43

The Chronicler begins the installation scene where the Samuel narrative ends, with the short reference to the communal feast following the completion of the ark transfer in 2 Samuel 6:17–19a, here in verses 1–3. But where the Samuel story shifts the scene from public festivities to the private confrontation between David and Michal (2 Sam. 6:20–23), the Chronicler carries forward in greater detail concerning the installation ceremony. He separates the report of the feast (vv. 1–3 = 2 Sam. 6:17–19a) from the report of the departure of the people and the return and blessing of David (v. 43 = 2 Sam. 6:19b), and uses the latter to bring the whole episode of the transfer of the ark to a close. In between the brackets of the Samuel narrative the Chronicler has added three new units: the appointment of Levitical ministers to serve before the ark in Jerusalem (vv. 4–7), the great hymn composed and sung on the occasion of the ark's installation (vv. 8–36), and the establishment of a shrine at Gibeon (vv. 37–42).

1. Worship before the ark, 16:1–7. In appointing the Levites to minister before the ark, David specifies the duties they are to perform. They are to "invoke, to thank, and to praise the LORD, the God of Israel," employing harps and lyres, cymbals, and trumpets—the same instruments used in the procession of the ark from Kiriath-jearim to Jerusalem. Lest it be thought that this was a one-time celebration, the Chronicler makes clear that they are to make this musical supplication and praise "regularly, before the ark of the covenant of God" (v. 6). Readers mindful of Levitical function throughout the period of the monarchy will note the absence of any instruction regarding Levitical participation in sacrifices. However, since there is no permanent altar and no Temple as yet, there can be no sacrificial ritual for the Levites in Jerusalem to maintain; hence, their duties here are confined to prayer and praise

2. David's hymn, 16:8–36. Clearly, the centerpiece of the chapter is the great hymn sung by David on the occasion of the installation of the ark. The hymn serves two purposes in this context: First, it preserves a sense of the nature of hymnody in the Temple of the Chronicler's own day, and second, it serves to advance one of the Chronicler's theological claims. The hymn is composed of all or portions of three psalms: Psalm 105:1–15 (=1 Chron. 16:8–22), Psalm 96:1–13 (=1 Chron. 16:23–33), and Psalm 106:47–48 (=1 Chron. 16:35–36). That these three psalms are included in the text of Chronicles tells us that at least several individual psalms, and probably groups of psalms, were already in writing and liturgical use by the mid-fifth century B.C. How much older they may be than this is impossible to ascertain, but their use here points to the conclusion that the psalms as we know them were important pieces of the worship life of Israel in the postexilic period. The Chronicler's decision to place these psalms on the lips of David also points to the conclusion that the tradition of David as hymnist and liturgist predates the Chronicler. The Chronicler uses this tradition as part of his overall presentation of David as the founder of Israel's faith. David not only provides for the work of the Levitical singers but also teaches Israel itself the songs to sing.

As a view of the Chronicler's theology, David's hymn is perhaps even more interesting both for what it says and for what it chooses not to say.

Once again, the Chronicler has heavily edited his source material in the service of his theme. The hymn presents us with a view of God shaping the course of history and creation to bring Israel into being, to "gather and rescue us from among the nations, that we may give thanks to your holy name" (Ps. 106:47 = 1 Chron. 16:35).

Framed as a call to thanksgiving and a summons to remember God's faithful acts, the first portion of the hymn is quoted directly from Psalm 105:1–15. It recites the covenant made by God with Jacob, including the promise to give Canaan to Israel as an inheritance (vv. 15–18) and the protection of the wandering patriarch as he moved throughout the land (vv. 19–22). However, the Chronicler omits the remainder of the psalm that rehearses Israel's sojourn into and exodus from Egypt. In its place he sets the second psalm, Psalm 96, which is used in its entirety. Psalm 96 is a hymn of praise to God as divine lord and judge over nations and peoples, and Israel is summoned to "worship the LORD in holy splendor" (Ps. 96:9 = 1 Chron. 16:29). God is praised particularly for God's greatness over other deities, using a phrase familiar to many Christians as an ascription of praise or call to worship: "Great is the LORD, and greatly to be praised; he is to be revered above all gods" (Ps. 96:5 = 1 Chron. 16:25). The final section of the hymn is the conclusion of Psalm 106; here the Chronicler has omitted a lengthy description of Israel's disobedience and faithlessness in the wilderness (Ps. 106:1–46) and cited only the psalmist's cry for deliverance: "Save us, O LORD our God, and gather us from among the nations" (Ps. 106:47 = 1 Chron. 16:35). He also changes the verb tenses of Psalm 106:48 so as to give the sense that 1 Chronicles 16:36b is a response by the people to the foregoing psalm ("Then all the people said, 'Amen!'"), rather than simply liturgical instructions to make a response ("Let all the people say, 'Amen'").

The effect of all this editorial activity is to create a hymn that celebrates the sovereignty and majesty of God over creation and nations, affirms God's faithfulness and grace in establishing a covenant with Jacob and his descendants, and entreats God to continue God's saving work in gathering the people "from among the nations." Written out of and for the liturgy of a people still struggling with their identity as a people of God among the nations and seeking to reestablish their religious traditions in a new Temple, such a hymn must have been a powerful tool for claiming that identity: Israel is chosen and precious to God. By setting it on the lips of David, the Chronicler gives this composite celebration of Israel's self-understanding in the present the authority of the sacred past. Israel is taught to sing this hymn of its identity and importance to God by the very founder of the faith, David. What greater warrant could there be to sing that hymn in the Chronicler's own day?

3. Care for the tabernacle at Gibeon, 16:37–43. Despite the installation of the ark in Jerusalem, David maintains the ritual of worship in Gibeon, insuring that sacrifices continue there. Gibeon is situated to the north of Jerusalem in the hill country of Benjamin, where an altar had been established in earlier times. Gibeon's importance as a cultic shrine is highlighted by the fact that the tabernacle is located there. The Chronicler, ever mindful of ancient precedent, is aware of the importance of the tabernacle as the locus of the presence of God with Israel as the people wandered through the wilderness. Since there is as yet no permanent Temple to which all Israel is to come to "seek the LORD," David acts appropriately to insure the continuation of worship there.

David appoints some of the priests, especially Zadok, to administer the sacrificial ritual at Gibeon, and he assigns Levites under the leadership of Heman and Jeduthun to serve as musicians there (vv. 39–42). The Chronicler is careful to note that at Gibeon, the morning and evening sacrifices are offered as prescribed in Exodus 29:38–42 and Numbers 28:3–8. The legal requirements from Exodus and Numbers specify that each day two lambs should be sacrificed on the altar, one in the morning and the other in the evening, each with accompanying grain offerings and libations. The Chronicler is careful to have David adhere closely to the requirements of the Torah, once again demonstrating the obedience of David in liturgical matters. The combined information about the musical accompaniment of the ark and the sacrificial ritual at the altar in Gibeon also allows us an insight into the operation of the Temple in the Chronicler's own day. The music, prayers, praises, and daily sacrifice envisioned by David's obedience to the Torah in 1 Chronicles 16 must surely reflect the Chronicler's own experience of the Temple. By placing their origins in David's establishment of the faith and liturgy of Israel, the Chronicler accords them the highest authority and importance.

5. David's Reign Established
1 Chronicles 17:1–22:1

With David established on the throne of the joined kingdoms of Israel and Judah and the ark of the Lord brought under David's personal protection in Jerusalem, the Chronicler now turns to the great theme of 1 Chronicles: the building of the Temple. In one way or another, virtually everything else in 1 Chronicles is related to the theme of the Temple construction and especially to David's role as founder of the faith of Israel. In exploring this theme, the Chronicler has to overcome the central problem with his view of David: Why was it not David but Solomon who built the Temple? The Chronicler's answer to this question is stated at the beginning of chapter 17, but it is developed as we watch the events of David's reign unfold.

THE DYNASTIC PROMISE AND DAVID'S PRAYER
1 Chronicles 17:1–27

17:1 Now when David settled in his house, David said to the prophet Nathan, "I am living in a house of cedar, but the ark of the covenant of the LORD is under a tent." ² Nathan said to David, "Do all that you have in mind, for God is with you."

³ But that same night the word of the LORD came to Nathan, saying: ⁴ "Go and tell my servant David: Thus says the LORD: You shall not build me a house to live in. ⁵ For I have not lived in a house since the day I brought out Israel to this very day, but I have lived in a tent and a tabernacle. ⁶ Wherever I have moved about among all Israel, did I ever speak a word with any of the judges of Israel, whom I commanded to shepherd my people, saying, Why have you not built me a house of cedar? ⁷ Now therefore thus you shall say to my servant David: Thus says the LORD of hosts: I took you from the pasture, from following the sheep, to be ruler over my people Israel; ⁸ and I have been with you wherever you went, and have cut

off all your enemies before you; and I will make for you a name, like the name of the great ones of the earth. [9] I will appoint a place for my people Israel, and will plant them, so that they may live in their own place, and be disturbed no more; and evildoers shall wear them down no more, as they did formerly, [10] from the time that I appointed judges over my people Israel; and I will subdue all your enemies.

"Moreover I declare to you that the LORD will build you a house. [11] When your days are fulfilled to go to be with your ancestors, I will raise up your offspring after you, one of your own sons, and I will establish his kingdom. [12] He shall build a house for me, and I will establish his throne forever. [13] I will be a father to him, and he shall be a son to me. I will not take my steadfast love from him, as I took it from him who was before you, [14] but I will confirm him in my house and in my kingdom forever, and his throne shall be established forever." [15] In accordance with all these words and all this vision, Nathan spoke to David.

[16] Then King David went in and sat before the LORD, and said, "Who am I, O LORD God, and what is my house, that you have brought me thus far? [17] And even this was a small thing in your sight, O God; you have also spoken of your servant's house for a great while to come. You regard me as someone of high rank, O LORD God! [18] And what more can David say to you for honoring your servant? You know your servant. [19] For your servant's sake, O LORD, and according to your own heart, you have done all these great deeds, making known all these great things. [20] There is no one like you, O LORD, and there is no God besides you, according to all that we have heard with our ears. [21] Who is like your people Israel, one nation on the earth whom God went to redeem to be his people, making for yourself a name for great and terrible things, in driving out nations before your people whom you redeemed from Egypt? [22] And you made your people Israel to be your people forever; and you, O LORD, became their God.

[23] "And now, O LORD, as for the word that you have spoken concerning your servant and concerning his house, let it be established forever, and do as you have promised. [24] Thus your name will be established and magnified forever in the saying, 'The LORD of hosts, the God of Israel, is Israel's God'; and the house of your servant David will be established in your presence. [25] For you, my God, have revealed to your servant that you will build a house for him; therefore your servant has found it possible to pray before you. [26] And now, O LORD, you are God, and you have promised this good thing to your servant; [27] therefore may it please you to bless the house of your servant, that it may continue forever before you. For you, O LORD, have blessed and are blessed forever."

In many ways, 1 Chronicles 17 is a pivotal chapter for 1 and 2 Chronicles. It contains the great dynastic promise of God to David that David will have a son on the throne of Judah in perpetuity and that God will always maintain a relationship of "steadfast love" (v. 13) with him. It also explains that, contrary to expectations developed so far by the Chronicler, David will not be the one to build the Temple. Finally, it begins the task of enhancing the reputation and role of Solomon as a great king in his own right. All this is done within a structure shaped largely by a play on words, one that, remarkably, works as well in English as it does in Hebrew.

The narrative of 1 Chronicles 17 depends heavily on the parallel story in 2 Samuel 7. Indeed, as we have seen in other places, the language is so similar that the few places where the two diverge stand out in sharp relief and point to the theological agenda of the Chronicler. The chapter has two sections: Nathan's prophecy to David (vv. 1–15) and David's prayer to the Lord (vv. 16–27).

1. Nathan's prophecy, 17:1–15. The initial motivation for the story of the Lord's promise through Nathan is David's desire to construct a permanent structure to contain the ark of the covenant. Such a move is understandable from at least two perspectives. First, David is already living in a palace; the continued presence of the ark in an impermanent structure implies a lack of concern for the symbols of Israel's God. Second, building a permanent structure to contain the ark further solidifies the position of Jerusalem and David as the proprietary center of Israel's religious life. Once the Temple is built, if one wishes to worship the Lord, one must come to the Lord's house in David's city.

The center of this section of the story is a play on the word "house" that runs the length of the prophecy. In brief, three senses of the term are employed here: house = palace; house = temple; and house = dynasty. In verses 1–2 when David uses the term, he means it literally: a palace. Nathan's reaction to David's proposal in verse 2 is intended to convey permission and general approval on the part of the prophet rather than a specific command from God.

In verses 3–6, the sense of "house" shifts to an extended meaning: house = temple. In this section, God responds to David's proposal with a vision to Nathan, beginning with the simple and startling prohibition: "You shall not build me a house to live in" (v. 4). Implied in this statement are two important ideas. First is the declaration that David will not be the one to build the house of the Lord. As the Chronicler and his audience knew, Solomon is the builder of the Temple. Second, God has no need of a house, and at no time throughout the history of God's relationship with Israel has God required the people to construct one (vv. 5–6).

Having dispensed with the notion that God has need of a temple, the prophecy turns in verses 7–15 to the third sense of "house": house = dynasty. The section begins with a prophetic announcement formula: "Now therefore thus you shall say to my servant David" (v. 7), followed by a recitation of the deeds of the Lord on behalf of David to secure him from his enemies. In verses 9–10a, God promises the security and peace of Israel, rest from those who assail the people, and, again, the subjugation of all enemies. After this recitation comes the central promise of the prophecy in verses 10b–14: the establishment of the "house of David" as a dynasty whose members shall sit on the throne in Jerusalem in perpetuity.

Several important themes echo through these verses. Foremost among them is the promise to David that God will create a "house," a dynasty, from among his sons. The language of the promise is careful. God promises the establishment of the kingdom not to David but to David's son, and identifies him as the builder of the Temple. Yet the promise of a dynasty is couched as a gift *to David* rather than to Israel. God guarantees David a place in the life of Israel in perpetuity, even if it is not the place of Temple builder. The terms of the promise are also important. God will establish the throne of the son, guaranteeing succession within the dynasty. God promises "steadfast love" to the son, which will not be withdrawn as it was from Saul (see 1 Chron. 10:13–14). The term translated "steadfast love" here is elusive, defying precise translation. It occurs most often in relationships, especially those sealed with covenants, and may be taken to mean a commitment to faithfulness and reliability on the part of the covenanters. In this context, however, the range of the term is extended by the foregoing promise that the relationship between God and the Davidic king will be that of a father and a son. The notion of the adoption of the king as the divine son is not original to the Chronicler; Psalm 2 has God declare to the king, "You are my son; today I have begotten you." Christians will also recognize this language in the words of the heavenly voice to Jesus on the occasions of his baptism and transfiguration. The term should not be taken to imply that Israel regarded its king as divine (later Christian usage aside), as was the case in ancient Egypt, but that a special relationship existed between God and the king that served the well-being of the entire nation.

2. David's prayer, 17:16–27. David's response to the prophecy of Nathan regarding the establishment of his dynasty is a prayer. The prayer has two main sections: verses 16–22 and verses 23–27. The first section mirrors the content of the first part of the prophecy. Where the prophecy rehearses God's benevolence to David (vv. 7–8), David's prayer responds in praise to God for God's latest benevolence to him in the promise to "build a house," specifically identifying the establishment of the dynasty as one of the "great deeds" of God (vv. 17–19). Where the prophecy recounts God's promises of peace and security to Israel (vv. 9–10a), David's prayer rehearses the exodus and conquest events, culminating in a reference to the covenant relationship between God and Israel (vv. 20–22).

The second section of the prayer is a rather audacious demand for God to be as good as the divine word. David's request in verse 23 to "let [the dynasty] be established forever" amounts to a fervent "Amen!" following which he urges that God live up to the promise. Remarkably, David suggests that the fulfillment of God's promise will redound not only to David's benefit but, more importantly, to God's. As long as there are Davidic kings to care for the Temple in Jerusalem, the praise of God in Israel will not be silenced and the Lord will be known as "Israel's God." The interconnected nature of these two elements is visible in verse 25. The revelation of the security of David's house has enabled David's prayer to God; God's faithfulness to that promise down through the generations enables that prayer and praise to continue. In blessing David and his house, God is blessed.

Once again, it is difficult to overestimate the importance of this chapter in the Chronicler's larger theological scheme. Two of the great themes of Chronicles—the centrality of David as the founder of Israel's faith and life, and the centrality of the Temple as the locus of the worship of God—are joined here in the dynastic promise to David.

For American readers, the assumptions of the text of an intimate relationship between religious life and civil authority may seem to run counter to our commitments to the separation of church and state; indeed, they *are* counter to our way of thinking. The notion that there is a clear line to be drawn between the authority of the king to govern, wage war, and conduct the life of the kingdom on the one hand, and the lordship of God on the other, would have been incomprehensible to the ancient Israelites. God is Lord, and the king is the divinely adopted son, which implies that the king is the human representative of God. His authority is divine authority, and the continued survival of the Davidic line is therefore an appropriate object of God's benevolence. We ought to be careful to distinguish, however, between a theology of divinely sanctioned kingship and the modern American "civil religion," which understands God as the guarantor of the American dream. In the Chronicler's view of Israel, king and kingdom exist as the direct expression of God's will and intent; they are blessed and experience prosperity as long as they serve that intent. But when king and kingdom stray from God's intent—as is often the case throughout the Chronicler's story of Israel—the same God who blesses Israel can and does withdraw that blessing. For the Chronicler, God is the sovereign Lord of Israel ("The LORD of hosts, the God of Israel, is Israel's God"), not the servant of Israel.

DAVID'S ENEMIES DEFEATED
1 Chronicles 18:1–20:8

First Chronicles 18:1–20:8 is the Chronicler's presentation of David defending and even expanding his realm through exploits on the fields of battle. As before, the Chronicler has drawn heavily on the resources of the accounts in 2 Samuel of David's wars; once again, he has edited and arranged them under the guidance of his overarching vision of David as the builder of the nation.

Structurally, these chapters should be understood as a large unit divided into three sections, each beginning with the same temporal clause, "Some time afterward." (Even though translated differently in the NRSV, the Hebrew phrase that begins 20:4 is the same as that in 18:1 and 19:1.) The Chronicler uses this phrase to mark the beginning of material from a different section of his source. However, its use gives the impression that this section is a sequential account of David's wars, and this is very likely not the case. Most scholars would argue that this section is really a compendium of accounts of David's military exploits over many years in his reign and should not necessarily be regarded as chronologically accurate. The three sections of this material are: the "four campaigns" (18:1–17), the war with Ammon and Aram (19:1–20:3), and heroic deeds against the Philistines (20:4–8).

1. Four campaigns, 18:1–17. Like the source from which it is drawn (2 Sam. 8:1–17), 1 Chronicles 18:1–17 falls into two parts. The first (vv. 1–13) contains notices of four military campaigns against neighboring kingdoms; the second (vv. 14–17) is a short list of military and civilian high officials in David's administration.

The Chronicler portrays David engaged in expansionist campaigns against the Philistines (v. 1), the Moabites (v. 2), the king of Zobah (vv. 3–8), and Edom (vv. 12–13). The Philistines are the best known of the four groups; they were originally a seafaring culture that settled on the southeast coast of the Mediterranean and began expanding eastward into Palestinian hill country at the expense of Israel. The Philistines were a loosely organized coalition of five cities, among them Gath, the most eastward and therefore the one most frequently in conflict with Israel. The Chronicler claims that David captured Gath and its surrounding villages. It may be that the notices of heroic activity on the part of David's men in 1 Chronicles 20:4–8 are properly to be associated with this campaign.

Moab was located on the east side of the Dead Sea, opposite Judah. The two kingdoms vied for control of the southern end of the Jordan Valley, near the ancient city of Jericho, for most of the period of the kings. David was able to gain control of the Jordan Valley and the southern

Transjordan during his reign, as the Chronicler indicates in verse 2. Part of that control was the extraction of an annual tribute payment from Moab and the recognition that the Moabite king owed fealty to David. Israel maintained this overlord-vassal relationship with Moab until the latter was able to separate itself and organize as an independent state in the mid–ninth century B.C.

The campaign against Zobah is the most complex of the narratives in this section. Zobah was located to the north of Israel, in the region more generally known in the ancient world as Hamath (hence the note in v. 3 that Zobah is "toward Hamath"). Most probably, it was situated in the southern end of the Bekaa, the great rift valley in Lebanon between the ranges of the Lebanon and Anti-Lebanon Mountains. Zobah and Hamath were part of a large, loosely confederated group of kingdoms in what is now Lebanon and Syria, known generally as Aramean states. The largest and most historically significant of these kingdoms was called Aram (although older translations of the Bible and also secondary literature more often use the term "Syria" to describe this kingdom), with its capital city at Damascus.

The origins of David's war with Zobah, which ultimately embroiled Aram and Hamath as well, are obscure. Both 2 Samuel 8:3 and 1 Chronicles 18:3 indicate that David attacked the king of Zobah, Hadadezer, "as he went to set up a monument at the river Euphrates." There are two ways to read this text. The first is to assume that "he" is Hadadezer, who is pressing a territorial claim north from the Bekaa to the Euphrates. If we read the text in this way, it is difficult to see what difference such a claim would have made to David, whose kingdom was located further south. The second way to understand this text is to assume that it is David who is on his way north to the river Euphrates to establish a monument marking his northern territorial claim, a claim certain to have been disputed by Zobah. Most modern scholars would dispute such a claim as well, noting that it is unlikely that the hegemony of Israel ever extended further north than the upper Jordan region above the Sea of Galilee.

Whichever of these two readings is the case, it is clear that war resulted from the action and that its outcome was an Israelite victory and no small amount of plunder for David. On this latter point, the Chronicler makes a significant addition to his 2 Samuel source, noting that David brought back from the battle "a vast quantity of bronze; with it Solomon made the bronze sea and the pillars and the vessels of bronze" (1 Chron. 18:8). According to the Chronicler, the vast bronze urn set in front of the Temple and the pillars and other vessels used in sacred service in the Temple were fashioned from captured booty brought home by David.

The final campaign noted in this section is against Edom, the desert kingdom located south and east of the Dead Sea. Edom is represented in the Old Testament as a traditional enemy of Israel. By bringing Edom under David's control, the Chronicler depicts David as having defended Israel from attack on every side and as having expanded its frontiers at the expense of its neighbors.

2. War with Ammon and Aram, 19:1–20:3. Again employing almost verbatim the text of his source in 2 Samuel, the Chronicler provides a somewhat more detailed look at David's struggle against Ammon, a kingdom in the northern Transjordan, and its Aramean allies. Ammon was another Aramean kingdom that threatened Israelite interests in the Transjordan and, on the west side of the Jordan, in the Jezreel Valley in Israel. Given the composite nature of the source for this section (elements from 2 Sam. 10:1–19; 11:1; 12:26, 30 and 31 are employed by the Chronicler in this account), it is possible that more than a single campaign is summarized in this section. Some scholars suggest that this campaign actually precedes that described in 18:3–8, since there are Arameans from Zobah serving as mercenaries in the Ammonite army in this text, while in the previous narrative it is clear that David accepts the tribute and subjugation of Zobah (18:6).

War begins as the result of a misunderstanding. David has dispatched messengers to express official condolences to King Hanun of Ammon at the death of his father. His emissaries are received with suspicion and cynical distrust, however, and Hanun has them humiliated. Their beards are shaved and their clothing is cut in such a manner as to expose their genitalia. David's response is measured and temperate, however; he commands the messengers to wait in Jericho, at the edge of the Israelite kingdom, until their beards, the symbols of their manhood, are grown out. He strikes not in retaliation but only in response to a developing threat from the combined Ammonite and Aramean forces at Medeba (modern Madaba, in Jordan).

The Ammonite army, aided by Aramean mercenaries, surrounds Joab and the Israelites. Joab's response is to employ a tactic used to great effect millennia later by Robert E. Lee: He divides his forces in the face of a numerically superior enemy. The stratagem works for Joab, and the Ammonite-Aramean army is routed. But the center of this story is not the tactical acumen of Joab but his faith. Joab reminds the army in verse 13 that they fight "for our people and for the cities of our God," and he entrusts the outcome to the will of God: "may the LORD do what seems good to him." Without explicitly affirming it, the implication of the text is that the outcome is the result of Joab's trust in God.

The affair is not ended, however. The Arameans, now acting without their Ammonite allies, prepare for a second attack. As the battle approaches, David is informed of the situation and takes personal command. The outcome is yet another victory for David; exorbitant numbers of Aramean charioteers and infantrymen are killed. With the end of the fighting, the Arameans "became subject" to David. The same claim is made in 18:6 above. It is possible that this account represents a battle against an as yet unsubjugated group of Arameans, or that this statement is meant as a summary of both accounts of David's wars against Aram, or that the Chronicler has preserved two separate accounts of the same war. The end result is David's assertion of hegemony over Aram. It is unlikely, however, that David literally claimed the Aramean throne; the Bible records the names of several Aramean kings in later years. Probably some settlement was achieved by which Aram agreed to stay clear of regional conflicts between Israel and its Transjordanian neighbors.

The final episode in the narrative of the Ammonite war is the Israelite attack against the Ammonite capital at Rabbah (modern Amman, Jordan). A careful reading of the story produces questions. In 2 Chronicles 20:1 we are told that "David remained at Jerusalem," but by the next verse we have David in Rabbah trying on the Ammonite crown for size. (The term translated "Milcom" in the NRSV may be understood in three ways: as the proper name of a king, as the proper name of the Ammonite deity, or as the Hebrew word "their king.") How do we resolve the confusion over David's location?

The real problem with this text is not spatio-temporal but literary and editorial. The Chronicler has created this account by taking the opening and concluding frames of the Bathsheba narrative in 2 Samuel 11—12 and dropping out the stories of the affair between David and Bathsheba, David's complicity in the murder of Uriah, the prophecy of Nathan, and the birth and death of the child born as a result of the illicit union. In so doing, of course, the Chronicler changes the very nature of the source material he is using. The Chronicler, as we have noted, is not concerned to present a history of David's life and reign or to draw a close character study of David the man. Rather, his goal is to ground the faith and life of the nation in the life and work of David. It is not that he seeks to hide or diminish the fact of David's affair with Bathsheba or its disastrous consequences for David and his family; rather, paying attention to those accounts would divert the Chronicler from his purpose. The Chronicler's purpose was not to answer the question: Was David before the walls at Rabbah or at home in Jerusalem? Instead, he was committed to portray David as the builder and safeguard for the future of Israel, and he served this point by drawing on the Rabbah story only so far as it allows us to see David once again bringing home the spoils of war that enhance the wealth of Israel. We are therefore asked to accept the spatio-temporal inconsistency of the narrative in the service of the larger thematic issue.

3. Heroic deeds against the Philistines, 20:4–8. The final section of this unit is not an account of a single battle but a summary of the heroic deeds of David's men in battle against the Philistines. Drawn from 2 Samuel 21:18–22, this brief notice lists the exploits of three warriors: Sibbecai the Hushathite, Elhanan son of Jair, and Jonathan the nephew of David. All three are noted as having distinguished themselves in single combat against Philistine enemies identified as "giants."

The term "giant" is problematic. In 2 Samuel 21:18–22, the term rendered "giants" should probably be translated as a proper name: "Raphah." The men against whom David's men fought were thus probably descendants of a family or clan among the Philistines, the Raphaites, perhaps well known for their size, strength, and ferocity in battle. In transmitting this notice, however, the Chronicler has altered a letter in the spelling of the name, so that we read "Rephaim" rather than "Raphah" as in his source. The Rephaim are known from Deuteronomy 2:11–25 as mythic and gigantic warriors who populated Edom and Moab long before the arrival of Israel in the region. By altering the spelling of the name, the Chronicler subtly suggests that the Philistine warriors against whom David's men fought and prevailed were descendants of this fearsome race of giants who terrorized the land before the days of Israel. Their defeat at the hands of David's men implies that even the mythic horrors of the ancient past have been banished by the strength of David.

We should say a word about the reference to "Lahmi the brother of Goliath" in 1 Chronicles 20:5. Once again, the Chronicler amends the text of his source. The phrase in 2 Samuel 21:19 reads: "and Elhanan son of Jaare-oregim, the Bethlehemite, killed Goliath the Gittite." The problem implied in the source material, of course, is that in 1 Samuel 17 it is David, not Elhanan, who kills the warrior Goliath of Gath. The editor of 2 Samuel 21 simply leaves the matter unresolved. Not so the Chronicler. Omitting the fragment "-oregim" from the name of Elhanan's father and dropping the definite article and initial consonant from the place name "Bethlehem," the Chronicler reads "Elhanan son of Jair killed Lahmi the brother of Goliath the Gittite." The Chronicler thus preserves the tradition of David's defeat of Goliath. It is interesting to note, however, that this is the only reference made to the fight between David and Goliath; it is omitted because, as part of the lore of David before his accession as king, it is not pertinent to the Chronicler's portrait of David. But his treatment of it here is clear evidence of his awareness of the stories of David he chose not to use.

DAVID'S CENSUS AND THE PLAGUE
1 Chronicles 21:1–22:1

The story of the census of Israel commanded by David and the pestilential punishment of Israel by God does not occupy a central position in the 2 Samuel narrative. It is, in fact, relegated to late in the story of David's reign, in the final chapter of 2 Samuel (2 Sam. 24:1–25). For the Chronicler, on the other hand, the story has a much greater significance, and he enhances and clarifies that significance both by retelling—with skillful editing—the 2 Samuel story and by appending a new section of his own creation. In the hands of the Chronicler, the story of David's census and the plague that followed become the occasion for the selection of the Temple site, thus adding to the mounting theme of David as the founder of Israel's faith.

The story is composed of five sections: David's census (vv. 1–6), the prophecy of Gad (vv. 7–13), the plague (vv. 14–17), the purchase of the threshing floor and the end of the plague (vv. 18–27), and the selection of the site for the Temple (21:28–22:1).

1. The census, 21:1–6. To modern ears, the notion of a census is not morally charged, and so the clear implication of the text that the census violates the will of God seems strange to us. In the world of the Bible, however, a census served primarily to identify the number of men able to be called upon for military purposes. In other words, it was a draft system. The foundation of the idea is the assumption on the part of the king that all those of serviceable age are the soldiers (and to a certain extent, the property) of the king. But in Israel, at least as the traditions of Joshua, Judges, and Samuel understand it, the people of Israel belong not to the king but to God. When they rise up for battle, they do so not in the service of the whims of the king but in obedience to the will of God. Thus, David's command to count the number of men who "drew the sword" in Israel is "abhorrent" because it lays bare David's view of himself as a Middle Eastern potentate rather than the servant of God.

It is in this context that the opening line of the text should be understood. The rather bald declaration that "Satan stood up against Israel and incited David" is unique in Chronicles; "Satan" makes no other appearance in the entire book (and, for that matter, only twice more in the entire Old Testament, in Job 1–2 and Zech. 3:1). The traditional reading in English translations, followed here by the NRSV, implies that Satan rises up to tempt David to sin. This is a perfectly reasonable rendering of the Hebrew text and may be precisely what the Chronicler intended. However, one scholar has noted another possibility that deserves attention. In Job 1—2, a figure identified in the Hebrew text as "the satan" appears as part of the heavenly entourage; the function of this figure is to challenge the apparent goodness and piety of Job, to test the truth of the boasts God makes about him. Frequently, the term "satan" is translated "adversary." The suggestion is made that, rather than reading "Satan" here, we might read the word simply as "an adversary." Two arguments can be made to support such a reading. First, no other use of "Satan" is made in Chronicles, so the personification of temptation represented here is unique and unlike the regular treatment of sin in Chronicles. Second, if we read "adversary" here, there is nothing to prevent the assumption that the adversary is human, that is, an unnamed military threat, for which David is preparing to institute a draft system to raise an army. Such a reading would be completely consistent with the situation described by the census.

The Chronicler's account of the census differs from his source in two additional ways. First, the Chronicler displays no interest in the route taken by Joab through Israel (see 2 Sam. 24:5–8). For the Chronicler, this information is extraneous; the knowledge that the census was taken is sufficient to explain the punishment of Israel. Second, the census totals are considerably different in 1 Chronicles 21:5 than in 2 Samuel 24:9: 1,100,000 in Israel in Chronicles, compared to 800,000 in Samuel; and 470,000 in Judah in Chronicles, compared to 500,000 in Samuel.

2. The prophecy of Gad, 21:7–13. God responds to David's action with displeasure; he "strikes" Israel. The precise nature of the divine action is vague as yet, but it is clear enough to evoke from David a confession of sin. One expects, after David's confession, to hear that God has stayed the divine wrath, but instead, through the offices of David's court prophet Gad, David is forced to choose his own and his people's punishment for his sin. The choices are famine, invasion, or epidemic plague— all devastating and deadly. David's choice is the one that requires no human intervention; it is not a failure of farming nor a breach in the country's defenses but the direct application of the power of God. Perhaps the reasoning is that what God does most directly God can undo most rapidly. Perhaps, though, David's own statement reveals the motive: Since the sin was an affront to God and not a third human party, justice must come from God and not some other human source.

Implied in the Chronicler's treatment of the census and plague is a crucially important principle for the rest of Chronicles: the principle of moral responsibility. The Chronicler understands human behavior to have consequences for our relationship with God, and those consequences are not withheld within our lives. If we obey God, we prosper and are blessed; if we sin, we receive punishment. While the neatness of the Chronicler's system is often unconvincing to modern ears, there can be little doubt about the truth of the underlying theological principle. Our behavior, and especially our sinful behavior, does indeed have consequences that are not set aside merely because we regret having sinned. The Chronicler makes the point with the order of events in the story of the census: David, confronted with his sin, begs for forgiveness, and God responds by offering David three ways to deal with the disruption of the relationship between them. The ways are not painless, for David or for his people. But they are the means through which the relationship with God continues, and from that continuance springs something even more important than the sin.

3. The plague, 21:14–17.

21:14 So the LORD sent a pestilence on Israel; and seventy thousand persons fell in Israel. 15 And God sent an angel to Jerusalem to destroy it; but when he was about to destroy it, the LORD took note and relented concerning the calamity; he said to the destroying angel, "Enough! Stay your hand." The angel of the LORD was then standing by the threshing floor of Ornan the Jebusite. 16 David looked up and saw the angel of the LORD standing between earth and heaven, and in his hand a drawn sword stretched out over Jerusalem. Then David and the elders, clothed in sackcloth, fell on their faces. 17 And David said to God, "Was it not I who gave the command to count the people? It is I who have sinned and done very wickedly. But these sheep, what have they done? Let your hand, I pray, O LORD my God, be against me and against my father's house; but do not let your people be plagued!"

The Chronicler graphically depicts the onslaught of the pestilence sent by God—undoubtedly some form of infectious disease—using two images that eventually coalesce into one. The first is that the plague is the "sword of the Lord"; this image is employed in 1 Chronicles 21:12 in contrast to the "sword of your enemies." The second is an angel sent by God to destroy Jerusalem. In 1 Chronicles 21:16, the Chronicler combines the two images into a single terrifying vision: David sees this angelic destroyer standing between earth and heaven holding a drawn sword stretched out over the city. David's reaction, along with that of the elders, is to fall on his face in fear and worship, and again to entreat God for mercy.

The moment is significant, and the Chronicler invites us to contemplate it in all its terror and wonder: the destroying angel, doing the bidding of an angry God, poised to wreak havoc and stayed only by the command of God; David and his elders fallen on their faces in panic and awe. This is a theophany, an appearance of the divine breaking into the realm of the human. The vision of the angel transforms the place of the vision into a holy place, and what happens there takes on special meaning. The place is identified as the threshing floor of Ornan the Jebusite ("Araunah" in 2 Samuel 24:16), in all probability a remnant of the population of Jerusalem prior to David's capture of the city. Already, however, it is more than a threshing floor; it is the place where David has seen a vision of the heavenly powers. David cries out for mercy once again to the God behind the vision, taking on himself the responsibility for his action and pleading for the release and safety of his people. In so doing, he gives the place yet another significance: It is the place where David's prayer delivered Israel. The direction in which the Chronicler turns the story is becoming clear: What began as a story about David's sin and punishment is becoming a tale of a special place.

4. *David's purchase of the threshing floor and the end of the plague, 21:18–27.* For a second time in this narrative, God responds to David's prayer through the offices of the prophet Gad. This time the command to David is to erect an altar on the spot of the angelic vision. The Chronicler notes that Ornan and his sons have also seen the vision (v. 20). The theophany is therefore a public event and not a private moment of David's piety. As such, the place is now publicly important, and Ornan recognizes the appropriateness of David's request to convert it into a shrine. His offer to give it to David is rebuffed, however, by David's insistence that he must buy the place "for the full price" (v. 24). The reason is made clear as the negotiation between David and Ornan continues: "I will not take for the LORD what is yours, nor offer burnt offerings that cost me nothing." The Chronicler highlights the importance of the point with the high price David pays for field and oxen. In 2 Samuel 24:24, the price is fifty shekels of silver; the Chronicler raises it to six hundred shekels of gold (v. 25). In the Chronicler's scheme, the increased cost makes sense. As the place is more important for his story, so its price is higher.

Having purchased the field, David erects the altar and offers sacrifices for atonement. The Chronicler notes that David "called upon the LORD, and [the LORD] answered him with fire from heaven on the altar." The moment is again significant. In Leviticus 9:24, at the conclusion of the consecration of Aaron as priest, Aaron appeals to God, who sends fire from heaven to consume altar and sacrifice. A similar moment occurs in the contest atop Mount Carmel between Elijah and the prophets of Baal (1 Kings 18:38). Later, in 2 Chronicles 7:1, fire falls from heaven to consume Solomon's sacrifice at the conclusion of the Temple dedication. In all these narratives, the intent is to convey divine acceptance of the sacrifice. In this situation, God's acceptance of David's sacrifice signals the end of divine hostility toward David and Israel. God commands the angel to sheath the sword of wrath at last, and the episode of the plague is finished.

5. *The selection of the site for the Temple, 21:28–22:1.* The plague may be over, but the Chronicler is not done. In fact, in this final section he at last arrives at the purpose for which he has told this story. David's erection of the altar and offering of sacrifice, together with the awe-inspiring vision of the destroying angel, have sanctified the spot of Ornan's threshing floor. It is the place of David's encounter with God. But the ancient traditions of Israel maintain the notion that the presence of God is associated with the tabernacle, the "house of the LORD," now situated at Gibeon, to the north of Jerusalem. David declares that the two shall be brought together into a single shrine (22:1). A new house—a permanent one rather than a temporary shelter—should be built to service the altar now erected on the threshing floor of Ornan.

The effect of David's declaration is to advance the absorption of the ancient religion of Israel into the service of the Davidic monarchy. Having already moved the ark of God into Jerusalem, David now decrees the replacement of the temporary structure that once housed the ark with a new, permanent one. The altar on which wandering Israel once offered sacrifices is to be replaced by an altar built by David; use of it henceforth will recall David's deliverance of Israel from the plague by means of his prayers and piety. Truly, for the Chronicler, David and the religion of Israel are inextricably bound together.

The story of the census and plague, then, reflects on the themes of the sins of leaders and their consequences to the people they lead, a theme that continues to resound in the politics and piety of our own era, as it surely does in any. It offers up the truth that the sins we commit have consequences that we must face and from which we must learn. But it also suggests that out of the great calamity of sin and punishment there yet grows redemption and new possibility. Here it is the sanctification of a holy place that opens the vision of the future of Israel's faith, as a threshing floor becomes the locus of worship and an encounter with God that becomes in turn the great Temple of the Lord. For us, perhaps the physical place is less important than the spiritual location of that encounter: some failure or occasion of grief that becomes the occasion for receiving forgiveness or understanding grace. But what person of faith cannot look back over the course of his or her own life and find those awe-filled moments where the edges of judgment and redemption come together and in the midst of which the shape of the future is outlined?

6. David's Preparations for the Building of the Temple
1 Chronicles 22:2–29:22a

The final eight chapters of 1 Chronicles are focused on David's work in preparing for the construction of the Temple. Preparing the way for the Temple is David's crowning achievement in the Chronicler's view, and so the Chronicler lavishes attention on this aspect of David's career as he does on no other. Yet at the heart of the matter lies a problem: The Chronicler must account for the historical fact, fully known by his readers, that it was not David who built the Temple but Solomon. It would have served the Chronicler's purpose if David were in fact the builder. However, the Chronicler had to find a way to admit the historical truth without compromising one of the theological foci of his work: that David is the founder of Israel's faith. He found the answer to his dilemma in the vision of David as the master planner and preparer of the Temple. In these final chapters of the story of David, we see a king who assembles, devises, organizes, and establishes both the human and material resources that will allow the Temple to come into being. Solomon is here little more than David's agent for the Temple construction, executing David's plan with David's material and installing David's chosen servants in the roles David assigned for them.

Chapters 22 through 29 form a large unit that appears on the surface to be rather diverse. The material contained here is held together by two factors. First, all of it is focused on the subject of the preparations and organization of the Temple and its human servants. Most important among the latter are the Levites, who are for the Chronicler the central figures in the Temple's life. This is somewhat surprising, since elsewhere in the biblical tradition, in both Old and New Testaments, the priests occupy center stage with regard to the Temple. The Chronicler, however, has in mind to rehabilitate—or perhaps establish for the first time—the primacy of the Levites, and he does so by giving the bulk of his attention to their various functions, even to the extent of pointing out that the priests themselves are Levites. Second, bracketing the central chapters on human resources (1 Chronicles 23–27) are two chapters concerned with the assembling of material resources (22: 2–5 and 29:1–9) and by instructions to Solomon about the construction (privately in 22:6–16 and publicly in 28:1–21).

Structurally, 1 Chronicles 22:2–29:22a is composed of eleven units: (1) David's preparations for the Temple (22:2–5), (2) David's personal instructions for the Temple (22:6–19), (3) the organization of the Levites (23:1–32), (4) the organization of the priests (24:1–31), (5) Temple musicians (25:1–31), (6) gatekeepers (26:1–19), (7) other Levitical officers (26:20–32), (8) officers of the king (27:1–34), (9) David's public instructions for the Temple (28:1–21), (10) the offering of the people (29:1–9), and (11) David's blessing of the offering (29:10–22a).

DAVID'S PREPARATIONS FOR THE TEMPLE
1 Chronicles 22:2–5

22:2 David gave orders to gather together the aliens who were residing in the land of Israel, and he set stone cutters to prepare dressed stones for building the house of God. ³ David also provided great stores of iron for nails for the doors of the gates and for clamps, as well as bronze in quantities beyond weighing, ⁴ and cedar logs without number—for the Sidonians and Tyrians brought great quantities of cedar to David. ⁵ For David said, "My son Solomon is young and inexperienced, and the house that is to be built for the LORD must be exceedingly magnificent, famous and glorified throughout all lands; I will therefore make preparation for it." So David provided materials in great quantity before his death.

The Chronicler begins his presentation of David's work toward the Temple with a summary of the material resources David collects for its construction. Stone and cedar form the major part of the material. Stone was quarried and dressed within Israel in ancient times, and it continues to be an important building material. The quarrying and dressing was, according to the Chronicler, the work of "aliens" (i.e., foreigners) living within Israel, implying perhaps that David had some system of draft labor for those considered to be non-Israelites (see also 2 Chron. 2:1–2, 17–18; 8:7–10 and commentary). Cedar was not found in large quantities in ancient Israel, but it was an important export of the ancient kingdoms of Tyre and Sidon (modern Lebanon). Iron and bronze serve as nails, hinges, and fasteners of various sorts. All these materials are long-lasting and strong, leaving the clear sense that the structure was intended to be permanent, enduring, and formidable—the very things the tabernacle could not be.

The Chronicler's explanation in verse 5 of David's actions is important to his theme. The magnitude and grandeur of the project are essential, both because they are testimony to the power and wealth of David's kingdom and because they must reflect the greatness of Israel's God, who is greater than all other gods. This explanation alone might have sufficed, but the Chronicler frames it with a reference to Solomon as "young and inexperienced." The Chronicler thereby explains that David must do the great majority of the preparation for the Temple because Solomon cannot yet be entrusted with the task.

The final sentence of the section is also significant. David goes about the task of preparation "before his death." It is, in the Chronicler's view, David's last act, and as such, it is also his greatest. Once the tasks of procuring materials, making plans, organizing personnel, and collecting money are accomplished, there will be no further or higher service David can render, and his reign will end at its apogee. True to his theory, the Chronicler notes the death of David at the end of 1 Chronicles 29, after his final words of blessing and benediction.

DAVID'S PERSONAL INSTRUCTIONS FOR THE TEMPLE
1 Chronicles 22:6–19

22:6 Then he called for his son Solomon and charged him to build a house for the LORD, the God of Israel. ⁷ David said to Solomon, "My son, I had planned to build a house to the name of the LORD my God. ⁸ But the word of the LORD came to me, saying, 'You have shed much blood and have waged great wars; you shall not build a house to my name, because you have shed so much blood in my sight on the earth. ⁹ See, a son shall be born to you; he shall be a man of peace. I will give him peace from his enemies on every side; for his name shall be Solomon, and I will give peace and quiet to Israel in his days. ¹⁰ He shall build a house for my name. He shall be a son to me, and I will be a father to him, and I will establish his royal throne in Israel forever.' ¹¹ Now, my son, the LORD be with you, so that you may succeed in building the house of the LORD your God, as he has spoken concerning you. ¹² Only, may the LORD grant you discretion and understanding, so that when he gives you charge over Israel you may keep the law of the LORD your God. ¹³ Then you will prosper if you are careful to observe the statutes and the ordinances that the LORD commanded Moses for Israel. Be strong and of good courage. Do not be afraid or dismayed. ¹⁴ With great pains I have provided for the house of the LORD one hundred thousand talents of gold, one million talents of silver, and bronze and iron beyond weighing, for there is so much of it; timber and stone too I have provided. To these you must add more. ¹⁵ You have an abundance of workers: stonecutters, masons, carpenters, and all kinds of artisans without number, skilled in working [16]gold, silver, bronze, and iron. Now begin the work, and the LORD be with you."

[17]David also commanded all the leaders of Israel to help his son Solomon, saying, [18]"Is not the LORD your God with you? Has he not given you peace on every side? For he has delivered the inhabitants of the land into my hand; and the land is subdued before the LORD and his people. [19]Now set your mind and heart to seek the LORD your God. Go and build the sanctuary of the LORD God so that the ark of the covenant of the LORD and the holy vessels of God may be brought into a house built for the name of the LORD."

1. David's instructions to Solomon, 22:6–16. The two sets of commands given by David here, one to Solomon (vv. 6–16) and one to the leaders of Israel (vv. 17–19), serve two purposes. The first purpose is to explain at last why Solomon has been chosen to build the Temple. The second is to connect the construction of the Temple with obedience to the law. The fact of the choice of Solomon as builder has been known since 1 Chronicles 17, but no explanation of that choice has been rendered until now. In verses 7–10, that explanation is finally offered. Simply put, it is because David has been a warrior, and the Temple must be built by one who is a "man of peace." But, as with most of the Chronicler's explanations, it is more subtle than simple.

The Chronicler's reasoning rests on the language of Deuteronomy 12:10–11. Moses commands the Israelites waiting on the east bank of the Jordan regarding the place on which they are to offer sacrifice and worship God:

> When you cross over the Jordan and live in the land that the LORD your God is allotting to you, and when he gives you rest from your enemies all around so that you live in safety, then you shall bring everything that I command you to the place that the LORD your God will choose as a dwelling for his name.

For the Chronicler, the pivotal term here is "rest"; it is the same Hebrew word he employs in 1 Chronicles 22:9 to describe Solomon: "He shall be a man of rest [NRSV: "peace"]. I will give him rest [NRSV: "peace"] from all his enemies on every side." David, by contrast, is a man of blood, having "shed much blood in [God's] sight on the earth." This does not necessarily imply disapproval of David's wars but only serves to explain why David is not chosen as the builder of the Temple. The Chronicler uses the Deuteronomic language to imply that a "man of rest" shall be the builder of the Temple, during a time when God has given "peace from all his enemies on every side." He then shifts the language of "rest" to "peace"—by noting in verse 9 that the name Solomon—*Shlomoh* in Hebrew—is rooted in the word *shalom*, "peace." Through this "peaceful one"—Solomon—God will give "peace"—*shalom*—to all Israel. Finally, the Chronicler returns to the language of Nathan's prophecy in 1 Chronicles 17:12–13, recalling the promise both of the establishment of David's "house" (i.e., dynasty) in Solomon and the building of the "house" (i.e., Temple) of the Lord by Solomon.

The second purpose for the instructions of David is to connect the act of building the Temple with the commitment to obedience to the law of God. Verses 11–16 are bracketed by the benediction, "may the LORD be with you," and in each case the benediction is connected to an encouragement to undertake the task of building the Temple. The Chronicler is careful in verses 12–13 to set the task in its proper context: To build the Temple is to obey the law. David's wish for "discretion and understanding" for Solomon anticipates the vision Solomon will have of God at Gibeon in which he asks specifically for "wisdom and knowledge" by which to govern Israel (2 Chron. 1:10). However, David's wish for wisdom is grounded in obedience: It is wisdom and understanding so that "you may keep the law of the LORD your God." As the story of the building of the Temple unfolds in 2 Chronicles 2—7, it will be clear that, to the Chronicler, the construction of the Temple is first and foremost an act of obedience to the law.

Having explained Solomon's role as builder to him and grounded the command to build in the concept of obedience, David points out the enormity of the material preparation made for the Temple. The numbers—equal to 3,750 tons of gold and 37,500 tons of silver—are so exaggerated as to be unbelievable. Their purpose can only be to overwhelm the reader with the sheer magnificence and opulence of the project. It comes as a surprise, then, to hear the Chronicler command Solomon to "add more" to this already fantastic total. One suspects that the intent here is not literal but theological; the task of preparing for the service of the Lord can never be completed, nor can one decide that enough has been done and no more is needed.

2. David's instructions to the leaders of Israel, 22:17–19. David also instructs the "leaders of Israel" (tribal leaders, as in 1 Chron. 27:16–22) to support Solomon in his efforts to carry out the project. Two interpretations are possible. One is implied in the statement that "Solomon is young and inexperienced" (22:5). The help of wiser, more experienced leaders is necessary to insure the success of the project. The other is perhaps more cynical: This may be a form of loyalty oath extracted by David from the "leaders" on Solomon's behalf. Seen in this light, the leaders would be promising to accept Solomon's succession as legitimate and committing their support both to Solomon's rule and to the Temple project. David reminds the leaders that the peace "on every side" is due directly to the fact that God has "delivered the inhabitants of the land into my hand." Moreover, as with Solomon earlier, the command to build the Temple is connected with obedience to the Lord, and, once again, that obedience is couched in the language of Deuteronomy. David's command, "Now set your mind and heart to seek the LORD your God," recalls the great Deuteronomic summary of religious life: "You shall love the LORD your God with all your heart, and with all your soul, and with all your might" (Deut. 6:5). Indeed, to "seek the LORD" is the recurring description of piety and faithfulness throughout 1 and 2 Chronicles.

ORGANIZATION OF THE LEVITES
1 Chronicles 23:1–32

Chapters 23—26 are the Chronicler's presentation of the Levites, organized for service in the Temple. For the Chronicler, the Levitical structure is the heart of David's preparation for the Temple. As such, it occupies the largest part of this section devoted to those preparations (1 Chronicles 22—29).

It is quite likely that in the hands of the Chronicler, the Levites are redefined as a much more significant liturgical group than they were before the exile. Indeed, the Levites play no role in the narratives of Samuel and Kings, and they are not mentioned in the Kings account of the building and dedication of the Temple. Outside of 1 and 2 Chronicles, Ezra, and Nehemiah, the Levites figure largely only in the book of Numbers, much of which is postexilic in origin as well. The prominent place accorded by the Chronicler to the role and function of the Levites, and their absence from the older narratives in Samuel and Kings, has led many scholars to conclude that Chronicles is an apology for the Levites as a new force in the liturgical heart of the Second Temple rather than a description of their role in the First Temple. Perhaps what we have in these chapters is a sort of charter describing that role and function in the Second Temple. By writing them into the era of David, the Chronicler grounds them in the sacred history so that their strong presence in his own time may seem to have historical precedent.

This is the second time the Chronicler has turned to the subject of the Levites; he provided a Levitical genealogy in 1 Chronicles 6, grounding their origins in the sons of Levi. The present chapter is in substantial agreement with the information in 1 Chronicles 6. The differences are perhaps due to changes in the prominence of Levitical houses from one period of Israel's history to another, or to the possibility that the Chronicler works here from different sources than those of chapter 6. There are two additional places where lists of Levites figure into the story, 2 Chronicles 29 and 31, both of which are part of the reforms of Hezekiah.

The present chapter has three parts: an introduction and general overview of the roles of the Levites (vv. 1–6), a list of the Levitical "divisions" (vv. 7–23), and the redefinition of the function of the Levites (vv. 24–32).

1. Introduction and overview of the roles of the Levites, 23:1–6. The opening lines of chapters 23—26 provide a time frame for the organization of the Levites, and they situate this task as one of David's last acts as he approaches his death and the succession of Solomon. Verse 1 thus ought not to be regarded as the announcement of Solomon's coronation but rather as a temporal reference for David's work: He organizes the Levites (and makes other preparations for the Temple) as part of his preparations to turn the kingdom over to Solomon.

The Chronicler organizes the Levites in two ways. First, they are organized according to function. The outline of Levitical functions here will be the structuring principle for the remainder of chapters 23—26: 24,000 Temple servants "in charge of the work in the house of the LORD (see 1 Chron. 23:24–32), 6,000 "officers and judges" (see 1 Chron. 26:20–32), 4,000 gatekeepers (see 1 Chron. 26:1–19), and 4,000 musicians (see 1 Chron. 25:1–31).

Second, the Chronicler also organizes the Levites into "divisions" based on the lineage of Levi in 1 Chronicles 6 ("Gershon" here is an alternate spelling of "Gershom" in 6:1). The term "division" will continue to play a role in the discussion of the personnel of David's reign and of the Temple. Levites serving as Temple servants, priests, and gatekeepers, and also David's military leadership are organized into divisions. Characteristic of each such organization is the fact that divisions come in multiples of twelve. It is thus likely that some sort of annual rotation through the twelve months of the year is implied by the term. One or two divisions of Levites would serve their functions for a month, and then would be replaced by another.

2. The Levitical divisions, 23:7–23. The names of the sons of Levi in 1 Chronicles 6:1 form the structure for this section: divisions named for descendants of Gershon are listed in verses 7–11, those of Kohath in verses 12–20, and those of Merari in verses 21–23. While tracing the specific lineage is not necessary, several details of the lists are worthy of comment.

In the Gershonite list in verses 7–11, two houses are listed—Ladan ("Libni" in 6:17) and Shimei. Sons of Shimei appear to be listed twice, once in verse 9 and then again in verse 10. It is likely that the phrase "sons of Shimei" in verse 9 should be regarded as a scribal error and removed, leaving Ladan with six descendants. Four sons of Shimei are then listed in verse 10, for a total of ten divisions from the lineage of Gershon.

Similar difficulties arise in the lineages of Kohath and Merari. Kohathite houses number four: Amram, Izhar, Hebron, and Uzziel. Moses and Aaron are the sons of Amram, but the sons of Aaron are designated as priests (6:3–15) and so are not numbered among the Levitical divisions; they are numbered separately in chapter 24. Counting the final generation listed for each of the houses of Kohath, we arrive at a total of nine. In the Merarite list, the sons of Mahli are Eleazar and Kish, but the text makes clear that there were no male descendants from Eleazar. The sons of Kish, however, married and had sons by the daughters of Eleazar (a custom called "levirate marriage"), thereby preserving the house. The total number of Merarite divisions is thus five, yielding a grand total of twenty-four divisions of Levites among the three groups.

We should also note the special care given to the treatment of the descendants of Moses and Aaron in verses 13–14:

> 23:13 . . . Aaron was set apart to consecrate the most holy things, so that he and his sons forever should make offerings before the LORD, and minister to him and pronounce blessings in his name forever; [14] but as for Moses the man of God, his sons were to be reckoned among the tribe of Levi.

The calling of the Aaronides to "consecrate the most holy things" deliberately recalls the assignment of function to sons of Aaron in Exodus 30:29–30. After instructing Moses to anoint with oil all the various furnishings and utensils used in the tabernacle, God commands:

> [y]ou shall consecrate them, so that they may be most holy; whatever touches them will become holy. You shall anoint Aaron and his sons, and consecrate them, in order that they may serve me as priests.

For the Chronicler, this text serves as warrant to regard the Aaronides as separate, endowed with a consecrated and consecrating function: to handle the instruments of the Temple. In an era in which few objects are regarded as holy, and especially in the Protestant tradition in which holiness is not often bestowed on material things, such words sound strange. Still, they evoke a vision of an almost tangible holiness of God, in which not only God but everything associated with the presence of worship of God is imbued with the power of the divine. To touch such objects is to transgress on the territory of the holy, and in Israel one did not do so lightly or without thought.

Yet, even with the special function to handle the holy, the Aaronides are still clearly within the Levitical system. This is also undoubtedly part of the Chronicler's agenda: to make it clear that, even though the priests occupy an elevated status in the Temple hierarchy, they are nonetheless part of the larger system and brothers of those Levites who serve in less exalted ways alongside them. The Chronicler's view of priesthood is thus strikingly egalitarian and serves both as a control on the claims of the priests and as a guarantee of the importance of the Levites.

Also striking, but for a different reason, is the inclusion of the sons of Moses in the Levitical list. Moses is called "man of God" here, but his sons are treated without deference. The inevitable conclusion is that, unlike the priesthood, which is passed from generation to generation, the prophetic status of Moses is charismatic. It is bestowed by God upon specific individuals and not inherited or gained by virtue of office. Prophets such as Nathan and Gad have already played a role in the Chronicler's narrative; others will play larger and more prominent roles still as the story moves on. The Chronicler is clear, however, that the prophetic role cannot be established or organized; it occurs as God wills it and on no other schedule.

3. Redefinition of the functions of Levites, 23:24–32.

23:24 **These were the sons of Levi by their ancestral houses, the heads of families as they were enrolled according to the number of the names of the individuals from twenty years old and upward who were to do the work for the service of the house of the LORD. 25 For David said, "The LORD, the God of Israel, has given rest to his people; and he resides in Jerusalem forever. 26 And so the Levites no longer need to carry the tabernacle or any of the things for its service"—27 for according to the last words of David these were the number of the Levites from twenty years old and upward—28 "but their duty shall be to assist the descendants of Aaron for the service of the house of the LORD, having the care of the courts and the chambers, the cleansing of all that is holy, and any work for the service of the house of God; 29 to assist also with the rows of bread, the choice flour for the grain offering, the wafers of unleavened bread, the baked offering, the offering mixed with oil, and all measures of quantity or size. 30 And they shall stand every morning, thanking and praising the LORD, and likewise at evening, 31 and whenever burnt offerings are offered to the LORD on sabbaths, new moons, and appointed festivals, according to the number required of them, regularly before the LORD. 32 Thus they shall keep charge of the tent of meeting and the sanctuary, and shall attend the descendants of Aaron, their kindred, for the service of the house of the LORD."**

Verse 24 serves as both the conclusion to the previous section and the introduction to the current one; it makes reference to the enrollment of

Levites and to the work they are to do in the service of the Temple. One notes, however, a difference with verse 3: Here the Levites are registered from age twenty and upward, while in verse 3 the age of registration is thirty. The difference is probably the result of the Chronicler's use of his sources. The function of the Levites is defined in Numbers 1—4, as part of a census of Israel in the wilderness. In Numbers 1, the census minimum age is twenty; probably the wording of this current section depends on this passage. But in Numbers 4, in the census of the three houses of Levi (Kohath, Gershon, and Merari), the census minimum age is thirty; it is likely the Chronicler was depending on Numbers 4 as he prepared 1 Chronicles 23:2–6, and thus used thirty in verse 3 as it appeared in his source. The reference to "twenty and upward" as part of the "last words of David" in verse 27 is difficult. Probably the best explanation is to understand this verse as a scribal note in the margin of an ancient copy of the text that was subsequently included here by mistake. Removing it restores an uninterrupted and sensible reading of David's words here.

The purpose of verses 25–32 is to redefine the role of Levites, a role that is otherwise defined in Numbers in relation to Israel's worship in the tabernacle. For the Chronicler, that role is completed now that David has installed the ark in Jerusalem, and a new vision of the function of the Levites is needed. Their functions, according to Numbers 1:48–53, were all associated with the care and movement of the tabernacle and its furnishings. They were to put up and take down the tent, transport it while the people were on the move, and stand guard over it while they were encamped. However, as the building of the Temple gets underway, all those functions will soon become obsolete, and so the Chronicler portrays David assigning new functions. The Levites are to be responsible for the maintenance of the Temple, clearing and cleansing, and also with the management of the vast quantities of grain, flour, and oil necessary to prepare the ceremonial breads for the grain offerings (see Leviticus 2). In addition, they are assigned to offer thanksgiving and praise during festivals and Sabbath worship. Their responsibilities are summarized by the two phrases of verse 32: They are to "keep charge of the sanctuary" and to "attend the descendants of Aaron, their kindred."

The Chronicler sees the Levites as an order of lay leaders in the Temple whose function is complex and intertwined with that of the priests. On the one hand, they are clearly cast in the role of assistants to the priests; on the other, they control the accomplishment of a wide variety of tasks without which the Temple could not function. Thus, the Chronicler describes a Temple that is not the sole province of the priests but that belongs to God's people as a whole and to the Levites in particular. By placing redefinition on the lips of David, the Chronicler raises the status of these lay leaders to a new prominence. Modern readers will recognize similar roles in the functions of elders and/or deacons in the New Testament church and in modern Protestant and (to an increasing extent) Catholic churches. The underlying principle of shared leadership between clergy and laity is at work in both ancient and modern contexts.

ORGANIZATION OF PRIESTS
1 Chronicles 24:1–31

Having established the general functions of the Levites and redefined their roles in the operation of the Temple, the Chronicler now turns to the organization of the priesthood. Chapter 24 is composed of two parts: the presentation of the divisions of the descendants of Aaron (vv. 1–19) and a list of additional Levites not otherwise assigned in the Levitical system of chapters 23—26 (vv. 20–32).

1. The divisions of the priests, 24:1–19. Like the Levites in 1 Chronicles 23, the priests are described first according to genealogical group (vv. 1–6) and then organized into twenty-four divisions (vv. 7–19).

The Chronicler seems to have drawn on Numbers 3:2–4 as his source for verses 1–6. In both contexts, Aaron has four named sons, only two of which live to have sons of their own. But Numbers 3:4 provides us the reason for the premature deaths of Nadab and Abihu: They "died before the LORD when they offered illicit fire before the LORD in the wilderness of Sinai." The reference here is to an incident described in Leviticus 10:1–2 in which Nadab and Abihu make an unauthorized use of censers sacred to worship in the tabernacle and are slain by fire sent from God. Harsh though the incident seems, it has faded into insignificance for the Chronicler; he omits any reference to it except to note the childless deaths of the two. For his purpose, it matters only that there are two ancestral lineages of Aaronide priests: Eleazar and Ithamar. Of the two lineages, Eleazar is clearly dominant, and this dominance is reflected in the divisional organization: sixteen divisions or ancestral houses for the lineage of Eleazar and eight for that of Ithamar.

The list of priestly divisions in verses 7–19 contains several names that occur in other Persian era materials, especially Ezra and Nehemiah. Jedaiah (v. 7) is known from Ezra 2:36 (=Neh. 7:39), Harim (v. 8) appears three verses later in Ezra 2:39 (=Neh. 7:42), Hakoz (v. 10) is also mentioned in Ezra 2:61, and Jeshua (vv. 11–12) is mentioned as one of those who returned with the Persian-appointed governor of Jerusalem, Zerubbabel, in the early postexilic period (Ezra 2:2; see also Haggai 1:1). It seems clear from the presence of these names that the list from which the Chronicler composed the priestly divisions was a late list, reflecting the priestly leadership of his own time.

2. The list of additional Levites, 24:20–32. Appended to the end of the priestly divisions is a list of otherwise unattached Levites. The list seems to repeat some of the information provided in the Kohathite and Merarite divisions of 1 Chronicles 23:12–20 and 21–23. In each case, however, additional names are provided that are otherwise unknown and serve no apparent purpose. It may be that this is a fragmentary list in the Chronicler's possession that he wanted to preserve; it may also be that some alternate Levitical genealogy has been appended here by a later editor. At this stage no clear answer to the questions of provenance and purpose have emerged. Whatever the origin of this material, some attempt has been made in 1 Chronicles 24:32 to include the names in the Levitical system simply by noting that they were organized by "lots corresponding to their kindred, the descendants of Aaron."

TEMPLE MUSICIANS
1 Chronicles 25:1–31

Following a pattern now familiar, the Chronicler lists the Levites set aside as Temple singers and instrumentalists first by describing the various genealogical groups descended from Levi (1 Chron. 25:1–7), and then by listing the groups by which the musicians were assigned to service in the Temple (vv. 8–31). Earlier, in 1 Chronicles 6:31–48, the Chronicler had provided a genealogy of the Temple musicians descended from the three Levitical families of Kohath, Gershon, and Merari to the Davidic era. Those genealogies end with Heman of the Kohathites (6:33), Asaph of the Gershonites (6:39), and Ethan of the Merarites (6:44). Here the first two names are the same, but Ethan is rendered "Jeduthun" in 25:1–6. In all likelihood, "Ethan" is a shortened or alternate from of a longer "Jeduthun," but the possibility does exist that by the Chronicler's day a new line of musicians known by the name "Jeduthun" had replaced the lineage of Ethan.

The list of sons of Heman, Asaph, and Jeduthun in chapter 25 represents not a genealogy but a division into ancestral houses of the sort already seen with the Levites (chap. 23) and the priests (chap. 24). The term "divisions," however, does not occur in this grouping. It may be that the corps of Temple musicians was better fixed in the traditions associated with the Temple and therefore the Chronicler does not need to portray them as being organized by David. Readers familiar with Psalms will recall the superscriptions of many of the psalms that bear the names of

Asaph (Psalms 50, 73—83), Ethan/Jeduthun (Psalms 39, 62, 89) and Korah, an ancestor in Heman's lineage (1 Chron. 6:37; Psalms 42—49, 84—85, 87—88). While the purpose of these names at the beginning of the psalms is not entirely clear, it seems very likely that they are names of collections of psalms known by the names of groups of Levitical musicians listed here in 1 Chronicles 25. If this is true, taking these psalms together with the musicians' lists here in the present chapter affords us a glimpse into the life of the Temple of the Chronicler's day. At the very least, we can say that the Temple musicians played a vital role in the worship of Israel. As verses 8–31 indicate, they were organized into twenty-four groups of twelve musicians each (thus the repeated phrase "X, his sons and his brothers, twelve," which occurs throughout vv. 7–31; the exception is v. 9, where it has apparently been accidentally omitted). The organization implies once again some annual rotation system of service in the Temple. The musicians were not only singers but instrumentalists, accompanying the psalms with "lyres, harps, and cymbals" (vv. 1, 6). If we understand the psalm superscriptions correctly, it seems likely that each group had something like a hymnal at its disposal in which were the lyrics that have come down to us as individual psalms in the Psalter. They were sung to familiar tunes, now lost to us except by exotic sounding names: "Lilies" (Psalms 45) and "The Deer of the Dawn" (Psalms 22).

It is perhaps in this context that we should understand the rather striking occurrence of the term "prophesy" in 1 Chronicles 25:1–2. Modern readers of the Bible are familiar with this term in two senses. The first is as it applies to the ecstatic activity of individuals caught up in a temporary frenzy identified with the "spirit of the Lord," as is the case with Saul in 1 Samuel 10:9–13. Second, and more commonly, we use the term to refer to the activity—either oral or written—of Old Testament figures identified as "prophets," such as Isaiah or Amos. The present use of the term seems to fall into neither category. Rather than being characterized by ecstatic frenzy, the work of the Temple musicians is the result of learning and discipline, as may be indicated by the phrase "teacher and pupil" in 1 Chronicles 25:8. And, if we are correct about the relationship between the psalms and the guilds of musicians, then even the words employed by the singers are not their own but part of a larger tradition. In what sense, then, is the work of the Temple musicians prophecy?

Perhaps the answer lies in the role played by the Temple musician in the worship life of Israel. Through the music of the psalms are offered to God the joys, praise, complaints, laments, and thanksgiving of individuals and the community of faith. Through that same music are offered to the worshipers the responses of God, promises of deliverance, assurances of pardon, condemnations of wrongdoing. In a very real sense, the

Temple musicians stand at the interface between the worshiping community and the God it worships, speaking to one on behalf of the other. Perhaps it is in this sense that we should understand the "prophecy" of the Temple musicians: They are the agents of the divine-human conversation in music. Surely their prophetic work in this sense is not greatly different from the concourse with God carried on by the church for millennia through its hymnody. To chant the psalms, to sing the great hymns of faith or celebration, to offer prayers through sung refrains, to respond to the Word preached with resounding hymnic affirmations of self dedication—surely this is no less a prophetic speech than was the music of the Levites of the Chronicler's Temple.

GATEKEEPERS
1 Chronicles 26:1–19

The next Levitical service defined by the Chronicler is the gatekeepers. As with other Levites, the gatekeepers are organized by divisions according to ancestral house, and once again there are three groups. However, only two represent lineages known from previous Levitical lists: Korahites (vv. 1–3), descended from Kohath (see 6:22), and Merarites (vv. 10–11). The third group is the sons of Obed-edom (vv. 4–8), who appear to have no overt connection with the Levitical genealogy and may even be an intrusion into a list that originally included only the two houses mentioned in verse 19. As the list stands, however, it is the house of Obed-edom that dominates the Chronicler's system. This fact has led some scholars to argue that the function of gatekeeper was not originally a Levitical one at all but rather one assigned to warriors or other military or police figures. Thus, the family of Obed-edom, whose name is familiar from having cared for the ark after David's initial and abortive attempt to move it to Jerusalem (see 13:13–14), may have stood guard over the ark at the Temple gates as a reward for having protected it in Kiriath-jearim. There may be some support for this view in the description of various members of Obed-edom's family as "able men" (v. 8). The adjective translated "able" in the NRSV is more often used to describe physically powerful warriors (see 1 Sam. 16:18; 31:12; and 2 Sam. 24:9). It would be reasonable to assume that the task of tending the massive doors of the Temple gates would require physical strength and thus those who are strong fighters would have been identified early as suited to the work. Only later was the function of gatekeeper understood as a Levitical one, perhaps as late as the Chronicler's own day.

The gatekeepers were posted by lot to various assignments, and once again the number twenty-four emerges. The east gate of the Temple, presumably the largest and most impressive (as was the case in most ancient Near Eastern temples), received six gatekeepers, while four each were assigned to the north, west, and south gates. In addition, four gatekeepers were assigned duty on the western approach road and two in the colonnade.

OTHER LEVITICAL OFFICERS
1 Chronicles 26:20–32

The remainder of 1 Chronicles 26 describes the functions of Levites engaged in a variety of other smaller functions. The first function is that of the treasurers who maintained the treasuries of "dedicated gifts." As the Chronicler envisions it in verses 26–28, these gifts were largely booty seized in battle by the leaders of Israel's armies, from the level of battalion commander upward, and from the days of Samuel and Saul to David. Rather than treating them as personal property, the victors offered them as thanksgiving offerings to God. The gifts were stored in the Temple treasuries, and thus came under the supervision and care of the Levites. Other Levites are described as "appointed to outside duties," apparently as governmental and judicial agents of the government stationed abroad in the countryside.

The reference in verse 20 to "Ahijah" as the one in charge of the treasuries is a small problem. This information would seem immediately to be contradicted by verses 21–25, in which various members of the lineages of Gershon and Kohath are listed as treasurers. The problem is resolved if "Ahijah" is read as "their brothers," a reading requiring only a very small change in the Hebrew text and supported by ancient translations. The succeeding verses then go on to spell out which Levitical families served as treasurers.

Of special interest is the reference to Levites appointed to "outside duties for Israel" in verses 29–32. The text is tantalizing but ultimately unclear about the functions of these Levites, calling them only "officers and judges" and assigning some to posts in the area west of the Jordan and some in the Reubenite, Gadite, and Manassite country east of the Jordan. In both areas, the officers and judges appear to have dual responsibilities: They serve both "the work of the LORD" (v. 30) and the "affairs of the king" (v. 32). It is likely that the distinction between sacred and secular responsibility is a great deal sharper in modern minds than in the minds of the Chronicler and his audience. Israel of the Persian era was permitted a fairly limited self-governmental power, mostly centered in matters of religious life. It would have been perfectly natural, therefore, to see the authority of the state and the authority of the Temple exercised through a single agency. Modern, though imperfect, examples of this theocratic style of government are visible in Calvin's Geneva or Puritan New England. For the Chronicler and his people, no clear line distinguished church from state, and thus civil administration could appropriately be understood as a Levitical function.

OFFICERS OF THE KING
1 Chronicles 27:1–34

With the end of 1 Chronicles 26, the Chronicler concludes the organization and assignment of Levitical duties he began in 1 Chronicles 23. However, before turning to the concluding instructions regarding the Temple, he has three additional lists of officers to add to the administrative structure of David's kingdom: a list of military leaders (vv. 1–15), a list of tribal leaders (vv. 16–24), and a list of various royal officers and advisors (vv. 25–34). None of these officers or leaders is identified as a Levite, and thus we assume that the Chronicler's purpose here is archival; he includes these lists so that a complete picture of David's administration is preserved.

1. The list of military divisions, 27:1–15. This list is organized around an annual rotational system, with twelve officers leading twelve divisions. The first verse of the chapter is quite explicit about this: The divisions "came and went, month after month throughout the year." The divisions are listed according to a repetitive pattern: first the name of the commander, including any special information about him, then the name of the chief officer, and then the size of the division (always twenty-four thousand). Several of the names appearing in the division list are known from the list of David's warriors in other places: Jashobeam, Dodai (although in 11:12 he is Eleazar son of Dodo; the Chronicler may have abbreviated the name in the present context), Benaiah (commander of Cherethites and Pelethites in 18:17), Helez (11:27), Sibbecai (20:4), and Asahel, brother of Joab. This last name is problematic, since according to 2 Samuel 2:18–23, Asahel was killed by Saul's general Abner before David gained control of Saul's throne. He could therefore not have served as one of David's divisional commanders. The inclusion of his name in this list is thus difficult to explain.

2. The list of tribal leaders, 27:16–24. The list of the leaders of the tribes provides an interesting view of Israel's composition as the Chronicler saw it. Of overriding importance to the Chronicler was to maintain the twelve-tribe system. Early descriptions associated with the distribution of land among the tribes omit Levi and compensate for the loss by dividing Joseph's portion between his sons Ephraim and Manasseh. The Chronicler has introduced two changes into this system. First, he restores Levi to the list, probably because of the importance he attaches to the place of the Levites in the life of Israel. Second, he lists Manasseh as two half-tribes rather than one, probably because Manassite territory was divided by the Jordan into eastern and western halves. These changes, however, require that two tribal names be omitted in order to maintain the total of twelve. The Chronicler chooses to omit Asher and Gad. The former's land was situated inland from Tyre and Sidon and was probably lost early to those strong powers. The latter's land lay between Manasseh and Moab in the Transjordan and was probably lost to Moabite expansion or to absorption into the larger Manassite claim.

3. *Royal officers and advisors, 27:25–34.* The Chronicler next provides a list of officials who have responsibility for husbanding the personal estate and resources of the king. The number of officials is twelve, leading one to suspect a certain artificial character to the list. Still, it is quite likely that David held considerable personal property and that such property would have required supervision that David himself could not have provided. Thus, even if this list is artificially organized, some such division of responsibility would have been necessary.

This section also includes a list of counselors and close associates of David, perhaps forming a sort of "cabinet" of advisors to the king. Some of the names are familiar as important characters in the story of David's reign. The names of Joab, David's commanding general, and Benaiah, commander of the elite units of David's army, are already familiar. Of special interest are Ahithophel and Hushai, listed here as David's "counselor" and "friend." Because he omits all discussion of the revolt of David's son Absalom, the Chronicler masks the roles played by these two characters in those events (2 Sam. 15:32–37; 17:5–14). In the present list, Ahithophel and Hushai are listed alongside one another, as if none of the events of Absalom's revolt had occurred and both had rendered valuable service to David.

DAVID'S PUBLIC INSTRUCTIONS FOR THE TEMPLE
1 Chronicles 28:1–21

28:1 **David assembled at Jerusalem all the officials of Israel, the officials of the tribes, the officers of the divisions that served the king, the commanders of the thousands, the commanders of the hundreds, the stewards of all the property and cattle of the king and his sons, together with the palace** officials, the mighty warriors, and all the warriors. [2] Then King David rose to his feet and said: "Hear me, my brothers and my people. I had planned to build a house of rest for the ark of the covenant of the LORD, for the footstool of our God; and I made preparations for building. [3] But God said to me, 'You shall not build a house for my name, for you are a warrior and have shed blood.' [4] Yet the LORD God of Israel chose me from all my ancestral house to be king over Israel forever; for he chose Judah as leader, and in the house of Judah my father's house, and among my father's sons he took delight in making me king over all Israel. [5] And of all my sons, for the LORD has given me many, he has chosen my son Solomon to sit upon the throne of the kingdom of the LORD over Israel. [6] He said to me, 'It is your son Solomon who shall build my house and my courts, for I have chosen him to be a son to me, and I will be a father to him. [7] I will establish his kingdom forever if he continues resolute in keeping my commandments and my ordinances, as he is today.' [8] Now therefore in the sight of all Israel, the assembly of the LORD, and in the hearing of our God, observe and search out all the commandments of the LORD your God; that you may possess this good land, and leave it for an inheritance to your children forever.

[9] "And you, my son Solomon, know the God of your father, and serve him with single mind and willing heart; for the LORD searches every mind, and understands every plan and thought. If you seek him, he will be found by you; but if you forsake him, he will abandon you forever. [10] Take heed now, for the LORD has chosen you to build a house as the sanctuary; be strong, and act."

[11] Then David gave his son Solomon the plan of the vestibule of the temple, and of its houses, its treasuries, its upper rooms, and its inner chambers, and of the room for the mercy seat; [12] and the plan of all that he had in mind: for the courts of the house of the LORD, all the surrounding chambers, the treasuries of the house of God, and the treasuries for dedicated gifts; [13] for the divisions of the priests and of the Levites, and all the work of the service in the house of the LORD; for all the vessels for the service in the house of the LORD, [14] the weight of gold for all golden vessels for each service, the weight of silver vessels for each service, [15] the weight of the golden lampstands and their lamps, the weight of gold for each lampstand and its lamps, the weight of silver for a lampstand and its lamps, according to the use of each in the service, [16] the weight of gold for each table for the rows of bread, the silver for the silver tables, [17] and pure gold for the forks, the basins, and the cups; for the golden bowls and the weight of each; for the silver bowls and the weight of each; [18] for the altar of incense made of refined gold, and its weight; also his plan for the golden chariot of the cherubim that spread their wings and covered the ark of the covenant of the LORD.

[19] "All this, in writing at the LORD's direction, he made clear to me—the plan of all the works."

[20] David said further to his son Solomon, "Be strong and of good courage, and act. Do not be afraid or dismayed; for the LORD God, my God,

is with you. He will not fail you or forsake you, until all the work for the service of the house of the LORD is finished. [21] Here are the divisions of the priests and the Levites for all the service of the house of God; and with you in all the work will be every volunteer who has skill for any kind of service; also the officers and all the people will be wholly at your command."

The crowning moment of the Chronicler's presentation of David's preparations for the Temple comes in David's speech to the gathered leaders of Israel in Jerusalem. This chapter and the next gather the themes and material presented throughout chapters 22—27. All the leadership of Israel is gathered to hear David's instructions. David's speech returns to the themes of his instructions to Solomon in 1 Chronicles 22: the prophecy of Nathan that God will establish Solomon's throne, the reasons why David will not build the Temple, the entrusting of the task to Solomon, and the preparations made by David for the work. Chapter 28 has two parts: David's address assigning to Solomon the task of building the Temple (vv. 1–10), and David's delivery of the plans for the Temple to Solomon (vv. 11–21).

1. David's address, 28:1–10. The Chronicler begins this climactic moment toward which he has been building by assembling the official leadership of the kingdom before the king to hear the speech. Arrayed before the seated king are all those military and political leaders described in 1 Chronicles 27, those upon whom will fall the responsibility for marshalling the gathered resources to accomplish the Temple project. Absent from the assembled group are the Levites; in the Chronicler's scheme, their responsibility is the management of the Temple's life after its completion, not participation in its construction. As the Chronicler describes the scene, the king dramatically rises to his feet for his speech and commands the attention of the people.

David's words, "I had planned to build a house of rest for the ark of the covenant of the LORD" (28:2), make clear that the initiative for the Temple belongs to David; precisely how true this statement is will be made clear in the second section of the chapter. As they stand, however, they evoke the scene of 1 Chronicles 17 and David's intent to build a structure to house the ark. The rest of David's speech then builds on the same play on the word "house" that Nathan's speech in chapter 17 employs: David will not build a house (Temple) for the ark, but God will build a house (dynasty) for David. From the very outset, then, the direction of the speech is clear: It will be instruction to Solomon to build the Temple and also justification for the dynastic succession of Solomon to the throne. But in addition to the language of Nathan's oracle, the Chronicler also returns to the imagery of Deuteronomy 12:10. David's words in verse 2, "I had planned to build a house of rest for the ark," evoke the Deuteronomic foundation used in 1 Chronicles 22:6–9 to explain why David does not carry through with his plans. As we saw there, the Chronicler makes the case that the Temple, as a house of rest, cannot be built by one who has shed blood.

The next step the Chronicler takes here is surprising. Rather than claim for Solomon the title "man of rest," as he does in 1 Chronicles 22:9, the Chronicler moves all the way back to the genealogies to justify the election of Solomon. God chose Judah as leader of the tribes, and within Judah the house of David's father, and among the sons of Jesse David; the sequence evokes the narrowing effect of the Chronicler's genealogies in chapters 1—9. We are left with the notion that the will and intent of God for the people of Israel is vested in the single man David. By the end of verse 4, the Chronicler has brought us to something of a historical nexus: God's will has been focused among all the peoples of the earth in Israel, in Judah, and in David. And now, "of all my sons, and the LORD has given me many, he has chosen my son Solomon to sit upon the throne of the kingdom of the LORD over Israel." The effect of the Chronicler's arrangement of David's speech is that the selection of Solomon is inevitable, foreordained by the ancient will of God at work throughout the generations. Then, as if to buttress the point, the Chronicler has David remind us of the prophecy of Nathan again: "It is your son Solomon who shall build my house and my courts, for I have chosen him to be a son to me, and I will be a father to him."

Readers who know the story of 2 Samuel know that the process by which Solomon came to succeed his father was a torturous and bloody one, moved along by the deaths of one after another of David's other sons and characterized by intrigue and deception. The question thus naturally arises: Is the Chronicler unaware of all this, or has he chosen to ignore it? The answer is, in all likelihood, "no" to both. The Chronicler is fully aware of the story of Solomon's succession; he has on more than one occasion cited texts from the middle of that story. But the 2 Samuel story is the story of the historical-political process by which Solomon achieved his father's throne, and that is not the focus for the Chronicler. Rather, his interest is in a theological reading of the result of that process: that God has guided events so that a will set in motion long before Solomon or David or even Israel itself would come to fruition in Solomon's accession and the construction of the Temple. The Chronicler has no need to recount the very human story of that accession, but only to state clearly the divine intention that has brought it to pass.

It is, however, not an unconditional divine intention that places Solomon on the throne. Attached to David's citation of Nathan's oracle is an all-important condition in verse 7:

> I will establish his kingdom forever if he continues resolute in keeping my commandments and my ordinances, as he is today.

As in 1 Chronicles 22:12–13, David once again connects the promise of success as ruler with obedience to the statutes and commandments of the law, and he further connects obedience with the specific act of building the Temple. Once again, and now publicly, David makes clear that there is a direct line between the health and welfare of the kingdom and the accomplishment of the great task of building the Temple. The Temple, in the Chronicler's vision of Israel, lies at the very spiritual heart of the people's identity, just as it lies at the heart of their geographic location.

The language of the peroration of David's speech to the assembly in verses 8–9 evokes Deuteronomy again:

> You must follow exactly the path that the LORD your God has commanded you, so that you may live, and that it may go well with you, and that you may live long in the land that you are to possess. (5:33)

Having outlined the path by which the Lord has led Israel to the moment of David's speech, the Chronicler now points the way toward the future. That future—characterized by safety and security in "this good land" for both present and future generations—is guaranteed only by obedience.

2. David delivers the plans for the Temple, 28:11–21. Having finished the address, David now delivers into Solomon's hands the plans for the Temple. One is struck by the detail and specificity of David's planning. Not only are the architectural plans handed over, determining the size and shape of the building and its various courts and porticos, but concrete details concerning the design and weight of the gold and silver furnishings are described as well. Indeed, it seems that the gold and silver lampstands and showbread tables, utensils, and incense altars are of greater importance to the Chronicler than the structure that housed them. Given the Chronicler's interest in the role of the Levites into whose care these items are given, perhaps this is not surprising. Also not surprising is the fact that David delivers to Solomon the description of the organization and function of the Levites; indeed, they are treated as part of the plans for the Temple, no less important than the architecture. Taken together, the details about the Temple furnishings and the operation of the Levitical system provide a link between the Temple of Solomon and the Temple of the Chronicler's own day. The role of the priests and Levites, serving in the Temple among the gold and silver vessels, is not merely to be caretakers and functionaries; rather, as they perform "all the service of the house of God," they are a concrete connection between the present and the sacred past.

THE OFFERING OF THE PEOPLE
1 Chronicles 29:1–9

David's address in 1 Chronicles 29:1–9 is probably best seen as a continuation of the address in 28:1–10; however, it takes up a different theme. Though it begins with a lengthy description of all the wealth and material amassed by David for the sake of the Temple, its clear direction is the summons in verse 5 to the leaders of Israel to match David's contributions. Perhaps it is not too facetious to suggest that David's words here are the challenge gift for the mother of all capital fund campaigns.

In truth, the weights of precious stones and both precious and common metals assembled first by David and then by the leaders are nothing less than staggering and are certainly exaggerations. But their exaggerated character serves to make the Chronicler's point that the most, biggest, brightest, and best should be devoted to the Temple. The reason is stated in the opening lines of the speech: The Temple will not be for mortals but for God. This is also the reason that David undertakes this massive fundraising effort: because it is a task too large for the "young and inexperienced" Solomon. No half measures will be acceptable, and no failures due to errors of judgment will be tolerated. The Temple requires a maximum, all-out effort on the part not only of the king but also of the people.

No preacher or stewardship chair who has ever sat through a kick-off dinner for a capital funds campaign can fail to grasp the dynamics of this text. David's speech is not a boastful display of his own wealth; it is a challenge to his officers and leaders to be as committed to the Temple project as he is. And however much such occasions may degenerate into arm-twisting sessions, the point is not to squeeze liberality out of an otherwise ungenerous people. For eight chapters, the Chronicler has set before his readers the unfolding vision of the Temple in all its glory and complexity, and not merely the Temple as a building but as a living thing, the beating heart of Israel's religious life. Failure to commit to the strength of that heart is not mere laziness; it is disobedience to the commandments of the LORD. The vast, exaggerated totals and the heaped displays of David's opulence and wealth are for the Chronicler a challenge not simply to the Israel of Solomon's day but to the Israel of his own day as well. If they were committed to such an extent, he asks implicitly, how can we be less?

Two verbs stand out in this presentation, one at the end of David's speech and the other at the end of the people's offering. David asks in verse 5 for those willing to *consecrate themselves* to the Lord. The implication of the term is that not merely the gifts of the people but their entire lives are set apart for the sacred purpose of the Temple. The Chronicler's view permits no one to compartmentalize their understanding of their wealth: so much for God, so much for country, so much for self. David's question presumes that all of life—and therefore all of life's resources—are claimed by the sacred and devoted to the task of serving God. Then, in verse 9, the people *rejoice* at the single-minded willingness with which the vast store of money and material is assembled. Far from the grumbling and complaining that too regularly accompanies our conversations about generosity in the life of the church, the Chronicler shows us a vision of a king and community overjoyed at the results of their common self-dedication. In truth, what other response is appropriate to the powerful result of consecrated commitment?

DAVID'S BLESSING OF THE OFFERING
1 Chronicles 29:10–22a

29:10 Then David blessed the LORD in the presence of all the assembly; David said: "Blessed are you, O LORD, the God of our ancestor Israel, forever and ever. ¹¹ Yours, O LORD, are the greatness, the power, the glory, the victory, and the majesty; for all that is in the heavens and on the earth is yours; yours is the kingdom, O LORD, and you are exalted as head above all. ¹² Riches and honor come from you, and you rule over all. In your hand are power and might; and it is in your hand to make great and to give strength to all. ¹³ And now, our God, we give thanks to you and praise your glorious name.

¹⁴ "But who am I, and what is my people, that we should be able to make this freewill offering? For all things come from you, and of your own have we given you. ¹⁵ For we are aliens and transients before you, as were all our ancestors; our days on the earth are like a shadow, and there is no hope. ¹⁶ O LORD our God, all this abundance that we have provided for building you a house for your holy name comes from your hand and is all your own. ¹⁷ I know, my God, that you search the heart, and take pleasure in uprightness; in the uprightness of my heart I have freely offered all these things, and now I have seen your people, who are present here, offering freely and joyously to you. ¹⁸ O LORD, the God of Abraham, Isaac, and Israel, our ancestors, keep forever such purposes and thoughts in the hearts of your people, and direct their hearts toward you. ¹⁹ Grant to my son Solomon that with single mind he may keep your commandments, your decrees, and your statutes, performing all of them, and that he may build the temple for which I have made provision."

²⁰ Then David said to the whole assembly, "Bless the LORD your God." And all the assembly blessed the LORD, the God of their ancestors, and bowed their heads and prostrated themselves before the LORD and the king. ²¹ On the next day they offered sacrifices and burnt offerings to the LORD, a thousand bulls, a thousand rams, and a thousand lambs, with their liba-

tions, and sacrifices in abundance for all Israel; [22] and they ate and drank before the LORD on that day with great joy.

The final section in the narrative of David's preparations for the Temple is David's blessing of the offering. The words are offered as a prayer of thanksgiving and petition, in much the same manner as a minister or priest offers a prayer at the conclusion of an offertory in modern worship. The prayer is structured in two parts: an exaltation of the sovereignty of God (vv. 10–13) and a petition for guidance for people and king (vv. 14–19). Following the prayer is a description of the worship and sacrifices of the assembly (vv. 20–22a).

The prayer begins with a celebration of divine sovereignty and power, phrased in terms sounding very much like those of modern prayers. David's praise of God amounts to the gathering of several synonymous terms to describe God's lordship: greatness, power, glory, victory, majesty, followed by the acknowledgment that "all that is in the heavens and on the earth is yours; yours is the kingdom." The language has a familiar ring; Protestants will immediately recognize verse 11 as the source of the final line of the Lord's Prayer: "Thine is the kingdom, and the power, and the glory." Some late versions of the prayer in Matthew 6:13 in fact contain this line; most, however, do not, and it is often omitted in Roman Catholic recitations of the prayer. In this context, however, the language serves to point to the theological foundation of the prayer: that all the amassed glory and wealth gathered by Israel for the purpose of the Temple construction in fact belongs not to the people but to God.

This theological truth then becomes the centerpiece for the next section of the prayer, verses 14–19. Acknowledging the smallness of both king and people before a God of such glory and power (v. 14), David confesses that the people are but "aliens and transients" in the land. The confession evokes two images. The first is the image of the patriarchs and the wandering people in the wilderness, living on that which God alone provided for their sustenance. The second is the language of human mortality, such as we find in Psalm 90:

> For all our days pass away under your wrath;
>   our years come to an end like a sigh.
> The days of our life are seventy years,
>   or perhaps eighty if we are strong;
> even then their span is only toil and trouble;
>   they are soon gone, and we fly away.
> So teach us to count our days,
>   that we may gain a wise heart.
> (Ps. 90:9–10, 12)

The result of each is the acknowledgment of complete dependence on God and the awareness that such dependence leads to an "uprightness" that is pleasing to God. David places his own and the people's offering before God in the context of this humble uprightness; no pride of accomplishment or wealthy boastfulness can be allowed to intrude on the sacredness of the offering. Rather, David's prayer—which, of course, is the prayer the Chronicler offers on behalf of his own people and the church offers on its own behalf—is that such an awareness of dependence and humility might continue to guide the people, that God might "keep forever such purposes and thoughts in the hearts of your people, and direct their hearts toward you." For the Chronicler, the building of the Temple is more a matter of the heart than of the hand. The Temple is grounded in and built on the faith of Israel and is the expression of that faith in wood and stone and metal and jewel.

The prayer concludes with a petition on behalf of Solomon, echoing once again David's desire that Solomon be guided in single-minded obedience to the statutes and ordinances of the law. And once again, the explicit connection is drawn between the general language of obedience and the specific act of building the Temple. One final time, the Chronicler hammers home the point that obedience and worship are not separable acts but rather part and parcel of authentic faith in God.

7. Solomon's Accession and a Summary of David's Reign
1 Chronicles 29:22b–30

The conclusion of the great story of David in 1 Chronicles is composed of two short narratives, each with its own purpose. The second account is a standard regnal summary of the sort found throughout 1 and 2 Kings and 2 Chronicles. The first has a more polemical and apologetic tone and may have been introduced later to offer an alternate vision of Solomon's accession to the throne.

Unlike the story of Solomon's accession to David's throne in 1 Kings 1—2, a tale of intrigue and chaos surrounding David's last days, the narrative of Solomon's accession in 1 Chronicles 29:22b–25 is a story of the fulfillment of divine intent. Solomon is destined for the throne by God rather than attaining it through secret negotiations among palace conspirators (1 Kings 1:11–14). Solomon is proclaimed king by a vigorous David in full possession of his physical and spiritual powers rather than by a weakened and compromised old man (1 Kings 1:32–37). Further, "all the leaders and the mighty warriors, and also all the sons of King David, pledged their allegiance to King Solomon," instead of having half die in blood purges (1 Kings 2:13–46). The note that "they made David's son Solomon king *a second time*" was certainly added by someone who did not understand the Chronicler's intent in 1 Chronicles 23:1. There, as we noted above, the reference to Solomon's elevation to the throne is intended as a summary comment to point to the outcome of the entire unit of chapters 22—29. Apparently the present comment—and probably the section as a whole—was added by someone who did not understand how Solomon could be king while David continued to be vital and active, and who perhaps also wanted to defend Solomon against charges that he had stolen the throne away from its rightful heir, Adonijah.

The summary of David's reign in verses 26–30 has all the earmarks of the Deuteronomic editorial framework that appears at the end of each king's reign in 1 and 2 Kings. The principal differences here have to do with style rather than content. David is "son of Jesse" rather than simply king, recalling his origins as a shepherd of his father's flock in Judah. He dies in "good old age, full of days, riches, and honor," and is succeeded without incident (or at least without comment on incident) by Solomon. In every respect, it is the picture of a great king's peaceful passing from life into death and a fitting end to the Chronicler's treatment of the hero of Israel.

At the end of the summary, there appear for the first time references to source documents from which the Chronicler appears to have drawn material for his account and where additional information may be found. As we noted in the introduction to this commentary, there is considerable debate over the authenticity of these references. It may be that the "records of the seer Samuel" are the very books we know as 1 and 2 Samuel, from which, indeed, the Chronicler has drawn a great deal of the content of his narrative. As for the "records of the prophet Nathan" and the "records of the seer Gad," no such documents are known to exist. If they were (or are) actual writings, it is possible that some of what we now regard as material unique to the Chronicler is drawn from them. Without them, however, the frequent references here and throughout 2 Chronicles remain a mystery, and we must continue to assume that materials unparalleled in existing sources reflect the Chronicler's own contributions to the story and its undergirding theology.

The end of the David story brings us to the midpoint of the Chronicler's presentation of the story of Israel. Thus far it has been a story of emergence and rising: of Israel from among the nations and peoples of the world, of David as the hero of Israel and the founder of the faith, and of the Temple as the theological and physical center of that faith. The three themes are irrevocably intertwined. As David rises, Israel rises; as the Temple moves closer to actuality, Israel's faith takes on meaning and David's prestige grows. There is little so far in this story to regret; only the story of the census carries the implication of sin, and even that is turned toward the noble purpose of identifying the site for the Temple. So far, the Chronicler's story is a story of fulfillment: of David's vision, of Israel's destiny, and of God's will.

The next step in the story of Israel is also a story of triumph. Part III has as its subject the reign of Solomon, and at its center is the construction of the Temple itself. Chapters 1—11 of 2 Chronicles tell the story of the fulfillment of David's vision and Nathan's prophecy of the building of two houses—one for David and one for the Lord.

Part III: The Reign of Solomon

2 Chronicles 1—9

The story of Solomon's reign is in large measure the story of the construction of the Temple; throughout his reign, Solomon is either preparing for it, building it, or dedicating it. For the Chronicler, the Temple is the centerpiece of the narrative. In building the Temple, Solomon carries out the design of David and, more importantly, the will of God.

The Temple is more than a civil construction project; for the Chronicler, it is a fulfillment of the law of Moses and an act of obedience and faithfulness by Solomon. David's instructions to Solomon in 1 Chronicles 22:12–16 and his prayer in 1 Chronicles 29:19 make this clear: In both there is a direct connection between obedience to the "commandments, statutes, and ordinances" of God's law and building the Temple. The narrative of the Temple construction in 2 Chronicles 2:1–5:1 will point to the same connection by relying on the descriptions of the tabernacle in Exodus in addition to the descriptions of the Temple in 1 Kings to describe Solomon's actions. As the Chronicler's Solomon builds the Temple, he is fulfilling the Law of Moses for the sacred worship space of Israel.

A recurring theme throughout the narrative of Solomon's reign in 2 Chronicles 1—9 is the king's opulence. The Chronicler understands Solomon's wealth and prosperity not merely as the impressive collection of imperial power, the purpose of which is to awe client kings and queens such as the queen of Sheba (2 Chron. 9:1–12). Rather, Solomon's wealth, prosperity, and prestige are also the blessing bestowed upon him by God for his obedience. Simultaneously, they also enhance that obedience: The wealthier Solomon is, the more lavish a Temple he designs and builds.

We should also understand the tradition of Solomon's wisdom in a similar manner. Readers are familiar with the legends of Solomon's wisdom and insight in governance and justice and the stories of Solomon as a collector of proverbs and wise sayings. While in 1 Kings this material has a life of its own, in Chronicles it exists only to serve the larger point of Solomon's obedience. Solomon's wisdom is a reflection of his obedience to God; he is wise in that he is faithful and obedient.

The Chronicler's presentation of the reign of Solomon falls into four major sections. The middle two sections—by far the largest and most complex—are devoted to the construction and dedication of the Temple (2 Chron. 2:1–5:1 and 5:2–7:22, respectively); these middle sections are bracketed by descriptions of Solomon's greatness (2 Chron. 1:1–17 and 8:1–9:31).

8. Solomon's Greatness
2 Chronicles 1:1–17

At the conclusion of the notice of Solomon's accession to the throne, 1 Chronicles 29:25 notes: "The LORD highly exalted Solomon in the sight of all Israel, and bestowed upon him such royal majesty as had not been on any king before him in Israel." The apparent agenda of much of 2 Chronicles 1—9, and especially of chapters 1, 8, and 9, is to demonstrate the truth of that notice. The story of Solomon's reign is the story of wealth, wisdom, international power, and prestige. But Solomon's wealth and wisdom serve a purpose for the Chronicler. We are dealing here not with a Middle Eastern despot but rather with an obedient servant of God. Solomon's obedience to God in building the Temple is the foundation of and the reason for all his wealth and the source of all his wisdom.

In this regard, Solomon is the prototype for all the kings of Israel, in a way even that David was not. David must carve a kingdom out of the hands of enemies and so is forgiven being "a man of blood." Solomon, like all the Davidic kings who succeed him, inherits that kingdom, a gift from God to David. It is the kings' responsibility to nurture that gift and augment its blessing. To the extent that they accomplish this at all, they do so through obedience to God and specifically through attention to the Temple and the faith it celebrates. Those kings who keep faith and obey prosper in the Chronicler's story; those who do not suffer the consequences of God's withdrawal of blessing.

Solomon's insight into this truth is the foundation of his wisdom. That is the point of the story of his vision at Gibeon in 2 Chronicles 1:1–13. Appended to this story is an old tradition about Solomon's involvement in horse and chariot trading (vv. 14–17). The thrust of this material in the hands of the Chronicler is to demonstrate how the wisdom of Solomon results in international prominence and prestige.

SOLOMON'S VISION AT GIBEON
2 Chronicles 1:1–13

Second Chronicles begins by drawing to a conclusion all the developments of 1 Chronicles 22—29 in a single sentence. Solomon "established himself in his kingdom," says verse 1. The choice of the reflexive verb implies that Solomon now takes the reigns of power for himself, moving beyond his father David's legacy. Although he will certainly carry out the mission his father assigned to him, he will do so in a manner grander than anything David had imagined. His wealth and prestige will now outstrip David's, and his position on the international stage will reach greater prominence than his father attained. More importantly, though, "the LORD his God was with him, and made him exceedingly great." With this note, the Chronicler signals the fulfillment of the promise of David to Solomon in 1 Chronicles 28:20 and echoes the language of the enthronement announcement of 1 Chronicles 29:25. In all likelihood, the Chronicler intended this opening sentence to be something of a summary or programmatic statement for the entire presentation of Solomon's reign. In much of what follows, there will be repeated testimonies to the blessing of God upon the king and the greatness that proceeds from that blessing.

The story of Solomon's visit to Gibeon and the vision there serves to convey divine confirmation of Solomon's accession to the throne of David. Solomon's request to God in verse 9 to "let your promise to my father David now be fulfilled" amounts to a request for God's approbation of his succession. Without it, Solomon cannot legitimately be king; with it, there can be no legitimate challenge to his kingship. For this reason, the event is explicitly public; all the figures representing the people of Israel are present at Gibeon: the commanders of the army, judges, tribal leaders, and heads of ancestral families. Everyone is represented in this gathering, so that by extension everyone is committed to the kingship established here.

But there is more afoot here than the granting of divine imprimatur on Solomon's kingship. In fact, the Chronicler uses the vision at Gibeon to establish two important theological themes that will resound throughout the story of Solomon's reign. The first of those themes is the tabernacle tradition that appears in the identification of Gibeon. Gibeon is a "high place," or hilltop, where the tent of meeting, or tabernacle, was located (see 1 Chron.15:37–42). In addition to the tabernacle, the altar built by Bezalel in Exodus 31:2–11 that accompanied the tabernacle throughout Israel's wandering in the wilderness is also in Gibeon. Solomon's pilgrimage to Gibeon at the beginning of his efforts to build the Temple signals the programmatic inclusion of the structure of the tabernacle in the details of the Temple. The tabernacle is the only worship space whose details were dictated by God; as the Chronicler prepares to describe Solomon's Temple, he makes clear that Solomon's vision is guided by the vision of worship in the law.

The second theme the Chronicler establishes in this account is the relationship between Solomon's obedience, his wealth, and his wisdom. In the vision that he (and the rest of the leaders of Israel?) sees in verses 7–13, God asks Solomon what he wishes to receive from the divine hand as a symbol of God's confirmation of his reign. Solomon's response in verses 8–10 begins by noting God's graciousness toward David and seeks the same gracious approval for David's son. As a symbol of that approval, Solomon asks for "wisdom and knowledge" to rule "this great people of yours." God's answer, in verses 11–12, expresses delight at Solomon's choice and then grants not only the wisdom and knowledge but "riches, possessions, and honor" as well. For the Chronicler, Solomon's legendary wisdom and also his vast wealth and international status and prestige are the direct outgrowth of his desire to be obedient as a servant of God.

Perhaps as instructive as what he includes is what the Chronicler elects not to include here. Readers of 1 Kings 3:16–28 are familiar with the narrative of the two women, one of whose child has died in the night and who now falsely claims that the child of the other is actually her own. Solomon decides the case by threatening to divide the child in half with the sword so that both mothers might have a portion. The story is a practical demonstration of Solomon's wisdom; he knows that the real mother will surrender the child rather than see it killed. The Chronicler omits this story, with which he would certainly have been familiar, because it demonstrates Solomon's wisdom in the wrong way. Solomon's wisdom is evidenced by his obedience to the law in the building of the Temple rather than in clever demonstrations of common sense.

SOLOMON'S TRADE IN HORSES AND CHARIOTS
2 Chronicles 1:14–17

From the sublime exchange between God and king, we move to the rather mundane business of horses and chariots. The Chronicler's point in including this detail about Solomon's international trade is less economic than theological. Having just heard God promise Solomon "riches, possessions, and honor," the Chronicler now describes one form of God's deliverance on that promise, to the extent that "the king made silver and gold as common in Jerusalem as stone."

The mechanism of Solomon's fortune is international trade, here in horses and chariots. Horses were imported from Egypt and Kue (or Cilicia, in modern Turkey), and paired with chariots of Egyptian craftsmanship. Some of the chariots were apparently kept by Solomon to build up a chariot force that was housed in Jerusalem and the "chariot cities." These latter were cities in Israel where garrisons of soldiers and stables for horses were established (archaeologists have suggested that remains at Megiddo and Hazor may have suited this purpose, although the matter is not settled). Others were sold on the international market, creating the image of Solomon as arms merchant. The Chronicler, however, almost certainly did not attach the negative significance to such an image that we might. For him, the point was that Solomon played a key role in international events and processes, that he procured considerable wealth from that role, and that both the prestige and the wealth were the direct result of God's blessing of the king.

9. The Construction of the Temple
2 Chronicles 2:1–5:1

The centerpiece of the Chronicler's presentation of Solomon's reign is the description of the construction and dedication of the Temple. The present section accomplishes the first of those goals. Surprisingly, relatively few architectural details about the Temple are present in this account; apart from the barest dimensions of the Temple structure, we know nothing of its design. This may be due to the fact that the Chronicler's readers had the Second Temple before them and needed no description to support the image. But it may also be true that the Chronicler's interest is in conveying the theological idea of the Temple rather than the physical appearance of the place. One notes in reading this material that while physical description of the building is in short supply, there is no want of description of the ornamentation, decoration, and furnishings of the Temple. The point of the Chronicler's description of the Temple seems to be its lavishness, through which is conveyed the devotion of Solomon and Israel to God. For the Chronicler, establishing in the mind's eye of his readers the image of the Temple as a religious icon may well be more important than describing its physical appearance.

The Temple construction narrative falls into three sections. The first describes Solomon's preparation for the project; its center is an alliance with Huram of Tyre through which Solomon procures both building materials and the services of a skilled craftsman (2:1–18). The second section is concerned with the actual construction of the sanctuary, especially the "most holy place" where the ark of the covenant will be kept (3:1–17). The third section is a description of the various furniture and utensils created for use within the Temple (4:1–5:1).

SOLOMON'S PREPARATIONS FOR BUILDING THE TEMPLE
2 Chronicles 2:1–18

On top of the preparations already accomplished by David, Solomon now adds additional material and human energy; this is the focus of 2 Chronicles 2. The chapter describes the correspondence between Solomon and Huram, king of the Phoenician city of Tyre, through whom Solomon procures both cedar for construction and the services of a skilled craftsman (2:3–16). Bracketing this central story are references to Solomon's conscription of a labor force (2:1–2 and 17–18).

1. Solomon's forced labor conscription, 2:1–2 and 17–18. For ease of discussion, we shall examine these nearly identical references to Solomon's forced labor conscription as a single unit. The Chronicler will return to this subject in 8:3–10.

The opening sentence of the chapter is a summary statement rather than new information. The assemblage of labor and material described in this chapter is devoted to the construction of the Temple, about which much will be said, and also to the palace complex, about which we hear virtually nothing. Readers familiar with 1 Kings 7 will recall that Solomon's palace was actually a large multiunit complex, of which the Temple was probably one unit. For the Chronicler, however, the only important construction to which the resources of Israel are devoted is the construction of the Temple, and that is the only work that receives attention here.

The practice of forced labor sounds to modern ears like slavery, and it may have been such. However, lifelong, enforced labor is only one form of slavery practiced in the ancient world. Another possibility suggested by the term "conscripted" (v. 2) is that of a draft, not unlike that used for military service. In either case, however, the idea would not have been a popular choice; hence, there are "overseers" whose task is to keep the laborers at work. The Chronicler is careful to note in verse 17 that the population from which this conscription is taken is the aliens who live in the land rather than the Israelites themselves. When the Chronicler returns to this subject in 8:3–10, the matter is made still clearer: The conquered people still in the land are the source for all the conscript labor, and no Israelites are included in their number. The end result is that the Temple is built not by the hands of Israel but by those whom God has given into Israelite hands. In an extended sense, perhaps, the Temple is not the work of Israel but the gift of God to Israel.

The numbers of conscripted laborers are large; indeed, some scholars have questioned whether they are not inflated in an effort to impress the reader with the sheer size of the project. While the answer cannot be determined, certainly ancient construction projects on the grand scale of the pyramids in Egypt or the great palaces of Assyria, Babylon, and Persia required vast resources of human labor to accomplish.

2. Solomon's alliance with Huram of Tyre, 2:3–16. The Chronicler continues the theme of Solomon's international prestige in the narrative of the correspondence between Solomon and Huram, king of Tyre (the same figure as "Hiram" in 1 Chronicles 14:1; the names are interchangeable alternatives). On the surface, the letter from Solomon to Huram is a request for the Tyrian king to provide large quantities of cedar, cypress, and algum timber and a skilled artisan to work in a variety of construction media. In addition, Solomon pledges to send workers to the Tyrian hill country in Lebanon to assist in cutting and hauling the timber, and promises a very generous supply of food to support the project. Huram responds with expressions of willingness to provide what Solomon needs and to do so in a way that puts Solomon to the least trouble. He declines Solomon's offer of food supplies, encouraging Solomon to devote the promised food to the support of his own workers. Finally, Huram promises the services of one Huram-abi, a skilled artisan who meets and exceeds all Solomon's requirements. The exchange is the model of deference, with Huram taking the role of the vassal and Solomon the overlord, even though Solomon himself acknowledges that Huram's tenure on the throne is much longer than his own. The effect of the story is to emphasize Solomon's greatness by showing the deference with which he is treated by his contemporaries and peers.

Once again, however, there is more than the simple storyline to consider. The Chronicler has skillfully woven into the correspondence of the two kings important themes and ideas that serve his larger theological purpose. One is the notion that the Temple does not contain God's physical presence.

> 2:4 I am now about to build a house for the name of the LORD my God and dedicate it to him for offering fragrant incense before him, and for the regular offering of the rows of bread, and for burnt offerings morning and evening, on the sabbaths and the new moons and the appointed festivals of the LORD our God, as ordained forever for Israel. ⁵The house that I am about to build will be great, for our God is greater than other gods. ⁶But who is able to build him a house, since heaven, even highest heaven, cannot contain him? Who am I to build a house for him, except as a place to make offerings before him?

Note the careful language used by Solomon to describe the Temple in verse 4: It is "a house for the name of the LORD my God." Solomon's words to Huram in verse 6 make the point: Even the highest heaven cannot contain God; how much less then a house built by human hands, even the hands of the king? For the Chronicler, the Temple is not a house for God—at least in the commonly understood conventions of the ancient Near East, a place where the deity dwelled. Rather, it was a place where God's name dwelled. The language is classic Deuteronomic phraseology: In Deuteronomy, God does not physically dwell in the Temple in Jerusalem but chooses the city as the place where the "name of God" is to be worshiped. In Hebrew thought and in subsequent Jewish and Christian theology, God is not bound by limitations of space or time. It is thus possible to understand God as great and all-encompassing, to claim that there is no place on earth that does not fall under the sovereign rule of God, even while asserting that the central shrine wherein this God is worshiped is the Temple in Jerusalem.

The fact that God does not dwell in the Temple should not lead one to conclude that the Temple is small or unimportant, however. On the contrary, the Temple is "great, for our God is greater than other gods." Hence, the preparations Solomon makes and the material gathered for the construction are "abundant, for the house I am about to build will be great and wonderful." No expenditure is too lavish, no design too grand when rendered in the service of God. The Chronicler's emphasis on the ornate decorations and rich appointments of the Temple is testimony to this commitment that the Temple's opulence reflects the greatness of God and the magnitude of Israel's adoration of God.

But if the Temple, however grand, is not the dwelling place of God, what is its function? Again, Solomon's speech offers the Chronicler's answer. The Temple is dedicated to the purpose of offering "fragrant incense before him, and for the regular offering of rows of bread, and for burnt offerings," and so forth (v. 4). In other words, the function of the Temple is to be the point of contact between God's people and the presence of God, and the locus for the worship of God's people according to God's commands.

The sacrifices Solomon intends to be offered in the Temple are those prescribed by Leviticus: the grain offerings in Leviticus 2 (the "offering of rows of bread"), the whole burnt offerings in Leviticus 1, and the various weekly, monthly, and annual festivals in Leviticus 23 (the "sabbaths, new moons, and appointed festivals of the LORD"). In defining the function of the Temple as the locus for the Levitical sacrificial cult, the Chronicler advances the notion that the Temple is the fulfillment of the requirements of the law.

Fulfillment of the law is also the underlying message in Huram's identification of Huram-abi, the artisan sent to assist in the construction of the Temple. The Chronicler notes that Huram-abi (the name means

"Huram is my father") is the son of a woman who is a member of the tribe of Dan, the northernmost of the Israelite tribes. The information is significant; in Exodus 35:31–34, the craftsman Oholiab who works on the tabernacle, is also a Danite, and he and his coworker Bezalel are described in a manner similar to Huram-abi: men of "skill, intelligence, and knowledge in every kind of craft." Once again, the Chronicler insures that the connection between Solomon's Temple and the tabernacle traditions from Exodus are clear. The Temple built in Jerusalem will reflect the divine intention for Israel's worship space expressed in the law.

CONSTRUCTION OF THE TEMPLE
2 Chronicles 3:1–17

3:1 Solomon began to build the house of the LORD in Jerusalem on Mount Moriah, where the LORD had appeared to his father David, at the place that David had designated, on the threshing floor of Ornan the Jebusite. ² He began to build on the second day of the second month of the fourth year of his reign. ³ These are Solomon's measurements for building the house of God: the length, in cubits of the old standard, was sixty cubits, and the width twenty cubits. ⁴ The vestibule in front of the nave of the house was twenty cubits long, across the width of the house; and its height was one hundred twenty cubits. He overlaid it on the inside with pure gold. ⁵ The nave he lined with cypress, covered it with fine gold, and made palms and chains on it. ⁶ He adorned the house with settings of precious stones. The gold was gold from Parvaim. ⁷ So he lined the house with gold—its beams, its thresholds, its walls, and its doors; and he carved cherubim on the walls.

⁸ He made the most holy place; its length corresponding to the width of the house, was twenty cubits, and its width was twenty cubits; he overlaid it with six hundred talents of fine gold. ⁹ The weight of the nails was fifty shekels of gold. He overlaid the upper chambers with gold.

¹⁰ In the most holy place he made two carved cherubim and overlaid them with gold. ¹¹ The wings of the cherubim together extended twenty cubits: one wing of the one, five cubits long, touched the wall of the house, and its other wing, five cubits long, touched the wing of the other cherub; ¹² and of this cherub, one wing, five cubits long, touched the wall of the house, and the other wing, also five cubits long, was joined to the wing of the first cherub. ¹³ The wings of these cherubim extended twenty cubits; the cherubim stood on their feet, facing the nave. ¹⁴ And Solomon made the curtain of blue and purple and crimson fabrics and fine linen, and worked cherubim into it.

15 In front of the house he made two pillars thirty-five cubits high, with a capital of five cubits on the top of each. ¹⁶ He made encircling chains and

put them on the tops of the pillars; and he made one hundred pomegranates, and put them on the chains. [17] He set up the pillars in front of the temple, one on the right, the other on the left; the one on the right he called Jachin, and the one on the left, Boaz.

Solomon begins building the Temple in the fourth year of his reign. For its location, he chooses the hill known to the Judeo-Christian world as "Mount Zion," the prominence formed by the confluence of two valleys, the Kidron and the Central (or Tyropoeon) Valleys. The Chronicler identifies the location in three ways. First, it is "Mount Moriah," the place where, according to Genesis 22, Abraham took Isaac and prepared to offer him as a sacrifice to God in obedience to God's command. The location of the Temple on this site commemorates it as a place of obedience and faithfulness. Second, the site is the place where David saw the vision of the angel, where he built an altar for worship, and where the plague halted its advance against Israel. It is thus the site of David's deliverance of his people through worship. Third, it is the "threshing floor of Ornan," the place specifically selected and purchased by David for the Temple; building it there carries out the wishes of David.

After so long and so much accumulated expectation, the description of the Temple structure itself is surprisingly brief and simple. The Temple is essentially a rectangular box with an attached vestibule in front. No windows, towers, arches, or grand entranceways are described that might give a sense of architectural uniqueness or grandeur. We are told simply that the Temple measured sixty cubits by twenty cubits, "of the old standard." The definition of a cubit is a bit elusive; estimates of its length vary from eighteen to twenty-four inches. Most likely, it was originally a rough and irregular measurement, probably the approximate length of a man's forearm from elbow to fingertip. The "old standard," along with any subsequent newer standard, is now lost to us, and we can only estimate lengths given in cubits. Assuming a cubit of eighteen inches, then, the main structure of the Temple was ninety by thirty feet, about the size of a large ranch-style house in modern America. Attached to the front of the main sanctuary was a vestibule, whose width was identical to the width of the sanctuary: twenty cubits (thirty feet). The length of the vestibule has undoubtedly been conflated with the figure for its height, a figure now given as one hundred twenty cubits, or an impossible one hundred eighty feet. In all likelihood, we should understand the length of the vestibule to be ten cubits (fifteen feet) and the height to be twenty cubits (thirty feet); the two figures have been mistakenly taken together to read "one hundred twenty cubits," an error easily made in Hebrew.

The principal interest of the Chronicler is not in dimensions or architectural description, however. It is rather in transmitting the vision of a gilded palace for the deity, gleaming with golden glow in the sun and sparkling with jewels. Doors, beams, walls, thresholds, upper chambers— all are overlaid with gold. The obvious intent is to create a stunning image in the mind's eye and to communicate the idea that the Temple of God was a magnificent, marvelous place. Truly it is a "great" house, where greatness is measured less by size than by opulence. The gilded vision may be overmuch for modern sensibilities, but to ancient eyes the sight of the gleaming Temple set atop the hill in Jerusalem glinting like a precious jewel in the setting sun must have been a spirit-stirring sight. Surely nothing less than the stirring of the spirit can have been the Chronicler's intention.

The centerpiece of the Temple was the "most holy place," the inner sanctuary called "the holy of holies" in older English versions of the Bible. A separate chamber within the main sanctuary, the most holy place was set apart for a special sacred purpose: to house the ark of God. In this respect, it reflects the function of the inner sanctuary in the tabernacle (see Ex. 26:31–36), which was divided from the main chamber of the tabernacle by a curtain and wherein the ark of God was set.

The most holy place is divided from the rest of the Temple by two features. One is the curtain, made of blue, purple, and crimson fabric, again recalling the description of the curtain of the tabernacle (Ex. 26:31). The other feature is a pair of cherubim, angelic figures rendered in statuary and overlaid with gold; standing side by side, their wing tips reach from one wall to the other, creating an impressive barrier between the main sanctuary and the most holy place. The purpose of the cherubim is not solely to impress, however, for once again the Chronicler is evoking the tabernacle tradition. In Exodus 25:10–21, the description of the ark of the covenant, Moses is commanded to carve two cherubim and place them on top of the ark so that their wings overshadow the mercy seat, a throne-like structure meant to suggest the throne of God. The great cherubim of the Chronicler's Temple are far larger and grander than the cherubim atop the ark, but they surely evoke that vision by reminding the reader that beneath the wings of the cherubim sits the ark, ancient Israel's symbol for the presence of God.

The final detail of the Temple structure in this chapter is the description of the great twin pillars made of bronze (see 2 Chron. 4:12, where the pillars are listed among the bronzework of Huram-abi). Again, it is probable that some conflation of figures has occurred to produce the unlikely height of thirty-five cubits (fifty-two feet). The same pillars are described in 1 Kings 7:15–22, where their dimensions are eighteen cubits high and twelve cubits in circumference, and where they bear five-cubit capitals. The Chronicler appears to have combined the three figures into a single measure of thirty-five cubits and used that measurement as the height. The names of the pillars are obscure. "Boaz" is known as the husband of Ruth and the ancestor of David (see Ruth 3—4); "Jachin" is otherwise unknown, but means "he establishes." The reason for their use as names for pillars, to say nothing of why pillars should need to be named at all, eludes us. However, situated beside the main door of the Temple, they must have been impressive sights.

In the last analysis, impressiveness is what the description of the Temple is all about for the Chronicler. We are to be impressed with two interconnected realities: the splendor of the Temple and the degree to which the execution of its design is obedient to the law. The former is a witness to the greatness of the God whom Israel worships; the latter is a measure of Israel's—and Israel's king's—devotion to that God. In our own era, it may be easy to forget that church architecture was once intended to evoke spiritual awe and communicate religious truths about the sovereign majesty of God. Such esoteric values are easily lost in concerns over seat cushions and lighting schemes and sound systems. But anyone who has ever stood before the great rose windows of medieval cathedrals in Europe or been lifted on the notes of a towering pipe organ or carried away with devotion by the spirituality conveyed in ancient icons—anyone, in short, who has been moved by the sight of beauty in a house of worship—is kin to the Chronicler and knows his vision of the Temple.

THE TEMPLE FURNISHINGS
2 Chronicles 4:1–5:1

Chapter 4 of 2 Chronicles serves as an inventory of the items made for use in the Temple, some in bronze and some in gold. The Chronicler gives the impression that Solomon was the maker of most of these items since Solomon must surely be regarded as the antecedent of the pronoun "he" in verse 1. Yet in verses 11–18, a list of bronze and gold items, many of which have already been mentioned, is attributed to the artisanship of Huram (=Huram-abi) of Tyre. The explanation for this apparent duplication is found in the Chronicler's editing of his source for this section, 1 Kings 7:13–51. In that account, Huram (in Kings, "Hiram") is identified in verses 13–14, and then in verses 15–47 is described as the maker of the various Temple furnishings and architectural flourishes; in verses 48–51, Solomon reenters the picture in a summary statement. The Chronicler has already identified Huram in 2 Chronicles 2:13–14, and so he omits that detail here, beginning instead with the list of items fashioned by Huram (vv. 1–10, again edited from its original). He concludes with the summary account of 1 Kings 7:48–51 (=2 Chron. 4:19–5:1). The intent was probably not to create the impression that Solomon was the actual artisan who made the furnishings but rather that they were made at his instigation by Huram-abi. The structure of 2 Chronicles 4:1–5:1 may be described in three parts: the list of bronze and gold items and architectural flourishes for the Temple (vv. 1–10), the list of items made by Huram (vv. 11–18), and the summary statement (4:19–5:1).

1. Items of gold and bronze, 4:1–10. The two largest and most visible features of Solomon's Temple in the Chronicler's vision were the bronze altar and the molten sea. Both sat outside the Temple building in the courtyard. The altar, from which sacrifices were offered to God, was thirty by thirty feet in area and fifteen feet tall—a formidable structure. The molten sea was a large bronze bowl about fifteen feet in diameter and some seven-and-a-half feet in depth. The molten sea was supported by a series of bronze panels that rested in turn on the backs of twelve bronze oxen, three facing in each of the primary directions. The bronzework of the molten sea was heavy; its thickness was some four to five inches (a handbreadth), and it had a turned rim like a cup or bowl. The Chronicler claims that the sea could hold three thousand baths of water—about eighteen thousand gallons. The stated purpose of the molten sea was to serve as a lavatory in which the priests might wash.

In addition to the altar and molten sea, the Chronicler also describes ten basins, five each on either side of the altar. He also describes ten lampstands and ten tables, all of gold, five of each on either side of the Temple. The purpose of the basins was to wash the animals to be offered for sacrifice; the purpose of the tables was to hold the bread set aside for the grain offering.

Once again, however, more is afoot here than simply providing an inventory of the Temple furnishings. To anyone in the Chronicler's audience, the references to the altar, the sea, the lampstands, and the tables would have evoked memories of the tabernacle tradition in Exodus. In Exodus 30:1–10, there is mention of an altar, but it is considerably smaller than the massive structure envisioned by the Chronicler. Similarly, Exodus 30:18–21 envisions a great basin in which the priests are instructed to wash before coming into the presence of God, but it is nothing like the massive size of the molten sea of 2 Chronicles 4. Both the lampstands and the bread tables are mentioned in Exodus 25:23–31; in the tabernacle, however, there is only one lampstand and one table, while in the Chronicler's Temple there are ten, all made of gold. Clearly, the Chronicler is taking the vision of the tabernacle and writing it large on the face of Solomon's Temple. Solomon obeys and fulfills the expectations of the law on a scale grander than the law could have anticipated.

2. The work of Huram of Tyre, 4:11–18. This section of the text is a near copy of 1 Kings 7:40–47. Among the items listed as made by Huram are a number of small utensils, such as pots, shovels, and forks, almost certainly to be used on the altar in the sacrificial ritual. Also listed are structures already mentioned: the pillars of bronze, the complex latticework on the capitals of the pillars, the basins, and the molten sea with its twelve oxen. The implication of the list is that Huram was the artisan who created these various pieces at Solomon's instruction and command, not that Huram has created a second set of these items, duplicating ones already created by Solomon.

3. Summary of Solomon's work on the Temple, 4:19–5:1. The final section of the chapter reviews and reiterates the work of creating the Temple furnishings. In the process, several additional items are mentioned, such as flowers, snuffers, firepans, tongs, and ladles. All are made of gold; all add to the splendor of the Temple. From time to time, the Chronicler refers in the succeeding narratives to these "utensils of the house of the LORD" (see, for example, 2 Chron. 24:14; 28:24; 29:19; and 36:7, 10, and 18, translated "vessels"). One curious element is the reference to the doors to the most holy place in verse 21. According to 3:14, the inner sanctuary was separated from the main nave by a curtain rather than by doors. The explanation for this apparent conflict may be that the Chronicler is employing more than one source in crafting his vision of the Temple and is either unaware of such minor contradictions or considers them unimportant.

In the end, what is important in the Chronicler's presentation of the Temple is its magnificence and beauty. As we have noted above, the vast quantities of gold and bronze and the ornate decoration and ornamentation of the Temple may be off-putting to modern eyes, especially those accustomed to Protestant traditions of austerity and restraint. But to appreciate the importance of the Chronicler's vision, we must understand that such ornamentation and opulence were understood as gifts of gratitude and celebration to God, acts of devotion and obedience. In much the same manner that generations of medieval builders lavished their lives and fortunes on the construction of the great European cathedrals, the Chronicler sees Solomon lavishing himself and his wealth on the Temple as an act of love and faith. The key to understanding the Chronicler's vision of the Temple is not to get lost in the measurements or the verbiage, but to see in the glinting gold and gleaming bronze the reflection of Israel's devotion to God.

10. The Dedication of the Temple
2 Chronicles 5:2–7:22

The story of the Temple dedication is the climax of the account of Solomon's construction of the Temple. For that matter, it is the moment the preparations and instructions of David throughout 1 Chronicles have anticipated.

Prominent in the account of the Temple dedication is the Chronicler's theology of worship. The vehicle for this theology is Solomon's prayer in chapter 6, and especially his question in verse 18: "But will God indeed reside with mortals on earth?" With this question, already raised in Solomon's remarks to Huram of Tyre in 2 Chronicles 2, the Chronicler begins to articulate new thinking about the role of the Temple in the religious life of the nation. For the Chronicler, God is not to be found in the Temple, dwelling among mortals; rather, the Temple is a point of contact with the power of the divine, a locus of forgiveness and an arena for obedience.

The Temple dedication story has three sections: the establishment of the ark (5:2–6:2), the dedication ceremony (6:3–7:11), and God's response to Solomon's dedication prayer (7:12–22).

ESTABLISHMENT OF THE ARK IN THE TEMPLE
2 Chronicles 5:2–6:2

5:2 **Then Solomon assembled the elders of Israel and all the heads of the tribes, the leaders of the ancestral houses of the people of Israel, in Jerusalem, to bring up the ark of the covenant of the LORD out of the city of David, which is Zion. ³ And all the Israelites assembled before the king at the festival that is in the seventh month. ⁴ And all the elders of Israel came, and the Levites carried the ark. ⁵ So they brought up the ark, the tent of meeting, and all the holy vessels that were in the tent; the priests and the**

Levites brought them up. [6] King Solomon and all the congregation of Israel, who had assembled before him, were before the ark, sacrificing so many sheep and oxen that they could not be numbered or counted. [7] Then the priests brought the ark of the covenant of the LORD to its place, in the inner sanctuary of the house, in the most holy place, underneath the wings of the cherubim. [8] For the cherubim spread out their wings over the place of the ark, so that the cherubim made a covering above the ark and its poles. [9] The poles were so long that the ends of the poles were seen from the holy place in front of the inner sanctuary; but they could not be seen from the outside; they are there to this day. [10] There was nothing in the ark except the two tablets that Moses put there at Horeb, where the LORD made a covenant with the people of Israel after they came out of Egypt.

[11] Now when the priests came out of the holy place (for all the priests who were present had sanctified themselves, without regard to their divisions, [12] and all the levitical singers, Asaph, Heman, and Jeduthun, their sons and kindred, arrayed in fine linen, with cymbals, harps, and lyres, stood east of the altar with one hundred twenty priests who were trumpeters). [13] It was the duty of the trumpeters and singers to make themselves heard in unison in praise and thanksgiving to the LORD, and when the song was raised, with trumpets and cymbals and other musical instruments, in praise to the LORD,

> "For he is good,
>   for his steadfast love endures forever,"

the house, the house of the LORD, was filled with a cloud, [14] so that the priests could not stand to minister because of the cloud; for the glory of the LORD filled the house of God.

[6:1] Then Solomon said, "The LORD has said that he would reside in thick darkness. I have built you an exalted house, a place for you to reside in forever."

The present story represents the final chapter in the narrative of the movement of the ark begun in 1 Chronicles 13 and continued in chapters 15 and 16. The Chronicler is careful to note that the Levites and priests are the liturgical leaders and bearers of the ark as it makes its final journey into the Temple. The leaders of the tribes are all assembled to witness the installation of the ark. Through them, as we have noted before, all Israel is symbolically present, so that the establishment of the ark becomes an act of the whole people of God. In so doing, Solomon folds the history and tradition of tribal Israel, the era of the Judges, into the new faith focused on the Temple in the city of the king.

The Chronicler takes care to preserve the earlier traditions of Exodus and 1 Kings as he presents this account. This care results in a peculiar and rather anachronistic note about the poles of the ark (5:9). The poles are those mentioned in Exodus 25:13–15 by which the ark was to be carried;

the Chronicler already referred to them in 1 Chronicles 15:15, when David's Levites carry the ark so that the ark itself might not be touched by human hands. The older, preexilic account of 1 Kings 8 also refers to the ark being carried to the Temple and its resting place in the inner sanctuary on long poles that were then left in position. The Kings account makes clear that the poles were still visible in the Temple "to this day," that is, at the point of the composition of the 1 Kings account. This made some sense as long as the original Temple stood; by the time of the Chronicler's account, however, the Temple of Solomon had been destroyed and the ark taken as spoil by the Babylonians. The Chronicler's preservation of the detail that the poles could be seen from outside the Temple and "are there to this day" is thus impossible in a physical sense, but it preserves the traditions of the ark in Exodus and of its installation in 1 Kings.

The Chronicler also preserves the tradition that the ark contained only the two tablets of the law given to Moses at Mount Sinai. On the surface, this seems a curious note, but no disrespect or diminution of the importance of the law should be implied here. Rather, the Chronicler avoids the notion that the ark contained some magical power or conjurative amulets, as were to be found in many other ancient Near Eastern temples. The ark was not a totem filled with magical power but a symbol of the law and grace of God. As a historical artifact, it evoked for Israel the memory of God's presence with the people through the wilderness, the conquest of the land, and the period of the Judges. Theologically, the ark stood for God's covenant with Israel and the demand of obedience that lies at the heart of the Chronicler's message. The ark in the center of the Temple stands as a symbol of the grace and demand of God at the center of Israel's religious life.

The moment of the installation of the ark in the Temple is the occasion for a powerful sign from God: the filling of the Temple with the "glory of the LORD" (vv. 11–14). Unfortunately, the power of the moment is obscured by the clumsy phrasing of both the Hebrew and English texts here. We should understand verses 11–14 as one sentence, as it is in 1 Kings 8:10, the source for the basic narrative here. The Chronicler, however, has inserted the lengthy note about the positioning of the priests and Levitical musicians who lead the celebration of the moment (vv. 11b–13a). The NRSV places most of this note within parentheses, but it fails to include the entire note, which properly extends through the words "and thanksgiving to the LORD" (v. 13a). The result is a broken sentence (v. 11a) followed by a long and confusing note (vv. 11b–12) and then a new sentence that does not fit its context (v. 13a). A more sensible arrangement of the text would place the closing parenthesis after the divine name in verse 13a and resume the main sentence with a second temporal clause, so that the section reads as follows:

> Now when the priests came out of the holy place (All the priests who were present had sanctified themselves, without regard to their divisions, and all the Levitical singers, Asaph, Heman, and Jeduthun, their sons and kindred, arrayed in fine linen, with cymbals, harps, and lyres, stood east of the altar with one hundred twenty priests who were trumpeters. It was the duty of the trumpeters and singers to make themselves heard in unison in praise and thanksgiving to the LORD.) and when the song was raised, with trumpets and cymbals and other musical instruments, in praise to the LORD:
> "For he is good,
>   for his steadfast love endures forever,"
> the house, the house of the LORD, was filled with a cloud, so that the priests could not stand to minister because of the cloud; for the glory of the LORD filled the house of God.

The purpose of the inclusion of these details of liturgical leadership is to insure that the importance of the moment is properly noted. This is an occasion of worship; indeed, it is one of those rare moments when human and divine meet in the rarefied atmosphere of holiness. In the Chronicler's system of thought, priests and Levites are the mediators of these transcendent moments. Their presence, ministering before the ark, singing and "making a joyful noise" before God, is essential. By inserting these details into the narrative, even at the risk of grammatical confusion, the Chronicler marks this as a moment of high liturgical importance. The ark of the covenant, symbol of the presence of Israel's God and emblem of its ancient faith, is at last settled into its permanent place, where it will remain to represent the availability and accessibility of God in the Temple.

The lyric of the song sung by the musicians is one used by the Chronicler in several ceremonial occasions: at the removal of the ark to Jerusalem (2 Chron. 16:34), in three places here in the narrative of the Temple dedication (5:13; 7:3; and 7:6), and by the people of Judah after Jehoshaphat has prepared them for battle against the Ammonites (20:21). At its core is the affirmation of God's goodness; the implication of its use here is that the Temple is God's blessing toward the people.

When the ark is installed, the Temple fills with a cloud so thick that the priests who serve before the ark cannot stand in its presence but have to evacuate their posts. The Chronicler identifies the cloud as "the glory of the LORD" (v. 14). As he has done before, the Chronicler depends on the tabernacle tradition here. Exodus 40:34–35 preserves the tradition that, when the tabernacle was erected, the "glory of the LORD" filled the tent so that even Moses himself could not enter. There is no precise definition of this term. Like the Deuteronomic phrase, "the name of the LORD," it may serve as a way of identifying God's presence without physically locating God in the Temple (or anywhere else). But, in a sense that the Deuteronomic expression does not capture, the phrase "the glory of the LORD" does have a nearly physical component. It is almost an atmosphere, one sufficiently charged with the divine presence that it becomes intolerable for the priests. Indeed, the word "glory" in Hebrew may also be translated "weight" or "heaviness." The sense here is that the very air of the Temple seems full, heavy, weighted with a charged presence. Israel of the Chronicler's day would never have taken the position—and the Chronicler himself specifically denies it in 2 Chronicles 2:6 and 6:18— that God is housed or contained within the Temple. At the same time, however, the Chronicler and his people would have affirmed that the atmosphere of the Temple was laden with an intensity that bespoke God's holiness and presence. What a loss for us in the modern church who come increasingly to regard our own sanctuaries merely as "rooms" rather than as places electric with the possibility of encounter with God.

The installation of the ark in the Temple is only the beginning of the dedication ceremony, and it is not the central moment; that honor is reserved for Solomon's prayer. Yet it makes a crucial point in the Chronicler's thinking about worship and the service of God. By making explicit that the glory of the Lord does not fill the Temple until the Levites have celebrated the liturgy, the Chronicler inseparably connects liturgy and worship with the experience of God's presence. God's presence is encountered in the context of the gathered community of faith, offering itself in "praise and thanksgiving." There is nothing private or individualistic about this moment; it is public, communal, and inclusive. In an era such as our own, when so much debate focuses on the nature of worship and on whether it has any future place in the life of the community of faith, the Chronicler's testimony is worth hearing. God's powerful, overwhelming presence is experienced when the community gathers and sings its songs of praise and thanksgiving and makes itself heard in celebration of God's goodness. For the Chronicler, these public occasions claim central place in the life of faith.

THE DEDICATION OF THE TEMPLE
2 Chronicles 6:3–7:11

6:3 Then the king turned around and blessed all the assembly of Israel, while all the assembly of Israel stood. ⁴ And he said, "Blessed be the LORD, the God of Israel, who with his hand has fulfilled what he promised with his mouth to my father David, saying, [5]'Since the day that I brought my people out of the land of Egypt, I have not chosen a city from any of the tribes of Israel in which to build a house, so that my name might be there, and I chose no one as ruler over my people Israel; [6]but I have chosen Jerusalem in order that my name may be there, and I have chosen David to be over my people Israel.' [7]My father David had it in mind to build a house for the name of the LORD, the God of Israel. [8]But the LORD said to my father David, 'You did well to consider building a house for my name; [9]nevertheless you shall not build the house, but your son who shall be born to you shall build the house for my name.' [10]Now the LORD has fulfilled the promise that he made; for I have succeeded my father David, and sit on the throne of Israel, as the LORD promised, and have built the house for the name of the LORD, the God of Israel. [11]There I have set the ark, in which is the covenant of the LORD that he made with the people of Israel."

[12]Then Solomon stood before the altar of the LORD in the presence of the whole assembly of Israel, and spread out his hands. [13]Solomon had made a bronze platform five cubits long, five cubits wide, and three cubits high, and had set it in the court; and he stood on it. Then he knelt on his knees in the presence of the whole assembly of Israel, and spread out his hands toward heaven. [14]He said, "O LORD, God of Israel, there is no God like you, in heaven or on earth, keeping covenant in steadfast love with your servants who walk before you with all their heart—[15]you who have kept for your servant, my father David, what you promised to him. Indeed, you promised with your mouth and this day have fulfilled with your hand. [16]Therefore, O LORD, God of Israel, keep for your servant, my father David, that which you promised him, saying, 'There shall never fail you a successor before me to sit on the throne of Israel, if only your children keep to their way, to walk in my law as you have walked before me.' [17]Therefore, O LORD, God of Israel, let your word be confirmed, which you promised to your servant David.

[18]"But will God indeed reside with mortals on earth? Even heaven and the highest heaven cannot contain you, how much less this house that I have built! [19]Regard your servant's prayer and his plea, O LORD my God, heeding the cry and the prayer that your servant prays to you. [20]May your eyes be open day and night toward this house, the place where you promised to set your name, and may you heed the prayer that your servant prays toward this place. [21]And hear the plea of your servant and of your people Israel, when they pray toward this place; may you hear from heaven your dwelling place; hear and forgive.

[22]"If someone sins against another and is required to take an oath and comes and swears before your altar in this house, [23]may you hear from heaven, and act, and judge your servants, repaying the guilty by bringing their conduct on their own head, and vindicating those who are in the right by rewarding them in accordance with their righteousness.

[24]"When your people Israel, having sinned against you, are defeated

before an enemy but turn again to you, confess your name, pray and plead with you in this house, 25 may you hear from heaven, and forgive the sin of your people Israel, and bring them again to the land that you gave to them and to their ancestors.

26 "When heaven is shut up and there is no rain because they have sinned against you, and then they pray toward this place, confess your name, and turn from their sin, because you punish them, 27 may you hear in heaven, forgive the sin of your servants, your people Israel, when you teach them the good way in which they should walk; and send down rain upon your land, which you have given to your people as an inheritance.

28 "If there is famine in the land, if there is plague, blight, mildew, locust, or caterpillar; if their enemies besiege them in any of the settlements of the lands; whatever suffering, whatever sickness there is; 29 whatever prayer, whatever plea from any individual or from all your people Israel, all knowing their own suffering and their own sorrows so that they stretch out their hands toward this house; 30 may you hear from heaven, your dwelling place, forgive, and render to all whose heart you know, according to all their ways, for only you know the human heart. 31 Thus may they fear you and walk in your ways all the days that they live in the land that you gave to our ancestors.

32 "Likewise when foreigners, who are not of your people Israel, come from a distant land because of your great name, and your mighty hand, and your outstretched arm, when they come and pray toward this house, 33 may you hear from heaven your dwelling place, and do whatever the foreigners ask of you, in order that all the peoples of the earth may know your name and fear you, as do your people Israel, and that they may know that your name has been invoked on this house that I have built.

34 "If your people go out to battle against their enemies, by whatever way you shall send them, and they pray to you toward this city that you have chosen and the house that I have built for your name, 35 then hear from heaven their prayer and their plea, and maintain their cause.

36 "If they sin against you—for there is no one who does not sin—and you are angry with them and give them to an enemy, so that they are carried away captive to a land far or near; 37 then if they come to their senses in the land to which they have been taken captive, and repent, and plead with you in the land of their captivity, saying, 'We have sinned and have done wrong; we have acted wickedly'; 38 if they repent with all their heart and soul in the land of their captivity, to which they were taken captive, and pray toward their land, which you gave to their ancestors, the city that you have chosen, and the house that I have built for your name, 39 then hear from heaven your dwelling place their prayer and their pleas, maintain their cause and forgive your people who have sinned against you. 40 Now, O my God, let your eyes be open and your ears attentive to prayer from this place.

41 "Now rise up, O Lord God, and go to your resting place,
    you and the ark of your might.

Let your priests, O LORD God, be clothed with salvation,
and let your faithful rejoice in your goodness.
⁴²O LORD God, do not reject your anointed one.
Remember your steadfast love for your servant David."

⁷:¹When Solomon had ended his prayer, fire came down from heaven and consumed the burnt offering and the sacrifices; and the glory of the LORD filled the temple. ²The priests could not enter the house of the LORD, because the glory of the LORD filled the LORD's house. ³When all the people of Israel saw the fire come down and the glory of the LORD on the temple, they bowed down on the pavement with their faces to the ground, and worshiped and gave thanks to the LORD, saying,

"For he is good,
for his steadfast love endures forever."

⁴Then the king and all the people offered sacrifice before the LORD. ⁵King Solomon offered as a sacrifice twenty-two thousand oxen and one hundred twenty thousand sheep. So the king and all the people dedicated the house of God. ⁶The priests stood at their posts; the Levites also, with the instruments for music to the LORD that King David had made for giving thanks to the LORD—for his steadfast love endures forever—whenever David offered praises by their ministry. Opposite them the priests sounded trumpets; and all Israel stood.

⁷Solomon consecrated the middle of the court that was in front of the house of the LORD; for there he offered the burnt offerings and the fat of the offerings of well-being because the bronze altar Solomon had made could not hold the burnt offering and the grain offering and the fat parts.

⁸At that time Solomon held the festival for seven days, and all Israel with him, a very great congregation, from Lebo-hamath to the Wadi of Egypt. ⁹On the eighth day they held a solemn assembly; for they had observed the dedication of the altar seven days and the festival seven days. ¹⁰On the twenty-third day of the seventh month he sent the people away to their homes, joyful and in good spirits because of the goodness that the LORD had shown to David and to Solomon and to his people Israel.

¹¹Thus Solomon finished the house of the LORD and the king's house; all that Solomon had planned to do in the house of the LORD and in his own house he successfully accomplished.

The centerpiece of the dedication ceremony is Solomon's prayer (6:12–42). The prayer itself is bracketed by a benediction from the king upon the people (6:2–11) and a description of the dedication festival (7:1–11).

1. Solomon's benediction upon the people, 6:2–11. Solomon's speech at the installation of the ark is cast as a blessing upon Israel (v. 5), but it is more an affirmation of the Chronicler's theology than anything else. We are already familiar with such benedictory speeches occurring at significant moments in the story: David issued a blessing of Israel at the conclusion of the Temple preparations in 1 Chronicles 29:10–19. There the speech served to emphasize the notion that Solomon's construction of the Temple is obedience to the divine law. Here, at an even more important juncture, Solomon's blessing speech also rehearses important theological themes.

Two interconnected themes form the core of verses 3–11: the Davidic monarchy and the centrality of the Temple. In an extraordinary statement, Solomon rehearses for the people a word from God, a word not otherwise known or recorded. Solomon's speech here is thus something of a prophetic utterance. The speech begins with the earliest relationship between God and Israel: the release from Egypt. Since that day, Solomon quotes God as saying, God had not chosen either a city in which to build a house or a ruler to govern the people. Rather, the symbol of God's presence with Israel was the ark of the covenant, and the person selected to guide Israel on its journey was Moses. Now, however, God has changed the divine mind. Having not heretofore chosen a city, God has now chosen Jerusalem; having not heretofore chosen a ruler, God has now chosen David.

The second section of Solomon's speech carries matters a step further. Dealing first with the theme of the construction of the Temple, Solomon's speech rehearses the familiar notion that David was not permitted to build the Temple. Interestingly, the critique of David that he was a "man of blood" (1 Chron. 22:8) is nowhere to be found here; indeed, there is no critique of David spoken or implied. Rather, David is praised for having had the notion to build the Temple in the first place. All that is said is that the building of the Temple shall be left to David's son. And with this statement, Solomon's speech turns to the second theme, that of Solomon's succession to David's throne. The succession of the son to the father's throne is understood explicitly as the Lord having "fulfilled his promise that he made." Finally, the Temple now standing before the eyes of all the people, containing the ancient ark and the symbols of Israel's covenant with God, is also the fulfillment of the promise, because Solomon has built it, as God indicated he would. Thus, in a very nimble series of statements, the Chronicler positions Solomon's kingship as the fulfillment of a divine promise and the Temple as evidence of that fulfillment. God has changed the direction of the divine choice by choosing both Jerusalem as the place for the Temple and David as the ruler of Israel. God has furthered that direction by appointing Solomon to take David's place and to carry out the divine option for the Temple denied to David. And the evidence of the truth of the promise is the fulfillment in wood and stone and jewel: the finished Temple.

The final touch in Solomon's statement is the conclusion, which appears to do little more than state the obvious: Solomon has set the ark in the Temple. Once again, however, more is being said. The speech circles back so that it ends where it began: with reference to the ark of the covenant, the symbol of God's presence with earliest Israel. Now the ark has been located in the Temple, the one built on God's chosen site in God's chosen city by God's chosen successor to God's chosen ruler. Tying all the ends together, the Chronicler gathers all the symbols of God's promise: ark, king, and Temple. All are present, all are in one place, and all things appear ready for the high moment of the drama, the prayer of dedication.

2. Solomon's prayer of dedication, 6:12–42. Solomon's dedicatory prayer is really two prayers bracketed by an introduction and a conclusion. The introduction (vv. 12–13) places the king on a great bronze platform, outside the Temple in the court. The platform, not previously mentioned in the list of bronze items made for the Temple, serves both a practical and a theological function. Practically, it raises Solomon up so that the crowd can see and hear him. Theologically, it places Solomon outside the Temple; in the Chronicler's thinking about the Temple, only priests may enter the sanctuary. Important as he is to the execution of divine intent in Chronicles, the king is nonetheless not a priest and may not enter the sacred precincts. As the prayer begins, the Chronicler pictures Solomon dropping to his knees in a sign of worship and humility.

The first of the two prayers of dedication, verses 14–17, is centered on the theme of royal succession, continuing the theme of verses 6–11. However, Solomon seeks not only confirmation of his own rule but the rule of his own successors. Heretofore, we have seen prayers of this nature focused on the transfer of the throne from David to Solomon. In verse 16, Solomon appeals to the future, evoking God's promise that "there shall never fail you a successor before me to sit on the throne of Israel." While not a precise citation of the divine promise to David in 1 Chronicles 17:14 that "his throne will be established forever," the current statement does not stray far from its intent. Certainly it is an important element in the Chronicler's larger theological scheme: The throne of David is God's chosen instrument to govern God's people Israel.

One notes, however, that the promise invoked here by Solomon is not an unconditional one. The successor shall never fail to sit on the throne "if only your children keep to their way, to walk in my law as you have walked before me." Alongside the theme of the centrality of the Davidic throne the Chronicler thus places the theme of obedience to the divine law; indeed, as we have already seen in David's instruction to Solomon (1 Chron. 22:12–13), the two are inextricably intertwined. As the Chronicler knew fully, with the Babylonian destruction of Jerusalem in 587 B.C., the time did indeed come when there failed a successor to David to sit on the throne of Israel. The Chronicler's theology sought to explain that loss by pointing to the disobedience of the king and the people (see 2 Chron. 36:15–16).

The larger and theologically more significant of the two prayers begins in verse 18. The prayer begins with a central question that underlies the whole and that has already been posed (see 2 Chron. 2:6): "But will God indeed reside with mortals on earth?" The obvious answer to the king's question is in the negative, as is indicated in the next sentence: "Even heaven and the highest heaven cannot contain you, how much less this house that I have built!" But the negative answer begs the unspoken question: What then is the purpose of the Temple, if it is not to be a house for God? The answer to that question is the underlying theme of the rest of Solomon's prayer.

In brief, the answer is this: The Temple is to be a house for prayer. This theme is anticipated in Isaiah 56:7: "My house shall be called a house of prayer for all peoples." Jesus will later employ this theme in condemning and driving out the buyers and sellers in the Temple court in Mark 11:17. Note that neither the prophet nor the Chronicler makes the claim that the Temple is the "house of God." Any notions about God residing in or being confined to the Temple would have been wrecked in the destruction of the Temple by the Babylonians. For the Chronicler, however, the Temple was not the house of God but a house of prayer. One comes to the Temple not to meet God—God can be and is met anywhere in the world over which God is sovereign Lord—but to offer prayer and worship, to seek God's mercy and forgiveness, and to avail oneself of the grace and goodness promised by God. That mercy and goodness can be withdrawn if the people are disobedient; it can also be restored if the people repent. Above all else, the Temple is the place toward which the divine eye is always trained and the divine ear forever attentive, ready to hear the prayers of the penitent and worshipful, ready to forgive and restore.

Having established his main theme, that the Temple is the house of prayer, Solomon then plays out a series of situations out of which prayers might arise. Of course, these situations are anything but hypothetical; they are in fact the history of Israel, from the mundane to the cataclysmic. At the mundane end of the scale, the prayer anticipates the occasions where one individual sins against another, and in the process of adjudication and settlement the Temple becomes the place for oath taking and promise making (vv. 22–23). At a slightly higher level, the prayer envisions the entire people sinning, experiencing defeat, then confessing fault and seeking forgiveness (vv. 24–25). Drought, disease, famine, insect plague—all these natural disasters are in turn anticipated as occasions of prayer for relief (vv. 26–31). Finally, at the most cataclysmic end of the scale, the complete defeat of the people, the loss of their identity, and exile in a foreign place—even these are anticipated as the occasion for redemptive repentance and prayer (vv. 34–39). In each case, the formula is similar: the situation is stated as a condition, beginning "If" or "When," then the confession and repentance of the people are specified, followed by a plea to God for hearing and forgiveness.

The exception to this pattern is the petition regarding the prayer of foreigners in verses 32–33. Here the prayer asks God to listen to the pleas of non-Israelites who have come to the Temple "because of your great name, your mighty hand, and your outstretched arm." The motivation for hearing and granting these requests is explicit: "in order that all the peoples of the earth may know your name and fear you." In other words, God hears and responds to the prayers of foreigners who come in faith so that the renown and worship of God might be extended beyond Israel.

At the center of Solomon's prayer of dedication lies the Chronicler's theology of moral responsibility. As we have noted before, the Chronicler understands that obedience of God begets reward and blessing, while disobedience engenders suffering and rejection. While the relationship between cause and effect appears simple and almost mechanical, to leave the matter there does an injustice to the Chronicler's thought. In his way of thinking, blessing and curse are the natural outgrowths of obedience and disobedience, respectively, as surely as warmth is the result of sunlight or moisture the result of rain. It is not so much that God sits in heaven waiting to bless the good and "zap" the evil—indeed, the Chronicler is wise enough in the ways of the world to know that such is often not the case—but that blessing or suffering will eventually come and that those who approach life in faith and obedience find that even suffering can be a way of deepening and broadening the faith that will offer hope and meaning amid pain. For the Chronicler, however, the more important notion is the position of God in the dynamic of sin and consequence. As the dedicatory prayer makes clear through its almost rhythmic repetition, God is forever attentive to the possibility of confession and repentance, forever ready to forgive and restore. The heart of the Chronicler's theology is thus not a scheme of reward and punishment but the word of the possibility of forgiveness and new life. It is a word of grace set alongside the obligation of obedience, and the two cannot be separated if either is to be rightly heard.

The prayer concludes in verses 40–42 with the Chronicler's own composition. Rehearsing again the prayer's general theme that God's eyes are open and God's ears attuned to the prayers offered in the Temple, the Chronicler then quotes Psalm 132:8–10. This "royal psalm" celebrates the same themes that have been at the heart of the dedication ceremony: the twin elections of Jerusalem as the place for the Temple and the Davidic house as the ruler of Israel. The section chosen seems ideal for the moment: the summons to God to "rise up and go to your resting place, you and the ark of your might." Having ensconced the ark in the Temple built by the hand of God's chosen servant, Solomon now sees both the Temple and the throne as secured by the presence and promise of God.

3. *Concluding worship, 7:1–11.* God's response to Solomon's psalmic summons is fire that falls from heaven and consumes the sacrifices laid out upon the altar. Fire falling on a prepared altar is a symbol already familiar to the Chronicler's audience. Heavenly fire consumes prepared offerings in such diverse texts as Leviticus 9:22–23, the inauguration of Aaron's priesthood, and 1 Kings 18:38, the contest between Elijah and the prophets of Baal. But the most important precedent is the Chronicler's own narrative of heavenly fire consuming the altar of David at the threshing floor of Ornan, the very site on which now sits the Temple and the great altar of Solomon (1 Chron. 21:26). The symbolic gesture is unmistakable: The God who on this site expressed acceptance and mercy on David at the end of the plague now expresses that same acceptance and mercy for Solomon and the people of Israel.

The "glory of the LORD" that fills the house was the subject of some comment in the previous section. Its appearance here returns the story line of the dedication ceremony to the point at which Solomon began his speeches to Israel and to God, in 2 Chronicles 5:14. Thus, with 2 Chronicles 7:2 we resume the account of the people's festivities in connection with the dedication of the Temple. The people seem to recognize and affirm the importance of the occasion; they respond with the couplet "For he [i.e, the LORD] is good, for his steadfast love endures forever." As we have already noted, this couplet occurs in moments of great religious significance when the approbation of both God and people are present.

Having received divine approval for himself and his Temple, Solomon then offers sacrifices of gratitude. The numbers of animals slaughtered are probably exaggerated; the sheer time required to do the work of slaughter and ritual preparation would surely have exceeded the seven-day period allotted by the Chronicler for the festival. Again, what is operating here is the Chronicler's desire to express by magnitude and volume the overwhelming importance of the occasion. Nothing is too great, too large, too ornate, or too numerous to be expended on the Temple.

The sacrifice is accompanied by musical contributions by Levites and priests. The former play on instruments created for liturgical use by David (see 1 Chron. 23:5); the latter are trumpeters who were mentioned earlier in the story at the installation of the ark (2 Chron 5:12–13). Together with the people's response in verse 3, their presence here underscores the importance of liturgy in the worship of Israel. Worship in the Temple, like worship in the sanctuary of any Christian congregation, is not intended to be a spectacle for observation but an event that invites the participation of the people.

Verses 8–11 describe the concluding festival surrounding the dedication of the Temple. In all probability, the dedication festival is connected with the Festival of Booths, or Sukkot, since both occur in the seventh month (Tishri, approximately mid-September to mid-October; the beginning of the Jewish year in ancient times was in the spring). The Chronicler is careful to note that the dedication is celebrated for seven days, followed by the Festival of Booths for seven days, and is concluded with a solemn assembly on the eighth day of the Festival of Booths, the fifteenth day since the beginning of the dedication. This note is an attempt to conform to Leviticus 23:34, which requires that the Festival of Booths be observed for seven days in the seventh month, beginning on the fourteenth day, and that the festival be concluded on the eighth day with a solemn assembly or convocation. After the assembly, the people are dismissed to their homes, "joyful and in good spirits" because of the goodness of God shown to them in the beauty and splendor of the Temple. Worship thus concludes in a mood of celebration.

With the conclusion of the dedication festival, the last public events associated with the construction of the Temple are concluded, and the Chronicler provides a summary comment in verse 11 to signal this fact. The reader notes that it is not only the work on the Temple that is brought to a successful conclusion but also that on the royal dwelling. The Chronicler has so far had nothing to say about the palace of the king, and there will only be fleeting reference to it elsewhere (2 Chron. 8:11). The reason is simply that the royal palace, however grand, is not the focus of the Chronicler's energy or intent and so need not enter the picture. The Temple is the sole interest and the centerpiece of Solomon's reign, and to that alone the Chronicler is willing to devote attention.

GOD'S RESPONSE TO SOLOMON'S PRAYER
2 Chronicles 7:12–22

7:12 Then the LORD appeared to Solomon in the night and said to him: "I have heard your prayer, and have chosen this place for myself as a house of sacrifice. 13 When I shut up the heavens so that there is no rain, or command the locust to devour the land, or send pestilence among my people,

¹⁴if my people who are called by my name humble themselves, pray, seek my face, and turn from their wicked ways, then I will hear from heaven, and will forgive their sin and heal their land. ¹⁵Now my eyes will be open and my ears attentive to the prayer that is made in this place. ¹⁶For now I have chosen and consecrated this house so that my name may be there forever; my eyes and my heart will be there for all time. ¹⁷As for you, if you walk before me, as your father David walked, doing according to all that I have commanded you and keeping my statutes and my ordinances, ¹⁸then I will establish your royal throne, as I made covenant with your father David saying, 'You shall never lack a successor to rule over Israel.'

¹⁹"But if you turn aside and forsake my statutes and my commandments that I have set before you, and go and serve other gods and worship them, ²⁰then I will pluck you up from the land that I have given you; and this house, which I have consecrated for my name, I will cast out of my sight, and will make it a proverb and a byword among all peoples. ²¹And regarding this house, now exalted, everyone passing by will be astonished, and say, 'Why has the LORD done such a thing to this land and to this house?' ²²Then they will say, 'Because they abandoned the LORD the God of their ancestors who brought them out of the land of Egypt, and they adopted other gods, and worshiped them and served them; therefore he has brought all this calamity upon them.'"

The final word in the dedication ceremony for the Temple is, appropriately, God's word. In the night after the festivities are over, the Chronicler tells us, God appears to Solomon and responds to his prayer.

God begins by granting the request of the prayer to be heard: "I have heard your prayer, and have chosen this place" responds directly to 2 Chronicles 6:39. Following the promise that the king's prayer has been heard, God enumerates a series of disasters and difficulties out of which Israel may pray and to which God is committed to listen; drought, locusts, and pestilence are all mentioned in 6:28. To each God responds with the conditional promise: "If my people . . . humble themselves, pray, seek my face, and turn from their wicked ways, then I will hear from heaven, and will forgive their sin and heal their land." To those who show humility and faithfulness, God promises that the divine eyes and ears will remain open and attentive to prayers offered in the Temple and, in a powerful revelation of divine emotion, concludes, "my heart will be there for all time."

Once again, we meet here the Chronicler's theology of moral responsibility. Evil that befalls Israel, whether natural or political, is related to Israel's sin. In God's language to Solomon, "When I shut up the heavens . . . , or command the locust . . . , or send pestilence . . . ," God is author of the disasters, no less than God is the agent of restoration when confession and forgiveness occur. In the logic of the Chronicler's system, if God is the author of the crisis, then God is also the source of healing and hope from it. Restoration results from repentance that is offered in humble prayer to God from the Temple.

In verse 17, God speaks a word about royal behavior: "As for you," the speech begins, clearly addressing Solomon and, through him, his successors. The Chronicler returns to the classic Deuteronomic terminology we have seen already in earlier admonitions to the king. Once again, the promise is conditional: "If you will walk before me as your father David walked, doing all that I have commanded you and keeping my statutes and my ordinances, then I will establish your royal throne."

The word to the kings here is both a positive and a negative outworking of the Chronicler's theology. On the positive side, there stands in verses 17–18 the promise of establishment and permanence if the kings "walk in the way of David," that is, obey the law, statutes, and ordinances of the covenant of Moses, particularly as that covenant is understood in the language of Deuteronomy. On the negative side, verses 19–22 spell out the consequences for "turning aside and forsaking" the covenant, particularly in serving and worshiping other gods: God will "pluck you up from the land" (i.e., allow the people to go into exile or be destroyed). And the Temple around which so much celebration has occurred will become a "proverb and a byword among all peoples." That is to say, it will become a notorious example of false confidence and misplaced faith. Everyone will know, says God, what happens to those who abandon the Lord who nurtured Israel from its birth in Egypt.

The Chronicler's view of history is summed up here and grounded in his theology. Every king, every generation, has the opportunity to enjoy the blessings of God's graciousness and favor if he and they live in obedience and faithfulness. And indeed, some of the kings of Israel do so, and the Chronicler's account offers ample evidence of God's blessing. But as obedience fails, so also do the tokens of God's favor, and both king and people suffer the consequences. Yet through it all, reconciliation and restoration continue to be open possibilities for Israel, and the doorway to them is repentance.

Chronicles is occasionally characterized as a "graceless" book because it seems to some to understand little except a rigid scheme of reward and punishment. But beneath the surface of the Chronicler's system there is a mature understanding of the workings of grace. The Chronicler knows that "[the LORD] is good, for his steadfast love endures forever." His treatment of David and Solomon is evidence of the benefits of obedience and faithfulness. But the Chronicler also knows the other side of life too—that sin is a reality even in the life of the faithful and the redeemed and that it has dire consequences that cannot be avoided by facile claims of confession and repentance. In the Chronicler's world (and in our own), sin has an impact on the way we live, and that impact can neither be denied nor ignored. Yet it is also true that sin and its consequences do not have the final word in the divine economy. Beyond sin and suffering there stands always a God who "will hear their prayer from heaven, and will forgive their sin and heal their land." The Chronicler's God is interested finally not in moral scorekeeping but in keeping covenant, and within that covenant in building relationships with God's children.

11. Solomon's Greatness
2 Chronicles 8:1–9:31

The remaining chapters covered in part III, 2 Chronicles 8:1–9:31, focus attention on Solomon's wealth, importance, and international prestige. As we noted earlier, this information brackets the central presentation of the construction and dedication of the Temple. In 2 Chronicles 1, however, Solomon's monetary wealth is more hinted at than explicit; here the wealth, power, and prestige are in the center of our view of the king's reign. The reason for the shift is the Chronicler's theological commitment to the notion that Solomon's wealth is the outgrowth of his wisdom, and his wisdom is the result of his obedience to God. That obedience is demonstrated in the building of the Temple; now that it is accomplished, Solomon is permitted to enjoy the benefits of his faithfulness.

Second Chronicles 8:1–9:31 falls naturally into four main sections: Solomon's trade and public works projects (8:1–18), the visit of the queen of Sheba to Solomon's court (9:1–12), various demonstrations of Solomon's wealth and prestige (9:13–28), and the summary of Solomon's reign (9:29–31).

SOLOMON'S TRADE AND PUBLIC WORKS
2 Chronicles 8:1–18

One of the ways to measure the importance and quality of any government, ancient or modern, is to examine the extent of public works it accomplishes for the benefit of its constituency. Among the reasons Herod (36–4 B.C.) is remembered with the epithet "the Great" is the list of public buildings and projects undertaken for the improvement of Palestine during his reign: the cities of the Decapolis and Caesarea, the great aqueduct along the Mediterranean coast, and, most important of all, the renovation of the Temple in Jerusalem. The Chronicler provides a similar list here in 2 Chronicles 8 to emphasize the importance and value of Solomon's reign. The list may be divided into three units: public works construction (vv. 1–11), the installation of the Temple ritual (vv. 12–16), and the trade venture with Huram of Tyre in Ezion-geber (vv. 17–18).

1. Solomon's public works construction, 8:1–11. The Chronicler lists in this section a series of construction projects undertaken by Solomon; many of their specifics are now obscure and need not detain us. There are, however, several items in this section worthy of comment. The first is the reference to Solomon's rebuilding twenty cities given to him by Huram of Tyre. As the text stands, the intent is clear; Huram has ceded some cities to Solomon that Solomon renovates and in which Solomon settles Israelites, thereby expanding Israelite territorial claims. The curiosity arises when one compares this note to its parallel in 1 Kings 9:10–14. There, it is Solomon who cedes cities in the north of Israel to Hiram (=Huram) in payment of a debt Solomon owed. According to the 1 Kings account, Hiram finds the cities unacceptable and makes a disparaging remark that becomes the origin of the regional name, Cabul. The Chronicler permits no such image here. Solomon is never presented as a debtor to Huram in 2 Chronicles; quite the contrary, Huram is eager to donate both the materials and the craftsman Huram-abi for the Temple construction (see 2 Chron. 2:11–16). Neither God's chosen place wherein will dwell the divine name nor the ruler chosen to govern God's people are beholden to others. Both Temple and kingdom are understood in the Chronicler's theology as God's gift to the people, not loans from other nations.

The second item worthy of comment has to do with the list of towns within Israel built or rebuilt as "storage towns" or "towns for the cavalry." Apparently what is intended here is a network of garrisons and stores in support of Solomon's army. Archaeologists have uncovered remains in various towns and cities of ancient Israel that suggest to some that Israelite and Judahite kings garrisoned troops and chariots in the cities of the realm, and that several cities contained royal supply depots upon which the troops could draw in times of crisis. That Solomon constructed a series of such stores and garrisons is not at all unreasonable. More to the point, perhaps, it portrays Solomon as a king of some power, ruling a kingdom of strategic significance on the map of the ancient Near East.

The third item worthy of note is the reference to Solomon's conscription of forced labor in verses 7–10. This is the third time the Chronicler has mentioned the king's labor draft, and this is by far the most detailed presentation of the subject. As before, the Chronicler is at pains to point out that the labor conscription did not apply to Israelites, that only those who were "foreigners" living in the land were subject to conscription. In verse 7, the Chronicler lists these peoples: the Hittites, Amorites, Perizzites, Hivites, and Jebusites. This list of cultural groups is a familiar one to readers of the Old Testament; it is the standard list of subjected peoples who lived in communities within Israel, and it appears throughout Joshua, Judges, and 1 and 2 Kings. Occasionally, individuals from these communities rise to prominence in Israelite society: Uriah, husband of Bathsheba and a general in David's army, was a Hittite. But in the minds of Israelites, including the Chronicler, they remain "other" and are not absorbed into the community of Israel. Hence, they are "fair game" for conscription for public construction. Such conscriptions may have been only slightly elevated above outright slavery, although there is no indication that the imposed servitude was lifelong.

The final noteworthy item here is the reference in verse 11 to the house for Pharaoh's daughter. Solomon probably married the daughter of Pharaoh as part of a treaty with Egypt (see 1 Kings 3:1; 9:16, 24; and 11:1), and she moved into the royal compound in Jerusalem. The Chronicler here notes that she was removed from the king's house to a separate, presumably more distant, location. The reason given is that "the places to which the ark of the LORD has come are holy." The implication here is that Pharoah's daughter is not permitted to live in close proximity to the most sacred areas of Israel's religious life. Some have speculated that the reason for this prohibition is that she is a foreigner. This is unlikely, however, in view of the openness of the Temple to the prayers of devout foreigners in 2 Chronicles 6:32–33. More likely is the suggestion that Pharaoh's daughter continued to worship the deities of her native Egypt and that the presence of such practices could not be tolerated within close proximity to the most holy site of Israel's religion.

2. The installation of the Temple ritual, 8:12–16. This short section represents the consummation of the long and detailed work of David in 1 Chronicles 23—26, in which David established the various orders and duties of the Levites and priests. With the Temple now complete, Solomon now installs them in their places. Before doing so, however, Solomon first institutes the ritual of daily and festival sacrifice on the altar.

In noting the initiation of the regular liturgy of sacrifice, the Chronicler is careful to note all the occasions upon which such sacrifice is required throughout the year. Once again, the reference is to the law of Moses, in this case, Leviticus 23 and Numbers 28—29. Daily offerings of a lamb each morning and evening, along with a grain offering, are prescribed in Numbers 28:1–8. Sabbath sacrifice, of course, is a weekly event associated with the observation of the Sabbath, and calls for two lambs and a grain offering (Num. 28:9–10). New moon sacrifices occur at the beginning of each month, requiring two bulls, a ram, seven male lambs, and a grain offering (Num. 28:10–15). The Festival of Unleavened Bread (originally a separate festival from Passover; combined in the reigns of Hezekiah [2 Chron. 30:21] and Josiah [2 Chron. 35:17]) takes place through the third week of the first month of the year (Nisan, mid-March through mid-April, [Num. 28:16–25]). The Festival of Weeks, or Shavuot, associated with the beginning of the wheat harvest, occurs fifty days after the end of the Festival of Unleavened Bread, usually in early June; the Christian observation of Pentecost derives from this festival (Num. 28:26–31). The Festival of Booths, Sukkot, is the end-of-harvest thanksgiving, and takes place in the seventh month, Tishri (September–October).

Interestingly, careful as the Chronicler is to list the various festivals, he omits the Festival of Trumpets (in later tradition, Rosh Hashanah, the new year festival) and the Day of Atonement (Yom Kippur). There is no clear explanation for this omission, but at least one possibility is suggested by the arrangement of the festivals throughout the year. One notes that the festivals as described by Leviticus 23 and Numbers 28—29 presume that the new year begins in the spring. However, anyone familiar with the current Jewish calendar will recall that the new year begins in the fall, with the observation of Rosh Hashanah, usually in September. Many scholars have suggested that, early in Israel's life, the calendar was oriented around the harvest and so began in the fall. Rosh Hashanah and Yom Kippur would have been more important in that context. Later on, however, perhaps during the reign of Josiah (641–610 B.C.), the calendar may have been shifted to a spring new year, deemphasizing the importance of Rosh Hashanah and Yom Kippur. Only after the biblical period, when the original fall new year was reinstated, did these latter two festivals regain their former significance. Whether for this reason or some other, they did not play a central role in the Chronicler's vision of the liturgical calendar of Judaism.

Having arranged for the observance of the liturgical calendar in the Temple, Solomon installs the priests and Levites who will manage its observation. They are installed "according to the ordinance of his father David," that is, in the divisions arranged by David in 1 Chronicles 23—26. In summary fashion, the Chronicler reviews their functions: priests in "service" performing sacrifice, Levites in their dual role as assistants to the priests and singers of praise, and gatekeepers posted at the various entrances to the Temple. The placement of the priests and Levites now completes Solomon's fulfillment of David's instructions regarding the Temple; he has been obedient in all respects to his father's vision. The

Chronicler notes this accomplishment with another summary comment in verse 16, assuring his readers that "the house of the LORD was finished completely."

3. Trade venture with Huram of Tyre at Ezion-geber, 8:17–18; 9:10–11. This interesting and somewhat obscure note is mentioned in both 2 Chronicles 8:17–18 and 9:10–11; it may be that the Chronicler has taken a single account and divided it between chapters 8 and 9. The gist of the matter is this: Solomon and Huram participate jointly in building ships for merchant trade in the Red Sea and, presumably, the Persian Gulf. As the text makes clear, the sailors are all Tyrean; since Israel has no experience at shipbuilding, it is not unreasonable to suppose that shipwrights were also dispatched from Tyre. If so, then Solomon's sole contribution would have been safe passage through the land, thereby saving Huram's ships and sailors the impossibly long and probably unimaginable voyage around the horn of Africa. Yet, according to the Chronicler, the proceeds to Solomon are far greater than the cost of his contribution. The location of Ophir is unknown; it is possibly on the east African coast or perhaps the west coast of the Arabian peninsula, but may also simply be mythic (see Job 22:24; 28:16; Ps. 45:19). Here, it is the source of vast amounts of gold. It is also the source of "algum wood," an unknown material (perhaps a member of the sandalwood family). Whatever its nature and origin, the wood is sufficiently exotic to serve as a building material; Solomon uses it for the Temple steps and for crafting musical instruments of rare quality. The point here is, of course, to emphasize the wealth and impressive nature of Solomon's court; it commands even the gold and rare wood of faraway and exotic places for its construction, in much the same way we might speak of Italian marble or Asian teak or mahogany.

THE VISIT OF THE QUEEN OF SHEBA
2 Chronicles 9:1–12

The visit of the queen of Sheba to Solomon's court is arguably the most famous episode in the folklore associated with Solomon's reign. Depicted in art and dramatized in story and on screen, the tale has acquired romantic overtones. The Chronicler's version of the story, however, is uninterested in any personal relationship between Solomon and the queen, and focuses instead on the themes with which we are now familiar: the connection between Solomon's wealth and wisdom and God's blessing. Once again, the Chronicler develops the theme that Solomon is wealthy because he is wise, and he is wise because he is obedient and faithful.

Verses 1–4 of 2 Chronicles 9 describe the visit of the queen to Solomon's court. Sheba is not located, but it is probably one of the modern Arab states, possibly Yemen. People known as Sabeans appear in the historical inscriptions of various Assyrian and Babylonian kings and are located in the Arabian peninsula. For our purposes, it is helpful to note the great distance that the queen would have traveled to reach Solomon; her visit is truly the arrival of an exotic monarch from a distant kingdom. That the report of Solomon's wealth and wisdom has reached her in her own land is therefore a statement of the extent of Solomon's international prestige. She comes to test the king's wisdom with "hard questions," the content of which the Chronicler does not disclose. We are told only that Solomon answers all questions satisfactorily and that "there was nothing hidden from Solomon that he could not explain to her" (v. 2). As impressive as Solomon's wisdom was, however, even more impressive was the obvious opulence of his court. The Chronicler provides unusual detail in the queen's observations in verses 3–4; everything from the house in which he lived to the clothing worn by valets and servants is singled out for mention. So overwhelmed with the sheer splendor of it all is the queen that "there was no more spirit left in her."

The queen's speech in verses 5–8 provides the Chronicler the opportunity to offer a theological rationale for Solomon's wealth. The queen pronounces a beatitude on the people of Israel and particularly upon Solomon's servants: happy (=blessed) are they because they stand close enough to hear and benefit from Solomon's wisdom each day. Then she blesses God for having set Solomon on the throne. In the final sentence of the speech, she makes the connection between God's love for Israel, Solomon's reign, and the presence of justice and righteousness in the kingdom. In effect, the speech claims, Solomon's reign and its wealth and power are the gifts of a benevolent and loving God not merely to Solomon only but to all Israel. They are a sign of God's love and grace toward the people. The wisdom that is manifest in Solomon's construction of the Temple is visible also in his personal intelligence and his administration of justice and righteousness, and that wisdom is grounded in Solomon's obedience and faithfulness to God. All the king's wealth, which increases with the gifts of gold, rare spices, and precious gems, is the direct result of that obedience and faithfulness and is therefore an outward symbol of the king's true inner greatness. It is this interior greatness, the greatness of faith, to which the queen refers when she says, "Not even half of the greatness of your wisdom had been told to me." Only after meeting and questioning Solomon does she understand that the real greatness of his reign is not finally measured in gold or architecture but in faith.

The final summary of the episode comes in verse 12: Solomon grants every desire of the queen, so that she leaves Solomon's court richer than she came. The statement is rich with images of the great ancient Near Eastern potentate, who is not to be outdone by his guests and showers them with gifts far in excess of their own offerings. Similar images may be seen in the behavior of the pharaoh of Egypt and of Abimelech of Gerar toward Abraham in Genesis 12:10–20 and 20:1–18, respectively. The Chronicler's purpose in including it here is transparent: Solomon is the greatest of kings, and no other monarch—not even the fabled queen of Sheba—can be seen as having greater largesse than his.

SOLOMON'S WEALTH AND PRESTIGE
2 Chronicles 9:13–28

Following the visit of the queen of Sheba to the court of Solomon, the Chronicler places a series of short statements describing other ways in which Solomon's wealth, power, and international prestige are visible. The initial section is a catalogue of Solomon's income and some of the uses to which he put it (vv. 13–21); the latter section is a summary of the king's prestige and place in the international community (vv. 22–28).

The gold received into Solomon's treasuries "in one year" (v. 13) should probably be understood not as a single occurrence but as an annual one: Solomon received *annually* six hundred sixty-six talents of gold, in addition to that resulting from the Red Sea trade venture with Huram. Such numbers are almost certainly inflated for effect; six hundred sixty-six talents of gold equal nearly fifty thousand pounds, a fantastic amount of money, especially on an annual basis. Also, the Chronicler claims, "all the kings of Arabia and the governors of the land" provided gold and silver to the king. He is probably speaking here of various smaller, tributary monarchs and rulers in the Middle East rather than kings of tribes from across the Arabian Desert. Arabs have lived in the desert regions of the Palestine for millennia and are frequently mentioned in the inscriptions of Assyrian and Babylonian kings campaigning along the Mediterranean coast. The Chronicler's purpose is to show Solomon as imperial and sovereign over other kings of the region and to imply once again that all this wealth and prestige are the result of God's blessing of the king.

One interesting note in this catalogue of Solomon's wealth is the comment on Solomon's house and throne. Except for the brief reference to the house of the daughter of Pharaoh, there has been almost no mention of the royal palace. Here, however, we learn that Solomon used some of the gold to make five hundred shields, two hundred large and three hundred smaller, all covered with gold. The shields were then hung in the "House of the Forest of Lebanon," so named because it was constructed from Lebanese cedar (vv. 15–16). From 1 Kings 7:1–12, we know that the royal palace complex contained five buildings: the House of the Forest of Lebanon, the Hall of Pillars, the Hall of the Throne, the House of Justice, and the House of the Daughter of Pharaoh. Of these, apparently the first and last were residences, one for the king and the other for his Egyptian consort; the others apparently were public buildings. The Chronicler mentions only the king's residence in his description of Solomon's court, and it is here that he lodges the golden shields. These shields were taken by the Egyptian Pharaoh Shishak as part of a Palestinian campaign during the reign of Rehoboam, Solomon's son and successor (2 Chron. 12:9–11).

The Chronicler also locates the royal throne in the House of the Forest of Lebanon (9:17–20). The description of the throne—ivory overlaid with gold, with golden steps and a golden footstool and surrounded by carved lions—leaves no doubt that Solomon is to be understood as an imperial figure. Lions were an important symbol of royalty and power in the ancient world: Assyrian, Babylonian, and Persian art and architecture are rife with images of lions being hunted by the king or incorporated into emblems and seals. That Solomon employs them as symbolic guards around the royal throne communicates the power of his kingdom. Some commentators have noted the inconsistency between this passage and the second commandment's prohibition of the carving of engraved images of living beings (Ex. 20:4–5); it appears likely, however, that ancient Israel distinguished between images carved for essentially ornamental purposes and those created to serve as idols and objects of worship. The lions around Solomon's throne would fall into the former category and would therefore not be subject to the second commandment's prohibition.

Verses 22–28 are a summary comment on Solomon's international standing and prestige. "All the kings of the earth" seek out Solomon's wisdom and guidance, in much the same way that the queen of Sheba did. In the process, Solomon's treasury and wealth grow as rapidly as does his reputation for wisdom. One particular measure for this growth in wealth is the size of Solomon's horse herd for use with his chariot force. In 2 Chronicles 1:14–16, the Chronicler mentions the horse trade between Egypt and Kue (Cilicia, in modern Turkey). The same material is employed again in this section of Solomon's international relations. Here, however, the focus is not on trade activity but on the accumulation of wealth brought by visitors to Solomon's court. Hence, in this reference, all mention of prices or trading activity is omitted; only the accumulation of silver, cedar, and horses appears, creating the impression that all this income flowed into Solomon's coffers from obedient and overawed kings. The Chronicler makes the point plainly in verse 26: "[Solomon] ruled over all the kings from the Euphrates to the land of the Philistines, and to the border of Egypt." While the claim may be somewhat expansive—there is no evidence that Solomon or any other Israelite monarch ever controlled the affairs of north Syrian states along the upper Euphrates River—it serves to make the point that the Chronicler wants to leave with his readers: Solomon was the greatest king, not merely of Israel but of the world of his day.

SUMMARY OF SOLOMON'S REIGN
2 Chronicles 9:29–31

The final three verses of the Chronicler's account of Solomon are a regnal summary of the sort we have already seen regarding David (1 Chron. 29:26–30); such summaries will continue to appear in some form following the reign of each king in Jerusalem. Their purpose is to communicate basic data about length of reign (in Solomon's case, forty years—in all probability a round number for "about two generations") and manner of death. The Chronicler's summary comment here communicates that Solomon "slept with his ancestors and was buried in the city of his father David." There have been attempts to read this comment as an expression of approval for the king's reign, but this can hardly be the case. One notes, for instance, that Rehoboam receives only negative evaluation for the quality of his reign, but he sleeps "with his ancestors" and is buried in the royal cemetery (2 Chron. 12:14–16). It is likely that "he slept with his ancestors" is a statement that the king died in peace rather than in battle or by assassination. Burial in the royal cemetery may simply be a function of convenience, but it does occasionally carry a moral overtone (see the notes on the death of Jehoram [21:18–20] or Ahaz [28:27]).

Worthy of note are the references to other sources given here by the Chronicler. The Chronicler credits three documents that do not now exist: the "history of the prophet Nathan," the "prophecy of Ahijah the Shilonite," and the "visions of the seer Iddo concerning Jeroboam son of Nebat." All three are significant. Nathan was the court prophet to David; it was through his intrigues in 1 Kings 1 that Solomon achieved the throne rather than his brother Adonijah. Ahijah the Shilonite is the prophet in 1 Kings 11:26–40 who encourages Jeroboam, then an officer in Solomon's forced labor operations, to revolt against the king. Iddo, identified here as a "seer" but perhaps also a prophetic figure, is unknown outside of Chronicles. However, the Chronicler identifies the content of his visions as "concerning Jeroboam son of Nebat"; that is, having to do with the Jeroboam revolt that led to the separation of the northern and southern kingdoms. By mentioning these names, the Chronicler signals his awareness that his account of Solomon's reign has not told the whole story. As in his presentation of David, the Chronicler has narrowed his focus to Solomon's central act and its ramifications. For the Chronicler, Solomon reigns in fulfillment of God's promise to David and so that Solomon might build the Temple in obedience to the law. As both a means of enabling that obedience and a reward of it, Solomon receives great wisdom, vast wealth, and overwhelming international prestige.

The story of 2 Chronicles 1—9, then, is the story of the Temple. The Chronicler understands the attention and care lavished upon it by David, then Solomon, and finally all Israel, as the appropriate expression of faith in God and gratitude for God's goodness.

The Chronicler's message, of course, is not antiquarian but contemporary for his own people. He wants to build in postexilic Israel the same loyalty and adoration for the reconstructed Temple that now sits on the site of the former, grander Temple of Solomon. His account of Solomon's Temple is thus more theological than architectural: It is the expression of God's intent as told to Moses regarding the place where God is to be worshiped. The Chronicler has adhered to the vision of the tabernacle in Exodus, Leviticus, and Numbers, writing that vision into stone and precious metal here. Solomon's Temple in the Chronicler's eyes is more rooted in Israel's theological memory than in its physical memory.

The Chronicler has a point to make: God and the worship of God demand the very best of us. Lavishing gold, silver, bronze, and every imaginable treasure on the house of the LORD is not excess but a total commitment of self and resources to the glory of God. The often outlandish measurements of size and weight and numbers of sacrifices are ways of summoning his readers—ancient or modern—to a devotion that withholds nothing and offers everything in service to God. From the Chronicler's perspective, all that we have and are belongs to and comes from God to begin with; nothing less than total devotion will do in response.

Part IV: The Kings of Judah

2 Chronicles 10—36

With the death of Solomon, the Chronicler reaches a critical juncture in the narrative of Israel's history. The kingdom of David and Solomon has been a golden age, a time when God's blessing rested visibly on the king and the nation was united in the service of both king and God. The Chronicler's presentation of both David and Solomon has focused on their respective roles as founder of Israel's faith and builder of the great Temple. In the process, he has shown us the great rewards of obedience: David is granted a dynasty and Solomon uncountable riches and prestige without limit. The point has been clear: Those who obey the LORD reap the rewards of their faithfulness. The Chronicler has allowed nothing to distract attention from that point, not even the well-known failures of David with Bathsheba or Solomon with his various foreign wives.

But when the Chronicler turns to the successors of Solomon, beginning with Solomon's own son Rehoboam, it is clear that the terms of the presentation have changed. The golden age is past, and harsher realities prevail. The kings are no longer righteous without exception, and the resultant fortunes of Israel are no longer so favorable. Instead of ignoring the failures of faith and obedience on the part of king and nation, the Chronicler now seizes on them and uses them to explain the various political and theological calamities that befall the nation. Yet beneath the gathering gloom, the Chronicler's theology remains intact: Those who obey find favor and blessing with God, and those who disobey find hardship and calamity. In the Chronicler's story of the kings, the sin and failure of Israel's monarchs from Rehoboam to Zedekiah will account for the suffering and struggle of Israel. Yet in that same story, the occasional piety and repentance of some of those same monarchs will continue to hold out hope for the redemption and peace of the nation.

This, of course, is precisely the point the Chronicler wishes to make for his audience of postexilic Jews, who are trying to rebuild for themselves their identity as a people of God. Despite the catastrophes of history, Israel of the Persian era has the opportunity for peace and wholeness, the opportunity once again to be the people upon whom God's favor rests. The key to that opportunity is the same as it was for Israel of the golden age, the same key too often forgotten throughout the story of the kings: obedience—"walking in the ways of David, keeping the statutes, the commandments, and the ordinances" of the law of God.

12. The Reign of Rehoboam
2 Chronicles 10:1–12:16

The story of the reign of Rehoboam is, above all else, the story of the division of Israel into two kingdoms, one in the north and one in the south. The southern kingdom is Judah, taking its name from the tribal group whose territory constitutes the majority of its land. The northern kingdom retains the name "Israel," although other names also attach to it, in particular, "Ephraim." In the literature of the Old Testament, therefore, the name Israel is used in two ways. It may and often does refer to the political entity of the Northern Kingdom that begins with the schism during the reign of Rehoboam and continues until it is overwhelmed by the Assyrian army in 722 B.C. It may also continue to refer to the whole people of God, including not only the political kingdom of Israel, but also that of Judah.

The Chronicler uses the term in both ways. Behind the latter use lies the Chronicler's theological commitment that "Israel" is the name for the whole people of God, whose land is the land promised to Abraham and delivered through Moses and Joshua, whose legitimate ruler is David or David's descendant, and whose worship is centered in the Temple built by Solomon in Jerusalem. Those who claim participation in that heritage but live under the authority of another king or worship in another temple are members of the people of God but are in rebellion. Their sin is their disobedience and resistance; their punishment is their exclusion from the community of blessing. They may repent and be restored, but while they are apostate the story of Israel does not include them.

This accounts for the fact that, unlike the account of 1 and 2 Kings, 1 and 2 Chronicles is not the story of two kingdoms, Israel and Judah, proceeding along parallel tracks through history, but of a single people, Israel, who live in a single kingdom, Judah. There are others, particularly those who live under the authority of the rebellious kings of the North, who play roles in that story, but the Chronicler's story is not truly about them. Thus, the Chronicler does not include the editorial synchronisms of the reigns of Judahite kings with their Israelite counterparts that occur throughout Kings, nor do the northern prophets Elijah and Elisha play the central role in Chronicles that they do in Kings. Instead, the story of 2 Chronicles is focused on the affairs of Judah and how the faithfulness (or lack thereof) of king and people plays through those affairs. That story begins with the reign of Rehoboam, Solomon's son and successor, in 2 Chronicles 10—12.

The narrative of Rehoboam's reign is organized so that the beginning and end of Rehoboam's reign are times of the king's willfulness and disobedience but the middle is a time of obedience. The calamities of Rehoboam's reign thus befall him early and late, while in between is a period of blessing and apparent prosperity. The structure is threefold: the rebellion of Jeroboam and the schism (10:1–19), Rehoboam's success (11:1–17), and the invasion of Shishak of Egypt (12:1–12). A summary of Rehoboam's reign occurs in 12:13–16.

THE REBELLION OF JEROBOAM AND THE SCHISM
2 Chronicles 10:1–19

The kingdom brought into being under David and nurtured by Solomon dissolves under Solomon's son Rehoboam. Apparently expecting the acclamation of people living in the northern half of the nation, Rehoboam comes to Shechem only to provoke their rejection of his rule. By the story's end, the king who arrived in Shechem in pride departs in fear for his life, and the northerners have a new king, Jeroboam, and a new nation, Israel.

The Chronicler has arranged the story into several conversations that serve to structure the narrative. After an introduction brings both Rehoboam and Jeroboam to Shechem for the coronation (vv. 1–2), Jeroboam and the Israelites confront Rehoboam with their request for leniency in the first conversation (vv. 3–5). The second and third conversations are the heart of the narrative, in which Rehoboam seeks the counsel of first the older advisors who had served Solomon (vv. 6–8a) and then the younger advisors who were Rehoboam's peers (vv. 8b–11). The fourth and climactic conversation returns to the scene of the first as Rehoboam responds to the Israelites (vv. 12–15). The final scene concludes the episode with the dramatic withdrawal of the North from the Davidic union and Rehoboam's flight back to Judah (vv. 16–19).

1. Introduction, 10:1–2. Rehoboam's trip to Shechem is explicitly for the purpose of making him king over Israel. While there are superficial similarities with the beginnings of the reigns of both David and Solomon, there are key differences as well. In David's case, the people of the northern tribes come to him at the southern city of Hebron (1 Chron. 11:1–3); here, Rehoboam goes north to Shechem. Solomon makes a pilgrimage to Gibeon, which is a Benjaminite town north of Jerusalem, but the only confirmation of his reign Solomon sought comes from God rather than from human beings (2 Chron. 1:2–13); Rehoboam explicitly seeks the approbation of the northerners for his rule. These subtle but important changes signal two things. First, Rehoboam does not have the position of strength occupied by his father and grandfather; this fact is indicated both by his need to seek approval for his reign and by the absence of any token of divine favor. Second, the union of North and South under David and Solomon is apparently a fragile one, held together more by the force of will and power of the king than by any natural inclination of the two peoples. Thus it is that, two full generations after David's accession to the throne and after all the rhetoric about the divine grant of dynasty to David's heirs, David's grandson still finds it necessary to go north to Shechem to be proclaimed king.

The other character who comes to Shechem is Jeroboam son of Nebat, introduced briefly and without explanation at the conclusion of Solomon's reign in the regnal summary (2 Chron. 9:30). The Chronicler adds little more here, giving only the information that Jeroboam had fled to Egypt during Solomon's reign. The Chronicler gives no reasons for his flight and exile in Egypt. Readers of 1 Kings 11:26–40 will recall that Jeroboam was Solomon's chief of forced labor and had attempted to revolt against Solomon at the instigation of a prophet, Ahijah the Shilonite. By omitting this information, the Chronicler gives the impression that Jeroboam is nothing more than an outlaw and also removes any reference to servitude forced upon Israelites by Solomon for his construction projects. The Chronicler thus deprives the impending Israelite revolt of any justifiable political foundation.

2. First conversation: Rehoboam with the people of Israel, 10:3–5. Jeroboam and the people of the North meet Rehoboam at Shechem, but they withhold their acclamation of Rehoboam's rule until they receive the answer to a request: "Lighten the hard service of your father . . . and we will serve you." One notes the care with which the request is framed. There is no overt mention of rebellion here; the possibility that the ties between Israel and Judah might be severed is not explicit in their words. Knowing the outcome of the episode, it is difficult for us to avoid reading in an implied threat ("or else"), but the fact is that Israel presents not an ultimatum but a plea for mercy to Rehoboam: Make our lives easier, and we will be your servants. Its true character as an ultimatum is only revealed as events unfold.

Still, the Chronicler means to indict even the legitimacy of their request. After all, has he not been clear that no Israelites were employed in forced labor on Solomon's construction projects? How then can their service under Solomon have been "hard?" The explanation being assembled before us for the separation of North and South is that the northerners are in unlawful rebellion against the legitimate ruler of all Israel, the divinely appointed scion of the house of David. At this stage, this explanation is only implied; later in 2 Chronicles it will be explicit (see 2 Chron. 13:5–6).

   3. Second and third conversations: Rehoboam and his advisors, 10:6–11. Having sent Jeroboam and the Israelites away for three days, Rehoboam consults with his advisors about his response. The counselors are divided into two groups, older men who had served Solomon and younger men who are Rehoboam's contemporaries. This arrangement establishes at the outset a comparison between the two sets of advisors over the question of whose wisdom is greater.

10:6 **Then King Rehoboam took counsel with the older men who had attended his father Solomon while he was still alive, saying, "How do you advise me to answer this people?"** [7] **They answered him, "If you will be kind to this people and please them, and speak good words to them, then they will be your servants forever."** [8] **But he rejected the advice that the older men gave him, and consulted the young men who had grown up with him and now attended him.** [9] **He said to them, "What do you advise that we answer this people who have said to me, 'Lighten the yoke that your father put on us'?"** [10] **The young men who had grown up with him said to him, "Thus should you speak to the people who said to you, 'Your father made our yoke heavy, but you must lighten it for us'; tell them, 'My little finger is thicker than my father's loins.** [11] **Now, whereas my father laid on you a heavy yoke, I will add to your yoke. My father disciplined you with whips, but I will discipline you with scorpions.'"**

The response of the older advisors to Rehoboam's question, "How do you advise me to answer this people?" counsels kindness and conciliation. They specifically identify the promise made by the Israelites to serve the king if their yoke is lightened, and they urge that the king accept some limitation on his powers now in exchange for the continued tranquility of his kingdom. The older advisors seem to understand the implicit threat in the words of the Israelites to withdraw if their pleas do not receive favorable consideration. They do not make the assumption that the Davidic union of North and South is irrevocable; rather, they seem to understand that its continued existence depends at least partly on the wisdom and foresight of the king.

The younger advisors do not seem to apprehend the nature of the implied threat; they see the Israelites' request simply as an opportunity to demonstrate that Rehoboam is stronger than Solomon. Moreover, they assume, as their older counterparts do not, that the union is irrevocable and that the king may do as he wishes with any of his subjects without fear of reprisal or negative consequence. Their response is couched in the language of despotic power. It begins with a rather crude statement that casts a harsh, arrogant, and derisive tone for the entire response. But there is more than mere gutter humor here. In using such a statement, Rehoboam would claim to have more power in his little finger, the weakest part of his body, than Solomon possessed in his genitals, the part of the body that, in ancient culture, insured the progress of generations. Implicitly, Rehoboam would thus claim that he can insure the survival of the Davidic monarchy with far greater ease of effort than was required of his father, the great Solomon himself.

The next statement from the younger men responds directly to the request of the Israelites: Rather than lightening the load of service, Rehoboam is counseled to add to it. In many ways, this is a classic statement of despotic assumption. Not only does it deny the request for mitigation, it adds greater pain and suffering as punishment for the effrontery of the request. It makes the assumption that the king has an unchallengeable right to expect the absolute sacrifice of his subjects. It echoes the mood, if not the actual vocabulary, of Pharaoh's response to Israel's cries for relief in Exodus 5: Not only are the Israelites commanded to return to work making bricks but they are deprived of one of the essential ingredients, straw, with which to make them. "Bricks without straw" becomes the epitome of despotic intolerance; its tone is matched by the language of Rehoboam's advisors here.

The final statement counseled by Rehoboam's younger advisors is more metaphorical than literal. That Solomon's labor chiefs beat people with whips is now seen as mild, perhaps because they leave only scars. Now the weapon of choice will be not only pain but poison: the sting of the scorpion. Of course, it is the image rather than any literal reality the advisors are after here. One cannot easily punish another with scorpions; one can, however, use the image effectively as a symbol to induce fear. Taken together with the other claims advised by the younger counselors, this statement is the final blow. The advice of the younger counselors is the very picture of despotic arrogance. The text, of course, indicates which set of advice Rehoboam favors by telling us that Rehoboam "rejected the advice that the older men gave him" (v. 8).

4. Fourth conversation: Rehoboam and the people of Israel, 10: 12–15. The final conversation is not so much a conversation as a royal speech. Jeroboam and the Israelites return to the king on the third day, presumably expecting either to hear the good news of some respite or to negotiate with the king over the terms of their service. What they hear instead is the claim of absolute royal power counseled by Rehoboam's younger advisors. Omitting only the derisive comparison with Solomon, Rehoboam parrots his younger advisors and, as the text has it, "did not listen to the people." There is no negotiation and no conversation, only demand.

The Chronicler explains Rehoboam's refusal to listen to the people with the clause:

> . . . because it was a turn of affairs brought about by God so that the LORD might fulfill his word, which he had spoken by Ahijah the Shilonite to Jeroboam son of Nebat.

The presence of this clause in the Chronicler's account is extraordinary and problematic on two levels. First, as we noted above, the Chronicler omits the prophecy of Ahijah, found in 1 Kings 11:26–40, and mentions it only in passing in the regnal summary for Solomon in 2 Chronicles 9:30. Yet the Chronicler now relies on this unintroduced material to explain the king's behavior and, implicitly, the national calamity of schism that will result from it.

The theological claim made by verse 15 is the second problem presented by its presence. By omitting the description of the political tensions within Solomon's kingdom and stoutly maintaining that no Israelites were subjected to forced labor, the Chronicler paves the way for the claim that the withdrawal of the North from the Davidic union is nothing more than a lawless rebellion by servants against their rightful, divinely sanctioned ruler. But verse 15 makes clear that that rebellion is in fact the will of God, expressed through the word of the prophet, the very mouthpiece of God. How are these two perspectives to be resolved?

In point of fact, they are not resolved. Rather, the Chronicler allows both perspectives to stand and for the moment accepts the ambiguity between them. On the one hand, the division between North and South that is about to happen is sinful and disobedient behavior on the part of Jeroboam and those who support him. As the narrative progresses, the Chronicler will rely increasingly on this perspective, particularly to explain the continuation of the division. On the other hand, however, the Chronicler seems to have no difficulty in accommodating the position that the schism was simultaneously the will of God anticipated by the prophetic word. For the moment, the Chronicler thus appears willing to explain the schism on two levels. On the human level it is sin, from which repentance and return are possible; on the divine level, it is God's will, perhaps in consequence to the sin of Rehoboam.

5. Conclusion, 10:16–19. Rehoboam's decision to turn a deaf ear to the pleas of the northerners for respite produces the anticipated result: The people revolt against the king. The speech conveying the rebellion is in some respects a mirror of the speech the Chronicler places on the lips of Amasai at the formation of the Davidic union (see commentary on 1 Chron. 12:18). The opening claims of that speech ("We are yours, O David!") are exactly reversed in the present speech ("What share do we have in David?/ We have no inheritance in the son of Jesse."), and the final line of Amasai's speech ("and peace to the one who helps you!") is ironically inverted in the final cry here ("Look to your own house, O David!"). The Chronicler created the Amasai speech in 1 Chronicles 12:18 as an ironic foil for this one, which is firmly situated in the tradition. The speech signals the end of the Davidic golden age in Israel; henceforth, the story is one of brokenness. No longer content to live in the same "house" of David, the northerners now "depart to their own tents" and bring an end to the union. Rehoboam is still left to reign over the people of Israel, but only those "living in the cities of Judah."

Two other ironic notes stand out in this section. The first is Rehoboam's decision to send Hadoram, taskmaster over the labor force, to collect the labor conscripts Rehoboam believes he has a right to expect from among the Israelites. In the face of the foregoing events, Rehoboam's insensitivity to the situation is almost incredible. He is prepared to carry through with his threats to increase the labor burden, despite the fact that the threats have already produced a schism. Clearly, he "did not listen to the people," and the failure to understand their message costs Hadoram his life.

The second ironic note is the manner of the king's departure from Shechem. The king who had ridden into Shechem in royal procession and announced with his behavior his faith in his own absolute power now flees for his life from his people. Having foolishly expended the life of Hadoram, the king finally understands that even his own life is in jeopardy, and he abandons the field in fear and disgrace.

The Chronicler's final comment on the episode is a summary comment that reaches out of the history he describes into the reality to which he speaks. "So Israel has been in rebellion against the house of David to this day" finally places responsibility for the schism on the shoulders of the Israelites who withdrew allegiance from Rehoboam. At first blush, the statement may seem to fly in the face of the assertion in verse 15 that the schism was a "turn of affairs brought about by God." As we noted above, however, the Chronicler seems willing to tolerate the coexistence of both perspectives; that is, that the division between Israel and Judah was simultaneously God's will and the result of sinful disobedience on the part of Israel. About one thing the Chronicler will become increasingly clear, though: Whatever the causes of the schism, its continuation is an act of willfulness and lawlessness on the part of Jeroboam and his cosecessionists. As subsequent comments (11:13–15 and 13:8–9) will demonstrate, Jeroboam's decision to build new worship centers and replace David's priesthood with new, non-Aaronide priests are the particular manifestations of this sin about which the Chronicler is most aggrieved. The influence of the Chronicler's theology here is evident. The schism itself, and the resultant hardship imposed on Rehoboam by it, is the divinely ordained consequence of Rehoboam's own arrogance and unwillingness to "listen to the people" as David and Solomon had done. But once divided, the continued separation, and especially the alternative religious structures required by the separation, become themselves the sin of the Israelites.

REHOBOAM'S YEARS OF SUCCESS
2 Chronicles 11:1–23

In spite of his responsibility for the schism, Rehoboam is not without some redemptive qualities in the estimation of the Chronicler. Sandwiched between two less than flattering portrayals of Rehoboam's reign (2 Chronicles 10 and 12:1–12) is a composition of the Chronicler detailing the successes of Rehoboam's reign. The material in 2 Chronicles 11 falls into three sections: a description of the fortifications of Judah (vv. 1–12), an account of Rehoboam's reception of the refugee priests and Levites from Israel (vv. 13–17), and a list of Rehoboam's wives and children (vv. 18–23).

1. Rehoboam's fortification of Judah, 11:1–12. As one might expect, Rehoboam's response to the Israelite revolt upon returning to safe ground is to raise an army to go back and reclaim what he regarded as rightfully his. But "the word of the LORD" intervenes here, in the form of a prophet's speech, and Rehoboam and the people of Judah are dissuaded from the expedition. Instead, Rehoboam settles for fortifying his own territory against attack; he fortifies fifteen cities (many of the cities are already in existence by this time), building garrisons and stockpiling weapons and foodstuffs to withstand attack. By this stratagem, the Chronicler claims, he "held Judah and Benjamin."

The center of this narrative, and the foundation for all that goes well for Rehoboam in this chapter, is the fact that he and his army listened to the "word of the LORD" from the prophet rather than rushing to the attack. Such restraint would have been militarily advisable, given the much greater size and strength of the North in comparison with the South. The Chronicler, however, is interested in the theological point to be made. By hearing and obeying the prophet's warning, Rehoboam hears and obeys God. The prophets who appear on the stage of the Chronicler's history are always the mouthpiece of the Lord; the word they speak is the "word of the LORD." In the absence of some scriptural guidance from the legal tradition, the prophet serves to express the divine intent. Rehoboam's attention and obedience are rewarded with survival, success, and more: As we shall see in the next section, those who are similarly faithful abandon Israel and come to Judah to strengthen it for the next three years.

In the center of the prophetic word is the statement of God: "This thing is from me." The phrase echoes the words of 2 Chronicles 10:15: "a turn of affairs brought about by God." Here, as there, the Chronicler ascribes the schism between the kingdoms to the will of God. As we have seen and will see again, however, this does not excuse Jeroboam or Israel from their culpability in dissolving the Davidic union, nor does it excuse their theological error in not worshiping at the Temple in Jerusalem. The Chronicler simply accepts two parallel but distinct explanations for the schism: God's will and human sinfulness.

It is also noteworthy that those against whom Rehoboam prepares to do battle are not treated as though they were a foreign enemy; rather, they are "your kindred." The prophet thus signals the divine perspective that the northerners are wayward members of the family of God's people, not appropriate targets for conquest and subjugation (see also 28:8–15, in which the same message is conveyed to Israelites in regard to Judahites). Rehoboam's willingness to "stand down" rather than follow through with his invasion plans thus avoids internecine war. While the Chronicler is not squeamish about the prospect of Judah and Israel doing battle with each other (see 13:13–19), he insists that it be done on the proper theological foundation. Rehoboam's behavior to date has demonstrated not faith and piety but arrogance and pride, and these are not worthy grounds from which to chastise the rebels of the North.

Instead of invading, Rehoboam fortifies a network of cities in Judah. The cities listed here are located in the west and east of the kingdom, even though the most obvious route for invasion from Israel came from the north. The explanation may be that Rehoboam had concentrated his army in the north, anticipating either an invasion from Israel or into Israel. The fortified cities would then have been intended to guard the invasion routes into Judah from other directions. In the west, Lachish and Azekah formed a line of defense against invasion from Philistia. In the northwest, Soco, Gath, Adullam, and Mareshah guarded the likely invasion routes against Philistine or Phoenician forces, or from flanking attacks from Israel. In the east, Bethlehem, Tekoa, Etam, and Beth-zur provided some protection from Moabite or Ammonite incursions across the Jordan. Hebron, in the center of Judah south of Jerusalem is less likely to have been a border fortress than a supply depot; Hezekiah and possibly also Josiah used Hebron in this way in later years. Some scholars have questioned, in fact, whether this list of fortifications is not actually from a later period such as the reign of Hezekiah (727–698 B.C.). While the matter cannot be settled with finality, it is certainly reasonable to suppose that Rehoboam might have sensed that his kingdom, weakened now by the loss of a significant population and territory, was now vulnerable to attack by its neighbors, and acted to protect it in this way.

   2. The defection of Israel's priests and Levites, 11:13–17.

11:13 The priests and the Levites who were in all Israel presented themselves to him from all their territories. 14 The Levites had left their common lands and their holdings and had come to Judah and Jerusalem, because Jeroboam and his sons had prevented them from serving as priests of the LORD, 15 and had appointed his own priests for the high places, and for the goat-demons, and for the calves that he had made. 16 Those who had set their hearts to seek the LORD God of Israel came after them from all the tribes of Israel to Jerusalem to sacrifice to the LORD, the God of their ancestors. 17 They strengthened the kingdom of Judah, and for three years they made Rehoboam son of Solomon secure, for they walked for three years in the way of David and Solomon.

The Chronicler now turns attention to the state of religious affairs between the kingdoms. Rehoboam receives into Judah priests and Levites from all over Israel who have fled their posts where they had served since the days of David and Solomon. There are obvious political reasons for the immigration. First, the Levites were officers of David's court put in place throughout the kingdom to assist David in keeping order (see 1 Chron. 26:29–32). Their loyalty to the house of David would have rendered them immediately suspect in the eyes of the new regime of Jeroboam. Second, it would have been in Jeroboam's obvious interest to establish worship centers within Israel as soon as possible and to staff them with priests who would be supportive of the northern view of God. Otherwise, northerners would have continued to go south to Jerusalem for the annual festivals, an obviously intolerable state of affairs.

   Still, the Chronicler is interested in the theological indictment of Jeroboam as he narrates the exodus of the priests and Levites from the north. The indictment is centered in the legitimacy of the new priests. Jeroboam "prevented [the priests and Levites] from serving as priests of the LORD, and had appointed his own priests for the high places." Even though such an action was an obvious political necessity, for the Chronicler it also violates the intent of God that service of the divine be conducted by Aaronide priests and Levites. Preventing legitimate priests from their service is equivalent in the eyes of the Chronicler to refusing to hear the word of the Lord from the prophet.

These priests demonstrate their illegitimacy in three ways. First, they offer service on "the high places." Prior to the establishment of the Temple, worship was conducted at a variety of shrines throughout Israel, many of them located on hilltops or mountains. Some of these shrines—Gibeon, Shechem, Shiloh, and Bethel, for example—became prominent sites for worship in early Israel; others fell into disuse over time. But the very fact of their widespread distribution was disturbing to the leadership in Jerusalem, which sought to centralize worship and regularize the theology of Israel. In later times, especially during the reigns of Hezekiah and Josiah, attempts were made to destroy high places and shrines outside Jerusalem (see 33:3 and 34:3). From the Chronicler's point of view, no worship of the Lord outside the Temple in Jerusalem is true worship.

Second, the priests of Jeroboam serve the "goat-demons" (or "satyrs," as older versions have it). The accusation here is not really that northern priests have taken up worshiping Greek mythological beasts; it is rather related to the fact that the sacrifice offered by northern priests at the high places is not regarded as sacrifice to the LORD, and must by definition be to other deities. The reference depends on Leviticus 17:1–7, where Aaron and his sons are commanded to see that all sacrifice takes place at the entrance to the tabernacle. Sacrifices offered in the "open field" are then regarded as "sacrifices for the goat-demons, to whom they prostitute themselves" (Lev. 17:7). In the Chronicler's appraisal, part of the sin of Jeroboam and those who follow him is that every sacrifice they offer is a sacrifice offered in an unacceptable place, that is, not the Temple.

Finally, the priests of Jeroboam offer service "for the calves that [Jeroboam] had made." The implication is that Jeroboam has created figures of calves as objects of worship for Israel's new shrines. There are two possible antecedents for such veneration. One is the golden calf created by Aaron in the wilderness while Moses was on Mount Sinai (Ex. 32:1–6). The other is the common representation of the Canaanite deity Baal as having the head of a bull. In either case, it is easy to understand the Chronicler's condemnation; one repeats the sin of Israel's ancient past at the very foot of the mountain where the people received the law of God, and the other makes Israel religiously indistinguishable from its neighbors. In addition, the creation of calf figures for veneration is a violation of the commandments to "have no other gods before me" and to "make no idol, whether in the form of anything that is in heaven above or on the earth beneath" (Ex. 20:3–4).

By contrast, those in Israel "who had set their hearts to seek the LORD" abandon the heretic kingdom and come to Jerusalem, and by their presence they strengthen the kingdom and its king. The Chronicler makes plain that the strength of the kingdom is not grounded in the size of its army or the impregnability of its fortresses but in the faithfulness and obedience of its people. He employs here a phrase, to "seek the LORD," that will appear repeatedly throughout the narrative of the kings. To seek the Lord is to live a life of obedience to the terms of the covenant between God and Israel and to be faithful in worship. It is a theme the Chronicler plays throughout the course of the narrative, progressively so in the stories of the Judahite kings (see 2 Chron. 14:2–8 and commentary). Here, Rehoboam's obedience to the word of the Lord from the prophet has created a space where similarly obedient and faithful people might dwell; the overall effect of such obedience to God is strength.

3. Rehoboam's wives and children, 11:18–23. Verses 18–23 list the wives of Rehoboam and the numbers of sons and daughters issuing from the marriages. That the king had so many children may be taken as a sign of divine favor upon him, and this accounts for why this information is placed here rather than in the summary of the king's reign. Within the section, however, one note is of particular interest: that Rehoboam "dealt wisely, and distributed some of his sons through all the districts of Judah and Benjamin." Placing princes of the royal house in various administrative districts throughout the kingdom surely would have had the effect of extending the sense of royal presence through the realm, enhancing the position of the king. Rehoboam would certainly have seen the wisdom of uniting the kingdom behind the royal house. In addition, he would have seen the wisdom of designating one of his sons, Abijah, as crown prince ("chief prince among his brothers," v. 22), reducing the likelihood of internal unrest and clarifying the succession to the throne.

THE INVASION OF SHISHAK
2 Chronicles 12:1–16

12:1 When the rule of Rehoboam was established and he grew strong, he abandoned the law of the LORD, he and all Israel with him. ² In the fifth year of King Rehoboam, because they had been unfaithful to the LORD, King

Shishak of Egypt came up against Jerusalem ³ with twelve hundred chariots and sixty thousand cavalry. A countless army came with him from Egypt— Libyans, Sukkiim, and Ethiopians. ⁴ He took the fortified cities of Judah and came as far as Jerusalem. ⁵ Then the prophet Shemaiah came to Rehoboam and to the officers of Judah, who had gathered at Jerusalem because of Shishak, and said to them, "Thus says the Lord: You abandoned me, so I have abandoned you to the hand of Shishak." ⁶ Then the officers of Israel and the king humbled themselves and said, "The Lord is in the right." ⁷ When the Lord saw that they had humbled themselves, the word of the Lord came to Shemaiah, saying: "They have humbled themselves; I will not destroy them, but I will grant them some deliverance, and my wrath shall not be poured out on Jerusalem by the hand of Shishak. ⁸ Nevertheless they shall be his servants, so that they may know the difference between serving me and serving the kingdoms of other lands."

⁹ So King Shishak of Egypt came up against Jerusalem; he took away the treasures of the house of the Lord and the treasures of the king's house; he took everything. He also took away the shields of gold that Solomon had made; ¹⁰ but King Rehoboam made in place of them shields of bronze, and committed them to the hands of the officers of the guard, who kept the door of the king's house. ¹¹ Whenever the king went into the house of the Lord, the guard would come along bearing them, and would bring them back to the guardroom. ¹² Because he humbled himself the wrath of the Lord turned from him, so as not to destroy them completely; moreover, conditions were good in Judah.

¹³ So King Rehoboam established himself in Jerusalem and reigned. Rehoboam was forty-one years old when he began to reign; he reigned seventeen years in Jerusalem, the city that the Lord had chosen out of all the tribes of Israel to put his name there. His mother's name was Naamah the Ammonite. ¹⁴ He did evil, for he did not set his heart to seek the Lord.

¹⁵ Now the acts of Rehoboam, from first to last, are they not written in the records of the prophet Shemaiah and of the seer Iddo, recorded by genealogy? There were continual wars between Rehoboam and Jeroboam. ¹⁶ Rehoboam slept with his ancestors and was buried in the city of David; and his son Abijah succeeded him.

Chapter 12 is the final chapter in the narrative of Rehoboam's reign, and the theme returns to the negative here. After growing strong and secure, king and people forget their allegiance to God and are made to pay for their waywardness through the medium of the Egyptian pharaoh Shishak.

The Chronicler borrows the seed for the narrative of Shishak's invasion from a short notice that appears in 1 Kings 14:25–28; in fact, he uses these verses verbatim in 2 Chronicles 12:9–11. But the Kings narrative is really only a point of departure for the Chronicler. In 1 Kings 14, the invasion of Shishak is noted principally as an explanation for the creation of the bronze shields carried by the king's guard. In Chronicles, Shishak becomes the instrument for an object lesson in the theology of moral responsibility.

In point of fact, Shishak's invasion is one of the few places where there is an extrabiblical source to describe an incident known in scripture. "Shishak" is actually Sheshonq I (ca. 945–ca. 924 B.C.), an Egyptian pharaoh and founder of the Twenty-second Dynasty in Egypt. Late in his reign, he conducted a military campaign through Palestine, a region traditionally claimed by Egypt before the rise of Israel and the Philistine states. Sheshonq/Shishak recorded his version of the campaign on a memorial stele at the sacred site in Karnak, and although there is some confusion about its contents, it is legible enough to indicate that the primary Egyptian targets in Palestine were not Jerusalem but various northern cities. The explanation is probably that Jerusalem, tucked away in the hill country, was deemed not worthy of the time and effort necessary to take it and so was bypassed. Alternatively, and more consistent with the biblical information, Shishak may simply have received a ransom in exchange for the security of Jerusalem, paid perhaps in the form of the golden shields of Solomon. In either case, from the Egyptian perspective the focus of the campaign was not Jerusalem. The Chronicler, however, sees the story from a different vantage altogether. For him, the explanation of Judah's survival is to be found in the operation of God's will in the drama of human sinfulness.

Verses 1–8 comprise what might be called a preamble for the notice of Shishak's invasion, the point of which is to explain the invasion in theological terms. The episode begins with the explanation that, after a period of strength, Rehoboam "abandoned the law of the LORD." In the Chronicler's theological system, every calamity is rooted in some sin or failure and every blessing in obedience and righteousness. Having shown Rehoboam enjoying the blessings of obedience to the prophet, he must now explain why those blessing have ended in hardship. The explanation is this accusation that the king and "all Israel with him" ceased to abide by divine law; Shishak's invasion is the consequence of that failure. The size and complexity of the Egyptian army are intended to convey their irresistibility (historically, Egyptian armies were made up of several nationalities in much the way the Chronicler indicates in v. 3); no one but God alone could save Judah from them. Their approach drives Judah's princes back into the temporary shelter of Jerusalem, but one gains the clear impression that the city's fall is merely a matter of time.

It is here that the Chronicler places the intervention of the prophet Shemaiah, already known as the prophet who prevented Rehoboam from invading Israel in 11:2–3. Once again, the prophet has a word from God, this time a word of judgment. Playing on the charge leveled against the king in verse 1 that he had "abandoned the law," God makes the punishment fit the crime: "You abandoned me, so I have abandoned you." And once again, the response of the king and people is obedience. They "humble themselves," acknowledging the justice of the charge. Seeing their self-humiliation, God relents and spares the city total destruction.

Yet if all is forgiven, all is not forgotten. Verse 8 leaves in place a portion of the judgment originally planned—that Judah will be the servant of Shishak. More striking perhaps is the reason offered: so that they will learn the "difference between serving me and serving the kingdoms of other lands." What is remarkable about this comment is the fact that it sees the calamity of Shishak's invasion not only in punitive terms, as consequence for disobedience, but also in didactic terms: It may serve to teach the people a lesson they have not yet learned, that serving God is better than serving others. It is a lesson Judah will forget again and for which it will pay dearly in the exile in Babylon. Part of the theological agenda of the Chronicler is to teach that lesson to his own generation so that the errors of the past will not continue to repeat themselves.

Following the moral point about obedience, the Chronicler places the notice from 1 Kings 14:25–28 concerning Shishak's invasion. The loss of the shields made by Solomon (see 9:15–16) is now the servitude imposed by God on Judah and not simply the explanation for Rehoboam's creation of bronze shields. They serve as reminders of both the consequences of the king's waywardness and the mercy of God to spare the city from a worse fate. The Chronicler appends a final reminder that this mercy resulted from the self-humiliation and repentance of the people, and so "the wrath of the LORD turned from him." Indeed, the account concludes, "conditions were good in Judah," a last assertion of the benefits associated with obedience.

The account of Rehoboam's reign ends with its regnal summary (12:13–16). According to the Chronicler, Rehoboam's seventeen-year reign extended well beyond the years described in 2 Chronicles 10—12, but only these early years are of importance to the Chronicler's purpose. Rehoboam receives a mixed verdict on his reign from the Chronicler. He is arrogant and wayward in chapters 10 and 12, and this sinfulness results in dire consequences for Judah: the loss of the North and the invasion of Shishak. But in between the calamities, Rehoboam is depicted as obedient, and even amid the punishment for his sinfulness, he is capable of repentance and humility. He is thus not an irredeemably negative character. Still, the Chronicler's final assessment of his reign is more negative than positive: He "did evil, for he did not set his heart to seek the LORD" (v. 14). The records of Rehoboam's reign written by Shemaiah and Iddo are, like most of the records mentioned by the Chronicler, nonexistent; indeed, apart from their mention here in Chronicles, we would know nothing of them at all.

13. The Reign of Abijah
2 Chronicles 13:1–14:1

The story of Abijah's reign is the story of a single incident, a battle between Israel and Judah. The account is without parallel in 1 Kings. As with most other such material, there is less revealed about Israel's history than about the Chronicler's theology. After a short introduction (13:1–2a), the centerpiece of the chapter is a sermon preached by Abijah to the opposing forces as the two armies gather for battle (vv. 2b–21). The sermon rehearses the Chronicler's perspective on the schism between North and South, argues for the moral and spiritual superiority of southern theology, and urges northerners not to resist the efforts of Abijah to reclaim the hegemony of the house of David. The account of the battle and its aftermath follows the sermon, and the chapter concludes with the summary of Abijah's reign (13:22–14:1).

1. Introduction, 13:1–2a. Abijah is introduced as the son of Rehoboam and Micaiah, even though the list of Rehoboam's wives and children specifies that Abijah's mother was Maacah. It is possible that the two are variant spellings of each other; it is perhaps more likely that the confusion derives from the Chronicler's use of his source in 1 Kings 15. In 1 Kings 15:2, the mother of Abijam (=Abijah) is Maacah, but later in the same chapter Maacah is listed as the mother of Asa and is therefore Abijah's wife (1 Kings 15:10).

2. Abijah's sermon to the Israelites, 13:2b–12. "There was war between Abijah and Jeroboam," the Chronicler tells us. He uses this information, based on the language of 1 Kings 15:6, as the point of departure for his story of Abijah's confrontation with Jeroboam. The encounter described here is probably the creation of the Chronicler's theological imagination rather than an account of a historical battle. Two factors support such a conclusion. First, the notion that one king might preach across the battle lines to another is certainly far-fetched. Second, the casualty numbers listed for Israel in verse 17, five hundred thousand slain, are obviously exaggerated; American casualties in the four years of involvement in World War II totaled only four hundred thousand slain.

Abijah's "pulpit" is the slope of Mount Zemaraim, a hill in southern Ephraim, just north of the area regarded as Benjamin. The significance of the location is that it is in territory claimed by the Northern Kingdom. Abijah has invaded the North in order to lay the claim of God and the house of David to the loyalties of Israel.

13:4 Then Abijah stood on the slope of Mount Zemaraim that is in the hill country of Ephraim, and said, "Listen to me, Jeroboam and all Israel! ⁵ Do you not know that the LORD God of Israel gave the kingship over Israel forever to David and his sons by a covenant of salt? ⁶ Yet Jeroboam son of Nebat, a servant of Solomon son of David, rose up and rebelled against his lord; ⁷ and certain worthless scoundrels gathered around him and defied Rehoboam son of Solomon, when Rehoboam was young and irresolute and could not withstand them.

⁸ "And now you think that you can withstand the kingdom of the LORD in the hand of the sons of David, because you are a great multitude and have with you the golden calves that Jeroboam made as gods for you. ⁹ Have you not driven out the priests of the LORD, the descendants of Aaron, and the Levites, and made priests for yourselves like the peoples of other lands? Whoever comes to be consecrated with a young bull or seven rams becomes a priest of what are no gods. ¹⁰ But as for us, the LORD is our God, and we have not abandoned him. We have priests ministering to the LORD who are descendants of Aaron, and Levites for their service. ¹¹ They offer to the LORD every morning and every evening burnt offerings and fragrant incense, set out the rows of bread on the table of pure gold, and care for the golden lampstand so that its lamps may burn every evening; for we keep the charge of the LORD our God, but you have abandoned him. ¹² See, God is with us at our head, and his priests have their battle trumpets to sound the call to battle against you. O Israelites, do not fight against the LORD, the God of your ancestors, for you cannot succeed."

The southern king begins by restating the claim of the house of David to a divinely sanctioned authority over all Israel. It is phrased as a rhetorical question: "Do you not know . . . ?" The answer, of course, is affirmative; the Davidic claim to the throne of God's people is not news to those who have rebelled against it. For the Chronicler, this leaves no room for any other explanation of the ongoing separation of the kingdom than the sinfulness of the northern rebels. The point is emphasized with the affirmation that the gift of the kingship is a "covenant of salt." This figure of speech occurs in Numbers 18:19; Moses receives God's instruction that sacrifices and worship of God are always to be offered through the agency of the priests, and this instruction is a "covenant of salt." The implication is that the ordinance is a permanent one, not subject to change by anything less than divine proclamation. The Chronicler understands the ordination of the Davidic family as kings of Israel to be no less permanent. The phrase "a covenant of salt" thus implies a permanence built on divine intent.

Abijah's indictment of the rebellion of the North has three parts. First is the rebellion of Jeroboam, "a servant of Solomon," against his rightful lord, Solomon, who is identified specifically as "son of David" (v. 6) The language is plain and direct here: Jeroboam is nothing more than a rebellious servant, committing treason against his lawful master.

The second phase of the rebellion is the gathering of "worthless scoundrels" around Jeroboam to defy the authority of Rehoboam (v. 7). The Chronicler has told this story in 10:1–19, and there he offers a mixed picture of responsibility. Rehoboam is depicted as rash and arrogant, and the departure of Israel from the union is at least somewhat justified as "a turn of affairs brought about by God." The Chronicler now seems to back away from that judgment to a degree; Rehoboam is partly excused for his behavior by the fact that he was "young and irresolute." The implication is that Jeroboam took advantage of the inexperience and vulnerability of Rehoboam to wrest the greater part of the kingdom from him. He is joined in this effort by people whose moral character is low, a charge based on their willingness to participate in denying Rehoboam his rightful kingship. The Chronicler offers the judgment that the revolt that began in treason continues in brigandage.

The third stage is the current moment. "And now," begins the king, indicating that the charges now turn to the present (v. 8). Abijah rehearses the Chronicler's charges from 11:13–17 against Jeroboam's regime: an illegitimate priesthood and idolatrous worship. As a result, those who come to worship in the shrines of the North worship what are "no gods"; that is, they have become idolaters. What began as treason and became brigandage has now become apostasy.

The Chronicler signals the contrast between the sin of Israel and the faithfulness of Judah with the adversative phrase, "But as for us . . ." In contrast to Israel, for Judah, "the Lord is our God, and we have not abandoned him." In fact, the people of Judah are faithful at precisely the points at which Israel is apostate. The priests of Judah are members of the family of Aaron, and they are assisted in liturgy by Levites, precisely as commanded by Moses and established by David. In addition, the sacrifices offered in the Temple are those required by the law, and attention is paid to the sacred bread and the lamps, again as prescribed by Moses and established by David. Judah's faithfulness to the true worship of God leads the king to the inevitable conclusion that "God is with us at our head" and that opposition to the intent of God is futile and self-destructive.

3. The battle between Israel and Judah, 13:13–21. Abijah's sermon apparently falls on deaf ears. The Chronicler records no oral response on the part of Jeroboam but tells us instead that while Abijah was sermonizing, Jeroboam was strategizing. Israel lays an ambush for Judah, and having politely waited for Abijah to finish preaching, they spring the trap. Judah suddenly discovers that the "battle is in front of them and behind them" (v. 14). Their reaction to this unnerving discovery is central to the Chronicler's message here. Rather than devise some stratagem such as dividing forces or developing an escape, Judah "cried out to the LORD, and the priests blew the trumpets." In other words, the response to the crisis is not a military one but a religious one. In part, the Chronicler is building again on the language of Israel's sacred legal tradition. Numbers 10:9 is part of the description of the silver trumpets God commands Moses to make for summoning the congregation to assembly:

> When you go to war in your land against the adversary who oppresses you, you shall sound an alarm with the trumpets, so that you may be remembered before the LORD your God and be saved from your enemies.

By evoking the memory of this text, the Chronicler points up the expectation of divine deliverance in battle. The victory is accomplished by God rather than by human effort: "God defeated Jeroboam and all Israel before Abijah and Judah" (v. 15). This fact is important for two reasons. First, the Chronicler wants to be clear that the victory is due to the faith and obedience of Abijah and Judah, not to any military stratagem on their part. Second, the victory accomplished by God is understandable as a divine punishment for the sinfulness and disobedience of Jeroboam and Israel rather than as internecine slaughter by one part of the people of God against another. In order that there remain no confusion on the point, the Chronicler brings the description of the battle to a close with the summary statement in verse 18: "Thus the Israelites were subdued at that time, and the people of Judah prevailed, because they relied on the LORD, the God of their ancestors."

After the battle, the Chronicler tells us, Judah claimed several towns and small villages in the south of Israel, most notable among them Bethel. This can at most have been a temporary southern occupation of the town, because Bethel eventually became an important religious center in the Northern Kingdom and the principal Israelite alternative to the Temple in Jerusalem. Bethel is the site of the confrontation between

Amos and the Israelite high priest Amaziah and is identified there as a royal chapel (see Amos 7:10–17).

Of more interest, and also of greater difficulty, is the reference in verses 20–21 to the respective fates of Jeroboam and Abijah. According to the Chronicler, Jeroboam "did not recover his power" and was "struck down" by the Lord. In contrast, Abijah "grew strong" and had a number of wives and children, a sign of divine blessing. The implication, although the text is not explicit on this point, is that Jeroboam died not long after the battle, while Abijah lived a long and fruitful life. However, the Chronicler began the description of Abijah's reign by declaring in 13:1–2 that Abijah's reign in Judah began in the eighteenth year of Jeroboam's reign in Israel and lasted three years; we know from 1 Kings 14:19 that Jeroboam reigned twenty-two years. If we take these data seriously, we must conclude that Jeroboam outlasted Abijah rather than the other way around. In all likelihood, we ought to see the editorial hand of the Chronicler at work once again here. It is clearly consistent with the Chronicler's theological program to have Abijah's faithfulness rewarded with longer life than Jeroboam's rebellion, even if the chronological data do not support such a claim. The Chronicler has thus carefully worded the statement of Jeroboam's demise so that it conveys a sense of the northern king's decline as compared with the southern king's ascendance: "Jeroboam did not recover . . . . But Abijah grew strong." The text notes only Jeroboam's decline during Abijah's life, not his death; the notice that "the LORD struck [Jeroboam] down, and he died" is not specifically connected to any particular point in Abijah's life. Since the Chronicler omits any further synchronism between Jeroboam and either the death of Abijah or the accession of Abijah's son Asa to the Judahite throne, he is able to leave the impression with his readers that Abijah was rewarded with longer life than his counterpart without explicitly saying so in contradiction to his sources.

Perhaps of greater concern is the question implied but not addressed by the narrative of the battle and its aftermath: After such a defeat, how is it that Judah and Israel continue as separate kingdoms? The answer may lie in the Chronicler's complex view of the nature of the schism itself. As we have noted before, the Chronicler understands the schism on two levels. On one level, it is the result of ongoing Israelite sinfulness and disobedience to the law of God given to Moses and fulfilled through David and Solomon. On another, the schism is the result of divine intent, as a consequence for the arrogance of Rehoboam. But in either case, the schism is for the Chronicler not a political issue but a theological one. The division between Israel and Judah derives from Israel's disobedience, and it will not be resolved apart from Israel's repentance. Military victories of the South against the North are seen by the Chronicler as expressions of the consequences of northern sinfulness; military victories of the North against the South are expressions of divinely ordained consequence for Judah's failure to obey (see 25:17–24). But only a national change of heart on the part of the people of Israel living in the North will heal the division and restore unity to the people of God.

4. Summary of Abijah's reign, 13:22–14:1. Abijah dies in peace and is buried in the city of Jerusalem. He is succeeded by his son Asa, whose reign will last a lengthy forty years. Moreover, the Chronicler tells us that the first ten years of Asa's reign were years of rest, implying that there was no war or military conflict during the period. The Chronicler intends the information about the peaceful death of Abijah, the smooth succession of power, and the period of rest to be understood in the same way as the relative strength of Abijah over against Jeroboam: as the consequence of Abijah's piety and faithfulness. The record of his deeds to be found in the writings of Iddo are, of course, unknown to us, as is anything said or done by the prophet of that name.

14. The Reign of Asa
2 Chronicles 14:2–16:14

The Chronicler's presentation of the reign of Asa is among the most positive portraits he paints of the Judahite kings; only Hezekiah and Josiah are reviewed more appreciatively than Asa. The account of Asa's reign is developed from material in 1 Kings 15:13–24, but the Chronicler embellishes the story greatly and along lines entirely consistent with his theology. The Asa narrative has the following components: Asa's piety and its rewards (14:2–8), the Ethiopian invasion of Judah (14:9–14), Azariah's prophecy and the covenant (15:1–19), and the alliance with Aram and Asa's death (16:1–14).

ASA'S PIETY AND ITS REWARDS
2 Chronicles 14:2–8

The Chronicler begins his portrait of Asa with the general assessment that he "did what was good and right in the sight of the LORD his God." The direct result of this obedience was that "the land had rest for ten years" under Asa's leadership. Asa's obedience takes the form of cultic reforms in Judah aimed at removing the influence of other deities. Verse 3 uses various terms associated in biblical literature with worship of other gods: "high places," "pillars," and "sacred poles." High places are hilltop shrines that once dotted the landscape throughout Israel. Some of them were devoted to the worship of Baal, the chief deity of the Canaanite pantheon; some, however, were devoted to the worship of the Lord (cf. the "high place" at Gibeon to which Solomon goes in 2 Chron. 1:3). The problem therefore seems to be less their association with other deities than the fact that they divert religious attention away from Jerusalem. Pillars are often called "standing stones" in other translations of the text; perhaps that is a more descriptive term. We ought not to think here of columns of carved stone but rather of large slabs of unhewn rock set erect in the ground and used for cultic purposes. The precise nature of their use is still unclear, but they were a common feature of hilltop shrines and thus came to be associated negatively with the worship of gods other than the Lord. Sacred poles, or "asherim," are clearly associated with the worship of Baal; "Asherah" was also the name of Baal's female consort in Canaanite mythology, and the poles called by her name stand for her presence at the shrine.

Having removed the influences of other deities, Asa also commanded his people to "seek the LORD." The Chronicler introduced this theme in the Rehoboam narrative (see 11:16); here it takes on greater importance, serving as the pivot for the entire Asa narrative. It is because they "sought the LORD" that the people were given both rest and success at fortifying the kingdom (v. 7); to "seek the LORD" is a major theme in the address of the prophet Azariah (15:2, 4) and in the covenant made by the people in response to the prophet's speech (15:12–13, 15). Finally, that Asa did not "seek the LORD" is the charge laid against the king at the end of the narrative (16:12). To "seek the LORD" is more than seeking oracular guidance in the midst of a dilemma; the term also includes worship in the Temple, obedience to the law, and reliance on God's grace and delivering power in crisis. It is a term of passion, implying deep religious commitment of the whole self, especially when it is used in the phrase "to seek the LORD with all [the] heart (15:12). Asa's reform thus carries with it a hortatory component not unlike the style of Deuteronomy. More than the administrative dictum to remove the physical signs of influence by non-Israelite deities, Asa's reform urges the nation toward a new relationship with God, a relationship built of trust and faithfulness and the confident reliance upon God amidst crisis.

The results of Asa's piety are felt in three ways. First, as already noted, "the land had rest." The Chronicler notes this in three places (vv. 3, 6, and 8), and in all three the rest and peace are clearly understood as gifts from God resulting from the faithfulness of king and people. Second, Asa and the people of Judah are able to use the period of rest to build and fortify cities around the kingdom. Once again, however, the construction of the cities is understood explicitly as the result of the gift of peace from the hand of God (v. 8). Finally, Asa is permitted to build a large army of infantry and bowmen, totaling five hundred eighty thousand troops, "all mighty warriors." The numbers are impressive and in all probability significantly exaggerated. However, in comparison to the outrageous size of the Ethiopian army about to be introduced in 14:9, the Judahites are grossly outnumbered.

THE INVASION OF ZERAH THE ETHIOPIAN
2 Chronicles 14:9–15

A test of Asa's piety is not long in coming. An Ethiopian force under the command of Zerah and numbering one million troops invades Judah. Asa's only recourse in the face of such a crisis is to appeal for divine aid; he does so, and the text is clear that "the Lord defeated the Ethiopians." The invaders are routed from the field and pursued until every one of them is slain. Having dispatched their opponents, Asa and his army remain in the plain of Gerar (the southwestern coastal plain, near Gaza) and conduct raids for plunder before returning to Jerusalem.

The account of the Ethiopian invasion is otherwise unknown. That is not to say that there were not threats posed to the security of Palestine by Ethiopian armies; much later in history, in 701 B.C., a large force of Ethiopian and Egyptian troops met the Assyrian army in battle in this general region. During Asa's reign, however, no record of an Ethiopian incursion into Palestine exists. One would imagine that so large an army could not have marched through Egypt and Palestine without leaving its mark on recorded history.

In all probability, then, the Chronicler has developed this story for theological purposes. The appearance of so large an invading force so soon after having described Judah's own sizeable army should be seen as a test of Judah's and Asa's piety: Faced with a truly grave crisis, will king and people trust in God or in their own strength? Asa passes the test:

> 14:11 **Asa cried to the Lord his God, "O Lord, there is no difference for you between helping the mighty and the weak. Help us, O Lord our God, for we rely on you, and in your name we have come against this multitude. O Lord, you are our God; let no mortal prevail against you."**

Asa begins this prayer by suggesting to God that, from the divine perspective, there is no difference in aid to the strong and to the weak. The comment seems to recognize that God, in sovereign freedom, may aid whomever God wills to aid, whether great or small. Why then should God deign to aid the weak? It is because the weak—and specifically Judah—rely upon God for strength rather than trusting in their own might. Asa's next statement makes the case: Judah, and not her opponents in battle, relies upon God. Like the term "seek," the word "rely" echoes through the Asa narrative. The prophetic criticism of Asa in the wake of the later Israelite invasion and the alliance with Aram is aimed at Asa's failure to "rely on the Lord" (16:7). Here, the great hope for Judah is precisely that it does rely on the Lord, whose help alone is sufficient to meet the threat. Finally, Asa makes clear that Judah has come out to battle not for its own glory but "in your name." The implication of this fact is then spelled out in the plea to "let no mortal prevail against you." A Judahite defeat by the Ethiopians is not merely a human loss but a divine defeat as well. The reliance of Judah on its God is thus cast almost as much as a test of the reliability of God as of the faithfulness of the people.

The victory won over the Ethiopian army is won by God rather than by Asa and his army. It is God who defeats Zerah; Asa and Judah merely "mop up" after the issue is decided. In the wake of the defeat, Judah also plunders the cities of southwestern Palestine. One notes that "the fear of the LORD was on them," indicating again that the Judahite army really represents the presence of God. The end result of this narrative is a vindication of both Asa's piety and faithfulness and the Chronicler's theme that trust in the Lord is rewarded with success, even in the face of overwhelming odds.

AZARIAH'S PROPHECY AND THE COVENANT
2 Chronicles 15:1–19

15:1 The spirit of God came upon Azariah son of Oded. [2] He went out to meet Asa and said to him, "Hear me, Asa, and all Judah and Benjamin: The LORD is with you, while you are with him. If you seek him, he will be found by you, but if you abandon him, he will abandon you. [3] For a long time Israel was without the true God, and without a teaching priest, and without law; [4] but when in their distress they turned to the LORD, the God of Israel, and sought him, he was found by them. [5] In those times it was not safe for anyone to go or come, for great disturbances afflicted all the inhabitants of the lands. [6] They were broken in pieces, nation against nation and city against city, for God troubled them with every sort of distress. [7] But you, take courage! Do not let your hands be weak, for your work shall be rewarded."

[8] When Asa heard these words, the prophecy of Azariah son of Oded, he took courage, and put away the abominable idols from all the land of Judah and Benjamin and from the towns that he had taken in the hill country of Ephraim. He repaired the altar of the LORD that was in front of the vestibule of the house of the LORD. [9] He gathered all Judah and Benjamin, and those from Ephraim, Manasseh, and Simeon who were residing as aliens with them, for great numbers had deserted to him from Israel when they saw that the LORD his God was with him. [10] They were gathered at Jerusalem in the third month of the fifteenth year of the reign of Asa. [11] They sacrificed to the LORD on that day, from the booty that they had brought, seven hundred oxen and seven thousand sheep. [12] They entered into a covenant to seek the LORD, the God of their ancestors, with all their heart and with all their soul. [13] Whoever would not seek the LORD, the God of Israel, should

be put to death, whether young or old, man or woman. [14] They took an oath to the LORD with a loud voice, and with shouting, and with trumpets, and with horns. [15] All Judah rejoiced over the oath; for they had sworn with all their heart, and had sought him with their whole desire, and he was found by them, and the LORD gave them rest all around.

[16] King Asa even removed his mother Maacah from being queen mother because she had made an abominable image for Asherah. Asa cut down her image, crushed it, and burned it at the Wadi Kidron. [17] But the high places were not taken out of Israel. Nevertheless the heart of Asa was true all his days. [18] He brought into the house of God the votive gifts of his father and his own votive gifts—silver, gold, and utensils. [19] And there was no more war until the thirty-fifth year of the reign of Asa.

Second Chronicles 15 is the centerpiece of the Chronicler's account of Asa's reign, and at the heart of the chapter is the covenant made by king and people with the Lord at the instigation of the prophet. The chapter is easily divisible into two main sections: Azariah's sermon (vv. 1–7) and the covenant and reforms (vv. 8–19).

1. *Azariah's sermon, 15:1–7.* Once again, the Chronicler introduces into the narrative an otherwise unknown prophet, who confronts Asa and the returning army as they arrive at the gates of Jerusalem. The prophet's speech is odd; part of it seems appreciative and congratulatory to Asa for his faithfulness and its rewards, and part seems threatening, ominous, and somehow out of place for the occasion in which the Chronicler places it. The sermon serves as a device for conveying the Chronicler's theological evaluation. Its point is clear enough: Those who seek God through obedience will find God; those who abandon God will be abandoned by God.

The prophet's speech echoes the themes of other canonical prophets. The summons to "seek [the LORD]" in verse 2 is familiar to readers of Isaiah: "Seek the LORD while he may be found, call upon him while he is near" (Isa. 55:6). Verse 7 reminds the reader of Zephaniah 3:16: "Do not fear, O Zion; do not let your hands grow weak." Between these two allusions to other prophetic speeches, the Chronicler sandwiches a peculiar description of Israel "without law" (vv. 3–6). The referent of this language is unclear. Does it refer to Israel in Egypt, prior to the exodus and the giving of the law at Sinai? Is it intended to describe the era of the Judges, when "there was no king in Israel [and] all the people did what was right in their own eyes" (Judg. 21:25)? In either case, the reference is at best a thinly veiled description of the Chronicler's own recent past, during and after the Babylonian exile. In that era, religious and political systems long established in Judah had broken down or were destroyed, and it might indeed have seemed that "it was not safe for anyone to go or come, for great disturbances afflicted all the inhabitants of the lands" (v. 5). The solution envisioned by the Chronicler to such social and political disorientation is to "seek the LORD."

The command to seek the Lord assumes a central place in this section. As we noted above, the term implies more than requesting oracular guidance for decision making, although that may have been part of it. Seeking the Lord is a matter of obedience to the law and instruction of God, of placing trust in God, and of committing one's life to the worship and service of God. Moreover, the choice to seek or not to seek the Lord carries certain consequences. We have already seen that the "peace on every side" experienced by Judah in 14:7 is the direct result of king and nation having sought the Lord. "Seek the LORD" now becomes the term of obligation for the covenant to be made in 15:12–13. Asa's failure to seek the Lord will also prove his undoing. In both the war with Israel and his final struggle with disease, the king's failure to seek the Lord and his seeking instead the aid of human agents is identified as the cause of his suffering and punishment. For the Chronicler, there is a direct connection between the faithfulness and religious devotion of king and people and their prosperity.

2. Asa's reform, 15:8–18. The religious reform undertaken by Asa and the covenant made by the people are the direct consequence of the prophet's speech. The reform begins "when Asa heard these words"; the words provide the "courage" needed for the king to do away with the symbols and practices of the worship of deities other than God. That such reform should require courage to undertake is noteworthy. The implication is that there was some political or social risk involved, probably due to the degree to which the worship of Baal and other Canaanite deities was entrenched in the life of the common people. Taking away a familiar facet of common life is inevitably a risky thing to do, even if the thing removed is patently harmful, as those in American society today who support legislation to control handguns can readily testify.

Asa's reform is achieved through three acts: (1) the removal of "abominable idols" throughout the land, (2) the repair of the altar in the Temple complex in Jerusalem, and (3) the making of a covenant among the people to "seek the LORD." A word should be said about each act.

The Chronicler is not specific about the nature of the "abominable idols" that Asa removes. In all likelihood, he uses the term to describe any shrine or altar not dedicated to God. For the most part, these would have been shrines or altars dedicated to the worship of Baal, the storm and fertility deity of Canaanite mythology. Worship of other deities persisted as well, especially in those periods when Israel or Judah were subservient to more powerful neighbors. One of the ways vassalage or subservience was recognized in the ancient world was the importation of the conqueror's gods into the conquered's temples and shrines. Regardless of the source of the idols, however, the Chronicler's point here is the depiction of Asa as a religious reformer and faithful worshiper of God. For the Chronicler, faithfulness to God leaves no room for divided loyalty but rather requires the removal of all influences toward other religious traditions.

Asa's repair of the altar identifies him as a king who takes seriously his responsibility to the official cult of Israel. In repairing the altar or otherwise attending to the physical condition of the Temple and its precincts, Asa places himself in the tradition of Solomon. Indeed, almost all the kings whom the Chronicler identifies as having "done what was right in the eyes of the LORD"—Jehoshaphat, Joash, Jotham, Hezekiah, Manasseh, and Josiah—engage in some form of physical repair to the Temple structure or reform of the practices within it. That a king accomplishes some restoration of the Temple is a sign of faithfulness in the eyes of the Chronicler.

The most important aspect of Asa's reform, however, is the covenant ceremony; the description of the covenant making and the contents of the agreement occupy a large block of verses (vv. 9–15) in the heart of the chapter. The covenant is made in the third month of the fifteenth year of Asa's reign; according to the calendar in use at the time of the Chronicler's writing, this would have been about the time of the Feast of Weeks (Pentecost), a time when large crowds of people would have been present in Jerusalem. The description of those present is important: not only those from Judah and Benjamin, already within the reach of the Judahite throne, but also "those from Ephraim, Manasseh, and Simeon who were residing as aliens with them." These "aliens" are present in Jerusalem for a reason: "Great numbers had deserted to [Asa] from Israel when they saw that the LORD his God was with him." The Chronicler's purpose here is to define the people of God in terms that have less to do with geography than obedience. Those who recognize that the Lord is to be found in Jerusalem at the Temple and that the only legitimate ruler over Israel is the scion of David are included within the covenant community. Those who deny these assertions or who live outside the community continue to live in rebellion against God. The definition of the people of God transcends political boundaries such as those between Israel and Judah; the people of God are defined by obedience, and obedience is at least partly measured by one's presence in the Temple at the times of celebration and festival each year. One is faithful to God and a member of the covenant community of God's people, regardless of where one lives, if one participates in the worship life of the people of God in the Temple.

The covenant ceremony (vv. 11–15) is described in three parts. First, there is the offering of vast sacrifices of oxen and sheep—so many that, once again, the numbers beggar belief. The sacrifices are taken from the "booty that they had brought" (v. 11), presumably the result of the campaign against Zerah and the depredations in southern Philistia (14:13–15). Next, the terms of the covenant are detailed: that all would "seek the LORD, the God of their ancestors, with all their heart and with all their soul," and that anyone refusing to do so would be put to death, regardless of age or gender (vv. 12–13). Finally, the covenant is sealed with an oath, announced with trumpet fanfare, and accompanied by great celebration (vv. 14–15).

As we have noted, at the center of the covenant is the obligation undertaken by the people to seek the Lord "with all their heart and with all their soul." The language here is directly related to the language of Deuteronomy 6:5: "You shall love the LORD your God with all your heart, and with all your soul, and with all your might." What is contemplated by the phrase "seek the LORD" is a total devotion of self and energy to obedience and faithfulness. The Chronicler understands "seeking the LORD" as a lifelong and life-consuming endeavor requiring the obligation of one's being to God. Nothing less than the entrusting of the self and one's resources to God will suffice; nothing less than complete reliance on the grace and deliverance of God is acceptable.

The Chronicler adds a final note, taken directly from 1 Kings 15:13–15, about Asa's religious and political reform. Asa removed his mother Maacah from the position of queen mother because she had participated in worship of Asherah, consort deity to Baal in Canaanite tradition. The title "queen mother" is as much a political office as a recognition that Maacah gave birth to the king; other women are described in this way in the Kings narrative (Bathsheba [1 Kings 1:15–21], Jezebel [1 Kings 17:21], and Athaliah [2 Kings 11:1–3]), and the Chronicler provides the name of the mother of each king of Judah through Hezekiah (2 Chron. 29:1). Although the duties are unknown, the position must have been significant enough in the life of the kingdom that the removal of its occupant was an event worthy of note. The Chronicler takes this as a sign of Asa's faithfulness, that he is willing to brave political upheaval in the service of obedience to God.

The summary comment that "the heart of Asa was true all his days" seems to indicate that Asa was faithful throughout his reign, a claim that the Chronicler is about to deny in the very next chapter. Its presence here is therefore curious. It is probably best explained by the fact that this section is taken almost verbatim from 1 Kings 15:13–15. Perhaps, however, it endures here as a signal that, despite the disobedience and failure that will mark the end of Asa's reign, the Chronicler's treatment is more complex and nuanced than a single verdict of "good" or "evil" will allow. The king may end his days in willfulness and transgression, but the Chronicler understands that beneath it all there beats the heart of a faithful man.

THE ALLIANCE WITH ARAM AND THE DEATH OF ASA
2 Chronicles 16:1–14

16:1 In the thirty-sixth year of the reign of Asa, King Baasha of Israel went up against Judah, and built Ramah, to prevent anyone from going out or coming into the territory of King Asa of Judah. ²Then Asa took silver and gold from the treasures of the house of the LORD and the king's house, and sent them to King Ben-hadad of Aram, who resided in Damascus, saying, ³"Let there be an alliance between me and you, like that between my father and your father; I am sending to you silver and gold; go, break your alliance with King Baasha of Israel, so that he may withdraw from me." ⁴Ben-hadad listened to King Asa, and sent the commanders of his armies against the cities of Israel. They conquered Ijon, Dan, Abel-maim, and all the store-cities of Naphtali. ⁵When Baasha heard of it, he stopped building Ramah, and let his work cease. ⁶Then King Asa brought all Judah, and they carried away all the stones of Ramah and its timber, with which Baasha had been building, and with them he built up Geba and Mizpah.

⁷At that time the seer Hanani came to King Asa of Judah, and said to him, "Because you relied on the king of Aram, and did not rely on the LORD your God, the army of the king of Aram has escaped you. ⁸Were not the Ethiopians and the Libyans a huge army with exceedingly many chariots and cavalry? Yet because you relied on the LORD, he gave them into your hand. ⁹For the eyes of the LORD range throughout the entire earth, to strengthen those whose heart is true to him. You have done foolishly in this; for from now on you will have wars." ¹⁰Then Asa was angry with the seer, and put him in the stocks, in prison, for he was in a rage with him because of this. And Asa inflicted cruelties on some of the people at the same time.

¹¹The acts of Asa, from first to last, are written in the Book of the Kings of Judah and Israel. ¹²In the thirty-ninth year of his reign Asa was diseased in his feet, and his disease became severe; yet even in his disease he did not seek the LORD, but sought help from physicians. ¹³Then Asa slept with his ancestors, dying in the forty-first year of his reign. ¹⁴They buried him in the tomb that he had hewn out for himself in the city of David. They laid him on a bier that had been filled with various kinds of spices prepared by the perfumer's art; and they made a very great fire in his honor.

The final chapter in the narrative of Asa's reign is dark. The king has so far been the paragon of piety and obedience; now he inexplicably turns away from his faithfulness and becomes arrogant, self-reliant rather than God-reliant, and bitter and angry. What explains so radical a shift in character?

The most likely answer is that the Chronicler drew on his source in 1 Kings for the information that alters the direction of his reading of Asa's reign. In 1 Kings 15:23, as part of the summary of the king's reign and after listing the impressive accomplishments of Asa, the narrator adds the line, "But in his old age he was diseased in his feet." To the Chronicler, with his commitment to moral responsibility that draws a direct connection between behavior and consequence, this datum poses both a problem and an opportunity. The problem is how to explain the ignominious disease at the end of the king's otherwise illustrious life: What had Asa done to warrant this conclusion to his life? The opportunity is the other side of the same equation between behavior and consequence. If the king has died in disease, there must be something in his life to account for this disease. The Chronicler finds the explanation for the king's demise in the narrative of the alliance with Aram. A careful reading of the story in 1 Kings 15:16–22 betrays no criticism of Asa for his stratagem with the Aramean king; if anything, it is seen as a clever and bold stroke that delivers the people of Judah. In the Chronicler's hands, however, the alliance with Aram becomes a moral failure on the part of Asa, a failure that then accounts for the suffering at the end of his life. The failure and its meaning are announced, as they frequently are in Chronicles, in a speech by an otherwise unknown prophet who appears at the crucial moment in the narrative to represent the Chronicler's moral and theological perspective.

The chapter may be organized into three subsections: the narrative of Asa's alliance with Aram in the face of threat by Israel (vv. 1–6), the speech of the seer Hanani and the reaction of Asa (vv. 7–10), and the regnal summary and account of the death of Asa.

1. The narrative of Asa's alliance with Aram, 16:1–6. Chapter 16 once again presents Asa and Judah in peril from an exterior foe: its northern neighbor, Israel. The story, which is the only extended narrative about Asa shared by both 1 Kings and 2 Chronicles, describes the efforts of the Israelite king Baasha to control access to Judah and Jerusalem by fortifying the town of Ramah, near the border between the nations. Perceiving the threat posed by a fortified city so near the border, Asa appeals to the king of Aram, once an ally of David, to forsake any agreements he might have with the Israelite king and to attack Israel from the north. Apparently the gold and silver, which Asa takes from the treasuries of palace and Temple, is sufficient to persuade the Aramean king, Ben-hadad; he attacks Israel, and draws Baasha and his forces away from their southern border to meet the northern threat. Asa then uses the respite to tear down Ramah and build Geba and Mizpah on the Judahite side of the border.

The Chronicler transcribes almost verbatim the account of the alliance with Aram found in 1 Kings 15:16–22, changing only a phrase or two. However, it is in the combination of the alliance story with the prophetic interpretation (vv. 7–10) that the hand of the Chronicler is clearest. Once we understand that Asa's stratagem is viewed as moral and spiritual weakness rather than strategic cleverness, two references in the story stand out as ironic. The first is the fact that the money to buy the services of Aram is taken from the Temple. Asa, in the Chronicler's view, is willing to use the Temple money to purchase security but is not willing to seek the protection of the God of the Temple. The second is the appeal to Ben-hadad to form an alliance "like that between my father and your father." The alliance mentioned here can only be that between David and Hadadezer in 1 Chronicles 19:19, formed after David defeats the combined forces of Ammon and Aram; it is, in other words, an alliance founded on David's strength. But in Asa's case, the Judahite king pleads from a position of weakness and supplication. The alliance Asa seeks is anything but like the one "between my father and your father."

2. *The speech of the seer Hanani, 16:7–10.* Having delivered his people from imminent danger once again, Asa is again met with a prophet with a message. Once again, the prophet is the mouthpiece for the Chronicler and a convenient means by which he can explain the meaning of the Aramean alliance.

The basic critique of the king's action is in the prophet's opening salvo: "Because you relied on the king of Aram, and did not rely upon the LORD your God . . ." As a result of this lack of faithfulness and trust, "the army of the king of Aram has escaped you" (v. 7). The implication is that, had Asa been faithful, a far greater prize than rebuilding Geba and Mizpah would have been his: not only the conquest of Israel but that of Aram as well. Once again, the reader is reminded of David's defeat of Aram and Ammon in 1 Chronicles 19. There, David's commander Joab encouraged his army to be "strong and . . . courageous for our people and for the cities of our God" (1 Chron. 19:13), and the result of their courage was a great victory. Here, the implied criticism of Asa is that, because he had not the courage of David, he will not have the victory either.

To make the point clearer still, the prophet reminds the king of God's deliverance of them from the Ethiopians. In that case, the mirror image of this one, the army of the enemy was innumerably large. Asa's response to that crisis was, in the Chronicler's view, the correct one: He trusted in and prayed to God. For that righteousness, he and Israel were rewarded with deliverance and great plunder. Here, however, Asa's failure to trust leads directly to greatly diminished rewards: In effect, he has at the end only what he began with. The Aramean alliance is thus the negative counterpoint to the positive portrayal of the rewards for faithfulness, obedience, and trust.

The next statement of the prophet's is perhaps the most curious: "For the eyes of the LORD range throughout the entire earth, to strengthen those whose heart is true to him." The first half of the statement is taken from Zechariah 4:10, where it serves as an affirmation of God's sovereign control over the events of human history. If a similar meaning is intended here, the Chronicler's point would be that the reason for entrusting ourselves to God is that God knows best and turns the course of history toward God's ultimate purpose. To trust God is thus to be aligned with that purpose; not to trust is to stand in its way. The Chronicler adds the second phrase, "to strengthen those whose heart is true to him," as a way of evaluating the faithfulness of people, whether in Asa's day or in the Chronicler's own. Those who trust in God are those whom God strengthens, and God in divine sovereignty never fails to see them or seek them.

The king's reaction to the prophet's judgment that "you have done foolishly in this" is understandable, even if it is out of character with the Asa we have seen so far. Imprisoning the prophet and placing him in stocks has other consequences than merely silencing him, however. The Chronicler understands the alienation and dissatisfaction growing between king and people over the inflicted cruelties of the king to be the result of the king's moral failure both to trust in God and to heed the prophet and repent. Clearly the king is on a downward spiral.

3. The regnal summary and the account of Asa's death, 16:11–14. The story of the alliance with Aram and the prophetic critique of the king bring the Asa narrative to a close. The Chronicler concludes the account of Asa's reign with the regnal summary information we have by now come to expect. We are given reference to the supplemental record of Asa's actions in the "Book of the Kings of Judah and Israel," a work now lost, unless the reference is to 1 and 2 Kings. The regnal summary information follows that given in 1 Kings 15:23–24, including the reference to the fact that in his old age, "Asa was diseased in his feet." The precise nature of the disease is unclear in both 2 Chronicles and 1 Kings. Speculation that the king may have suffered from diabetes that caused unhealed foot sores or from some circulatory disorder is pointless, as is speculation that "feet" is a euphemism for the genitalia, implying that Asa suffered from some form of venereal disease. For the Chronicler, the point is that the disease presents the king with a final opportunity to trust in and rely upon God for deliverance. He makes the point clear by adding the note that, despite the severity of the disease, the king elects to trust in human agency rather than divine grace. In so doing, the king demonstrates that the piety and faithfulness of his youth are truly lost and that the verdict of the prophet is just. Asa's death thus appears to follow as a consequence of his faithlessness.

Curiously, however, the Chronicler is not prepared to dismiss Asa to ignominy. Instead, he elects to add to the regnal summary several details about the funeral of Asa that communicate honor and respect. He was buried in a rock-hewn tomb, on a bier filled with various costly burial spices, and a great bonfire was lit in his honor. Were the Chronicler satisfied to consign Asa to the ranks of the reprobate, these details could easily have been omitted. That he chooses instead to relate them, especially in the context of remarks about Asa's failure, should indicate a certain ambivalence on the part of the Chronicler about Asa. He was a good king who went bad, but perhaps not so bad that his legacy of piety and faithfulness ought to be obscured. For the Chronicler, as for most of us, human life is rarely a simple matter of goodness or evil but rather a complex mixture of success and failure, faithfulness and faithlessness, honor and humiliation.

15. The Reign of Jehoshaphat
2 Chronicles 17:1–20:37

The chapters devoted to the reign of Jehoshaphat, 2 Chronicles 17—20, deal with one of the more important post-Solomonic kings of Judah. In the 1 Kings narrative, Jehoshaphat receives relatively light treatment, while the major attention is devoted to the conflict between his Israelite counterpart, Ahab, and the prophet Elijah. The Chronicler, in a manner consistent with his treatment of Israelite kings to date, deals with Ahab only insofar as he is involved in the telling of the Jehoshaphat story. Of the material familiar to the readers of 1 Kings, only the story of the prophet Micaiah and the defeat and death of Ahab in 1 Kings 22 is preserved here, along with fragmentary references from 1 Kings at the beginning and end of the Chronicler's presentation.

If the material is new, however, the themes are familiar. When the king demonstrates faithfulness and piety, he and the nation are rewarded with prosperity and peace. When the king does not trust in God and becomes entangled in foreign alliances, he is condemned and suffers reversal. Once again, the prophets are the agents by whom the condemnation is delivered. Interestingly, the Chronicler uses the story of Micaiah and the alliance with Ahab (2 Chron. 18:1–19:3) to reflect on the thorny problem of how to discern which prophet speaks for God when there is more than one prophetic witness.

The Jehoshaphat narrative has the following components: an introduction (17:1–6), Jehoshaphat's instruction in the law and its rewards (17:7–19), Micaiah and the alliance with Ahab, (18:1–19:3), Jehoshaphat's reforms of the judicial system (19:4–11), the Ammonite invasion (20:1–30), and the summary of the reign of Jehoshaphat (20:31–37).

INTRODUCTION TO THE REIGN OF JEHOSHAPHAT
2 Chronicles 17:1–6

The Chronicler's introduction to Jehoshaphat is, for all intents and purposes, new material; he uses only the last half of 1 Kings 15:24: "His son
Jehoshaphat succeeded him." The purpose of the section is to set the
theme for the whole presentation of the reign by drawing the connection
between piety and success, disobedience and failure. Verse 1 sets the
theme for the section: Jehoshaphat "strengthened himself against Israel."
Verse 2 elaborates a bit: The king builds fortified cities throughout Judah
and establishes garrisons in both Judahite and Ephraimite cities. Verses
3–4 then develop the theme of Jehoshaphat's piety as patron of the religion of his people. The Chronicler tells us that he

17:3 . . . walked in the earlier ways of his father; he did not seek the Baals,
⁴ but sought the God of his father and walked in his commandments, and
not according to the ways of Israel.

Several aspects of this description are worthy of note. First, the reading,
"walked in the earlier ways of his father," omits the name "David" that is
present in the Hebrew text of this verse ("of his father David"). The editors of the NRSV made the decision, on the strength of the adjective
"earlier" here, that the "ways" to which the text refers are the ways of
Jehoshaphat's own father, Asa, rather than those of David. There are several instances throughout 2 Chronicles where the ways of the king are
compared both to those of his biological father (26:4; 27:2) and to David
(28:1; 29:2; 34:2), so either reading is defensible.

Second, we note the recurrence here of the theme of seeking the Lord
that played such a prominent role in the Asa story. It will have a significant part in the Jehoshaphat narratives as well, serving as the primary
descriptive phrase for faithful reliance on God by king and people.

Third, Jehoshaphat acts in accord with the commandments of God
and specifically "not according to the ways of Israel." There has already
developed in 2 Chronicles a well-established accusation of impiety and
apostasy against the Northern Kingdom for its refusal to worship at the
Temple in Jerusalem and its use of the image of a calf or bull in the worship of God. These are the "ways of Israel" that Jehoshaphat righteously
avoids.

The reward of this piety and self-discipline is that "the Lord established the kingdom" in the hands of Jehoshaphat. The phrase echoes the
description of Solomon's assumption of power in 2 Chronicles 1:1. Along
with the establishment of his power and authority, Jehoshaphat also

receives "great riches and honor." Such gifts, given to other kings (Rehoboam, Uzziah, and even Hezekiah), are often the source of pride on the part of the king; they become the occasion on which the king turns away from reliance on God and trusts in human agents of deliverance. In the case of Jehoshaphat, the Chronicler's preliminary assessment is that this sort of pride will not develop, or at least will not permanently mar the king's achievements, because "his heart was courageous in the ways of the LORD."

THE KING'S INSTRUCTION IN THE LAW AND ITS REWARDS
2 Chronicles 17:7–19

The first specific action of Jehoshaphat to which the Chronicler calls attention is a fascinating one, both because it is unusual and because it serves as an example of the king's piety. In the third year of his reign, the king initiates a public instruction of the populace in "the book of the law." This is not the only occasion in the Bible when such public instruction in sacred law is given; the reading of the commandments at Mount Sinai (Ex. 34:33) and Ezra's reading of the law in Jerusalem (Neh. 8:1–8) are others. The unusual feature here is the sending of a team of roving teachers throughout the land to bring the instruction directly to the people. The effect is to communicate the belief that the sacred law is intended to pertain to everyday life and not merely to be confined to sacred acts within the Temple. At the same time, it gives the Chronicler another occasion to demonstrate the depth of Jehoshaphat's piety and commitment to obedience: He would have not merely himself but the whole of his kingdom instructed in the ways of God.

The "book of the law" mentioned in 2 Chronicles 17:9 is a difficult phrase. By the time of the writing of Chronicles, the phrase almost certainly referred to the Pentateuch (the biblical books Genesis through Deuteronomy). But prior to the exile, and especially as early as the reign of Jehoshaphat, no such collection of legal material existed. Probably we should interpret the phrase as the Chronicler anachronistically reading back the existence of the book of the law from his own day into the time of Jehoshaphat. Whatever is meant by the phrase, the point is undamaged; Jehoshaphat's commitment to faithfulness and obedience is so strong that he intends the behavior of the entire nation to reflect it.

The commissioning by the king of persons to teach the law is an unusual move; we know nothing of the individuals mentioned here, except that the Chronicler tells us that they come from three classes in Judahite society: the "officials" of the king, the Levites, and the priests.

These are, of course, the same classes of sacred and secular officers established by David in 1 Chronicles 23—26.

Jehoshaphat's piety and commitment to obedience are rewarded in the enhancement of the nation's security. Verses 10–19 demonstrate three ways in which that security is enhanced. First, the international prestige of Judah is reflected in the peace with surrounding nations that "did not make war against Jehoshaphat" and that brought payments of tribute in precious metals and livestock. Second, Jehoshaphat carries out large-scale public works projects throughout the land, including the building of fortified cities and storage depots for use in times of crisis. Third, the king develops the army. The Chronicler appears to describe a kind of conscription system, involving the recruitment of soldiers from the ancestral houses within the kingdom. The total number of soldiers recruited is impossibly large: over 1 million men, a force far larger than the capability of the king or the realm to maintain or support. The point of such exaggerated numbers is, as before, to portray a Judah blessed by God with an invincible strength. It is important to remember, however, that such strength exists only as long as the people are obedient; when the king or the people forget their need to rely upon God, that strength evaporates and defeat looms. This is precisely the point of the Chronicler's next narrative.

THE ALLIANCE WITH AHAB AND THE WAR WITH ARAM
2 Chronicles 18:1–19:3

18:1 Now Jehoshaphat had great riches and honor; and he made a marriage alliance with Ahab. ² After some years he went down to Ahab in Samaria. Ahab slaughtered an abundance of sheep and oxen for him and for the people who were with him, and induced him to go up against Ramoth-gilead. ³ King Ahab of Israel said to King Jehoshaphat of Judah, "Will you go with me to Ramoth-gilead?" He answered him, "I am with you, my people are your people. We will be with you in the war."

⁴ But Jehoshaphat also said to the king of Israel, "Inquire first for the word of the LORD." ⁵ Then the king of Israel gathered the prophets together, four hundred of them, and said to them, "Shall we go to battle against Ramoth-gilead, or shall I refrain?" They said, "Go up; for God will give it into the hand of the king." ⁶ But Jehoshaphat said, "Is there no other prophet of the LORD here of whom we may inquire?" ⁷ The king of Israel said to Jehoshaphat, "There is still one other by whom we may inquire of the LORD, Micaiah son of Imlah; but I hate him, for he never prophesies anything favorable about me, but only disaster." Jehoshaphat said, "Let the king not say such a thing." ⁸ Then the king of Israel summoned an officer

and said, "Bring quickly Micaiah son of Imlah." ⁹Now the king of Israel and King Jehoshaphat of Judah were sitting on their thrones, arrayed in their robes; and they were sitting at the threshing floor at the entrance of the gate of Samaria; and all the prophets were prophesying before them. ¹⁰Zedekiah son of Chenaanah made for himself horns of iron, and he said, "Thus says the LORD: With these you shall gore the Arameans until they are destroyed." ¹¹All the prophets were prophesying the same and saying, "Go up to Ramoth-gilead and triumph; the LORD will give it into the hand of the king."

¹²The messenger who had gone to summon Micaiah said to him, "Look, the words of the prophets with one accord are favorable to the king; let your word be like the word of one of them, and speak favorably." ¹³But Micaiah said, "As the LORD lives, whatever my God says, that I will speak."

¹⁴When he had come to the king, the king said to him, "Micaiah, shall we go to Ramoth-gilead to battle, or shall I refrain?" He answered, "Go up and triumph; they will be given into your hand." ¹⁵But the king said to him, "How many times must I make you swear to tell me nothing but the truth in the name of the LORD?" ¹⁶Then Micaiah said, "I saw all Israel scattered upon the mountains, like sheep without a shepherd; and the LORD said, 'These have no master; let each one go home in peace.'" ¹⁷The king of Israel said to Jehoshaphat, "Did I not tell you that he would not prophesy anything favorable about me, but only disaster?"

¹⁸Then Micaiah said, "Therefore hear the word of the LORD: I saw the LORD sitting on his throne, with all the host of heaven standing to the right and to the left of him. ¹⁹And the LORD said, 'Who will entice King Ahab of Israel, so that he may go up and fall at Ramoth-gilead?' Then one said one thing, and another said another, ²⁰until a spirit came forward and stood before the LORD, saying, 'I will entice him.' The LORD asked him, 'How?' ²¹He replied, 'I will go out and be a lying spirit in the mouth of all his prophets.' Then the LORD said, 'You are to entice him, and you shall succeed; go out and do it.' ²²So you see, the LORD has put a lying spirit in the mouth of these your prophets; the LORD has decreed disaster for you."

²³Then Zedekiah son of Chenaanah came up to Micaiah, slapped him on the cheek, and said, "Which way did the spirit of the LORD pass from me to speak to you?" ²⁴Micaiah replied, "You will find out on that day when you go in to hide in an inner chamber." ²⁵The king of Israel then ordered, "Take Micaiah, and return him to Amon the governor of the city and to Joash the king's son; and say, ²⁶'Thus says the king: Put this fellow in prison, and feed him on reduced rations of bread and water until I return in peace.'" ²⁷Micaiah said, "If you return in peace, the LORD has not spoken by me." And he said, "Hear, you peoples, all of you!"

²⁸So the king of Israel and King Jehoshaphat of Judah went up to Ramoth-gilead. ²⁹The king of Israel said to Jehoshaphat, "I will disguise myself and go into battle, but you wear your robes." So the king of Israel disguised himself, and they went into battle. ³⁰Now the king of Aram had

commanded the captains of his chariots, "Fight with no one small or great, but only with the king of Israel." [31] When the captains of the chariots saw Jehoshaphat, they said, "It is the king of Israel." So they turned to fight against him; and Jehoshaphat cried out, and the LORD helped him. God drew them away from him, [32] for when the captains of the chariots saw that it was not the king of Israel, they turned back from pursuing him. [33] But a certain man drew his bow, and unknowingly struck the king of Israel between the scale armor and the breastplate; so he said to the driver of his chariot, "Turn around, and carry me out of the battle, for I am wounded." [34] The battle grew hot that day, and the king of Israel propped himself up in his chariot facing the Arameans until evening; then at sunset he died.

[19:1] King Jehoshaphat of Judah returned in safety to his house in Jerusalem. [2] Jehu son of Hanani the seer went out to meet him and said to King Jehoshaphat, "Should you help the wicked and love those who hate the LORD? Because of this, wrath has gone out against you from the LORD. [3] Nevertheless, some good is found in you, for you destroyed the sacred poles out of the land, and have set your heart to seek God."

The centerpiece of the narrative of Jehoshaphat's reign is the story of the alliance with King Ahab of Israel in the war against Aram for control of Ramoth-gilead. Ramoth-gilead was a town in the northern Transjordan and was a point of contention between Israel and Aram throughout the history of the two nations. At the time of the narrative, Ramoth is under the control of Aram, and Ahab appears resolved to wrest it away and restore it to Israel. The Chronicler's version of the story is almost a copy of the narrative as it appears in 1 Kings 22, except that there are several key changes made by the Chronicler in the service of his theological aims. These will be noted in the discussion below. The narrative as it stands in 2 Chronicles 18:1–19:3 has three main sections: the prophetic consultation (18:1–27), the battle narrative and the death of Ahab (18:28–34), and the prophetic critique of Jehoshaphat (19:1–3). The third of these sections is unique to the Chronicler.

1. The prophetic consultation, 18:1–27. The basic plotline of the narrative in Chronicles is unchanged from its source in 1 Kings 22: Jehoshaphat of Judah has come "down" (i.e., from the higher elevation in Jerusalem to the lower plains where Samaria is located) to meet the king of Israel, Ahab. The latter seeks to persuade the former to participate with him in an attack on Ramoth-gilead; Jehoshaphat appears willing, but insists that before the attack commences a consultation of the prophets be made.

The Chronicler has provided a new introduction to the narrative that alters his source narrative in three important ways. First, he repeats the note of 17:5 that "Jehoshaphat had great riches and honor," but without the balancing comment about the purity of the king's heart. The effect is to imply that the economic security and prestige of Jehoshaphat has led him astray and will induce him to place his trust in places other than in God. Indeed, Jehoshaphat's response to Ahab's request is to make the people of Judah "your people" rather than to affirm that they are first and foremost the people of God. The very first phrase of the account thus creates the sense that the piety of Jehoshaphat is on the verge of going astray.

The second alteration is the Chronicler's note that Jehoshaphat "made a marriage alliance with Ahab." At issue here is the fact that such an alliance ensnares Judah in entanglements with a foreign power, and in particular with Israel, a group of people whom the Chronicler regards as apostate. This is the same concern we have already seen in the Chronicler's critique of Asa for becoming entangled with Aram against Israel (16:1–9). It will occur again at the end of the Jehoshaphat narrative (20:35–37). Clearly, the theme of avoiding alliances with foreign powers is a vital one for the Chronicler, and the Chronicler's own knowledge of history would lead him to be wary of such alliances. The conquests of Israel by the Assyrians and Judah by the Babylonians could be directly traced to the kingdoms' participation in hopeless alliances against larger powers.

The third alteration of the source narrative is not an addition but an omission. In 1 Kings 22:3, Ahab offers the justification that "Ramoth-gilead belongs to us, yet we are doing nothing to take it out of the hand of the king of Aram." The Chronicler omits this explanation of the war with Aram completely, leaving the impression that there are no grounds for the invasion and perhaps that it is altogether unprovoked. Should Jehoshaphat choose to participate in it, he will be the aggressor rather than the defender, and he does so at the risk of conducting war without divine approval.

In response to this concern for divine approbation of a military enter-prise, Ahab summons some four hundred prophets to pronounce bless-ing from God on Ahab's proposed enterprise. These appear to be "court prophets," seers and prognosticators in the employ of the king, presum-ably paid to pronounce the desired divine approval on the king's plans. Jehoshaphat's insistence on hearing another prophet betrays the distrust of these figures to speak the truth. But it also sets up a primary theme for the rest of the narrative: What happens when prophetic words conflict?

The conflict between prophetic messages is personified in Zedekiah son of Chenaanah and Micaiah son of Imlah. Which prophet speaks the truth? The story signals the answer by several means. First, Micaiah is cast as the lone voice of truth against the chorus of falsehood. Second,

Micaiah alone prophesies the word of disaster, an unpopular (and politically unsafe) word to speak, where all the others foretell success for the king—a word welcome to royal ears and therefore suspicious. Finally, the exchange between Micaiah and the messenger in verses 12–13 makes it clear that Micaiah will speak only "whatever my God says." Employing the strongest oath used in biblical literature—"as the LORD lives" (or "by the life of the LORD")—Micaiah binds himself to a testimony beyond his own decision.

It is all the more surprising, then, that Micaiah lies to Ahab when called upon to speak. However, he lies in so obvious a manner that even Ahab can recognize the falsehood. The effect is to place Ahab in the position of insisting on hearing a truth he must then choose to ignore: that if he carries through with the invasion, his army will wind up scattered and defeated with their leader dead. Having heard Micaiah's prophecy of disaster for king and people, Ahab cannot pretend to have piously obeyed the guidance of the prophets, for he knows that the truth has been spoken in his hearing.

The scene creates a theological problem: If prophets lie, how can their word be trusted as a guide to the will of God? The provisional answer offered by the text is that the truth is found in those prophets who speak "in the spirit" of God. This is the effect of the vision of the heavenly throne room Micaiah describes in verses 18–22. The scene provides the answer to the question: How can so many prophets be wrong and only one be right? Because all the prophets lie except that one whom God designs to speak the truth.

But the answer begs the next question, raised by the next scene—the confrontation between Zedekiah and Micaiah. Zedekiah's challenge to Micaiah is to prove that the spirit of God speaks through Micaiah and not through Zedekiah and his comrades. Micaiah's reponse is to point to the end result of the prophecy: Zedekiah will know which prophet spoke the truth in the spirit of God when his prophecies of victory turn sour and he seeks refuge in an inner chamber from those who would kill him. In the end, the Chronicler's solution to the problem of conflicting prophetic testimony is the classical solution offered in Deuteronomy 18:21–22: The true prophet is the one whose word proves true.

The problem, of course, is that this does not help in the moment of decision. Ahab must choose between prophetic promises, one of victory and the other of catastrophe. The Chronicler is clear, however, that he is not in the dark about the choice; indeed, he knows from the moment Micaiah first speaks that to carry through with his plans to invade is to act in a manner contrary to the will of God. That he chooses to do so is thus a sign of Ahab's sinful rebelliousness, a judgment confirmed by the prophet Jehu in 19:2.

Still, the dilemma is not completely resolved, even if the Chronicler leaves no room to exonerate Ahab. Those seeking to learn the lessons of the episode are still confronted with the need to choose between opposing prophetic counsels, and we are not often afforded the luxury of waiting until all is said and done before choosing. The best guide may be Karl Barth's advice to "listen for the command of God in the moment of decision." Inside those who are faithful and obedient, there is perhaps a sense of bearing and direction that resonates with truth and seeks to follow it. The presence of that sense is perhaps as much a sign of righteousness as its absence is a mark of sinfulness. Such an answer can hardly be regarded as fully satisfactory, but it is as much as the Chronicler—or any of us—is able to say.

2. The battle and the death of Ahab, 18:28–34. Once again, the Chronicler remains close to the source narrative in 1 Kings 22 in this portion of the story. Here, as in Kings, Ahab disguises himself but insists that Jehoshaphat wear his royal robes. Ahab appears in so doing to be hedging his bets; he is willing to disobey what he knows to be the will of God, but he seeks the shelter of disguise and anonymity in carrying out the deed. The sense that he does not have the courage of his own convictions is further evidence for the Chronicler of the weakness and wickedness of Ahab's character.

Ironically, it is this very weakness that both saves Jehoshaphat and condemns Ahab. Aramean troops press the battle against Jehoshaphat, whom they mistakenly assume to be the Israelite (rather than the Judahite) king. When they discover their error, they withdraw, because they have been commanded not to fight with anyone except Ahab. Amid the melee, however, Ahab is mortally wounded by a chance shot from an archer.

The Chronicler gives this section his own spin by adding the detail that, when set upon by the Arameans, Jehoshaphat cried out and "the LORD helped him. God drew them away from him." In the Kings narrative, Jehoshaphat's loud shout identifies him as the king of Judah and not the intended target of the Aramean's attack. In the Chronicler's version, however, Jehoshaphat's cry becomes a battlefield prayer, which God hears and to which God responds by "drawing away" the enemy. Jehoshaphat's deliverance is thus the direct result of his piety in Chronicles rather than the operation of coincidence as in 1 Kings 22.

Unlike Jehoshaphat, Ahab is not spared but rather wounded, and he dies late in the day. The Chronicler then omits the story of Ahab's chariot being brought back to Samaria bearing his body (1 Kings 22:37–38). Instead of returning in peace, as the king had assumed he would in 18:26, he does not return at all, even in death. Micaiah's word is thus found to be true in all its details.

3. The prophetic critique of Jehoshaphat, 19:1–3. The third section of the story is the Chronicler's own addition, unique to this presentation. Jehoshaphat, upon returning to Jerusalem, is greeted with condemnation by the prophet Jehu, son of Hanani (known from the Asa narrative in 16:7–10). Like his father before him, Jehu seizes the moment of the king's return from battle to criticize the king for becoming involved in foreign alliances and not relying on God. His question, "Should you help the wicked and love those who hate the LORD?" summarizes the Chronicler's characterization of Ahab. The Israelite king is sinful and in willful rebellion against the word and will of God. That Jehoshaphat allowed himself to become entangled with him is a sign of Jehoshaphat's own weakness; he is not the perfect king he has so far been portrayed to be. Still, there is enough righteousness and obedience in him, as witnessed by his commitment to religious purity, his eagerness to abolish the pagan shrines in the land, and his having "set [his] heart to seek God" to deliver him from the fate of Ahab. He is spared to learn from his mistakes.

JEHOSHAPHAT'S JUDICIAL REFORMS
2 Chronicles 19:4–11

Sandwiched between the account of the war with Aram and the battle with Ammon (20:1–30) is this short description of a national revision of the judicial system. The account has two parts: the appointment of judges in the outlying cities of the realm (vv. 4–7), and the appointment of judges in Jerusalem itself (vv. 8–11).

It is important to bear in mind that justice in ancient Israel was not sharply distinguished from religious obligation, as it is sometimes thought to be in the modern world. Rather, human judgment was understood to be a reflection of divine justice. To establish or uphold justice is to act in a manner consistent with the intent of God for the order of creation and human relationships. Indeed, the very name of the king implies the importance of God in the establishment of justice: "Jehoshaphat" means "Yahweh judges" in Hebrew. Human judges had a specific religious responsibility in adjudicating legal matters: They acted on behalf of God to establish and uphold the justice of God. Jehoshaphat's instructions to the judges in verse 6 are explicit about this:

> 19:6 . . . Consider what you are doing, for you judge not on behalf of human beings but on the LORD's behalf; he is with you in giving judgment.

The Chronicler is also explicit about the king's intent in reforming his judiciary. This is not an effort at either efficiency or enhanced royal control over decisions. It is salvific in nature; Jehoshaphat "went out again among the people . . . and brought them back to the LORD, the God of their ancestors" (v. 4). There is no separation of sacred piety and secular justice here; they are the same.

The king delivers admonitions both to the city judges (vv. 6–7) and the Jerusalem judges (vv. 9–11). The common element in both is the presence of the term "the fear of the LORD" (vv. 7, 9). This term is most often associated with worship and the sense of awe and wonder at the presence of God. We have also seen it used of the surrounding nations who paid tribute to Jehoshaphat because "the fear of the LORD fell" on them (17:10), and of the cities around Gerar in the wake of Asa's victory over the Ethiopians (14:14). In either usage, the term implies an overwhelming sense of the presence of God, whose word and will one dares not defy. It is out of this overwhelming sense of God's presence and power that the judges are to carry out their responsibility. There is no room, therefore, for the perversion of God's justice (v. 7) or for offering anything less than the whole heart and being to the task (v. 9).

As the Chronicler understands it, the purpose of judgment is instructive and protective:

> 19:9 . . . "This is how you shall act: in the fear of the LORD, in faithfulness, and with your whole heart; 10 whenever a case comes to you from your kindred who live in their cities, concerning bloodshed, law or commandment, statutes or ordinances, then you shall instruct them, so that they may not incur guilt before the LORD and wrath may not come on you and your kindred. Do so, and you will not incur guilt."

One cannot help but note the connection between the judge's execution of his responsibility to instruct in the law and his or her own fate. If the judge acts to instruct the people so that they amend their ways, guilt is avoided and wrath does not ensue. If, on the other hand, the judge fails sufficiently to convince the people of their error, guilt and wrath accrue not only to the people but to the judge as well.

Justice in the sense apprehended by the Chronicler is finally not punitive or even corrective; it does not seek ultimately to punish the wrongdoer for past crimes or to induce him or her to contemplate the error of his or her ways. Rather, for the Chronicler, justice is preventative. It stands as a buffer between human sin and divine wrath. By warning the sinner of the full consequence of his or her act, the judge not only sets to right individual inequities but also shields the whole community from divine wrath. Justice, in this sense, is an extension of grace rather than its opposite as is often thought. It is God forestalling the consequence of our actions so that the actions might be rectified. As for the judge, it is no small thing to stand in the breach between human sin and divine anger. Hence, the Chronicler's benediction seems altogether appropriate: "Deal courageously, and may the LORD be with the good!"

THE AMMONITE INVASION
2 Chronicles 20:1–30

The next episode in the Chronicler's account of Jehoshaphat is another military encounter, this time in facing an invasion from the east. In almost every way, it is the opposite of the Ramoth-gilead episode in 18:1–19:3. There, Judah agrees to participate in a foreign alliance; here Judah acts with the help of God alone. There, Judah is involved in an invasion of another country (the Chronicler having omitted reference to Israelite ownership of Ramoth-gilead); here Judah itself is being invaded. But most important, perhaps, there the king and people do not approach the battle with piety and single-minded devotion and trust in God; here, on the other hand, such piety and trust take center stage.

The narrative may be divided into four parts: the invasion and the reaction to it (vv. 1–4), Jehoshaphat's prayer (vv. 5–12), Jahaziel's prophecy (vv. 13–19), and the battle and its aftermath (vv. 20–30).

1. The invasion and reaction, 20:1–4. The narrative begins with the announcement that a coalition of people from the eastern and southern fringes of Judah has mounted an invasion into Judah and is threatening Jerusalem. Ammon and Moab are two cultures already well-known to readers of the Old Testament; they inhabited the plains and rolling hill country east of the Jordan River, with Ammon to the north and Moab to the south. The Meunites were a seminomadic culture that roamed the desert reaches around the southern borders of Judah; we have met them once before in 1 Chronicles 4:41 and will again in 2 Chronicles 26:7. The forces of the coalition approach Judah at its most vulnerable point: around the north end of the Dead Sea near En-Gedi. From En-Gedi, the road to Jerusalem through the Judahite hill country, while rugged, is not long, and an army with the advantage of surprise would be on the edges of the city very quickly. Small wonder, then, that the king and people react to the news with fear.

Still, Jehoshaphat's reaction is not a call to arms and a cry to man the defenses of the city; rather, it is a religious reaction. In the face of dire threat, Jehoshaphat proclaims a fast and "sets himself to seek the LORD." The people across the country respond in kind, so that three times in two verses (vv. 3–4), the narrative employs the phrase that has become emblematic of Judahite piety: "seek the LORD."

2. Jehoshaphat's prayer, 20:5–12. At the heart of the Chronicler's account of the nation's approach to the crisis is the king's prayer (vv. 5–12). The prayer is set in the Temple complex, in the "new court" (an otherwise unknown structure). Like Asa in facing the Ethiopian invasions (14:11), Jehoshaphat's prayer seeks deliverance from an overwhelming foe, affirming that the only source of such deliverance is God. Unlike Asa's prayer, however, Jehoshaphat utters a classical lament, carefully crafted and employing rhetorical flourishes of several sorts. The prayer has four sections, corresponding to the four major elements of a lament: the cry to God (vv. 6–9), the statement of distress (vv. 10–11), the appeal for vindication (v. 12a), and the expression of trust (v. 12b).

> 20:5 **Jehoshaphat stood in the assembly of Judah and Jerusalem, in the house of the LORD, before the new court,** [6] **and said, "O LORD, God of our ancestors, are you not God in heaven? Do you not rule over all the kingdoms of the nations? In your hand are power and might, so that no one is able to withstand you.** [7] **Did you not, O our God, drive out the inhabitants of this land before your people Israel, and give it forever to the descendants of your friend Abraham?** [8] **They have lived in it, and in it have built you a sanctuary for your name, saying,** [9] **'If disaster comes upon us, the sword, judgment, or pestilence, or famine, we will stand before this house, and before you, for your name is in this house, and cry to you in our distress, and you will hear and save.'** [10] **See now, the people of Ammon, Moab, and Mount Seir, whom you would not let Israel invade when they came from the land of Egypt, and whom they avoided and did not destroy—** [11] **they reward us by coming to drive us out of your possession that you have given us to inherit.** [12] **O our God, will you not execute judgment upon them? For we are powerless against this great multitude that is coming against us. We do not know what to do, but our eyes are on you."**

The prayer begins with a cry to God, calling for God's attention to the plight of the people (vv. 6–9). This section is composed of a series of carefully worded rhetorical questions, each of which anticipates an affirmative response from God: Are you not our God? Do you not rule over the nations? Did you not drive out the inhabitants of this land and give it forever to the descendants of "your friend Abraham?" The effect of the accumulation of these questions is twofold. First, it asserts faith in the sovereignty of God, whom Jehoshaphat understands has guided and shaped history toward the goal of giving and preserving the land in the possession of the people. Second, and more to the immediate point, it serves as a reminder to God of the divine covenantal obligation to the people.

Verses 8–9 make that obligation more explicit. In language deliberately reminiscent of Solomon's prayer in 2 Chronicles 6, Jehoshaphat reminds God that they have built a house for the name of the Lord and that God has agreed to hear prayers of distress from within it, and having heard, to save (7:12–14). The prayer has now made the strongest possible case for God's deliverance: Deliverance is in accord with the divine will for Israel; God has a historic covenantal obligation to Israel, born of the promise of God to Abraham; and the prayer for deliverance is uttered from the Temple, where God has agreed to hear and save those who pray.

Verses 10–11 now state the specific distress: the treachery of Ammon and Moab. Once again, the prayer relies on the sacred story for justification: God did not permit Israel to invade and destroy Ammon and Moab while the people wandered in the wilderness (see Deut. 2:1–22). Rather, the Ammonites and Moabites were spared, and now they repay that largesse with an attempt to drive the people out of "your possession that you have given us to inherit" (v. 11).

Verse 12a is a cry for vindication, in many ways the climactic moment of the prayer. As in the case of the initial cry to God in verses 6–9, the plea for vindication is stated in the form of a question: "Will you not execute judgment on them?" The form is the same as the rhetorical questions of verses 6–9, but this question is not rhetorical; it is rather the crux of the issue. However, the earlier questions have built up the sense of anticipation of affirmative response, and now that same anticipation emerges in the crucial moment. If God has affirmed all the other questions, will God not also now affirm this most important one?

Finally, the prayer affirms trust in God in verse 12b. It accomplishes this in two ways. First, the prayer reminds God that "we are powerless against this great multitude." This may seem an ironic statement in light of the claims in 17:10–19 that Judah possesses an army in excess of one million men; what nation need fear invasion with an army of that size? But once again, the issue for the Chronicler is not military strength but the strength of faith; that which delivers God's people is not the might of their arms but the might of God in whom they place their trust. Asa's prayer in 14:11 makes the same case explicitly: "We rely on you, and in your name we have come against this multitude." Like his father before him, Jehoshaphat now places his own trust in God.

Second, the prayer makes the explicit claim that "we do not know what to do, but our eyes are on you." Rather than watching the coalition forces that they fear, or looking to their arms, king and people remain focused on God in trust that the prayed-for deliverance will be forthcoming.

3. Jahaziel's prophecy, 20:13–19. The next section of the narrative represents the divine response, through the medium of a prophetic speech, to the king's prayer for deliverance. The speech is delivered by Jahaziel, who is identified as a Levite and whose lineage is carefully noted. It is unusual for a Levite to step out of liturgical office and assume prophetic responsibilities, but it provides the occasion to note that prophecy is not alien to liturgy in the Chronicler's view of faith but is at home in it.

In a word, the response to Jehoshaphat's prayer is that the deliverance prayed for will come. But along with the promise, the Chronicler advances some important ideas about his theology of war. The first of those ideas is that "the battle is not yours but God's" (v. 15). Warfare is a divine enterprise and not the tool of human greed. Its purpose is to clear away any threat to the safety, security, and well-being of God's people. It is not to be used for vengeance, acquisition, or self-aggrandizement. Its only service is to the will of God. This notion is foundational to the concept of "holy war," so often employed—and often misused—in history, and moderns ought always to be skeptical of human calls to divinely sanctioned war. But there can be no doubt that neither the Chronicler nor those about whom he wrote were squeamish about engaging in battle when they understood themselves called to do so.

The second notion about warfare is that the victory anticipated is in fact already won. "Stand still, and see the victory of the LORD on your behalf," urges Jahaziel in verse 17. The salient point here is that victory in divine warfare is already decided on the divine plane. God has won the victory, and all Israel must do is "stand still" and observe that victory being played out before them on the stage of human events. The Chronicler makes no room for the notion that human battles are the proving ground for conflicts between deities (a notion common in ancient Near Eastern mythology), and he would reject outright any claim that the people win victory on behalf of God. In fact, the reverse is the case; the victory is won by God on behalf of the people.

The third important notion about war is found in the often-repeated benediction, "The LORD is with you." In this particular context, it is the response to the expression of trust in the king's prayer: "Our eyes are on you." The prophet now claims that the Lord will be constantly visible to those watching eyes, so that their confidence in the promised victory never flags. The prophetic promise of God's presence amid the crisis of war is to reassure the people that, as God works out the divinely ordained vindication of the people, all is proceeding according to God's purpose.

In many ways, the Chronicler's notion of holy war is similar to apocalyptic thought about the great struggle between good and evil. There, as well as here, "the battle is not yours but God's," and the human role is faithfully to stand by in trust that, despite appearances to the contrary, the victory belongs to God. In apocalyptic literature as well as here in this speech, the goal is encouragement and reassurance that God is in control throughout the tempestuous events that threaten the security of God's people. And in both, the purpose of such speech is to teach and nurture radical reliance on God in the face of crisis. The attitude encouraged by the Chronicler is not one of passivity but of confident expectation of God's deliverance.

The response of the king and the people to Jahaziel's prophecy is again a model of piety: They bow down with faces to the ground. This is the opposite of warlike posturing; this is abject submission to authority and power. In the face of battle, Jehoshaphat and Judah declare themselves dependent upon God and submissive to the divine will. The Levites are alone in the assembly left standing on their feet; they do so in service of their function to offer praise to God. In short, the whole moment is the physical expression of trust in the promised deliverance of God.

4. The battle and its aftermath, 20:20–30. The next morning, king and people assemble at Tekoa, east of Jerusalem in the Judahite highlands. As they assemble, Jehoshaphat gives them what in other situations might have been battle instructions. Here, however, we have yet another religious admonition: "Believe in the LORD your God and you will be established." One final time, the Chronicler returns to the theme of trust. The language here is reminiscent of Isaiah 7:9: "If you do not stand firm in faith, you shall not stand at all" (the verb translated "stand firm" in Isaiah is the same as that translated "be established" here). The link between faith and victory is explicit: Belief, not strength of arms, is the key to the deliverance of God.

The people's response is the now familiar psalmic refrain, "Give thanks to the LORD for his steadfast love endures forever." We have seen this response used twice already, in 5:13 at the completion of the Temple construction and in 7:3 at the conclusion of Solomon's prayer of dedication. The Chronicler makes use of this refrain on those occasions when the people offer their affirmation of the divine will. Understood in this way, a similar claim is made of the divine will to deliver Judah from the enemy: The battle is God's, and in some measure the victory is already won.

Indeed, the beginning of the song is the occasion of victory, as the coalition of Ammonite, Moabite, and Meunite forces turn on each other in confusion and destroy each other, without Judah even being on the field of battle (vv. 22–23). By the time Jehoshaphat and his forces arrive, the enemy is dead and there is nothing to do but enjoy the spoils of the battle. Quite literally, then, the battle has been God's, and God has won the victory. As in the case of the Ethiopian invasion during Asa's reign (14:15), the plunder taken here is vast, including "livestock in great numbers, goods, clothing, and precious things" (v. 25).

Before returning home, Jehoshaphat and the army gather in the Valley of Beracah for worship and thanksgiving. This is the appropriate act on the part of one who has lamented to God and then been delivered from distress: One returns to God in worship to give thanks and to bless the name of the Lord. The name of the place where the king and people offer their worship is explained by the act of worship itself: "Beracah" is a form of the Hebrew word for "blessing," and the "Valley of Beracah" is thus the "valley of blessing." Having offered blessing in the valley, the king and people return with great rejoicing to Jerusalem, where the event concludes with a celebration of God's deliverance in the Temple, the place from which the prayer for deliverance went forth in the beginning. The arrival at the Temple is the sign that the episode has now come full circle and is concluded.

There remains only to note that the "fear of God" came upon the surrounding nations, convincing them that, with such a powerful ally as God, attacks against Judah are truly futile. The result is that "the realm of Jehoshaphat was quiet, for his God gave him rest all around" (v. 30). We recall in 17:10 that this is how the reign of Jehoshaphat began, after the people had been instructed in the law by the king's roving teachers; the surrounding nations were awed by the "fear of God" and brought tribute money to Jehoshaphat. Now, at the end of his account of Jehoshaphat's reign, the Chronicler brings us back to the same note.

SUMMARY OF THE REIGN OF JEHOSHAPHAT
2 Chronicles 20:31–37

At the close of the narrative of Jehoshaphat's reign, the Chronicler provides the now familiar summary of the king's life. The details are taken directly from 1 Kings 22:41–44. We are told the length of the king's reign (twenty-five years) and the name of his mother (Azubah daughter of Shilhi), that he "walked in the way of his father Asa" and did "what was right in the sight of the Lord." The Chronicler's summary retains the lone critique of Jehoshaphat, that "the high places were not removed," despite the fact that this contradicts the Chronicler's own account of the king's reign. Second Chronicles 17:6 makes the opposite claim, that he did remove the high places.

The Chronicler's version of the summary differs from the source material in three ways, however. First, 1 Kings 22:43 fills out the critique regarding the removal of high places with the detail that "the people still sacrificed and offered incense" on them. The Chronicler omits this detail and opts for the broader statement, "the people had not yet set their hearts upon the God of their ancestors."

The second difference is the Chronicler's outright omission of 1 Kings 22:44: "Jehoshaphat also made peace with the king of Israel." In its place, he substitutes the brief narrative regarding the abortive joint shipping venture with Ahaziah of Israel, son and successor of Ahab. Once again, however, the Chronicler edits the material for his own purposes. In 1 Kings 22:47–49, the project is all the idea of Jehoshaphat; Ahaziah asks to be included in the venture but is refused. The ships never accomplish their mission, however; they are wrecked at Ezion-geber. In Chronicles, the initiative for the project seems to come from Ahaziah, but Jehoshaphat joins him willingly. The Chronicler's comment that Ahaziah "did wickedly" is intended to account for the disastrous wreck of the fleet. The 1 Kings 22 description of the ships as "of the Tarshish type" has become the destination of the fleet—"ships to go to Tarshish"—despite the fact that sailing to Tarshish from Ezion-geber would require traveling around the southern end of Africa and then north to the western end of the Mediterranean.

The third and most significant change from the source narrative is the addition of the prophetic critique of the venture by Eliezer son of Dodavahu (v. 37). The prophet warns Jehoshaphat of the impending shipwreck and blames it on the fact that the king has chosen to participate with Ahaziah. Once again, then, the Chronicler plays the theme of the folly and sin of foreign entanglements, particularly those that involve the apostatic Northern Kingdom. That the Chronicler would have this be his last word on Jehoshaphat, otherwise one of the greater kings in the Chronicler's estimation, is indicative of the importance with which he regards this concern. For him, Israel (understood in the broad sense as the whole people of God) is a holy people, who are called apart from untoward contact with other nations and populations who might distract them from seeking the Lord.

16. The Kings from Jehoram through Ahaz
2 Chronicles 21—28

Second Chronicles 21—28 presents a less impressive series of reigns, which are dominated more by moral and military failure than by obedience and success. Throughout these chapters, a pattern emerges: A king comes to the throne of Judah and begins his reign in obedience to God and is rewarded with success. At some point, however, the king ceases to be obedient and meets with frustration and defeat. The pattern is not universal: Jotham (chap. 27) receives no negative assessment, while Ahaz (chap. 28) receives only criticism and judgment.

At work beneath the Chronicler's treatment of these kings is his omnipresent theology of moral responsibility. From his source in 1 and 2 Kings, he knows that both success and failure have befallen these kings. In his system of thought, success is the result of faithfulness, and failure follows disobedience. In those places where he judges the record of the king's religious life to justify the events that happen, he transmits that record with few significant changes. Where the king's record of religious activity does not seem to warrant his fate, the Chronicler augments his source with narrative material to explain the correlation. In the end, the Chronicler upholds with a high degree of consistency his notion that each individual's lot in life is directly connected to his or her devotion to God.

When one steps back still further from the stories of the kings in 2 Chronicles 21—28, another pattern is discernible, a pattern of moral and spiritual decline in Judah, a pattern that threatens the very soul of the nation. For the kings Jehoram through Joash, this decline results from the alliance of the Judahite monarchy, the house of David, with the Israelite house of Omri. At the center of the decline is a threat to the Davidic line; the focus of the threat is Athaliah, daughter of Ahab of Israel, wife of Jehoram of Judah, and mother of Ahaziah. The Chronicler has already condemned alliances with foreign powers as unholy entanglements; now he shows the grave results such entanglements produce.

With the deaths of all other visible claimants to the throne of David, Athaliah takes control, and for the first time in its history the house of David is disenfranchised, its only hope a small child hidden away in the Temple. For the kings Amaziah through Ahaz, the moral and spiritual crisis centers in apostasy, the abandonment of the worship of God in favor of religious innovation. King after king leaves the "ways of David" in favor of devotion to other deities.

The units within this section correspond to the narratives of the various kings' reigns: Jehoram (21:1–20), Ahaziah (22:1–9), the usurpation by Athaliah and the Temple coup (22:10–23:21), Joash (24:1–27), Amaziah (25:1–28), Uzziah (26:1–23), Jotham (27:1–9), and Ahaz (28:1–27).

THE REIGN OF JEHORAM
2 Chronicles 21:1–20

The narrative material about Jehoram is dependent on 2 Kings 8:16–22, but the Chronicler has significantly augmented it with the addition of a letter to the king from the prophet Elijah, otherwise unknown. The narrative falls into three sections: an introduction, containing summary information about the king's reign (vv. 1–7), the revolts of Edom and Libnah (vv. 8–10), and Elijah's letter and the death of Jehoram (vv. 11–20).

1. Introduction, 21:1–7. The account of Jehoram's reign in 2 Chronicles contains the basic information already known from 2 Kings 8:16–19, namely, that Jehoram began his reign at the age of thirty-two and reigned for eight years. But the Chronicler also makes several important changes. The first of these is the addition of the account of Jehoram's purge of his brothers, along with other Judahite officials, in verses 2–4. Jehoram, having established himself in power, conducts a blood purge of his brothers who might be potential claimants to the throne. (Two brothers appear in English to have the same name: Azariah. In fact, the names are distinct in Hebrew; the first is *Azaryah*, and the second is *Azaryahu*. It is also possible that the second name may be misspelled in the text; it may perhaps be *Uzziyahu*, or "Uzziah.") The account serves two purposes: to serve as grounds for Elijah's indictment of Jehoram in verse 13 and also to set the stage for the succession crisis in 2 Chronicles 22. There, after the deaths in rapid succession of both Jehoram and Ahaziah, no adult members of the house of David are left alive to claim the throne, opening the way for Athaliah, Jehoram's Omride queen, to seize control.

The language the Chronicler uses to describe Jehoram's purge is interesting. Although it is obscured in the NRSV, the Hebrew of verse 4 should probably be translated: "And Jehoram rose against the kingdom of his father and grew strong and killed all his brothers with the sword." The idiom to "rise against" is always negative in the Old Testament; it implies here that Jehoram's actions are an uprising against the interests and well-being of his own people. One obvious reason for seeing the king's actions in this way is that they reduce to a dangerously small number the strength of the house of David.

The Chronicler makes clear that Jehoram walks "in the ways of the kings of Israel"; that is, he participates in the Baal cult rather than the worship of God in the Temple. The Chronicler ascribes this apostasy to the fact that the wife of Jehoram is Athaliah, daughter of Ahab and Jezebel. Those familiar with the narrative of 1 and 2 Kings will recall that Jezebel was a Sidonian princess married to Ahab as part of an alliance between Israel and Sidon (1 Kings 16:31). Jezebel either introduced or, more likely, advocated for the already existing worship of the Canaanite deity Baal in Israel. Both Kings and Chronicles view the presence of Athaliah in Judah as a similar advocacy for Baal in the South. Thus, in the heart of the house of David, a dynasty personally bound by covenant to the Lord, the Baal cult is being openly practiced and encouraged. Small wonder that the Chronicler's evaluation of Jehoram is that "he did what was evil in the sight of the LORD." Only because of the covenantal bond between king and God does God refrain from destroying the house of David. Despite the rigid consistency with which the Chronicler often applies his theological system of moral responsibility, he does not have a wooden or mechanistic view of God. God is consistently gracious and merciful and, above all, faithful to the divine commitment to the house of David.

   2. The revolts of Edom and Libnah, 21:8–10. The political disasters of the revolts by Edom and Libnah are the only pieces of information provided about Jehoram in the source narrative in 2 Kings 8:20–22. The Chronicler faithfully transmits them here not only because they are present in this source but because the revolts of subject peoples against the king seem to follow as punishment for the king's apostasy. Edom, the kingdom to the south and east of Judah beyond the Dead Sea, is variously under and out of the control of Judahite kings throughout the monarchy. A revolt by the Edomites therefore would not have been so unusual. More disturbing, however, is Jehoram's inability to bring the Edomites to heel. In fact, Jehoram is ambushed by Edomite forces and forced to fight his way out. The Chronicler omits the datum from 2 Kings 8:21 that "his [i.e., Jehoram's] army fled home," thereby sparing the Judahites the indignity of cowardice. But there can be no doubt from the text that Jehoram's campaign was a failure.

Even more unsettling is the revolt of Libnah. Libnah had long been a Judahite city, located in the western hill country (the "Shephelah") north of Lachish. Several Judahite cities had long contained significant populations of Canaanite and perhaps Philistine people, and the Libnah revolt may be traceable to them as an effort to throw off an unwanted Jerusalemite hegemony. Whatever its origins, that a Judahite city should cast aside its loyalty to the throne of David is a signal of the weakness of the king.

3. Elijah's letter and the death of Jehoram, 21:11–20. The main thrust of the Chronicler's presentation of the reign of Jehoram is the letter from Elijah, an element unique to the Chronicler. Elijah was a northern prophet whose ministry was concurrent with the Israelite kings Ahab and his son Ahaziah; there is no record of his having ventured involvement in the political and religious life of the Southern Kingdom. However, according to the succession data in 2 Kings 1:17, Ahaziah's death occurs in the second year of the reign of Jehoram of Judah, and so perhaps some contact between the two is not impossible. Still, the language and theology of Elijah's letter here are so typical of the Chronicler that it is hard to see these verses as anything other than his composition.

The Chronicler justifies the unusual event of the prophetic letter by noting that Jehoram was specifically responsible for leading "the inhabitants of Jerusalem into unfaithfulness" and making "Judah go astray." That Jehoram is personally apostate is not bad enough; he must also instigate and abet the moral decline of his people as well. Jehoram's innovations with Baalism merit, in the eyes of the Chronicler, a rebuke from the greatest and most entrenched opponent of Baalism in Israel's history, Elijah.

21:12 A letter came to him from the prophet Elijah, saying: "Thus says the LORD, the God of your father David: Because you have not walked in the ways of your father Jehoshaphat or in the ways of King Asa of Judah, 13 but have walked in the ways of the kings of Israel, and have led Judah and the inhabitants of Jerusalem into unfaithfulness, as the house of Ahab led Israel into unfaithfulness, and because you also have killed your brothers, members of your father's house, who were better than yourself, 14 see, the LORD will bring a great plague on your people, your children, your wives, and all your possessions, 15 and you yourself will have a severe sickness with a disease of your bowels, until your bowels come out, day after day, because of the disease."

The prophet's letter contrasts two "ways": one the way of David, Jehoshaphat, and Asa, and the other the "way of the kings of Israel." The former is the way of obedience, leading people to covenant with the

Lord, seeking the Lord in the Temple; the latter is the way of apostasy with Baal and meddling in Canaanite tradition, which leads invariably to faithlessness and disaster. Elijah's charge against Jehoram is that he has chosen the latter—and wrong—way. In addition, Jehoram has committed fratricide within the royal house. The murder of his brothers is not merely murder; it is also an assault on the security of the throne of David. For these crimes, Jehoram and his people—and especially his wives and children—will suffer from a great plague (which will also affect "all [his] possessions," a curious notion). And as if that loss were not personal enough, a sickness described in graphic detail will assault the bowels of the king himself. No more personal and intimate a punishment for sin could be devised.

The remainder of the narrative spells out the fulfillment of Elijah's announcement in specific acts. Arabs and Philistines attack Jehoram, and they seem particularly bent on depriving the king of his family and possessions. The Chronicler's location of the Arabs and Philistines as "near the Ethiopians" is problematic. At the time of Jehoram's reign, Ethiopian control over Egypt and the Sinai was more than a century away; by the time of the Chronicler's own day, Ethiopians had been removed as players in Palestinian politics for more than two centuries. Perhaps the Chronicler follows a tendency already visible in 2 Kings to blur the distinction between Egypt and Ethiopia, especially in the later centuries of the Judahite monarchy. At any rate, the focused nature of the raid by Philistines and Arabs—an attack on the family and property of the king alone—seems strange and conveniently correspondent to the prophecy of Elijah. Even more obviously linked to Elijah's letter is the account of Jehoram's disease. No modern diagnosis need be applied here; for the purpose of the Chronicler, the king's malady is more theological than physical.

His death after an eight-year reign is apparently greeted with no outpouring of public grief. The people of Jerusalem "made no fire in his honor" as was made for Asa (16:14). More telling still is the unique and sarcastic comment, a rare revelation of the Chronicler's own personality perhaps, that "he departed with no one's regret."

THE REIGN OF AHAZIAH
2 Chronicles 22:1–9

As a preface to the comment on this section, we should note the ease with which names of kings are confused in this period. Names of kings in both Israel and Judah are similar, probably because members of the Omride dynasty of Israel were part of both royal families. Ahab's two successors are his sons, Ahaziah and Jehoram (also called "Joram" in both Kings and Chronicles). The latter is slain by Jehu in the coup and purge described in 2 Kings 9. Jehoshaphat of Judah, contemporary of Ahab, is also succeeded by kings named Jehoram and Ahaziah, but they are his son and grandson, respectively. Jehoram of Judah was married to Athaliah, the daughter of Ahab, and it is this same Athaliah who will seize the throne of David in Jerusalem after the death of her son Ahaziah of Judah.

The Chronicler's presentation of the reign of Ahaziah is a drastically abbreviated version of 2 Kings 8:25–10:14, the dominant feature of which is the coup by Jehu against Jehoram of Israel. The political upheaval of the Northern Kingdom, resulting in the death of the last of Ahab's sons and the murder of Ahab's wife Jezebel, spills over into the Southern Kingdom, as well. Ahaziah son of Jehoram of Judah has gone to visit the Israelite king and is killed as part of the purge of Ahab's descendants by Jehu. For the Kings narrative, the focus is on Jehu and his purge. For the Chronicler, the focus is on the death of Ahaziah and the creation of a succession crisis in Judah.

The account begins with the note that "the inhabitants of Jerusalem made [Jehoram's] youngest son Ahaziah king as his successor." In view of the normal practice of the inheritance of the throne by the eldest son, the elevation of Ahaziah is unusual and necessitated by the removal of all the other children by the invading Arabs and Philistines (see 21:17). Ahaziah is listed as forty-two years old at the time of his accession; this is clearly impossible if Jehoram was only forty at the time of his death (see 21:20). In all probability, the text is in error here and should read "twenty-two," as in 2 Kings 8:25. The Chronicler adds two phrases to the Kings description of Ahaziah: the notes that "his mother was his counselor in doing wickedly," and that the Omrides "were his counselors, to his ruin." The intent of these additions is to lay the blame for the moral and spiritual decay of Judah at the feet of Athaliah and the Omride influence she introduced into Jerusalem.

The disastrous invasion of Ramoth-gilead serves primarily to place Ahaziah within reach of Jehu. The wounding of Jehoram of Israel and Ahaziah's visit to his relative and colleague serve to situate both kings in the Jezreel Valley, where they are attacked by Jehu. This latter figure is, according to 2 Kings 9:1, anointed by agents of the prophet Elisha to overthrow the descendants of Ahab and rid Israel of the influence of the Baal cult. The Chronicler does not mention Jehu's prophetic backing, but he does make clear that Ahaziah's death was "ordained by God." In the 2 Kings 9 narrative, the killing of Ahaziah is almost an afterthought; it is necessary because, by virtue of his mother Athaliah, he is a member of the family of Ahab. In 2 Chronicles 22, on the other hand, the purpose of the narrative is the death of Ahaziah; the execution of judgment on the house of Ahab is dealt with in a temporal clause in a sentence focused otherwise on Ahaziah. Ahaziah, the king of Jerusalem, meets his end not in his own city but hiding in the city of his mother's family, Samaria. Nonetheless, he is treated with respect in death because he is the grandson of Jehoshaphat.

The account of Ahaziah's reign ends with the note that "the house of Ahaziah had no one able to rule the kingdom." After Jehoram's fratricides in 21:4 and the deportation of the royal family in 21:17, the death of Ahaziah leaves no one able to occupy the throne of David. The crisis of succession has now dawned, and into the power vacuum in Jerusalem steps the Omride queen mother, Athaliah.

ATHALIAH'S USURPATION AND THE TEMPLE COUP
2 Chronicles 22:10–23:21

These verses mark the only point at which a person not a lineal descendant of David sits on the throne of David in Jerusalem. For the Chronicler, whose view of David is that he and his house were elected by God for perpetual rule in Jerusalem, this is a crisis of the first order.

At center stage in this drama are three characters: two strong, decisive women, Athaliah and Jehoshebeath, and the priest Jehoiada. Athaliah, the daughter of the Israelite king Ahab and wife of Jehoram by virtue of an alliance between Jehoshaphat of Judah and her father, is with the death of her son Ahaziah the only adult claimant to the throne. She takes power, perhaps initially as a sort of regency, but then immediately moves to exterminate all remaining members of the Davidic royal line. Jehoshabeath, daughter of Jehoram and (half-?) sister of Ahaziah, stands over against Athaliah in allegiance to the house of David; she sees to it that the infant Joash, the last remaining Davidide, is stolen away from the killing of the others and kept in the Temple in secret throughout his early childhood. The Chronicler adds the note to his description of Jehoshabeath that she is not only a member of the royal family but also "wife of the priest Jehoiada"; she is thus doubly committed to the preservations of the twin institutions of monarchy and Temple that have characterized the best of Judah and Jerusalem. The priest Jehoiada is the instigator of the revolt against Athaliah. When the child king reaches the age of seven, Jehoiada decides that the time for action has come. Marshalling the forces of the Levites, he carefully reveals the identity of the king to them and arranges for the uprising that will place the child on the throne.

The Chronicler has drawn faithfully on his source narrative in 2 Kings 11 but again has edited and augmented his source in such a way as to produce a very different picture of the coup. Where the Kings narrative presents us with a small, secret cabal of killers who remove and execute Athaliah, the Chronicler makes clear that the events in the Temple are carried out by "all the people" of Judah and that the king is so acclaimed not by a small group of power brokers but by the nation as a whole. Where the work of guarding king and Temple is assigned to a military guard in Kings, in Chronicles it is the responsibility of the Levites to guard both.

1. The rescue of Joash, 22:10–12. We have noted above the strong priestly involvement in the rescue of the line of David. Not only is Jehoiada the central planner and commander of the coup but his wife Jehoshabeath is the guardian and caretaker for the infant king. There is also a subtler image to be seen here, in the fact that the Temple itself shelters and protects the child Joash.

22:12 **he remained with them six years, hidden in the house of God, while Athaliah reigned over the land.**

The child is quite literally nurtured in the Temple and there kept safe from the murderous intentions of Athaliah. It will be from this same house of God that the house of David will be re-proclaimed and its rule reestablished. One cannot read these verses without having in mind the divine promise to David in 17:10 that "the LORD will build you a house."

2. The coup and death of Athaliah, 23:1–15. After six years of nursing and guarding the child Joash, Jehoiada decides that the time has come to make his presence known and to challenge Athaliah for the throne of David. He makes a covenant with the leaders of Judah's army and through them the Levites, and all gather in the Temple for the dramatic revelation of the child king. Having seen him, they are told what positions to take up and what to do when the critical moment arises. The king is then presented to the people, and the noise of their celebration alerts Athaliah. She emerges from the palace to be captured by Jehoiada's strategically placed forces and is led away to be executed.

It is important to the Chronicler that the coup is led by a priest and conducted by the Levites, who are stationed by Jehoiada around the Temple and palace. In other words, its leadership is clerical rather than strictly political. Rather than allowing the retiring Levites to go off duty at the end of their watch, Jehoiada has them remain on station and uses their colleagues otherwise scheduled to take up their places as guards for the young king. The account is explicit that only Levites are permitted within the Temple, "for they are holy, but all the other people shall observe the instructions of the LORD" (v. 6). The Chronicler is careful to maintain the righteousness of the coup. Nothing less than careful obedience to the law will do; the dynasty founded upon the promise of God cannot be restored in disobedience to God's instructions. Both Temple and dynasty have been compromised by the incursion of the Baalist Athaliah; they cannot be restored by compromised obedience.

Jehoiada's presentation of the young king Joash in verse 3 should also be noted with some care:

> Here is the king's son! Let him reign, as the LORD promised concerning the sons of David.

A better translation of the Hebrew would be:

> "See, the son of the king reigns, just as the LORD promised concerning the sons of David."

Rendering the phrase in this way clarifies the point Jehoiada seeks to make here: that the child is none other than the son of Ahaziah and that, despite all expectations, he now reigns from David's throne. God has delivered on the divine promise to establish the throne of David.

The force of Levites guarding the young king is armed with spears and shields from the armory of David placed in the Temple. The source of these weapons is unclear; perhaps they were brought to the Temple as votive offerings after successful military campaigns (see 1 Chron. 26:26 and 2 Chron 15:8). What is important is not the source of the weapons but their symbolic value; they are, quite literally, the arms of David, brought from David's house, to protect the youngest scion of David's house.

Joash receives the crown of his office from the priest Jehoiada, yet another symbol of the religious foundation upon which the royal ideology of Judah rests. The people make a "covenant" with him, although the phrase would actually be better translated "bear a witness to him" in the sense that they agree that this one is of the house of David and is therefore the rightful heir to the throne. At this point, they publicly acclaim him with the ancient shout of "Long live the king!"

Athaliah now emerges onto the scene, decrying the coup as treason. The cry is certainly ironic. In the sense that any uprising against the monarch is treason, Athaliah is right; in the sense by which the Chronicler assesses justice, the coup is the righteous punishment for her own treason. For indeed, it was her "treason" against the rightful worship of God that led the heirs of Jehoram into this crisis of succession.

Respectful of the Temple and its laws, the Chronicler does not requite Athaliah's treason within the courts of the Temple but in the palace stable gate. No bloodshed thus tarnishes the Temple or renders it unclean.

3. The covenant and reforms of Jehoiada, 23:16–21. Having rid the city and kingdom of Athaliah and proclaimed Joash as king, Jehoiada proceeds to act as regent for the young king and to reform his kingdom. The first act of reformation is the making of a new covenant with the people to "be the LORD's people." The obvious implication of this covenant is the disavowal of the Baalism so recently practiced in the city; consequently, the crowd immediately acts to destroy the Baal temple in Jerusalem and execute the priest. Jehoiada then assigns Levites to their appropriate stations, offering burnt offerings in the Temple and standing watch at the gates, according to the instruction of Moses as ordered by David. With the reestablishment of the Levitical priests in their offices, the Temple restoration is accomplished. The military guard then escorts Joash to his throne, accompanied by the rejoicing of the populace. The city is then "quiet," and the sense of the text is that the peace of righteousness has at long last been restored. Tragically, it would be a short-lived peace.

THE REIGN OF JOASH
2 Chronicles 24:1–27

The Chronicler's evaluation of Joash, the young king in whom the hope of restoration and restitution is lodged, is initially a positive one: "Joash did what was right." However, the Chronicler qualifies the statement with the note that Joash's righteousness is limited to "all the days of Jehoiada." This one clause signals a change in the behavior and fortunes of the king; having begun well under the tutelage of the priest, Joash ends badly under his own guidance. The chapter falls easily into two parts: the first period while Jehoiada is still alive (vv. 1–16), and the second after the old priest's death (vv. 17–27).

1. The first period of Joash's reign, 24:1–16. Joash's reign begins well enough: After providing the initial information of age at the time of accession and mother's name, the Chronicler indicates that "Joash did what was right in the sight of the LORD all the days of the priest Jehoiada." The statement serves two purposes. As indicated above, it is a literary signal that the reign of Joash will go seriously awry after the death of the priest. But it is also a reminder that the king is a minor when he ascends to the throne and is thus under the regency of the priest, who sees to it that the king does "what is right." Jehoiada's care for Joash extends to the point of securing wives for him, with whom he might sire children to assure the continuation of the Davidic line, an important accomplishment in view of the recent crisis of succession (22:10–12).

Joash's first major act as king is to undertake repairs to the Temple. Not only is this a royal duty, but it is necessitated by the years of neglect of the Temple at the hands of Athaliah and her family (v .7). In order to effect the repairs, Joash assigns the Levites to

24:4 . . . "Go out to the cities of Judah and gather money from all Israel to repair the house of your God, year by year; and see that you act quickly."

Joash has a precedent for such a collection. Exodus 30:12–16 and 38:25–26 prescribe the collection on the Day of Atonement of a half-shekel tax for the maintenance of the tabernacle. Neither passage indicates how the tax is to be collected, however; furthermore, the initiative of the king in ordering the Levites out into the countryside to gather it may indicate that the collection of the tax had lapsed altogether. The addition of this responsibility may be the reason for the Levites' reluctance to obey the king; the Chronicler tells us in verse 6 that "the Levites did not act quickly." The king takes this as resistance to obeying not only his own commands but the dictates of Moses as well, and he upbraids Jehoiada for permitting the failure. It is a strained moment in the relationship between the king and priest.

The strain is resolved by the king: He orders the creation of a wooden chest for the collection of the tax. Abandoning the idea that the tax would be collected throughout the countryside (where the proceeds would have been larger), the king settles for allowing the half-shekel to be collected from those who come to the Temple (vv. 8–9). The Chronicler's note identifying the tax as the "tax that Moses the servant of God laid on Israel in the wilderness" (v. 9) serves to indicate that the Temple collection now takes the place of the king's order. The money is dropped in a chest created at the king's behest and set by the Temple gate. The people appear delighted to pay the tax, and soon the chest is overflowing with money. Agents of both the king and the priest are assigned to empty the box and count the money, again a sign that mistrust exists between them. Under mutual observation, however, the collection goes well, and the repairs are paid for in good order. So much is collected, in fact, that there is money left over to refashion the utensils for use within the Temple. The Chronicler's point in preserving this story seems to be both to hint at the growing rift between king and priest and to say that a common dedication on the part of both to the proper service of God results in the accomplishment of good things for Judah.

The death of Jehoiada brings this narrative to a close. The priest is buried with royal honors, perhaps because he has functioned as de facto king for much of his life. The Chronicler's evaluation of his life is particularly interesting: "He had done good in Israel, and for God and his house." In the end, the contribution of the priest is measured not by his political importance but by his ministry in the house of God on behalf of God and God's people.

2. The second part of the reign, 24:17–27. Although the first part of Joash's reign is positive, the second is negative; indeed, the negativity of the second so exceeds the righteousness of the first that it is hard to see the two as the reign of the same king. Bereft of his spiritual advisor, Joash relies on the counsel of "officials of Judah." Their advice is to abandon the worship of God in favor of the sacred poles and idols of the Baal cult. In a particularly ironic comment, the Chronicler tells us that the king and his advisors "abandoned the house of the LORD" (v. 18), the very same house that had sheltered and protected Joash during his infancy and childhood, from which he had been crowned and anointed king, and for the repairs of which he had gone to much trouble.

The "wrath" that falls upon Judah as a result of this apostasy is not specified, unless this is a summary comment referring to the Aramean invasion in verses 23–24. What the Chronicler seems more interested in explaining is that the waywardness of the king and the officials was the occasion for multiple warnings by various unnamed prophets. At stake in this section is a larger theme being built by the Chronicler as we turn toward the last chapters of the work: the theme of the ignored prophetic warning. For the Chronicler, the prophet is the mouthpiece of God, articulating the divine will and clarifying events in light of that will. That the warnings of prophets should go unheeded, as they do here, is equivalent to ignoring the word of God. In the end, it is this very tendency to ignore the prophetic warning and change the nation's ways that results in the destruction of Jerusalem and the downfall of the house of David (see 36:15).

As if to crystallize this problem, the Chronicler offers us the narrative of Zechariah, the son of Jehoiada the priest. That Joash will not listen even to this one, who is closest to the priest who nurtured and guided him, is evidence of the desperate nature of the king's decline.

24:20 Then the spirit of God took possession of Zechariah son of the priest Jehoiada; he stood above the people and said to them, "Thus says God: Why do you transgress the commandments of the LORD, so that you cannot prosper? Because you have forsaken the LORD, he has also forsaken you." [21] But they conspired against him, and by command of the king they stoned him to death in the court of the house of the LORD. ²² King Joash did not remember the kindness that Jehoiada, Zechariah's father, had shown him, but killed his son. As he was dying, he said, "May the LORD see and avenge!"

Zechariah's warnings are couched in the language of the Chronicler, except in negative form. The familiar refrain to "seek the LORD" became its antithesis in the charge, "you have forsaken the LORD"; the promise of David to Solomon that "the LORD is/will be with you" (1 Chron. 22:16; 28:20) becomes "[the LORD] has also forsaken you." Yet the warnings go unheeded again, and the king commands the murder of Zechariah. The stoning of the prophet is a criminal act on several levels. First, it is the murder of an innocent person, accomplished without process and at the whim of the king. Second, the murder of a prophet is always a criminal act, as it amounts to an assault on the being of God. Third, in murdering Jehoiada's son, Joash forgets his covenantal obligations with and to Jehoiada, obligations taken up on the day he was announced as king (23:16). Finally, the murder takes place "in the court of the house of the LORD," surely intended by the Chronicler as a final irony in light of the fact that Zechariah's father would not permit the slaying of Athaliah in the Temple. What was a safe and sacred place for Jehoiada becomes the dying place for Jehoiada's son.

Zechariah's death cry for divine vengeance is the theme for the rest of the Chronicler's narrative of Joash's reign. The defeat of Judah by the king of Aram is otherwise unrecorded but clearly serves the Chronicler's theological interest. The very officials who counsel Joash to apostasy are now destroyed. Moreover, the defeat of Judah's army comes at the hands of a numerically smaller Aramean foe. We have seen the theme of the smaller army defeating the greater because of the intervention of God, but heretofore the intervention has always been on Judah's behalf. Now God "delivered into their [i.e., the Arameans'] hand a very great army." The reason for the defeat and this reversed divine intervention is simple: "because they had abandoned the LORD" (v. 24).

Having been wounded in the fight, Joash falls victim to a palace conspiracy and is assassinated in his own bed. The reason given is vengeance for the execution of Zechariah. The method of assassination—stabbing to death—recalls the death of Athaliah in the palace stable gate. Once again, the irony is thick: The one who represented the hope for Jerusalem and Judah out of the darkness of apostasy has been stabbed to death in a manner little different from the way in which the queen died whose evil reign he was to have undone. The Chronicler finishes the evaluation with two other noteworthy comments. First, we are told that he was not buried with the kings, usually the sure sign by which the

Chronicler expresses his general sense of disapproval of a king's reign. Second, the Chronicler makes reference to the "many oracles against him" recorded in the "Commentary on the Book of the Kings."

THE REIGN OF AMAZIAH
2 Chronicles 25:1–28

The Chronicler presents Amaziah as another in the familiar series of good kings gone bad. The story of Amaziah's decline into apostasy and sin, told in verses 5–16, is largely the creation of the Chronicler. As we have noted before, in the Chronicler's theology of moral responsibility, the evil that befalls an individual must have its roots in some lack of faithfulness in that individual's life. The source narrative for the reign of Amaziah, 2 Kings 14:1–20, contains no account of Amaziah's unfaithfulness significant enough to warrant the defeat and imprisonment Amaziah suffers at the hands of the northern king Joash. The Chronicler therefore builds such an account from the reference to the invasion of Edom in 2 Kings 14:7.

The account of Amaziah's reign contains four sections: an introduction (vv. 1–4), the narrative of the invasion of Edom and the king's apostasy (vv. 5–16), the narrative of the invasion of Israel (vv. 17–24), and Amaziah's death and regnal summary (vv. 25–28).

1. Introduction, 25:1–4.

25:1 **Amaziah was twenty-five years old when he began to reign, and he reigned twenty-nine years in Jerusalem. His mother's name was Jehoaddan of Jerusalem.** [2] **He did what was right in the sight of the LORD, yet not with a true heart.** [3] **As soon as the royal power was firmly in his hand he killed his servants who had murdered his father the king.** [4] **But he did not put their children to death, according to what is written in the law, in the book of Moses, where the LORD commanded, "The parents shall not be put to death for the children, or the children be put to death for the parents; but all shall be put to death for their own sins."**

The Chronicler's evaluation of Amaziah is unique and striking; initially positive, it contains a note of foreboding: "He did what was right in the sight of the LORD, yet not with a true heart." The final phrase evokes both the language of Deuteronomy 6:5, "You shall love the LORD your God with all your heart," and of the piety of Asa (who led his people "to seek the LORD . . . with all their heart" [2 Chron. 15:12]). The phrase is a window into the Chronicler's understanding of true religious devotion; if such devotion is not carried through with the whole being, it is shallow and doomed to failure.

Having attained the throne, Amaziah predictably executes justice on those responsible for the assassination of his father, Joash. The Chronicler is careful to note, however, that the punishment is limited to the perpetrators themselves and does not extend to their families. In this he can claim for Amaziah a greater righteousness than the Omride-influenced Jehoram, Ahaziah, or Athaliah, each of whom conducted purges of their enemies upon coming to power. More important, however, Amaziah's actions are in this instance reflective of the system of divine mercy and justice as the Chronicler understands it, limiting the consequences of an evil deed to the lives of those directly responsible for it.

2. *The invasion of Edom and Amaziah's apostasy, 25:5–16.* The first of the two major episodes recorded for Amaziah's reign is the invasion of Edom. The king carries out a census of his people, undoubtedly oriented toward the development of a system of conscription, and recruits an army of some three hundred thousand men. While such a force would have been, in real terms, a sizeable army for the ancient Near East, in the orders of magnitude employed by the Chronicler for military strength it is comparatively small. Apparently seeking to augment his forces, Amaziah hires one hundred thousand Israelite mercenaries. This action brings swift reaction from an unnamed prophet ("a man of God") who demands that Amaziah dismiss the northerners because "the LORD is not with Israel." Behind the prophetic condemnation of the plan to use mercenaries lie two main objections the Chronicler has voiced before. First, by employing foreigners in a Judahite enterprise, Judah entangles itself in foreign alliances that invariably bring trouble (see 16:7–9; 19:2; and 20:35–37). Second, the involvement of foreigners to enhance the size of the army obscures the Chronicler's basic theological commitment about warfare, that is, that it belongs to God and is won not by military strength or stratagem but by faith and obedience. The prophet assures the king that only if he entrusts the battle to God will the outcome be favorable. The king agrees, but only after fretting about the money lost in wasted payment of the mercenaries; the prophet's response is to assure the king again that if he will entrust himself to God, all losses will be repaid. It seems worthy of note that, although Amaziah does indeed obey the prophet, the loss of the money is never recouped. This is probably attributable to the fact that Amaziah himself becomes unfaithful to God by the end of the narrative.

Amaziah's victory over the Edomites is dramatic: ten thousand killed and another ten thousand captured. The slaughter of the captives by pushing them off the top of a high cliff so that they are "dashed to pieces" (v. 12) is barbaric to modern sensibilities, particularly in an era in which nations at war are expected to adhere to conventions that include humane treatment of prisoners of war. However, from the perspective of the ancient world and of the Chronicler himself, the Edomites are the enemies of God whose appropriate fate is extermination. Admittedly, this explanation does little to make such executions more palatable. However, before we are too ready to criticize the ancient world from the values of the modern, we should perhaps recall that our own century has demonstrated no small facility with barbarism.

While Amaziah and his Judahite army are laying waste to the Edomites, Israelite mercenaries released from service with Judah are laying waste to cities between Samaria and Beth-horon. The reason for the raids is probably to be sought in the fact that, once released from the invasion force, they were denied any expectation of sharing in the spoils of the campaign. Apparently they decide to extract booty from their former employers. The Chronicler's inclusion of this detail appears to serve no purpose other than to provide a pretext for Amaziah's invasion of Israel (vv. 17–24). However, the cities ransacked by the Israelites hardly appear to be Judahite; territory between Samaria and Beth-horon was traditionally regarded as Israelite. It may be that some of these towns are among those captured by Abijah (13:19), although this cannot be determined.

What had been a successful campaign turns disastrous from the Chronicler's point of view when Amaziah decides to install in the Temple and worship the captured gods of Edom. It was not unusual for victorious kings to bring back religious statuary from conquered peoples; the installation of foreign deities in subsidiary positions in the sanctuary of the conqueror was understood as a symbol of the subjection of the defeated deity to the conquering deity. It may be that Amaziah does nothing more than this. But the Chronicler's radically monotheistic theology leaves no room for other gods, even conquered ones. The installation of foreign deities in the Temple of God is therefore tantamount to acknowledgement of their existence and permission to worship them. This is apostasy for the Chronicler and is completely unacceptable. It merits a sharp prophetic rebuke, the second time Amaziah has been corrected by the prophets.

The exchange between the prophet and the king in verse 16 employs a wordplay not immediately obvious in English:

25:16 **But as he was speaking the king said to him, "Have we made you a royal counselor? Stop! Why should you be put to death?" So the prophet stopped, but said, "I know that God has determined to destroy you, because you have done this and have not listened to my advice."**
17 **Then King Amaziah took counsel . . . .**

Rather than accepting the prophetic critique and adjusting his behavior as he had done before, the king challenges the prophet: "Have we made you a royal counselor?" The answer anticipated by this rhetorical question is, of course, negative; prophets do not have royal authority to make or critique royal policy. But the prophet's response takes the matter beyond the level of royal authority. The prophet needs no permission from the king; his authority is from God: "God has determined to destroy you." The verb translated "determined" by the NRSV is the same as the root for the word "counsel/counselor" in Hebrew; to translate as the NRSV does at this point may be clearer but obscures the wordplay intended here. Perhaps a better rendering would be "God has taken counsel to destroy you." Having rejected the prophet's "counsel," Amaziah turns to the "counsel" (v. 17) of others, a decision that leads directly to his ruin. This is the heart of the Chronicler's critique of Amaziah: Rather than seek the counsel of the Lord "with a true heart," he seeks other, more foolish counsel, which courts inevitable disaster.

3. The invasion of Israel, 25:17–24.

> 25:17 **Then King Amaziah of Judah took counsel and sent to King Joash son of Jehoahaz son of Jehu of Israel, saying, "Come, let us look one another in the face."** [18] **King Joash of Israel sent word to King Amaziah of Judah, "A thornbush on Lebanon sent to a cedar on Lebanon, saying, 'Give your daughter to my son for a wife'; but a wild animal of Lebanon passed by and trampled down the thorn bush.** [19] **You say, 'See, I have defeated Edom,' and your heart has lifted you up in boastfulness. Now stay at home; why should you provoke trouble so that you fall, you and Judah with you?"**
> [20] **But Amaziah would not listen—it was God's doing, in order to hand them over, because they had sought the gods of Edom.**

Amaziah's word to Joash of Israel, "Come, let us look one another in the face," is clearly intended to be provocative, either because it implies a military challenge or because it assumes that the two are equals, a claim Joash would surely deny. Joash's response in verse 18, therefore, should be understood as condescending and sarcastic. It is couched in the language of fable: A thistle makes bold to propose marriage to a great cedar but is trampled in the end by a forest animal. While attempts to read this parable as an allegory should be resisted, the parable's meaning is clear enough: Amaziah, like the thistle, is puffed up with pride, perhaps after his Edomite victory, and he believes himself stronger than he is. Joash makes the point in nonmetaphorical terms in the following verse, along with the counsel to "stay at home."

Joash's words are intended to be understood as wise counsel. That they come from someone outside Judah and not from a prophetic figure is somewhat striking. We will see this phenomenon again and at a more crucial juncture: Josiah will refuse to hear the wise counsel of the pharaoh of

Egypt in 35:22, and for his failure will lose his life. Here, also, Amaziah chooses to ignore the wisdom offered to him and pursues the foolhardy invasion of the North. Just as Joash promised, the invasion ends in ignominious defeat for Judah and for Amaziah personally. The army of Judah is completely demolished at Beth-shemesh (a town about fifteen miles southwest of Jerusalem, indicating that the battle was in Judahite, rather than Israelite, territory), and the demoralized Judahites flee the field, abandoning their king to capture. Worse still, Jerusalem itself is assaulted and violated, and the Temple treasuries are ransacked. The phrase "and Obed-edom with them" (v. 24) is curious; the caretaker of the ark from the era of David (see 1 Chron. 13:14 and 15:24) must have been long dead, so perhaps it is his remains that are mentioned here. On the other hand, the phrase may be sarcastic; "Obed-edom" means "servant of Edom," perhaps a snide reference to Amaziah's worship of the captured Edomite gods.

Amaziah's imprisonment by Joash is of uncertain duration; there is no clear indication in the text about its length. We know only that Joash took Amaziah with him as a prisoner while he ransacked Jerusalem. It may be that the "hostages" taken by Joash to Israel are taken in exchange for the king and that the king himself was freed when Joash returned to Samaria.

4. Amaziah's death, 25:25–28. The Chronicler records the death of Amaziah as the result of yet another palace conspiracy. That two such cabals have brought about the deaths of two consecutive kings, and these after the Jehoiada coup against Athaliah in 2 Chronicles 23, is indicative of the unrest that plagues Judahite history.

The Chronicler, of course, is not interested in questions of politics. In his system, that which drives events is the morality and faithfulness (or lack thereof) of God's people and their king. Amaziah's troubles, therefore, are traceable not to the pressures of international empires off the stage of action but rather to Amaziah's own faithlessness; they begin "from the time that Amaziah turned away from the LORD" (v. 27). As a final symbol of the distance between God and the king, when the conspiracy against him breaks out, he seeks shelter not in Jerusalem, traditional sanctuary of the king, but in Lachish. Of course, even there the king is not safe but is hunted down and slain. The narrative of Amaziah that began with such promise thus ends in dismal failure.

THE REIGN OF UZZIAH
2 Chronicles 26:1–23

Uzziah, the second-longest reigning king in Judah's history (Manasseh's reign of fifty-five years is the longest), is hurried to the throne in the wake of his father's assassination. The source for the Chronicler's account of Uzziah's reign is 2 Kings 15:1–7, a relatively short narrative when compared to the length of the present account. The reason for the difference between the two is that the Chronicler has significantly expanded on his source with the addition of two episodes. The first is an embellishment on 2 Kings 15:3 that he "did what was right in the sight of the LORD." The second is an effort to solve a theological problem presented to the Chronicler by the fact of Uzziah's leprosy. How could such a good king come to be cursed with lifelong leprosy so that he must spend that life as an outcast?

The narrative of Uzziah's reign may be treated in four sections: an introduction (vv. 1–4), the catalogue of Uzziah's accomplishments and blessings (vv. 5–15), the story of Uzziah's invasion of the Temple (vv. 16–21), and the account of his death and burial (vv. 22–23).

1. Introduction, 26:1–4. The Chronicler augments the usual information about the king's age at accession, length of reign, and mother's name with three notes. The first is that Uzziah recovered the town of Eloth (an alternate spelling for Elath, the port city on the Gulf of Elath, presumably lost during the Edomite revolt against Amaziah). The second is that he "did what was right in the sight of the LORD," the standard positive evaluative comment on a king's reign. The comment is qualified by the addition, "just as his father Amaziah had done." As we already know, Amaziah's obedience faltered as he became stronger; the same pattern is present for Uzziah, and this is probably what the Chronicler seeks to signal by using this phrase. The third note is that Uzziah "set himself to seek God," the Chronicler's special commendation of the king's piety and faithfulness. However, once again the praise is limited by qualification: "As long as he sought the LORD, God made him prosper." The implication is, of course, that Uzziah's good fortune is directly related to his commitment to right worship and obedience to the law and that once that obedience is violated, his fortunes will turn for the worse. This is precisely the pattern of Uzziah's reign, at least in the hands of the Chronicler, and thus his comment here might be seen as a "seeding" of the plot of the narrative.

2. The catalogue of Uzziah's accomplishments and blessings, 26:5–15. The Chronicler's first lengthy addition to his source serves to flesh out the summary comment of verse 5: "As long as he sought the LORD, God made him prosper." The construction projects, international repute, agricultural productivity, and military strength are all tangible evidence of God's blessing for Uzziah's faithfulness. That all these are divine blessings is signaled by the final, summary comment of the section: "He was marvelously helped until he became strong."

Uzziah's military activity is directed against old enemies: Philistines, Arabs, and Meunites in the west and south, and Ammonites in the east. He succeeds in campaigns against the former, "breaking down the walls" of Philistine cities. From the latter he is able to extract tribute, a payment of significant money in lieu of conquest and plunder. In neither case does the text support the claim that Uzziah conquered this territory for inclusion in any expansion of his borders; instead, the military activity appears to be more raid than systematic conquest. The sum total of the activity is that "he became very strong" (v. 8) and that his renown reached as far as Egypt.

Civic construction is a standard sign of a king's material prosperity, and Uzziah is credited with the construction of towers—in Jerusalem (part of the city's defenses) and in the wilderness (observation posts from which to see the approach of an enemy)—and cisterns (large water storage facilities). Uzziah is credited with large herds and significant agricultural resources in the form of farmlands and vineyards. While these would certainly have supplied the king's table, they are also probably for the support of the army.

Uzziah's army is not as large as some fielded by Israelite or Judahite kings, at least as claimed by the Chronicler, but it is sizeable enough to be seen as a blessing and a source of strength. The Chronicler's principal interest seems to be in describing the armament employed by the army. The list of weapons includes nothing out of the ordinary for an army of the day: Shields, spears, bows, and sling stones were all standard weapons. "Coats of mail," however, has an anachronistic flavor. The intent here is almost certainly not to describe material made of interlocking metal rings of the type worn by knights of the Middle Ages but rather body armor made of leather, perhaps with some sheets of beaten metal to protect against arrow pierces. Most interesting, however, is the reference to machines set up on the walls of Jerusalem. The description is curiously elliptical; "devices, the devising of devisers" is a literal translation of the Hebrew phrase rendered more sensibly by the NRSV: "machines, invented by skilled workers." They appear to be catapults, although if both arrows and large stones were thrown by the same mechanism it would have been an unusual catapult. Whatever their nature, it is clear that they were defensive in purpose because they were posted on the walls and vulnerable corners of the city.

As we noted above, the summary comment in verse 15 speaks for the entire section in describing God's help to Uzziah to grow strong. However, the comment has a double edge: As the next episode will show, Uzziah's achievement of strength and security is the occasion of his sin against God in the Temple. This is another of the Chronicler's themes in the stories of the kings: that with strength and security too often come greed and self-aggrandizement. As long as the king understands his position to be tenuous, he recognizes the need for divine aid and is sustained by it; when there is no longer a visible threat, a certain spiritual pride seems to set in that leads to his undoing.

3. Uzziah's invasion of the Temple and his leprosy, 26:16–21. Verses 16–21 are the second major addition of the Chronicler to his source material. They serve to resolve the theological problem posed by the fact that an otherwise good king contracts lifelong leprosy. The Chronicler's answer to the problem is to explain Uzziah's leprosy as a result of his pride. Specifically, it is the result of an attempt on Uzziah's part to take over the priestly function of sacrifice and liturgical leadership.

> 26:16 **But when he had become strong he grew proud, to his destruction. For he was false to the LORD his God, and entered the Temple of the LORD to make offering on the altar of incense.** [17] **But the priest Azariah went in after him, with eighty priests of the LORD who were men of valor;** [18] **they withstood King Uzziah, and said to him, "It is not for you, Uzziah, to make offering to the LORD, but for the priests the descendants of Aaron, who are consecrated to make offering. Go out of the sanctuary; for you have done wrong, and it will bring you no honor from the LORD God."** [19] **Then Uzziah was angry. Now he had a censer in his hand to make offering, and when he became angry with the priests a leprous disease broke out on his forehead, in the presence of the priests in the house of the LORD, by the altar of incense.** [20] **When the chief priest Azariah, and all the priests, looked at him, he was leprous in his forehead. They hurried him out, and he himself hurried to get out, because the LORD had struck him.** [21] **King Uzziah was leprous to the day of his death, and being leprous lived in a separate house, for he was excluded from the house of the LORD. His son Jotham was in charge of the palace of the king, governing the people of the land.**

Involvement in the care and operation of the Temple, and at least general religious leadership and sponsorship, is the responsibility of the king. Solomon built the Temple, Joash repaired and renovated it, Asa led the people in the making of a new covenant of faithfulness, and both Hezekiah and Josiah will carry out major reformations of Judah's central religious ritual, Passover. But the limitation imposed on the king from earliest days, and certainly recognized by the Chronicler with his sharply defined system of liturgical leadership, is that the king may not invade on sacerdotal function. In the end, the king is not a priest but one of the people, and he must stay outside.

Uzziah's entry into the Temple to offer sacrifice on the incense altar is a political challenge to the power and autonomy of the priests. If the king may enter the Temple to offer sacrifice, then what need is there of priests, who may occasionally speak critically of the king's policies or behavior? It may be, then, that the danger perceived by the priests is a threat by the king to the security of their position. But more likely, and of paramount importance to the Chronicler, the king's intrusion into the Temple violates the boundary between sacred and profane, between the realm of the holy within the Temple and the secular world outside it. By entering the Temple to offer his own sacrifice, the king claims in effect to know who is the appropriate agent to conduct sacred ritual. "It is not for you, Uzziah, to make offering to the LORD" may be understood to carry either concern or both, but in any case the offense is serious.

The result is equally serious: The king becomes a leper. The moment is a dramatic one, and the Chronicler describes it with the skill of a novelist. The king stands, censer in hand, confronted by the phalanx of priests that bar his progress. He is angry. But no sooner does he become enraged at the priests than his forehead breaks out in a "leprous disease," and he is hustled out of the Temple. What began as a prideful show of royal power ends as an ignominious retreat into seclusion.

The "leprosy" of which the text speaks may or may not be what modern medicine calls "Hansen's disease," a disorder of skin and tissue that results in severe disfiguration and often loss of appendages. In the ancient world, any outbreak on the skin was referred to as leprosy. Such disorders were (and are) common in a world susceptible to bacteriological infections due to poor sanitation and hygiene. Leprosy was understood as curable in some cases, and Mosaic law provides for priestly recognition of the restoration of health to a leper as a precondition of his return to society. Thus, that Uzziah was "leprous to the day of his death" is a particularly onerous judgment on the king.

Ensconced in a "separate house" for the remainder of his reign, Uzziah can no longer exercise any of the public functions associated with kingship, such as hearing cases for judgment or attending the festivals at the Temple. Though probably still the behind-the-scenes decision maker, the king cedes all public functions of rule to his son Jotham. Whether Jotham was in fact a co-regent who shared royal power with his father, as many scholars have claimed, is doubtful; there is little clear evidence that such an arrangement ever existed in Israel. What is clear is that Jotham was placed "in charge of the palace of the king," that is, that he governed the day-to-day affairs of the palace and that he exercised some authority over the people.

4. Uzziah's death and burial, 26:22–23. Having spent the rest of his days set apart from but close beside his kingdom because of his leprosy, Uzziah spends eternity in a similar condition. Upon his death, Uzziah is buried "near" but not "with" his ancestors in the royal cemetery in Jerusalem. The reason given is the same as the reason for his separation in life: "He is leprous."

Some years ago, excavations in Jerusalem uncovered a late second- or early first-century B.C. marker bearing the inscription: "Here are the bones of Azariah [= Uzziah] king of Judah. Do not open." Apparently the tradition of Uzziah's leprosy endured and was respected well into early Judaism.

THE REIGN OF JOTHAM
2 Chronicles 27:1–9

The Chronicler's account of Jotham sticks fairly close to the information provided in the source narrative of 2 Kings 15:32–38, adding only brief notices regarding his reign and international prestige. This is in itself striking, in view of the unqualified positive evaluation the Chronicler awards Jotham: "He did what was right in the sight of the LORD" even to the extent of avoiding the sin of Uzziah. As a result, he is rewarded with success in building defenses and in warfare against the Ammonites—two signs of divine approbation in the Chronicler's scheme. The only semblance of a critique offered by the Chronicler is that during his reign "the people still followed corrupt practices," implying the continuation of Baal worship in Judah. But the waywardness of part of the population does not appear to tarnish the reputation of the king.

It is hard to explain, therefore, why the Chronicler does not make more of a positive example out of Jotham than he does. The absence of attention to Jotham is probably traceable to his nearly blank identity. Throughout his reign, Jotham labors in the shadow of the more vibrant Uzziah, the absentee king locked away with a leprosy that forever memorializes his violent but colorful character. Jotham, on the other hand, though visible, seems almost transparent. He is something of a cipher; he appears to stand for nothing so vigorous as anger or sin. In the end, the best the Chronicler can find to say for him is that he "became strong because he ordered his ways before the LORD his God."

THE REIGN OF AHAZ
2 Chronicles 28:1–27

28:1 Ahaz was twenty years old when he began to reign; he reigned sixteen years in Jerusalem. He did not do what was right in the sight of the LORD, as his ancestor David had done, 2 but he walked in the ways of the kings of Israel. He even made cast images for the Baals; ³ and he made offerings in the valley of the son of Hinnom, and made his sons pass through fire, according to the abominable practices of the nations whom the LORD drove out before the people of Israel. ⁴ He sacrificed and made offerings on the high places, on the hills, and under every green tree.

⁵ Therefore the LORD his God gave him into the hand of the king of Aram, who defeated him and took captive a great number of his people and brought them to Damascus. He was also given into the hand of the king of Israel, who defeated him with great slaughter. ⁶ Pekah son of Remaliah killed one hundred twenty thousand in Judah in one day, all of them valiant warriors, because they had abandoned the LORD, the God of their ancestors. ⁷ And Zichri, a mighty warrior of Ephraim, killed the king's son Maaseiah, Azrikam the commander of the palace, and Elkanah the next in authority to the king.

⁸ The people of Israel took captive two hundred thousand of their kin, women, sons, and daughters; they also took much booty from them and brought the booty to Samaria. ⁹ But a prophet of the LORD was there, whose name was Oded; he went out to meet the army that came to Samaria, and said to them, "Because the LORD, the God of your ancestors, was angry with Judah, he gave them into your hand, but you have killed them in a rage that has reached up to heaven. ¹⁰ Now you intend to subjugate the people of Judah and Jerusalem, male and female, as your slaves. But what have you except sins against the LORD your God? ¹¹ Now hear me, and send back the captives whom you have taken from your kindred, for the fierce wrath of the LORD is upon you." ¹² Moreover, certain chiefs of the Ephraimites, Azariah son of Johanan, Berechiah son of Meshillemoth, Jehizkiah son of Shallum, and Amasa son of Hadlai, stood up against those who were coming from the war, ¹³ and said to them, "You shall not bring the captives in here, for you propose to bring on us guilt against the LORD in addition to our present sins and guilt. For our guilt is already great, and there is fierce wrath against Israel." ¹⁴ So the warriors left the captives and the booty before the officials and all the assembly. ¹⁵ Then those who were mentioned by name got up and took the captives, and with the booty they clothed all that were naked among them; they clothed them, gave them sandals, provided them with food and drink, and anointed them; and carrying all the feeble among them on donkeys, they brought them to their kindred at Jericho, the city of palm trees. Then they returned to Samaria.

¹⁶ At that time King Ahaz sent to the king of Assyria for help. ¹⁷ For the Edomites had again invaded and defeated Judah, and carried away captives. ¹⁸ And the Philistines had made raids on the cities in the Shephelah and the Negeb of Judah, and had taken Beth-shemesh, Aijalon, Gederoth, Soco with its villages, Timnah with its villages, and Gimzo with its villages; and they settled there. ¹⁹ For the LORD brought Judah low because of King Ahaz of Israel, for he had behaved without restraint in Judah and had been faithless to the LORD. ²⁰ So King Tiglath-pilneser of Assyria came against him, and

oppressed him instead of strengthening him. [21] For Ahaz plundered the house of the LORD and the houses of the king and of the officials, and gave tribute to the king of Assyria; but it did not help him.

[22] In the time of his distress he became yet more faithless to the LORD—this same King Ahaz. [23] For he sacrificed to the gods of Damascus, which had defeated him, and said, "Because the gods of the kings of Aram helped them, I will sacrifice to them so that they may help me." But they were the ruin of him, and of all Israel. [24] Ahaz gathered together the utensils of the house of God, and cut in pieces the utensils of the house of God. He shut up the doors of the house of the LORD and made himself altars in every corner of Jerusalem. [25] In every city of Judah he made high places to make offerings to other gods, provoking to anger the LORD, the God of his ancestors. [26] Now the rest of his acts and all his ways, from first to last, are written in the Book of the Kings of Judah and Israel. [27] Ahaz slept with his ancestors, and they buried him in the city, in Jerusalem; but they did not bring him into the tombs of the kings of Israel. His son Hezekiah succeeded him.

Ahaz, as the Chronicler treats him, is the worst of the kings of Judah—worse even than Manasseh, who holds that distinction in 2 Kings but whom the Chronicler rehabilitates. Ahaz is evaluated with a totally and unremittingly negative assessment.

During Ahaz's reign, Judah emerges as a player—albeit in a minor role—on the stage of ancient Near Eastern politics. Assyrian interest in the southeast Mediterranean is growing, and the expansionist Assyrian king Tiglath-pileser III (not "-pilneser" as the Chronicler misspells it) begins to bring Judah and the Philistine states into the Assyrian sphere of influence. Typically, though, the Chronicler shows little interest in these great affairs of politics and of Judah's role in the larger history of the ancient Near East. Rather, he is interested in the all-important connection between behavior and consequence in the life of the king and the people. As a result, the Chronicler's story of Ahaz differs sharply from the source in 2 Kings 16:1–20. Where the 2 Kings story is the tale of the king of Judah trapped in the rising tide of Assyrian pressure on the region, the Chronicles story is a saga of sin and punishment. The great kingdoms vying for control of the ancient world—here Aram, the Philistines, and Assyria—are merely tools in the divine hand honed for the punishment of a sinful and faithless Ahaz.

The Chronicler's presentation of the reign of Ahaz has five sections: an introduction (vv. 1–4), Judah's defeat by Aram and Israel (vv. 5–7), the return of the Judahite captives (vv. 8–15), the Assyrian attack against Judah (vv. 16–21), and Ahaz's apostasy and death (vv. 22–27).

1. Introduction, 28:1–4. Unlike any of his predecessors, Ahaz's sixteen-year reign is without any redemptive feature. Not only does Ahaz "not do what was right in the sight of the LORD" but he actively pursues the Baal apostasy of the Israelite kings, as well as other "abominable practices." The Chronicler is specific about at least some of them: Ahaz cast images of the Baals (the deity Baal in Canaanite religion had multiple specific manifestations; hence the use of the plural here), he made various sacrifices and offerings at countryside shrines and high places, and he engaged in some poorly defined ritual in the "valley of the son of Hinnom." The valley mentioned here is the dry torrent valley west and south of the city of Jerusalem. The origins of the name are obscure, but by the time Judah controlled the region it was clearly associated with religious practices of which the orthodox leadership of the Temple sharply disapproved. These practices may have included child sacrifice; the reference to Ahaz having "made his sons pass through fire" is often interpreted to imply such a ritual. Similar comments are made in Jeremiah 7:30–31 and in 2 Chronicles 33:6 about subsequent kings that lend credence to this suggestion. However, the matter is still debated, and the most that can be said with any certainty is that the Chronicler (along with other biblical writers) regarded the rituals in the valley of the son of Hinnom as "abominable practices," the strongest and most ardent condemnation offered by the Bible.

The heart of the Chronicler's accusation against Ahaz is not merely apostasy but undoing the work of God. By resurrecting Canaanite practices such as child sacrifice (if indeed such is the case) and restoring the images and shrines of the Baal cult to positions of prominence and respect throughout the country, Ahaz puts back what God banished in the conquest of the land by Joshua and of the city of Jerusalem by David.

2. Judah's defeat by Aram and Israel, 28:5–7. The source narrative for the Chronicler's portrait of Ahaz, 2 Kings 16:5–9, describes Judah under simultaneous assault from two directions. In the north, Aram and Israel have combined forces and marched southward, intent on overthrowing Ahaz and replacing him with another king. In the south, the Edomites are active again, probably seeking to regain control of the port city of Elath. The former of these two threats was by far the more serious, provoking royal panic and requiring the prophet Isaiah to calm Ahaz's nerves and strengthen his resolve to trust in God (Isa. 7:1–14). Apparently at stake was Judah's participation in the resistance against Assyria led by Aram and Israel; Ahaz had been reluctant to join the anti-Assyrian coalition for fear of Assyrian depredations, and the two coalition leaders were resolved to force Ahaz to "join or else."

The Chronicler treats this episode very differently than does the narrator of 2 Kings. First, he separates the two fronts and treats them as different wars. Second, it is possible to read verse 5 to imply two different campaigns rather than a single united invasion of Judah by the joint Aramean-Israelite army. Thus, Ahaz is defeated not once but twice. Third, and most important, the defeats are the result of God having given Ahaz "into the hand" of the enemy so that the background for the defeats by Aram and Israel is not to be sought in the realm of international politics but rather in the faithlessness and corruption of Ahaz himself. To the extent that Judah suffers more broadly than the king alone, it is because "they had abandoned the LORD, the God of their ancestors" (v. 6). But the king is singled out for particular punishment in verse 7, with the deaths of his son, his palace commander, and his second-in-command. Once again, the Chronicler upholds his theory of moral responsibility, deriving the justification for the suffering of an individual or group from their own behavior.

   3. The return of the Judahite captives, 28:8–15. This section is unique to the Chronicler and presents an unusual opportunity to reflect on the understanding of the relationship of individual northerners to "Israel," that is, to the people whom the Chronicler would broadly identify as the "people of God." The narrative describes the capture of some two hundred thousand Judahites—surely an exaggerated number—by their northern counterparts, presumably as part of the war between the two kingdoms. The captives and the booty taken along with them are brought to Samaria, where they are prevented from entering the city by a prophet, Oded. Oded's critique is not of the war itself; he recognizes that the defeat of Judah was the result of divine intent to punish Judah for its apostasy and disobedience. But the prophet decries the wanton killing of the Israelites' Judahite kindred "in a rage that has reached up to heaven." Moreover, he castigates Israel for its intent to enslave its kindred and points out that Israel has no claim to moral superiority over Judah that might warrant such treatment. Instead, the North has nothing in its religious heritage to show except "sins against the LORD your God." The prophet orders the captors to release their prisoners and allow them to return. The prophet is joined in his stand by several individual Israelites, whose names the Chronicler carefully registers. It is they who see to it, after the Judahites are released, that they are fed and clothed and returned in safety to Jericho, the city at the north end of the Dead Sea near the border between the kingdoms.

   Two interconnected realties are worthy of note in this narrative. First, the clear presumption of Oded's speech is that God is Lord of Israel no less than of Judah. Second, particular individuals within the Northern Kingdom show themselves to be faithful and obedient to the direction of God through the word of the prophet; this is undoubtedly why the Chronicler goes to some pains to identify them clearly. They represent the understanding that, even though the northern nation and its leadership as a whole are in rebellion against the proper worship of God and the proper allegiance to the house of David, individual northerners may still show themselves to be faithful and find inclusion in the covenant community. Such ideas would have been important in the Chronicler's own day, as Jews struggled to define the limits of "Israel" in the wake of the return from exile; indeed, something of the same issues are at stake in modern discussions of Jewish identity. Is membership in the covenant community founded upon physical lineage or geographic location, or is it a matter of faith and obedience to the word and will of God? For the Chronicler, the answer is the latter: "Israel" is that community that identifies itself by its obedience to the law and its worship of God in the Temple.

The return of the captives places a limit on the chain of suffering begun by Ahaz's apostasy. From the Chronicler's perspective, there must be an end to the pain and punishment endured by the people on account of their king. The release and return of the captives brings about that end and makes a future possible. But the return also serves to foreshadow the larger and more important return from exile in Babylon by those taken in 587 B.C. (or their descendants). The final two verses of 2 Chronicles (36:22–23) indicate that such a return will be possible; by the time of the Chronicler's writing that return was at least well underway if not largely complete. Like the end of the punishment resulting from Ahaz's sins, the great return from exile will signal the end of the suffering from the sin of the nation as a whole. And like the future promised by the restoration of the captives to their families, the restoration of Israel to the land promises a new future. It is that future that the Chronicler seeks to build as he tells the story of Israel's past.

4. The Assyrian attack on Judah, 28:16–21. As he has done throughout the narrative of Ahaz's reign, the Chronicler once again takes a small portion of the source material—2 Kings 16:6—and builds it into a larger account that suits his theological purposes. The particular text is the invasion of Judah's southern and western regions by Edomite and Philistine forces. For the Chronicler, these encounters mark a low point in Judah's life, brought about by the intent of the Lord to punish Ahaz for his unrestrained sinfulness and disobedience to the law.

It is also the occasion for introducing the Assyrians onto the stage of the Chronicler's narrative. The Assyrian empire was an ancient people whose capital was situated at Nineveh, in the northern end of the Tigris-Euphrates Valley. Landlocked and without means of growth except by conquest, the Assyrians learned early that their survival depended on their ability to control ports of trade on the eastern Mediterranean and at the mouth of the Euphrates. Hence, Assyrian kings were constantly engaged in expansionist military campaigns aimed at bringing new territory within the sphere of their influence. In the latter half of the eighth century B.C., under the leadership of Assyria's most aggressive king, Tiglath-pileser III (the Chronicler misspells the name as "Tiglath-pilneser"), Assyria began asserting its hegemony along the great trade routes leading through Aram, Israel, and to a lesser extent Judah, and down the eastern Mediterranean coast. Speaking from the vantage point of history, it is unlikely that any kingdom ever appealed to the Assyrians for aid against their neighbors in a minor conflict, since the cost of Assyrian "aid" was often the loss of national identity and even of life itself. To put the matter bluntly, the Assyrians were quite capable of taking whatever they regarded as advantageous to own or control, and they were guided in their actions by a policy of economic self-interest that hardly ever wavered.

It is therefore highly unlikely either that Ahaz appealed to Assyria for aid against Edom and the Philistines in the border wars of his time or that the Assyrians required any such pretext to show up on the scene. On the other hand, it is known from contemporary Assyrian records that, in the years 734–732 B.C., Tiglath-pileser III did conduct an extensive military campaign in Palestine. The campaign resulted in the destruction of Aram, the debilitation of Israel and the execution of its king, and the suppression of several Philistine and Phoenician states along the eastern Mediterranean coast. In the final stages of the campaign, the Assyrian king conducted an expedition as far south as "the river of Egypt" (probably the Wadi Besor, south of Gaza; possibly the Wadi el 'Arish in the Sinai), where he claims to have set up his monument. That such an expedition would have made contact and perhaps even extracted tribute from Judah is not at all unlikely. Hence, the comment in verse 21 that "Ahaz plundered the house of the LORD and the houses of the king and of the officials, and gave tribute to the king of Assyria" is not in the least implausible.

Once again, however, it is not the accurate rendering of a historical account that is the Chronicler's main agenda here but the teaching of a theological lesson. The invasions of Edom and the Philistines are the result of God's intervention to punish Ahaz for his apostasy. Instead of learning from the punishment, however, Ahaz deepens his own guilt by appealing for foreign aid against God's own judgment. Becoming entangled in yet another foreign alliance, Ahaz is vulnerable to oppression by the Assyrians. This oppression—in the least financial and perhaps also military—is precisely the result. The Chronicler's point is clear: Not only does Ahaz not accept the righteous correction of God for his sinfulness but he aggravates that sin by becoming enmeshed in destructive foreign entanglements. The Chronicler's judgment on the whole affair is succinct and clear: "It did not help him."

5. *Ahaz's apostasy and death, 28:22–27.* From the Chronicler's perspective, Ahaz could have used the occasion of his suffering at the hands of the Assyrians to reconsider his ways and return to the Lord; that he does not do so even "in the time of his distress" is thus a further indictment of his faithlessness. Rather than turning to the God of David and Solomon, Ahaz turns instead to the gods of Aram, following the logic that, if they were helpful to the Arameans, they would be helpful to him. But the king does not leave the matter there; he dismantles the cult of the Temple in two important ways. First, he destroys the Temple utensils, cutting them in pieces so as to render them useless. The action is not a sign of neglect of the Temple but rather of assault against it; it is a rejection of the Temple and the God it professes. The action of the king recalls the Chronicler's comment that the children of Athaliah had broken into the Temple and used all the Temple paraphernalia for the Baal cult (24:7), but it goes one step further in rendering the Temple utensils useless even for apostasy. Second, he "shut up the doors of the house of the LORD," blocking the promised access of the people to God through prayers to the house. The king's actions represent a crime against the faith of Israel of the highest order: Not only has he abandoned the historic patronage of the king toward the Temple in favor of other deities but he has assaulted the Temple itself, voiding the promise of Solomon that the Temple would be a house of prayer wherein the people could always offer themselves and their situation to God. The sentence represents a stunning and tragic moment in the Chronicler's narrative; small wonder that Ahaz is accused of "provoking to anger the LORD, the God of his ancestors."

Ahaz's death is noted without comment, except that he was buried in the city of Jerusalem but not in the royal cemetery.

17. The Reign of Hezekiah
2 Chronicles 29:1–32:33

With the exceptions of David and Solomon, Hezekiah is the most important king in the story of Israel and Judah. Through his reforming piety and unwavering faithfulness, Hezekiah brings Judah back from the brink of self-destructive apostasy. Recalling the image of David, Hezekiah revitalizes the Levites and reorganizes the operations of the Temple. Recalling the image of Solomon, he restores and readies the Temple structure itself. At the center of his reign, according to the Chronicler, is a new observation of the Passover, now an occasion of nationwide joy centered in Jerusalem. Grounded in Hezekiah's strong faith and trust in God, Judah is able to withstand the assaults of Sennacherib, king of Assyria. In virtually every way, the Chronicler's presentation of Hezekiah's reign is a picture of the dawn of righteousness and restoration after a long night of sin and waywardness.

The Hezekiah narrative is divided easily into sections corresponding to the current chapter divisions in the book: the sanctification of the Temple (29:1–36), the celebration of the Passover (30:1–27), plans for the support of the Temple clergy (31:1–17), and the invasion of Sennacherib and the end of Hezekiah's reign (32:1–33).

SANCTIFICATION OF THE TEMPLE
2 Chronicles 29:1–36

The first and most urgent task Hezekiah faces is to reopen the doors of the Temple and to restore it to use and order. Given the Chronicler's primary focus on the Temple and its role in the life of the people of God, it is hardly surprising that he places this task at the top of the list for the new king. The work is multilayered; not only must the Temple be "cleansed" (i.e., the paraphernalia of non-Yahwistic religions be removed) but the Temple must also be "sanctified" (i.e., prepared and set apart for its sacred use as the dwelling of the name of the Lord). Before this task can be undertaken, however, those who can do the job must be gathered, organized, and sanctified. The story of Hezekiah's sanctification of the Temple and the restoration of worship may be divided into three subsections: the introduction to Hezekiah's reign (vv. 1–2), the cleansing and sanctification of the Temple (vv. 3–19), and the restoration of worship in the Temple (vv. 20–36).

1. *Introduction to Hezekiah's reign, 29:1–2.* The brief introduction to Hezekiah's reign is nearly identical to the information provided in 2 Kings 18:1–2, with the exception of an alternate spelling of his mother's name (there, "Abi; " here, "Abijah"). The one remarkable note about the introduction, especially in comparison to its recent predecessors, is that it is unqualifiedly positive. Not only does Hezekiah do "what was right," but he does so in a manner "just as his ancestor David had done." No other king to date has received so positive an evaluation; no other except Josiah (34:2) will receive one for the rest of the Chronicler's story.

2. *Cleansing and sanctifying the Temple, 29:3–19.* Hezekiah must reverse the disastrous course of apostasy that resulted in Ahaz closing the doors of the Temple and leading the nation into the worship of other deities. This is a task for the king not merely because the previous king was responsible for creating the crisis but because patronage of the Temple had been the responsibility of the king since the inception of the Davidic monarchy. To accomplish the task of cleansing and restoring the house of God, the king marshals those to whom David assigned the task of operating the Temple: the priests and the Levites.

29:4 **He brought in the priests and the Levites and assembled them in the square on the east.** [5] **He said to them, "Listen to me, Levites! Sanctify yourselves, and sanctify the house of the LORD, the God of your ancestors, and carry out the filth from the holy place.** [6] **For our ancestors have been unfaithful and have done what was evil in the sight of the LORD our God; they have forsaken him, and have turned away their faces from the dwelling of the LORD, and turned their backs.** [7] **They also shut the doors of the vestibule and put out the lamps, and have not offered incense or made burnt offerings in the holy place to the God of Israel.** [8] **Therefore the wrath of the LORD came upon Judah and Jerusalem, and he has made them an object of horror, of astonishment, and of hissing, as you see with your own eyes.** [9] **Our fathers have fallen by the sword and our sons and our daughters and our wives are in captivity for this.** [10] **Now it is in my heart to make a covenant with the LORD, the God of Israel, so that his fierce anger may turn away from us.** [11] **My sons, do not now be negligent, for the LORD has chosen you to stand in his presence to minister to him, and to be his ministers and make offerings to him."**

Hezekiah's speech to the Levites is cast in three parts. The first part is the command to prepare and carry out the cleansing and sanctification of the house (v. 5). Attention to detail is important to the Chronicler. The priests and Levites must first sanctify themselves before beginning work on the house. There is obvious logic here; the Temple cannot be restored to ritual cleanliness by those who are themselves unclean. What is striking is the implication of the command: that the priests and Levites, whose task it is to remain ritually clean and ready to serve in the house of God, have in fact allowed themselves to lapse into uselessness by virtue of inactivity. It is not merely the king who has wandered from the faith but the clergy as well.

The terms "cleanse" and "sanctify" mean more than merely the removal of dirt. To cleanse the sanctuary was to remove all traces of pollution (the text uses the unusually strong term "filth") introduced by the idols and icons of foreign deities. To sanctify was then to follow ritualized procedures for setting the sacred space apart to the worship of God, consecrating it so that it is markedly different from all other space.

The second part of Hezekiah's speech is a rehearsal of the sins of the ancestors who brought Judah to this low point in its religious history (vv. 6–9). Throughout this portion of the speech, "our ancestors" refers not to ancestors of the distant past but to Ahaz and those of his generation, whose religious innovations instigated the crisis. Verse 6 states in general terms the theological indictment against that generation: They have done what was evil and forsaken the Lord, "and have turned away their faces from the dwelling of the LORD, and turned their backs." This last phrase is of particular importance; in effect, it reverses the position vis-à-vis the Temple prescribed for the people in Solomon's prayer of dedication in 2 Chronicles 6 to "turn toward" and "pray toward this place." Ahaz and his cohort have undone the dedication of Solomon, and the house so dedicated must now be restored. Verse 7 then offers a bill of particulars on how the Temple was allowed to fall into disrepair: They "shut the doors of the vestibule and put out the lamps, and have not offered incense or made burnt offerings."

Verses 8–9 rehearse the judgment of God on Judah for its sins: the wrath of the Lord. While the Chronicler's language here is nonspecific, the reference is clearly to some catastrophic defeat resulting in the deportation of large numbers of Judahite prisoners. So far in the narrative, the only such catastrophe worthy of the name is the Assyrian invasion during Ahaz's reign (28:20–21); this invasion, however, did not result in large-scale losses for Judah. The language employed by the Chronicler is a near quotation of Jeremiah 29:18, which refers to the defeat of Judah and exile at the hands of the Babylonians more than a century after Hezekiah. In all probability, the Chronicler is telescoping several events and accounts into a single reference: He uses the Assyrian campaign of 734 B.C. as the occasion for describing the fall of the Northern kingdom, an event that did not occur until 722/21, five years into the reign of Hezekiah. Moreover, he borrows language employed by Jeremiah to describe the Babylonian destruction of Jerusalem in 587 to describe the Assyrian invasion of a century before. In this way, he plants the seeds to explain the Babylonian debacle as the result of Judah's continuing faithlessness to God. The effects of the defeat of 587 are still being felt in the Chronicler's own time, and the prayers of his own people still ascend for the return and restoration of their families living in exile.

Verses 10–11 describe Hezekiah's intent to "make a covenant with the LORD, the God of Israel." Central to the execution of that covenant is the cooperation of the clergy in restoring the Temple to its proper function; hence, the king urges them not to be "negligent, for the LORD has chosen you to stand in his presence." Once again, the Chronicler is preaching to his own audience here. One of the lingering problems of the postexilic era was the negligence and laxity with which the rebuilding and reestablishment of the Temple function took place. Through the voice of Hezekiah, the Chronicler urges his own people not to make the same mistake again and to renew the covenant of their own hearts to the service of the LORD.

The response of the Levites is one of action rather than of words. They spring to the tasks of self-preparation and then of cleansing and sanctifying the Temple. The Chronicler lists Levites representing each of the three main Levitical clans—Kohath, Merari, and Gershon—as well as representatives of the three families of Levitical singers—Asaph, Heman, and Jeduthun. A seventh group is also identified, that of Elizaphan. The list is not intended to be exhaustive; the text is clear that they "gathered their brothers" to undertake the task before beginning to carry out the king's command. The Chronicler is careful to note that only priests enter the inner sanctuary where the ark of the covenant and other sacred objects reside; the cleansing of the sanctuary is thus carried out with attention to the rules of order and cleanness. Once the objects of foreign religious significance are removed, they are disposed of in the Kidron Valley, a riverbed to the east of Jerusalem where other objects of idolatry are thrown (see 2 Chron. 15:16; 2 Kings 23:4, 6, 12).

The Chronicler is quite specific about the timing of the cleansing of the Temple. We are told when the work began (on the first day of the first month), when it began in the vestibule or interior of the Temple (on the eighth day of the first month), how long the cleansing of the interior of the Temple took (eight days), and when the entire project was completed (on the sixteenth of the month). There are two reasons for this specificity about dates. First, because the cleansing is not finished until the sixteenth of the month, Passover must be postponed; the festival is normally scheduled to begin on the fifteenth day of the first month. The Chronicler thus provides a ready explanation for the delayed Passover inaugurated by Hezekiah in the next chapter. Second, the fact that the cleansing of the interior of the Temple requires eight days (from the eighth to the sixteenth) recalls the dedication of the Temple by Solomon (7:8–9). This is one of several ways in which the Chronicler implies that the reign of Hezekiah should be understood as comparable with that of Solomon.

3. Restoration of worship in the Temple, 29:20–36. Once the Temple has been cleansed, it can be rededicated to its sacred purpose. As the Chronicler presents it, there are two stages in this dedicatory process. First, the altar must be rededicated and purified of the sin of idolatry that stains king, Temple, and nation (vv. 20–30). Second, the ritual of thanksgiving and self-dedicatory offerings can be resumed (vv. 31–36).

The Chronicler draws on Numbers 7:84–88 for his account of the rededication of the altar. In the Numbers text, Moses has completed the establishment of the tabernacle and proceeds to the dedication of the altar. The dedicatory sacrifice consists of bulls, rams, lambs, and male goats—the same list of animals offered in the Chronicler's account of Hezekiah's ritual. Once again, as he did so often in the account of Solomon's construction of the Temple, the Chronicler reaches back into the sacred story of the tabernacle to find precedent and foundation for the obedience of the present. At the same time, however, he makes the Numbers sacrifice fit the needs of the narrative moment by telling his readers that the sacrifices were "a sin offering for the kingdom and for the sanctuary and for Judah." What transpires here is not merely the rededication of the altar but the expiation of the guilt of the community. The royal house that instigated the apostasy, the Temple in which the objects of the Baal cult were stored, and the nation that accepted the cult are all in need of cleansing from the stain of guilt, and so the Chronicler makes clear that the sin offering made by Hezekiah pertains to all. The dashing of blood against the altar is a purgation rite, cleansing the altar and Temple symbolically by the power of blood. Blood was considered the locus of life and vitality in Hebrew thought and thus is the agent for restoring life to those "dead in trespasses" (Col. 2:13); Christians are familiar with such imagery from the traditions of the Eucharist and the language of atonement. Hezekiah and the officers lay hands on the head of the male goats not as a sign of fondness but as a symbolic gesture; by this contact the sins of king and people are transferred to the animals and atoned.

The Chronicler's other significant innovation in his account of the rededication of the altar is the role played by the Levitical singers in worship. We have seen before that the Chronicler consistently provides a place in important liturgical moments for the Levites and especially for the musicians and singers; the present case is no exception. Levites with various instruments and singers who offer songs of thanksgiving accompany the sacrifices being offered, just as they did when Solomon dedicated the Temple (7:6).

With the announcement to the priests and Levites that "you have now consecrated yourselves," the offerings of thanksgiving and self-dedication can now resume (vv. 31–36). Thank offerings are offered upon occasions of deliverance, perhaps from illness or some crisis, or in the case of national deliverance from military threat. The volume of sacrifice quickly overwhelms the priests, however, who cannot keep up with the responsibility to skin and prepare the animals. The Levites must come to the aid of the priests. While no direct criticism of the priests is stated, one is at least implied in the Chronicler's comment that "the Levites were more conscientious than the priests in sanctifying themselves." The apparent meaning of the comment is that more Levites than priests took seriously the king's command to sanctify themselves and were thus ready to assist in the sacrifices when the priests were not. The Chronicler will return to this theme again in 2 Chronicles 30 in discussing the Passover celebration. At the end of the present chapter, however, he offers what may be something of an excuse to the priests in his statement that "the thing had come about suddenly" (v. 36). The immediate purpose of the comment is to explain the surging popularity of the sacrifice, but a secondary agenda may be to explain why fewer priests than were needed were available and thus to take away some of the rebuke that they were sanctified in insufficient numbers to meet the need of the moment.

CELEBRATION OF THE PASSOVER
2 Chronicles 30:1–27

30:1 **Hezekiah sent word to all Israel and Judah, and wrote letters also to Ephraim and Manasseh, that they should come to the house of the Lord at Jerusalem, to keep the passover to the Lord the God of Israel. ² For the king and his officials and all the assembly in Jerusalem had taken counsel to keep the passover in the second month ³ (for they could not keep it at its proper time because the priests had not sanctified themselves in sufficient number, nor had the people assembled in Jerusalem). ⁴ The plan seemed right to the king and all the assembly. ⁵ So they decreed to make a proclamation throughout all Israel, from**

Beer-sheba to Dan, that the people should come and keep the passover
to the LORD the God of Israel, at Jerusalem; for they had not kept it in
great numbers as prescribed. ⁶So couriers went throughout all Israel and
Judah with letters from the king and his officials, as the king had commanded, saying, "O people of Israel, return to the LORD, the God of
Abraham, Isaac, and Israel, so that he may turn again to the remnant of
you who have escaped from the hand of the kings of Assyria. ⁷Do not be
like your ancestors and your kindred, who were faithless to the LORD
God of their ancestors, so that he made them a desolation, as you see.
⁸Do not now be stiff-necked as your ancestors were, but yield yourselves
to the LORD and come to his sanctuary, which he has sanctified forever,
and serve the LORD your God, so that his fierce anger may turn away
from you. ⁹For as you return to the LORD, your kindred and your children
will find compassion with their captors, and return to this land. For the
LORD your God is gracious and merciful, and will not turn away his face
from you, if you return to him."

¹⁰So the couriers went from city to city through the country of Ephraim
and Manasseh, and as far as Zebulun; but they laughed them to scorn, and
mocked them. ¹¹Only a few from Asher, Manasseh, and Zebulun humbled
themselves and came to Jerusalem. ¹²The hand of God was also on Judah
to give them one heart to do what the king and the officials commanded by
the word of the LORD.

¹³Many people came together in Jerusalem to keep the festival of
unleavened bread in the second month, a very large assembly. ¹⁴They set
to work and removed the altars that were in Jerusalem, and all the altars
for offering incense they took away and threw into the Wadi Kidron. ¹⁵They
slaughtered the passover lamb on the fourteenth day of the second month.
The priests and the Levites were ashamed, and they sanctified themselves
and brought burnt offerings into the house of the LORD. ¹⁶They took their
accustomed posts according to the law of Moses the man of God; the
priests dashed the blood that they received from the hands of the Levites.
¹⁷For there were many in the assembly who had not sanctified themselves;
therefore the Levites had to slaughter the passover lamb for everyone who
was not clean, to make it holy to the LORD. ¹⁸For a multitude of the people, many of them from Ephraim, Manasseh, Issachar, and Zebulun, had not
cleansed themselves, yet they ate the passover otherwise than as prescribed. But Hezekiah prayed for them, saying, "The good LORD pardon all
¹⁹who set their hearts to seek God, the LORD the God of their ancestors,
even though not in accordance with the sanctuary's rules of cleanness."
²⁰The LORD heard Hezekiah, and healed the people. ²¹The people of Israel
who were present at Jerusalem kept the festival of unleavened bread seven
days with great gladness; and the Levites and the priests praised the LORD
day by day, accompanied by loud instruments for the LORD. ²²Hezekiah
spoke encouragingly to all the Levites who showed good skill in the service
of the LORD. So the people ate the food of the festival for seven days,

sacrificing offerings of well-being and giving thanks to the LORD the God of their ancestors. 23 Then the whole assembly agreed together to keep the festival for another seven days; so they kept it for another seven days with gladness. 24 For King Hezekiah of Judah gave the assembly a thousand bulls and seven thousand sheep for offerings, and the officials gave the assembly a thousand bulls and ten thousand sheep. The priests sanctified themselves in great numbers. 25 The whole assembly of Judah, the priests and the Levites, and the whole assembly that came out of Israel, and the resident aliens who came out of the land of Israel, and the resident aliens who lived in Judah, rejoiced. 26 There was great joy in Jerusalem, for since the time of Solomon son of King David of Israel there had been nothing like this in Jerusalem. 27 Then the priests and the Levites stood up and blessed the people, and their voice was heard; their prayer came to his holy dwelling in heaven.

The Chronicler's presentation of Hezekiah's Passover celebration changes the meaning of the festival in two important ways. First, by centralizing the observation of the festival in the Temple and Jerusalem, the king transforms it from a small family-oriented table festival (see Ex. 12:1–20) into a national occasion of celebration. In the process, he focuses the attention of the nation on the king's house and the king's chapel, sites sure to stir patriotic support for king and nation. Second, and more important for the Chronicler's theology, Hezekiah's Passover becomes the occasion for inviting the remnant of Israel back to Judah, back to the worship of God in the Temple, in an effort to heal the breach created by Jeroboam's rebellion against Rehoboam.

The account of the Passover, and particularly the invitation to the "remnant" of Israel to return to Jerusalem (v. 6), assumes that the Northern Kingdom had ceased to exist as a political entity. In fact, Israel was subsumed under the Assyrian empire in 722/21 B.C. But the beginning of Hezekiah's reign is probably five years earlier, in 727. The Chronicler appears to ignore this datum, however, in the interest of presenting Hezekiah's reign as the ideal moment to reclaim the lost northerners.

The structure of the account of the Passover is twofold: verses 1–12 recount the preparations for the Passover; verses 13–27 are the celebration of the Passover itself.

1. Preparations for the great Passover, 30:1–12. The king's preparations for the celebration of the Passover are described in three parts: the decision to celebrate the Passover in the second month and to invite to the celebration the remnant of the Northern Kingdom (vv. 1–5), the king's message conveyed throughout the kingdom (vv. 6–9), and the various reactions to the announcement (vv. 10–12).

The first section, the decision to celebrate the Passover, is bracketed in verses 1 and 5 by the information that the Passover should be open to all throughout the kingdom, including "all Israel" and especially those in "Ephraim and Manasseh" (v. 1) and, more broadly, "from Beersheba to Dan" (v. 5). Ephraim and Manasseh are the two tribes immediately to the north of Benjamin and therefore closest to Judah. The phrase "from Beer-sheba to Dan" describes the full extent of classical Israel, from the southernmost city (Beer-sheba) to the northernmost (Dan). The theme is thus set: This will be a Passover like no other, because it will be a great reunion of the people of God. Within the brackets, verses 2–4 serve to explain why the Passover is being celebrated in the second month rather than the first, as prescribed. Numbers 9:9–11 allows for individuals who are traveling or are ritually unclean to delay the observation of the Passover by one month, and the Chronicler now employs this excuse on behalf of the whole nation. The explanation offered relies on the comment in 2 Chronicles 29:34 that an insufficient number of priests had made themselves ritually clean to handle the work of sacrifice before the altar in the Temple. In addition, the Chronicler notes that the people had not assembled in Jerusalem, perhaps a reference to the provisions for travel as reasons for delaying the Passover in Numbers 9:9–11. The plan meets the approval of the king and his officials, who seem to be in charge of the event (as opposed to the clergy), and the decision is made.

The next phase of preparation is the announcement of the decision. Once again, the Chronicler employs a bracketing technique in composing the speech to be delivered by the messengers. Verses 6 and 9 contain the promise that if the people of the North will "return to the LORD," God will reward their faithfulness. In verse 6 the promise is couched in general terms: The Lord will "turn again to the remnant of you who have escaped . . . the kings of Assyria." In verse 9 the promise is explicit: Your kindred and your children will find compassion with their captors, and return to this land." But if the bracketing verses offer mercy, the center verses are full of accusations. Verses 7–8 remind the Israelites that their ancestors were faithless to God in turning their backs on Jerusalem and that only by reversing that "stiff-necked" rebellion and returning to the place where God is to be found can they remove the curse of suffering and defeat that has befallen them. The theology is fully consistent with what we have seen throughout Chronicles: Those in the past have sinned, and they have suffered for it. But before you now lies the chance for obedience; be faithful and live. For the Chronicler, of course, this is not merely a matter of historical curiosity. In his own time, the people of Israel were widely dispersed throughout the ancient world, and the

Chronicler nourished the hope that, like the Israel of Hezekiah's Passover, they would hear the invitation to "return to the LORD" and come back to Jerusalem. It was not to be, of course, for either Hezekiah or for the era of the Chronicler; Jews remained and remain scattered. But the Chronicler's hope is nonetheless remembered in the closing words of the Passover celebration, when Jews vow to celebrate the Passover "next year in Jerusalem."

Reaction to Hezekiah's invitation is mixed at best. In Israel, north of the Judahite border, it meets largely with scorn and disdain; it is even mocked. Such response confirms the Chronicler's judgment on the North that, by and large, they deserve the fate of destruction and dispersal because of their ongoing rebellion against the houses of God and David. But some are receptive and "humble themselves" to come to the festival. The comment makes clear that more is at stake here than merely attending a festival; to come to Passover in Jerusalem as an Israelite is publicly to bear witness to a change of heart and religious commitment. Within Judah, of course, the festival is met predictably with great joy and excitement. The Chronicler is clear that this is the doing of the "hand of God," which blessed Judah so that the people were of "one heart" to obey the command of king and God. Still, one cannot avoid the conclusion that this will not be the great reunion of the people of God it was intended to be. That occasion will have to wait for the Passover celebration of Josiah's reign (2 Chronicles 35).

2. Celebration of the Passover, 30:13–27. As people gather in Jerusalem for the celebration of the festival, the first act to be undertaken is the purification of the city from the vestiges of Baal worship (vv. 13–14). The act parallels the cleansing of the Temple, except that this time the cleansing is accomplished by the laity rather than the clergy. As before, cult objects and idols are removed and thrown into the Wadi Kidron, the dry river bed to the east of the city. With the city purified of non-Yahwistic influences, the celebration is ready to begin.

The Chronicler again draws attention to the role of the Levites, this time in carrying on the sacrifice for the multitude. In accordance with the provisions of Exodus 12:1–20, the Passover lambs are slaughtered on the fourteenth day of the month, the "day of preparation." However, the large number of celebrants causes a problem: There are still insufficient numbers of priests to handle the task of slaughtering so many animals. The Chronicler comments that "the priests and Levites were ashamed" (v. 15) and that they responded by sanctifying themselves in sufficient numbers to handle the task. Taking their "accustomed posts," the priests and Levites at last restore the Temple to its full and proper function. In verse 17, the Chronicler explains the importance of this: The arrival of so many pilgrims from the North means that most of the participants in the ceremonies are themselves unclean, so they cannot offer their own sacrifice. Instead, the work of ritual slaughtering must be done for them by the Levites.

The arrival of so many unclean pilgrims from Israel creates another problem for the Chronicler: Not only are they ritually unclean to offer the sacrifice but they are also unclean to eat the sacred meal that accompanies it. This is a problem that Levitical intervention cannot solve. The solution is provided, however, through the intercession of the king; his theologically innovative prayer is found in verses 18–19. Having noted that those from the Israelite tribes of Ephraim, Manasseh, Issachar, and Zebulun were unclean yet were eating the meal anyway, the king could halt the celebration until the pilgrims could be made clean, or he could ignore the violation of the laws governing ritual purity. In fact, he chooses a third option. Hezekiah's prayer asks God to "pardon all who set their hearts to seek God, the LORD the God of their ancestors, even though not in accordance with the sanctuary's rules of cleanness." The prayer acknowledges that a violation of the law exists and that the people understand their guilt; it further asks that God pardon their uncleanness from God's own grace. Perhaps most important of all, it implies that the commitment of the heart is more important than strict ritual obedience. Those who, in the classic phrase used by the Chronicler to express deep piety and commitment, "set their hearts to seek God, the LORD the God of their ancestors" should be accepted, even if they are not strictly obedient to the letter of the law. The divine response to Hezekiah's logic is apparently positive; verse 20 indicates that "the LORD heard Hezekiah, and healed the people," implying that the action of God was to take away the guilt caused by the violation of the law.

The final section of the chapter is yet another example of religious innovation: having celebrated the festival for a week, the people decide— again, apparently without clergy involvement—to continue the celebration for a second week. The Chronicler intends this as an expression of the overwhelming popular support for and engagement with the festival. He also intends for the reader to recall that Solomon's ceremony of dedication also lasted fourteen days (7:9) and thus once again to suggest that Hezekiah is a king like Solomon. The king and the royal court supply animals for sacrifice and feasting, and priests prepare themselves for service in sufficient numbers to meet the needs of the celebration. The Chronicler notes that "the whole assembly"—even those who were resident aliens—rejoiced throughout the festival, a sign of God's blessing of the people's faithfulness. The joy of the people was unequalled by anything since the time of Solomon, according to the Chronicler. In making this comment, he finally makes explicit the comparison between Hezekiah and Solomon that underlies this entire narrative.

The Chronicler concludes the account of the Passover with a final note: that the blessing of the people by the priests and Levites was "heard; their prayer came to [God's] holy dwelling in heaven." The implication of the comment is that the priests and Levites have finally been restored to their proper places and in appropriate numbers, and that the Temple is once again functioning as it should. Hezekiah has accomplished his goal: He has reversed not only the depredations of his father but has made the Temple the center of Israel's life in a way it has not been since the days of Solomon.

The account of the great Passover is a clear example of religious innovation at its best. Carefully attending to tradition and insuring that laws of purity and cleanness are remembered and observed, the king and Levites nonetheless find creative ways to solve problems created by the people's violation of those laws. Whether it be the Levitical intervention in the act of ritual slaughter when their priestly brothers were ill-prepared, or the king's solution to ask for pardon for an unclean nation to eat the sacred meal, the story of Hezekiah's Passover shines with the commitment to permit the popular expression of religious fervor to proceed ahead, undeterred by legalities. The Chronicler's devotion to tradition and law will not permit him to ignore violations, but his passion for those who set their hearts on seeking the Lord will not allow him to stand in the way of true faith. The demands of the present require him to envision innovations in worship, obedience, and even theology. Surely much the same thing can be said of the modern church. The great temptation for the church is always to hold tightly to its time-honored and cherished traditions, even when they have become more barrier than channel to the expression of meaningful faith. The struggle before the church of the present (if indeed this has not always been the church's struggle) is how to hold on to the past loosely, allowing it to guide our way through the present without halting our progress altogether. Tradition and innovation must be for us what they are for the Chronicler: partners, not opponents, in the quest to express the faith of the people of God.

PLANS FOR SUPPORT OF THE TEMPLE CLERGY
2 Chronicles 31:1–21

With the restoration of the Temple function completed and the great Passover celebration accomplished, Hezekiah's duties to the Temple now turn to its infrastructure. Second Chronicles 31 is devoted to matters related to the task of provisioning the clergy who serve the Temple. Once again, the structure is simple and readily perceived. After a brief description of the completion of the destruction of idols (v. 1, which may perhaps belong with the previous chapter), verses 2–19 record the means by which the king provides foodstuffs for the Levites. Within this account are two smaller units, the first concerning the offering of food supplies by king and people (vv. 2–10) and the second concerning the provision of storage for the food and for its management and distribution (vv. 11–19). The chapter concludes with the Chronicler's summary of Hezekiah's reign (vv. 20–21).

1. Completion of the destruction of idols, 31:1. Having recommitted themselves to the worship and service of God, the people now move out through the cities of Judah to remove the traces of the worship of other gods. The cultic objects they cut down and remove are "pillars" and "sacred poles," two standing pieces that are part of the accoutrements of Canaanite worship. But the cultic reclamation of the outlying areas is not confined to Judah; the people remove high places and cult objects in nearby Ephraim and Manasseh as well. These were the same areas from which Israelite participants in the great Passover came, so the Chronicler pictures them as sympathetic to the aims of the religious reforms of Hezekiah.

2. Provisions for the priests and Levites, 31:2–10. Hezekiah's first task after the celebration of the Passover is the reorganization of the Temple clergy. During the period of Ahaz's apostasy, priests and Levites had apparently become nonfunctional, so that, as noted in chapters 29 and 30, it was necessary to reconsecrate them in large numbers before the ritual of sacrifice could resume. Having now accomplished that reconsecration, Hezekiah reestablishes the rotation of duty for the clergy. It is not clear from the text whether the "divisions" in verse 2 are the same as those established by David in 1 Chronicles 24 and Solomon in 2 Chronicles 8:14 or if this represents a new organizational structure. The basic structure of responsibilities remains the same, however: Priests are responsible to conduct the sacrifices, and Levites are to assist the priests and to care for the operation and cleaning of the Temple. Verse 2 also mentions the two main subsidiary functions of the Levites—gatekeeping and music.

The king is generous in providing for the support of the clergy. His donations for the various offerings and festivals—sacrifices at morning and evening, on the Sabbath and at the beginning of the month ("new moon")—form the foundation of the sacrificial ritual, assuring that it will go forward. But the king commands further that the law of the tithe

(Deut. 14:12) be observed as well. The law required that the people bring a tenth of the produce of the land—grain, wine, livestock, and so forth—to the Temple for offering to the Lord. The offering was then shared among priests, Levites, and participants as a sacrificial meal. This may have been an issue for the Chronicler's own day: Malachi 3:8–10 urges the people to "bring the full tithe into the storehouse," an exhortation fully consistent with the description of this chapter. Malachi is a late prophet, active during the postexilic period, and may have been pointing to some lack of participation on the part of the people in support of the Temple and its sacrificial ritual.

In the Chronicler's description, the response of the people is again abundant (vv. 6–7); so much is brought in that it quickly overwhelms the storage capacities of the Temple, and the excess is piled up "in heaps" on the Temple grounds. The piles of provisions are, to the eyes of the Chronicler, evidence of God's blessing and of the people's faithfulness, and this is made explicit in the comment of the priest Zadok to the king in verse 10: "The LORD has blessed his people, so that we have this great supply left over."

3. Provisions for storage and distribution, 31:11–19. Hezekiah's response to the blessing of God through the abundance of the tithe is to build storehouses. These store facilities are constructed not only in Jerusalem but, as verse 15 indicates, in the other cities where there were communities of priests. Hezekiah takes various Levites from their duties and assigns them responsibility to oversee the construction and operation of the stores, including the distribution of food to the non-Jerusalem clergy. Priests and Levites whose divisions were not on duty in the Temple would not have shared in the sacrificial meal, and they and their families would therefore have been deprived of food. The Chronicler is careful to note that provision is made for their support as well, so that serving the Lord is not a penalty or an occasion of undue suffering. The king takes care to insure that the entire registry of priests, Levites, and their families is recorded and supplied as a way of rewarding the diligence of the clergy who "were faithful in keeping themselves holy." In other words, the provisioning of the clergy allowed them to maintain their ritual purity and readiness to serve in the Temple, so that the crisis of unsanctified clergy that hampered the celebrations of chapters 29 and 30 did not occur again. The principle is not foreign to Christians, who support through their contributions their clergy so that the clergy do not have to provide a separate living for themselves in addition to their pastoral responsibilities.

4. Summary comments on Hezekiah's reign, 31:20–21. The Chronicler concludes this section with effusive praise for all that Hezekiah has accomplished. Looking back over the restoration of the Temple, the revitalization of the Passover, and the reorganization of the Temple clergy, his conclusion is that the king "did what was good and right and faithful before the LORD his God" (v. 20), praise offered no other king. In addition, the Chronicler judges that Hezekiah did these things not with ulterior motives or seeking to aggrandize his position but "with all his heart." The result is predictable to those who understand the Chronicler's theology: "he prospered" (v. 21).

It is odd, however, that such a summary comment appears here rather than at the conclusion of the Hezekiah narrative, where we might have expected it. The reason for its inclusion here is probably that this concludes the Chronicler's own composition about Hezekiah's reign. Much of what follows in chapter 32 is drawn from his source in 2 Kings 18:13–19:37, and although the Chronicler has significantly reworked it according to his own theological and stylistic preferences, it is not the creation of his own vision in the way that chapters 29–31 are. In addition, the account in 2 Chronicles 32 contains the only critical comment to be found in the Chronicler's presentation of Hezekiah (32:25), and perhaps the Chronicler felt that such glowing and enthusiastic endorsements of the king as appear in 31:20–21 could not be written after that criticism.

SENNACHERIB'S INVASION
AND THE END OF HEZEKIAH'S REIGN
2 Chronicles 32:1–33

The story of Sennacherib's invasion of Judah is the one place in the Hezekiah narratives where the Chronicler draws heavily from the source in 2 Kings 18:13–19:37. Even so, he presents the material in his own way, editing and augmenting to craft a portrait consistent in every way with his theology.

The Sennacherib invasion is also one of the few places in Chronicles for which we have nonbiblical contemporaneous material, in this case in the form of Assyrian royal inscriptions that describe the campaign. While the Assyrian inscriptions have their own bias that serves their interests, they do provide an alternate image of the events of the campaign.

Sennacherib (who reigned from 705 to 681 B.C.) was the fourth in a series of expansionist kings to rule the Assyrian empire. The abrupt death of his predecessor, Sargon II, while on a military campaign in the Caucasus Mountains, brought Sennacherib to the throne amid widespread revolt, both among the provinces of the empire and within the palace itself. Judah appears to have participated in one such revolt, along with several Phoenician and Philistine states. Between 705 and 702, Sennacherib was occupied with matters at home and elsewhere in the empire, but in 701 he conducted a massive retaliatory and disciplinary campaign among his rebellious vassals in Palestine. According to his accounts of the events, Sennacherib laid siege to the city of Lachish, destroyed a large number of cities and towns in the countryside of Judah, and "shut Hezekiah up like a bird in a cage." Sennacherib extracted from Hezekiah a large monetary tribute before withdrawing his army. Sennacherib returned to Assyria, where he had a successful reign of more than twenty years. In 681, however, amid a palace coup, Sennacherib was assassinated by his own sons.

The Bible presents two accounts of the invasion of Judah by Sennacherib, 2 Kings 18:13–19:37 (reproduced nearly identically in Isaiah 36:1–39:8) and the present chapter in 2 Chronicles 32. Most scholars would agree that the account in 2 Kings itself contains at least two separate narratives. One is a short notice, 2 Kings 18:13–16, in which Hezekiah strips the Temple treasuries in order to collect tribute money that will save Jerusalem from destruction (this is in essential accord with Sennacherib's accounts). The other is a much longer and highly dramatic account, 2 Kings 18:17–19:37, that describes an Assyrian siege of Jerusalem, boastful challenges to Hezekiah's leadership by Sennacherib's officers, and finally a miraculous delivery of the city by divine intervention.

Second Chronicles 32 is similar to the larger account of 2 Kings 18:17–19:37, but it is by no means identical. Among the differences between the two are:

- the addition of a description of Hezekiah's defenses (32:1–8);
- the omission of any reference to an alliance with Egypt, an important point in 2 Kings 19:8–13;
- the omission of any reference to the payment of tribute;
- the collapse of three Assyrian speeches into one speech and a letter;
- the omission of Hezekiah's prayer; and
- the significant reduction in the role of the prophet Isaiah.

The Chronicler also follows his source in making reference to two other events in Hezekiah's reign: the king's illness (2 Kings 20:1–11; 2 Chron. 32:24–26) and the reception of envoys from Babylon (2 Kings 20:12–19; 2 Chron. 32:31). In each case, however, the accounts are drastically shortened in the Chronicler's version and make different theological points than in Kings. The end result is that, while using his source material faithfully, the Chronicler has crafted his own narrative of Hezekiah's reign and Sennacherib's invasion with its own distinct meaning for the story of Israel.

Chapter 32 is composed of the following parts: the account of Hezekiah's defensive preparations (vv. 1–8), Sennacherib's speech and letter (vv. 9–19), the defeat and death of Sennacherib (vv. 20–23), Hezekiah's illness (vv. 24–26), and the summary of Hezekiah's reign and account of his death (vv. 27–33).

1. The account of Hezekiah's defensive preparations, 32:1–8. The invasion of Sennacherib is introduced with the rather striking temporal clause, "After these things and these acts of faithfulness" (v. 1). The purpose of the clause can only be to dispel any notion that the invasion is due to some misdeed on Hezekiah's or the nation's part. So far in Chronicles, foreign invasions of Judah have served the function of punishing the sinfulness of king and people. But in the case of Hezekiah, the Chronicler has gone to considerable lengths to establish the piety and faithfulness of both. We are thus forced to see the invasion in a different light. For the Chronicler, the outcome of the invasion—the absolute defeat of Sennacherib by miraculous intervention—is the result of the Assyrian king's arrogance and ignorance about the power and uniqueness of Israel's God. This point will be fully developed by the end of the story, but the way is prepared for it in the first verse.

Hezekiah's response to learning of the invasion is to prepare his people for their own defense. His actions represent the classic steps in defensive siege warfare: gathering supplies, protecting resources, and marshalling strength. In his plan "to stop the flow of the springs" (v. 3), Hezekiah protects the city's water supply. Apparently, spring openings outside the city wall were blocked with rock and dirt and camouflaged, and the water redirected though new conduits inside the city walls. There exists today in Jerusalem a water conduit cut through the solid bedrock beneath the city often referred to as "Hezekiah's Tunnel" that probably dates from this period and may be the redirected water supply of which the Chronicler speaks here and in verse 30. By disguising the water supply in this way, Hezekiah would have both deprived the Assyrians of a ready water supply and insured accessible, safe water for the city's defenders.

The king further prepares the city by rebuilding broken sections of the wall and constructing a new outer wall for added security. A number of years ago, excavations in the Jewish Quarter of the Old City of Jerusalem uncovered a section of wall that some archaeologists have dated to the period of Hezekiah's reign; it may be that this is evidence of the accuracy of the Chronicler's narrative on this point. Repairs to the "Millo" (v. 5) probably involve shoring up the terrace walls on the south end of the city below the Temple complex. The final stage of material preparation is rearmament of the populace, in verse 5.

After seeing to the physical aspects of defense, Hezekiah turns his attention to the spiritual:

32:6 **He appointed combat commanders over the people, and gathered them together to him in the square at the gate of the city and spoke encouragingly to them, saying,** 7 **"Be strong and of good courage. Do not be afraid or dismayed before the king of Assyria and all the horde that is with him; for there is one greater with us than with him.** 8 **With him is an arm of flesh; but with us is the** LORD **our God, to help us and to fight our battles." The people were encouraged by the words of King Hezekiah of Judah.**

This speech draws on the Chronicler's theology of warfare. It features two emphases: (1) the reassurance that God is with Hezekiah and his people as reason not to fear, and (2) the promise that God will "fight our battles." The former is a familiar theme from David's assurances to Solomon in 1 Chronicles 22:16–17 and 28:20. The latter echoes the Chronicler's notion that war is the province of God and that God is the victor on behalf of the faithful (see 2 Chron. 14:9–15; 20:5–30 for examples of this theology in action). The speech has the effect of expressing basic trust in God's deliverance and divine strength, the very aspect of God's character most severely challenged by Sennacherib's messages to Judah and Jerusalem. The Chronicler is beginning to fill in the picture of the reason for the invasion: What is being tested is Hezekiah's trust in God's power to deliver God's people. The people who hear Hezekiah's acclamation of trust are "encouraged" by his words; they will need that encouragement in the face of the theological onslaught to come.

2. Sennacherib's speech and letter, 32:9–19. The messages sent verbally and in writing from Sennacherib to the people of Jerusalem can best be described as a propaganda campaign designed to undermine the faith and trust of the people against their king and God. That it fails is attributable to the strong centralizing power of the Passover and the popular commitment to faith detailed in chapters 29—31. In many respects, chapter 32 is the reason why Hezekiah has devoted so much effort to the revitalization and centralization of the faith of the nation; without it, there is no commitment to the preservation of the core institutions of Judah, the Temple, and the Davidic monarchy.

32:9 After this, while King Sennacherib of Assyria was at Lachish with all his forces, he sent his servants to Jerusalem to King Hezekiah of Judah and to all the people of Judah that were in Jerusalem, saying, 10 "Thus says King Sennacherib of Assyria: On what are you relying, that you undergo the siege of Jerusalem? 11 Is not Hezekiah misleading you, handing you over to die by famine and by thirst, when he tells you, 'The LORD our God will save us from the hand of the king of Assyria'? 12 Was it not this same Hezekiah who took away his high places and his altars and commanded Judah and Jerusalem, saying, 'Before one altar you shall worship, and upon it you shall make your offerings'? 13 Do you not know what I and my ancestors have done to all the peoples of other lands? Were the gods of the nations of those lands at all able to save their lands out of my hand? 14 Who among all the gods of those nations that my ancestors utterly destroyed was able to save his people from my hand, that your God should be able to save you from my hand? 15 Now therefore do not let Hezekiah deceive you or mislead you in this fashion, and do not believe him, for no god of any nation or kingdom has been able to save his people from my hand or from the hand of my ancestors. How much less will your God save you out of my hand!"

16 His servants said still more against the Lord GOD and against his servant Hezekiah. 17 He also wrote letters to throw contempt on the LORD the God of Israel and to speak against him, saying, "Just as the gods of other nations in other lands did not rescue their people from my hands, so the God of Hezekiah will not rescue his people from my hand." 18 They shouted it with a loud voice in the language of Judah to the people of Jerusalem who were on the wall, to frighten and terrify them, in order that they might take the city. 19 They spoke of the God of Jerusalem as if he were like the gods of the peoples of the earth, which are the work of human hands.

The Assyrian assault begins with a message to the inhabitants of Jerusalem, delivered by Assyrian royal servants while Sennacherib is still at Lachish. In 2 Kings 18, the speakers are identified as royal officers, and their titles—Rabshakeh and Rabsiris—are given. The Chronicler depersonalizes them, so that it seems that the message is spoken directly to the Jerusalemites by Sennacherib himself. The focal point is Sennacherib's challenge to the lordship and power of God and the trustworthiness of Hezekiah. In other words, Sennacherib assaults God and king, the very two institutions Hezekiah has worked to strengthen. The speech begins with the question, "On what are you relying?" (v. 10)—precisely the central question of the Chronicler's narrative. Indeed, one might argue that this question underlies the whole story of Israel in the hands of the Chronicler; upon whom does Israel— its kings and its people—place its trust: the Lord God of its ancestors or other deities of the nations? Sennacherib's challenge to Jerusalem thus reaches not merely the ears of the people on the other side of the wall but those of the whole community of faith throughout history. For the Chronicler, only one answer to that question leads to deliverance and peace: God is with us.

Sennacherib's challenge is that God will not, in fact, deliver Judah from his hand. The speech offers two reasons: (1) God is offended by Hezekiah's religious reforms, especially by the removal of the high places and sites of Baal cultic worship and the centralization of worship in Jerusalem; and (2) God is unable to withstand Assyrian might, for "no god of any nation or kingdom has been able to save his people from my hand" (v. 15). Regardless of which is true, the people have, according to Sennacherib, been misled by Hezekiah into foolish resistance.

From the Chronicler's perspective, Sennacherib commits two serious theological mistakes. First, he misunderstands the nature of worship in Israel. From the Chronicler's point of view, the Temple in Jerusalem is the one divinely ordained place of worship; far from being offended by the centralization of the cult, the God of Chronicles regards it as a necessary and faithful commitment to obedience. Second, Sennacherib misunderstands the nature of God, believing that the God of Israel is "like the gods of the peoples of the earth," a ludicrous notion for the Chronicler since all other gods are merely "the work of human hands" (v. 19). The second error is repeated in the letter to be read to the inhabitants of Jerusalem (vv. 16–17). The clear message in both speech and letter is "God will not save you."

A word should be said about the comment in verse 18 that the readers of the letter shouted "with a loud voice in the language of Judah." The source text in 2 Kings 18:26 portrays a conversation between the Assyrian officials and the officers of Hezekiah in which the Judahites ask the Assyrians to use Aramaic rather than Hebrew so that the people do not understand the threats being made and lose heart. Here the Chronicler has no such concerns for the commitment of the people to resistance. From verse 8 onward, the people of Judah and Jerusalem are the backbone of the resistance, and the Chronicler has no fear that they will be disheartened in their cause by the obviously erroneous words of a foreigner. For the Chronicler, the issue at stake here is precisely the faithfulness and trust in God of the king and people. Let them hear, the Chronicler seems to assume; the end result will not change.

3. Sennacherib's defeat and death, 32:20–23. The response of the king to the speech and letter of Sennacherib is to cry out to the Lord, which, in the view of the Chronicler, is exactly the correct response (see

14:11, Asa's cry in the face of the Ethiopian invasion, or 20:5–12, Jehoshaphat's prayer before the Moabite and Ammonite invasion). Basic to the Chronicler's notion of warfare is that victory is not won by strength of arms but by strength of faith; those who trust in the Lord prevail. The Chronicler has such implicit trust in Hezekiah's faith that he needs only to mention the fact of the king's prayer; he does not transmit the entire text of the prayer from the source (see 2 Kings 19:15–19). Moreover, the Chronicler does not even use this occasion as an opportunity to insert a prophetic oracle, even though one is readily available in 2 Kings 19:21–34. In fact, the role of Isaiah son of Amoz, which is quite prominent in the 2 Kings presentation of these events, is reduced to the single reference here in verse 20 that he shared the king's prayer. The Chronicler's view of Hezekiah is that his faith is strong enough to require no prophetic support.

The fate of Sennacherib is presented in a single verse, almost as if it were an afterthought. There is no military confrontation, no battle of tactical skills; there is only the angel who "cut off all the mighty warriors and commanders and officers in the camp of the king of Assyria" (v. 21a). The simplicity and matter-of-fact quality of the statement makes the Chronicler's point by understatement: Sennacherib thought he was stronger than the God of Israel, and he was wrong. With that fact established, there is nothing else for Sennacherib to do but return home "in disgrace," where in "the house of his own god, some of his own sons struck him down" (v. 21b). The irony is rich. The God whom Sennacherib assumed could not protect his enemies from his hand in fact quite handily did so, but the god in whom Sennacherib trusted for protection could not protect him from the hands of his own family. As if to make the point obvious, the Chronicler reminds us that "the LORD saved Hezekiah and the inhabitants of Jerusalem from the hand of King Sennacherib of Assyria" (v. 22).

As we noted above, Assyrian records make it plain that Sennacherib reigned another twenty years after the 701 B.C. campaign, and his assassination did not take place until 681. Thus, the cause-and-effect relationship implied by the Chronicler between Sennacherib's boastful arrogance and his death is a bit strained in reality. But, as we have also noted before, the Chronicler often demonstrates little interest in what our era might regard as solid historical reasoning, preferring instead to read the story of Israel theologically. From this perspective, it matters little whether the interim between the siege at Jerusalem and Sennacherib's death was twenty years or two weeks; the one is the direct result of the other, and both were the result of the work of God. Faith wins the day in this story, and the arrogant boasts of the Assyrian king of superiority over

God are met in the end with the quiet (if finally violent) assertion of divine superiority over the king. At the last, it is Hezekiah who reaps the rewards of international repute and good fortune, while Sennacherib goes down to ignominious defeat.

4. Hezekiah's illness, 32:24–26. This narrative, like the story of Sennacherib's invasion before it, is taken from the source narrative (2 Kings 20:1–11) but in a dramatically altered form. In Kings, Hezekiah's illness occasions a despondency on the part of the king to which Isaiah responds by offering the king a sign: The shadow on a sundial will move backward as a sign that the Lord will favor Hezekiah and heal him (2 Kings 20:9). In the Chronicler's version, Isaiah makes no appearance at all, the sign is left unspecified, and it is to the sign rather than to the illness that Hezekiah responds inappropriately, so further punishment rather than immediate healing is the result. An unspecified "wrath" is sent upon king and populace, and abates only after the king "humbled himself for the pride of his heart" (v. 26).

Hezekiah's illness creates a theological problem for the Chronicler similar to that of the Sennacherib invasion. Like foreign invasion, illness has been one of the means by which divine displeasure with the king has been expressed (see 16:11–12 and 26:16–21). But Hezekiah has done nothing with which God is explicitly displeased, and the Chronicler offers no explanation for the onset of the illness. In all probability, the Chronicler again wants to use this episode to teach a moral lesson. The moral lesson of the Sennacherib invasion is that trust in God delivers Israel. The moral lesson here is that God is receptive and responsive to the repentance of the faithful.

What has Hezekiah done for which he needs to repent? The Chronicler is never specific about this, offering only the explanation that "Hezekiah did not respond according to the benefit done to him, for his heart was proud" (v. 25). We are not told what the nature of the inappropriate response was or what an appropriate response might have been. Instead, we are told only that the king's heart was proud and that it is precisely this pride of which he must repent in order to turn back the divine wrath. That he does so and is forgiven is most likely the Chronicler's point here; Hezekiah thus serves as a moral example even when he sins.

There is probably one final reason for the inclusion of this episode, and it is to be found in the final clause of verse 26: "The wrath of the LORD did not come upon them in the days of Hezekiah." Royal pride and apostasy have been a consistent problem throughout 2 Chronicles 10—36; indeed, they are the major reasons why Judah is finally overwhelmed by the great powers of the ancient Near East. Judah and Jerusalem are spared annihilation this time, in the "days of Hezekiah," but the day is coming when divine patience finally runs out and the tides of history overwhelm the city and its kings. The illness of Hezekiah becomes for the Chronicler another opportunity to comment on the danger of human pride and to warn that God's patience with human sin does not last forever. The day of reckoning for Judah is approaching, even if it "did not come upon them in the days of Hezekiah."

5. *Summary of Hezekiah's reign, 32:27–33.* The list of Hezekiah's achievements in verses 27–30 is intended to indicate the breadth of God's blessing upon the king. All the standard measures of wealth and success as a monarch are present: monetary and material wealth, military strength, and civic construction. The conclusion to which the reader is inevitably led is that "Hezekiah prospered in all his works" (v. 30) because God blessed him as a result of his great faithfulness.

The one striking element of this summary of Hezekiah's reign, especially for those familiar with the account in 2 Kings 20:12–19, is the Chronicler's brief description of the arrival of the envoys from Babylon. In Kings, the Babylonian envoys are allowed by an overzealous and naïve Hezekiah to inspect every aspect of the king's treasuries, the Temple, and the various fortifications of the city of Jerusalem. The prophet Isaiah chastises him for his foolishness, explaining that he has now given the Babylonians a reason to conquer Jerusalem. The Chronicler omits the entire story and merely mentions that the envoys from Babylon arrived, explaining that they were sent to "inquire about the sign that had been done in the land" (presumably the same sign mentioned in v. 24). We are not told what the envoys learned or what Hezekiah revealed, and Hezekiah does not appear naïve or foolish as he does in the source narrative. Rather, we know only that the whole matter was the occasion for a divine test, "to know all that was in his heart" (v. 31). We are not told what God learned.

The death of Hezekiah is accompanied with the standard reference to additional material in other sources. This time, however, we may possess at least some of what the Chronicler refers to; Isaiah 36—39 provide an account essentially parallel to the one in 2 Kings 18:13–20:19 and may be what the Chronicler means in verse 32 by the "vision of the prophet Isaiah son of Amoz." After his death, the king is buried with full honors in his ancestral cemetery, a sign of the esteem with which he is held by his people.

Hezekiah's death brings to a close the last flowering of Judah's glory before the precipitous fall to the end of the kingdom. There will be one other momentary glimpse of the former glory of Solomon in Josiah (2 Chronicles 34—35), but in the Chronicler's treatment it is a lesser moment. Hezekiah's reign holds for the Chronicler many messages he deems it important for his own time to hear: the possibility of return from exile (30:6–9), the necessity of a revitalized Temple, cleansed of its brokenness, and a reunited people healed of their divisions (chaps. 29—30), and the witness that one withstands a great enemy not with force of arms but armed with faith (chap. 32). It is no surprise, therefore, that with the close of Hezekiah's death, the Chronicler's vision turns dark as he contemplates a Judah that did not learn from its teacher's example but slowly slid into chaos.

18. The Reigns of Manasseh and Amon
2 Chronicles 33:1–25

Throughout the story of the kings of Judah, the Chronicler never wavers in his commitment to the doctrine of individual responsibility. At the same time, he has continued to hold out faith in the possibility of repentance and redemption. Nowhere is that commitment and faith clearer than in the present narrative, the story of Manasseh. Following the picture of Manasseh painted in 2 Kings 21:1–9, the opening verses of 2 Chronicles 33 portray a Manasseh whose evil and apostasy reach monumental proportions. But the Chronicler's story then takes a dramatic and unexpected turn, showing a repentant Manasseh restored to his kingdom and faithful to his God. The worst of Judah's kings thus becomes in the hands of the Chronicler an example of the possibilities of repentance and divine forgiveness.

Viewed from the perspective of the Chronicler's theology, such a turn of events is necessary. The source narrative credits Manasseh with a reign of fifty-five years, the longest of any Judahite monarch. For the Chronicler, long years of life and reign are a sign of divine favor and blessing, but the Manasseh we meet in 2 Kings 21:1–9 deserves neither. So the Chronicler is faced with the necessity of rehabilitating the reputation of Judah's most apostate king, a feat accomplished by the story of Manasseh's capture, repentance, and restoration (2 Chron. 33:1–9).

The chapter has four sections: Manasseh's apostasy (vv. 1–9), Manasseh's repentance and restoration (vv. 10–17), Manasseh's death and regnal summary (vv. 18–20), and the regnal summary for Amon (vv. 21–25).

1. Manasseh's apostasy, 33:1–9. Manasseh's accession to the throne occurs at age twelve. But he wastes no time in undoing the work of his father.

33:3 **For he rebuilt the high places that his father Hezekiah had pulled down, and erected altars to the Baals, made sacred poles, worshiped all**

the host of heaven, and served them. ⁴ He built altars in the house of the
LORD, of which the LORD had said, "In Jerusalem shall my name be forever." ⁵ He built altars for all the host of heaven in the two courts of the
house of the LORD. ⁶ He made his son pass through fire in the valley of the
son of Hinnom, practiced soothsaying and augury and sorcery, and dealt
with mediums and with wizards. He did much evil in the sight of the
LORD, provoking him to anger. ⁷ The carved image of the idol that he had
made he set in the house of God, of which God said to David and to his
son Solomon, "In this house, and in Jerusalem, which I have chosen out
of all the tribes of Israel, I will put my name forever; ⁸ I will never again
remove the feet of Israel from the land that I appointed for your ancestors, if only they will be careful to do all that I have commanded them,
all the law, the statutes, and the ordinances given through Moses."
⁹ Manasseh misled Judah and the inhabitants of Jerusalem, so that they
did more evil than the nations whom the LORD had destroyed before the
people of Israel.

Within the first few verses it is clear that Manasseh's evil will rival that of
Ahaz; indeed, the language used by the Chronicler echoes that used to
describe Ahaz. Manasseh "did much evil in the sight of the LORD" and
particularly in following "the abominable practices of the nations whom
the LORD drove out before the people of Israel" (v. 2). By restoring the
cultic practices of peoples driven from the land through Israel's arrival
and settlement, Manasseh, like Ahaz, undoes the work of God. The conquest of Canaan was, in the eyes of ancient Israel, God's gracious gift to
his people of a safe place where they might live in peace and follow the
commandments of their God without temptation from other religions.
To restore those very religions is to undermine the gracious gift of safety
and security from God to the people.

The specifics of Manasseh's restoration of the Canaanite Baal cult are
detailed in verses 3–8. He rebuilt high places (i.e., non-Temple worship
shrines in outlying areas) torn down by Hezekiah during the great reform
of Hezekiah's first year, and erected altars to Baal and "sacred poles," all
of which are forbidden in Israel. He "worshiped all the host of heaven"
(v. 3), probably a reference to another ancient Canaanite ritual whose
details are now unclear. The passing of his son "through the fire in the
valley of the son of Hinnom" (v. 6) is the same rite practiced by Ahaz
(28:3). In addition, Manasseh patronized various practitioners of necro-
mantic arts: wizardry, communion with the spirits of the dead, and so
forth, all of which are sharply forbidden because they violate the boundary between the realm of the human and the realm of the divine (cf. Deut.
18:9–13). The point of this list of crimes and misdeeds seems to be that
Manasseh has undone as effectively as possible the reforms of his father

and returned to the practices of his grandfather; it is as if the reforms of Hezekiah had never occurred.

The nadir of Manasseh's descent into apostasy is the establishment of a carved idol in the midst of the Temple. The significance of this act goes beyond its violation of the commandment prohibiting engraved or carved images (Ex. 20:4–6). The Chronicler uses this occasion to recite in some detail the theology of the location of the divine name in the Temple and in the city of David precisely because that theology is abrogated by the idol. The Temple is called into being by God's decision to place there the divine name (see, among other texts, 2:4–6); in the Chronicler's vision it is to be the place where for all time God's name should be held in respect and awe, and to which all Israel should appeal for aid and comfort in hardship. Indeed, the Temple is something of a symbol for Israel's vitality: As long as the people keep the covenant by obeying "all the law, statutes, and ordinances" (v. 8), God will hold their place in the land secure. But Manasseh's brazen act of apostasy abrogates that promise and unsettles Israel in the land God has given them to settle. It is for this reason that the Chronicler concludes that Manasseh has "misled" the people of God into folly and death.

2. Manasseh's repentance and restoration, 33:10–17. The divine reaction to Manasseh's sin is carried out through the offices of the Assyrian empire: Manasseh is carried away in chains to Babylon, to the court of the Assyrian king (Sennacherib, after conquering Babylon, used the city as a royal capital for some years). Verse 10 provides a summary of prophetic warnings that go unheeded, offering further justification still for the punishment Manasseh receives. The imprisonment of the king was used as punishment for impiety and disobedience once before, when Amaziah was imprisoned in the North in the wake of his foolhardy aggression against the northern king Joash (25:20–24).

What is striking about Manasseh's imprisonment is that his punishment also becomes the occasion for his redemption:

33:10 **The LORD spoke to Manasseh and to his people, but they gave no heed. 11 Therefore the LORD brought against them the commanders of the army of the king of Assyria, who took Manasseh captive in manacles, bound him with fetters, and brought him to Babylon. 12 While he was in distress he entreated the favor of the LORD his God and humbled himself greatly before the God of his ancestors. 13 He prayed to him, and God received his entreaty, heard his plea, and restored him again to Jerusalem and to his kingdom. Then Manasseh knew that the LORD indeed was God.**

The Chronicler's vision of Manasseh is as a moral example of the possibility of forgiveness: The evil king is punished, but in his punishment sees the error of his ways and repents. The Chronicler employs the phrase we have seen already to signal the sincerity of Manasseh's repentance: The king "humbled himself" (see also 11:12 and 32:26). The divine response is hearing and acceptance, and the result is that Manasseh is restored to the kingdom (v. 13).

Is the episode of Manasseh's repentance historical? There is no information in Assyrian records from the reigns of Sennacherib or Esarhaddon (Assyrian king, 681–669 B.C.) to indicate that Manasseh was ever imprisoned; indeed, the only mention of Manasseh is complimentary of his regular tribute and provision of soldiers and supplies for Assyrian campaigns against Egypt. It thus does not appear likely that Manasseh was taken in chains to Babylon. The possibility, of course, exists that Manasseh made some sort of state visit to the Assyrian court, a reward perhaps for being a loyal vassal, and that the Chronicler has taken license with the visit for his own purposes. In the end, of course, we have only the Chronicler's narrative, and it serves a theological rather than a historical aim: We are to see in this story the possibility of redemption even for the most hardened of apostates.

The list of good things done by Manasseh after his repentance (vv. 14–16) counterbalances and reverses the evil done before (vv. 3–7). After strengthening the defenses of city and countryside, Manasseh tears down all the altars he erected in city and countryside alike, removes the foreign gods from the city, and does away with the idol he had set up in the Temple. He restores the sacrificial ritual to operation as his father Hezekiah had done, initiating it with sacrifices of well-being and thanks (see 29:31–36). All these acts are among those typically regarded by the Chronicler as the achievements of a worthy king and as the symbols of God's blessing on the king's reign.

3. Manasseh's death and regnal summary, 33:18–20. The last words of the Chronicler on the subject of Manasseh's reign are, appropriately, mixed. Manasseh's apostasy and disobedience are not forgotten; rather, they are specifically recalled and recorded in the writings of "seers" unnamed. But remembered as well is Manasseh's repentance, that he "humbled himself" (v. 20) and prayed to God. In fact, a reference among the records cited by the Chronicler mentions the prayer of Manasseh. A document bearing the title, "The Prayer of Manasseh," is among the texts included in the Apocrypha, the writings regarded as noncanonical by Protestants but included in the Roman Catholic and Greek Orthodox canons. The Chronicler's account of Manasseh's death mirrors this mixed verdict as well: It is peaceful, and he is buried in Jerusalem, but without mention of honor.

4. The reign and regnal summary of Amon, 33:21–26. The Chronicler's account of Amon's reign and its evaluation is drawn nearly verbatim from 2 Kings 21:21–22, except that remarks in the Kings account that denigrate Manasseh have been withdrawn in Chronicles. The Chronicler sees Amon's reign as evil without mitigation and specifically without any of the repentance or redemption in Manasseh's life. It is hardly surprising that the Chronicler expresses no outrage at the assassination of Amon by his servants. In the Chronicler's system, evil begets evil.

We do take note of the people who emerge to deal with the crisis of succession posed by Amon's assassination. The text identifies them as the "people of the land." Scholars have for some time debated who these people are but have arrived at no consensus. Are they wealthy landowners who form a sort of Judahite aristocracy? Are they some royal council or other governmental body? Are they some power block within the political system of Judah that stands over against the king but are still loyal to the kingdom? Nothing can be determined with certainty except that they seem to emerge in crises of succession, that they seem empowered or perhaps self-empowered to execute justice on those they deem responsible for the crisis, and that they appear able to appoint a king to ascend to the vacant throne. They escort the boy king Joash to his throne (23:20); they settle the succession by appointing Josiah king in the wake of Amon's assassination, and they make Jehoahaz king after Josiah's death in battle (36:1). All that can be said with any clarity is that this group, shrouded as they are in mystery, plays a crucial role in late Judahite politics.

19. The Reign of Josiah
2 Chronicles 34:1–35:27

The Chronicler's presentation of Josiah in 2 Chronicles 34—35 is built on the form and content of his source narrative in 2 Kings 22—23, but the final portraits of the king in the two are strikingly different. In Kings, Josiah is the greatest of the kings of Judah, exceeded only in righteousness and importance by David and Solomon. He is a nationalistic hero and religious reformer who reunites his people, divided since the days of Rehoboam, and restores the proper worship of the Lord in the Temple. In Chronicles, on the other hand, Josiah has a less impressive place. To be sure, he reorganizes the Passover celebration so that it is a national festival centered in Jerusalem and focused on the Temple, but in this he is less an innovator than a systematizer. In Chronicles, the credit for understanding the importance of Passover as a festival of national significance goes to Hezekiah (2 Chronicles 30). It is Hezekiah and not Josiah who first hits upon the notion of including the former Northern Kingdom in the great celebration in Jerusalem, and it is Hezekiah who develops the Passover as a centralized, Temple-oriented event rather than a small, family-oriented gathering. Josiah's contribution to the Passover is organization and systematization. What "came about suddenly" (29:36) and rather haphazardly under Hezekiah's innovation is now in Josiah's hands carefully planned. The priests and Levites are sanctified and ready in sufficient numbers to handle the demands of the sacrifice, the observation of the festival occurs on the proper day of the proper month, and there are no embarrassed prayers asking for divine forbearance with those who have violated the laws of ritual cleanness.

For all that, however, there is still the sense in 2 Chronicles 34—35 that the fervor of Hezekiah is missing in Josiah. Perhaps the best clue to this truth is the difference in the description of the popular response to the two celebrations. The accounts of Hezekiah's Passover are replete with the signs of popular pleasure: The people "rejoiced" (29:36), they shame the priests by their devotion (30:15), they overwhelm the sacrificial process by their numbers (30:18–20), they extend the festival an additional seven days "with gladness" (30:23), and they experience "great joy" in the celebration (30:26). Josiah's Passover, for all its propriety, lacks a single reference to popular joy or zeal.

It is difficult to avoid the conclusion that the Chronicler offers a more sympathetic picture of Hezekiah than of Josiah, thus reversing the pattern of evaluation found in his source in 2 Kings. For the Chronicler, the passionate piety and devotion of Hezekiah appears preferable to the careful ordering of religious observation in Josiah. That both are important to the story is without question, but perhaps in an era when the people of God have lost some of the sense of the power and transformative quality of worship, what most needs recovery are the passions that impel them to sanctuary and altar rather than the rules that govern their behavior when they get there.

JOSIAH'S RELIGIOUS REFORMS
2 Chronicles 34:1–33

34:1 Josiah was eight years old when he began to reign; he reigned thirty-one years in Jerusalem. 2 He did what was right in the sight of the LORD, and walked in the ways of his ancestor David; he did not turn aside to the right or to the left. 3 For in the eighth year of his reign, while he was still a boy, he began to seek the God of his ancestor David, and in the twelfth year he began to purge Judah and Jerusalem of the high places, the sacred poles, and the carved and the cast images. 4 In his presence they pulled down the altars of the Baals; he demolished the incense altars that stood above them. He broke down the sacred poles and the carved and the cast images; he made dust of them and scattered it over the graves of those who had sacrificed to them. 5 He also burned the bones of the priests on their altars, and purged Judah and Jerusalem. 6 In the towns of Manasseh, Ephraim, and Simeon, and as far as Naphtali, in their ruins all around, 7 he broke down the altars, beat the sacred poles and the images into powder, and demolished all the incense altars throughout all the land of Israel. Then he returned to Jerusalem.

8 In the eighteenth year of his reign, when he had purged the land and the house, he sent Shaphan son of Azaliah, Maaseiah the governor of the city, and Joah son of Joahaz, the recorder, to repair the house of the LORD his God. 9 They came to the high priest Hilkiah and delivered the money that had been brought into the house of God, which the Levites, the keepers of the threshold, had collected from Manasseh and Ephraim and from all the remnant of Israel and from all Judah and Benjamin and from the inhabitants of Jerusalem. 10 They delivered it to the workers who had the

oversight of the house of the LORD, and the workers who were working in the house of the LORD gave it for repairing and restoring the house. ¹¹ They gave it to the carpenters and the builders to buy quarried stone, and timber for binders, and beams for the buildings that the kings of Judah had let go to ruin. ¹² The people did the work faithfully. Over them were appointed the Levites Jahath and Obadiah, of the sons of Merari, along with Zechariah and Meshullam, of the sons of the Kohathites, to have oversight. Other Levites, all skillful with instruments of music, ¹³ were over the burden bearers and directed all who did work in every kind of service; and some of the Levites were scribes, and officials, and gatekeepers.

¹⁴ While they were bringing out the money that had been brought into the house of the LORD, the priest Hilkiah found the book of the law of the LORD given through Moses. ¹⁵ Hilkiah said to the secretary Shaphan, "I have found the book of the law in the house of the LORD"; and Hilkiah gave the book to Shaphan. ¹⁶ Shaphan brought the book to the king, and further reported to the king, "All that was committed to your servants they are doing. ¹⁷ They have emptied out the money that was found in the house of the LORD and have delivered it into the hand of the overseers and the workers." ¹⁸ The secretary Shaphan informed the king, "The priest Hilkiah has given me a book." Shaphan then read it aloud to the king.

¹⁹ When the king heard the words of the law he tore his clothes. ²⁰ Then the king commanded Hilkiah, Ahikam son of Shaphan, Abdon son of Micah, the secretary Shaphan, and the king's servant Asaiah: ²¹ "Go, inquire of the LORD for me and for those who are left in Israel and in Judah, concerning the words of the book that has been found; for the wrath of the LORD that is poured out on us is great, because our ancestors did not keep the word of the LORD, to act in accordance with all that is written in this book."

²² So Hilkiah and those whom the king had sent went to the prophet Huldah, the wife of Shallum son of Tokhath son of Hasrah, keeper of the wardrobe (who lived in Jerusalem in the Second Quarter) and spoke to her to that effect. ²³ She declared to them, "Thus says the LORD, the God of Israel: Tell the man who sent you to me, ²⁴ Thus says the LORD: I will indeed bring disaster upon this place and upon its inhabitants, all the curses that are written in the book that was read before the king of Judah. ²⁵ Because they have forsaken me and have made offerings to other gods, so that they have provoked me to anger with all the works of their hands, my wrath will be poured out on this place and will not be quenched. ²⁶ But as to the king of Judah, who sent you to inquire of the LORD, thus shall you say to him: Thus says the LORD, the God of Israel: Regarding the words that you have heard, ²⁷ because your heart was penitent and you humbled yourself before God when you heard his words against this place and its inhabitants, and you have humbled yourself before me, and have torn your clothes and wept before me, I also have heard you, says the LORD. ²⁸ I will gather you to your ancestors and you shall be gathered to your grave in peace; your eyes shall not see all the disaster that I will bring on this place and its inhabitants." They took the message back to the king.

²⁹ Then the king sent word and gathered together all the elders of Judah and Jerusalem. ³⁰ The king went up to the house of the LORD, with all the people of Judah, the inhabitants of Jerusalem, the priests and the Levites, all the people both great and small; he read in their hearing all the words of the book of the covenant that had been found in the house of the LORD. ³¹ The king stood in his place and made a covenant before the LORD, to follow the LORD, keeping his commandments, his decrees, and his statutes, with all his heart and all his soul, to perform the words of the covenant that were written in this book. ³² Then he made all who were present in Jerusalem and in Benjamin pledge themselves to it. And the inhabitants of Jerusalem acted according to the covenant of God, the God of their ancestors. ³³ Josiah took away all the abominations from all the territory that belonged to the people of Israel, and made all who were in Israel worship the LORD their God. All his days they did not turn away from following the LORD the God of their ancestors.

After a general introduction to the reign of Josiah (vv. 1–2), the narrative of Josiah's religious reforms follows a simple, three-part structure: The Chronicler describes the purging of the land of idolatrous worship (vv. 3–8), followed by the discovery and interpretation of the book of the law (vv. 9–28), and concludes with a covenant renewal ceremony between king and people (vv. 29–33).

1. Purging the land of idolatry, 34:1–8. The Chronicler introduces the reign of Josiah with the standard formula, taken directly from 2 Kings 23:1–2, relating the age of Josiah's accession to the throne and the length of his reign. But then he diverges from the order of his source material. In 2 Kings 23:3–20, the first event in Josiah's reign is the discovery of the book of the law in the Temple; both the religious reforms and the celebration of the Passover are the result of this discovery. In 2 Chronicles 34, on the other hand, it is the religious reforms that come first, followed by the discovery of the law book. The effect is to reduce the importance of the law book in the estimation of the Chronicler. It is not the foundation of the king's reforming activity. Rather, the king's zeal for reform grows out of his own personal faith and piety, which are described in verse 3: At age sixteen he "began to seek the God of his ancestor David," and four years later, at age twenty, he began the purge of the land.

The reforms conducted by the king (vv. 4–8) are focused on the removal of the worship of Baal from the kingdom. A comparison between the description of the reforms in 2 Kings 23:4–20 and in the present text shows that the Chronicler has considerably abridged his source, devoting only five verses to the reform. We should trace some of this foreshortening to the fact that much of the cultic purge of Judah took place under Manasseh in the Chronicler's scheme (2 Chron. 33:14–17); only that

which Amon had time to restore in the brief two years of his reign needs
to be removed. But perhaps we should also attribute the brevity of the
reform account to the Chronicler's view of Josiah as not so much a
reformer as an organizer.

The reforms are thorough. Images and carvings and sacred poles to
Asherah, all part of the cultic furniture of the Baal cult, are pulled down
and destroyed. The vehemence is notable: They are not merely thrown
out as before but ground into dust so as to render them permanently irre-
trievable. Moreover, the dust is then spread upon the graves of those who
worshiped at the altars and adored the images, surely a sign of defilement
of the graves of those whom the reformers considered apostate. The
bones of priests—Baalist priests surely, although the text is not explicit
about this—are burned on their own altars, so that the priests become an
ironic sacrifice to their own apostasy. The reform is extended beyond the
borders of Judah into Manasseh, Ephraim, and Simeon and as far north
as Naphtali, the northernmost of the ancient tribal territories. The overall picture of the reform is one of meticulous care taken to demolish all
evidence of impurity and allegiance to other gods.

2. Discovery of the book of the law, 34:8–28. Out of the reform comes
the discovery of the book of the law. The Chronicler sets the stage for the
discovery narrative by indicating that "when he had purged the land and
the house," the king turned to the matter of repairs. In this he follows the
pattern already familiar from Hezekiah's reign: purification first, then
preparations and restorations to service. Having removed the evidence of
apostasy, Josiah now turns to preparing the Temple for use in the worship
of God and in that context discovers the book of the law.

The initial elements of the story resemble Joash's repairs to the
Temple in 24:4–14. Here, as well as there, the repairs to the Temple are
to be financed through the tax collected from the people when they enter
the Temple gates, and transmitted to the priests and Levites to oversee
the work. However, unlike Joash's repairs, no allegations of inactivity in
collection or arguments over the method of appropriating the money
mark Josiah's repairs. Instead, the king's messengers deliver the money,
collected by the Levites in an orderly manner, to the priest Hilkiah (v. 9),
and from there it is placed in the hands of the supervisors and workers on
the Temple project. The work is done "faithfully" (v. 12), and overseen
by Levites.

In the context of the repairs, Hilkiah discovers "the book of the law of
the LORD given through Moses" (v. 14). But what are the contents of the
book? For most of the last two centuries, scholars have assumed that the
book in question is Deuteronomy, or at least some significant portion
thereof. This claim is bolstered by the reference later in 2 Chronicles

34:24 to the "curses that are written in the book." Deuteronomy 27:9–26 and 28:15–68 contain well-known imprecations to fall upon an Israel that does not obey the covenant. More recently, however, challenges to the assumption that Deuteronomy was the law book discovered in the Temple have been raised by a number of scholars, so that its degree of certainty is now less than before. Indeed, the Chronicler's description of the book as "the book of the law of the LORD given though Moses" would more commonly be used in the Persian period to describe the contents of the entire Pentateuch (the first five books of the Bible). It is perhaps the case that, for the Chronicler, what is intended by the phrase "book of the law" is the Pentateuch (or some version of it), since by the time of Ezra (ca. 450 B.C.; see Neh. 8:1–8) such a work almost surely was being read in Jewish circles.

The process of transmission of the book of the law from Hilkiah to the king (vv. 15–18) carries the sense of increasing foreboding and dread. The priest delivers the book to Shaphan, the royal secretary, without comment, as if he wishes to be rid of it. Shaphan reports the finding to the king, but only after informing the king that his commands have been or are being satisfied, as if to soften the blow of the contents of the book. Only after reporting his success does Shaphan broach the subject of the book of the law with Josiah. Even then, the secretary shifts the responsibility for the origin of the book away from himself: "The priest Hilkiah has given me a book" (v. 18). After distancing himself in this way, Shaphan reads the contents of the book to the king.

The royal reaction is dramatic. Tearing the clothes is a common act of mourning and despair often associated with the news of a death or other irreparable tragedy. That Josiah should choose such a gesture to express himself is an indication of the gravity of the indictment posed by the book. Clearly its contents are upsetting. The king's second act is less emotional and more analytical: He commands a delegation of five officials to "inquire of the LORD for me and for those who are left in Israel and in Judah, concerning the words of the book" (v. 21). The reason already points to the result: "for the wrath of the LORD that is poured out on us is great."

Verses 22–28 are the inquiry of the Lord commanded by the king. To "inquire of the LORD" is to consult a prophet concerning the propitious nature of a situation; we have already seen Ahab and Jehoshaphat make such an inquiry by means of prophetic consultation in 18:4–20 (see especially vv. 4 and 7). More often than not, such prophetic consultations result in warnings of ill fate rather than promises of good fortune (see Jer. 28:8–10). Certainly the present consultation is no exception. Huldah (a female prophetic figure—perhaps rare but not unknown in the Old

Testament) declares disaster upon Judah and Jerusalem, fulfilling directly the "curses that are written in the book" (v. 24). The reason for this judgment is simple and already anticipated by the king in verse 21: the apostasy of the ancestors. Huldah's message from God is more specific: Israel has forsaken God, made offerings to other gods, provoking the divine wrath that will now be "poured out upon this place and will not be quenched" (v. 25).

Careful readers of this text will wonder how the Chronicler, with his commitment to a doctrine of individual moral responsibility, can permit the sins of the "ancestors" to be visited upon the generation of Josiah, which has sought to be faithful. The answer has at least two parts. First, the prophecy of Huldah is careful to note that Josiah himself will not suffer the disaster but will "be gathered to your grave in peace; your eyes shall not see all the disaster that I will bring on this place and its inhabitants" (v. 28). Thus, the reward for Josiah's faithfulness and obedience is a forestalling of the calamity until after Josiah's death. Second, even the Chronicler's theology of individual responsibility does not preclude a divine accounting for the whole accumulation of Israel's sin and waywardness. In a very important sense, the events of 587 that bring Judah to its end are the result of the aggregation of guilt and sin from the beginnings of the nation until its final days. That guilt and sin are epitomized in the depravity of the final kings of Judah (see 2 Chronicles 36), but they are not confined there. Smaller obediences have been rewarded individually and smaller apostasies have been punished individually, but the great final accounting of Israel's self-conduct in the land still awaits. Thanks to the obedience of Josiah, it waits for a while longer.

The king responds to Huldah's confirmation of his worst fears with what may seem like whistling in the dark. He gathers the elders and people together before the Temple, reads the book of the law to them (v. 30), and then covenants with God to follow the terms of the book—even quoting the classical Deuteronomic language for those terms: "commandments," "statutes," and "decrees." He commits himself to it fully and without reservation: "with all his heart and all his soul" (v. 31), a phrase that evokes the language of Deuteronomy 6:4–5. Having committed himself to the covenant, the king then requires the same of all the people as well, and for the rest of the life of the king, claims the Chronicler, the covenant was obeyed. In this manner, the amnesty granted the king from the disaster threatened in Huldah's prophecy is broadened to include all the people of Judah and Benjamin and in the city of Jerusalem. As a sign of good faith toward the covenant, Josiah destroys Baal cultic sites in Israel, requiring the people to worship God rather than to follow the Baal traditions. Yet, in spite of covenant and reform, the warning of Huldah hangs over the text like a cloud: One day the curse will fall upon Judah. It is only a matter of time.

CELEBRATION OF THE PASSOVER AND THE DEATH OF JOSIAH
2 Chronicles 35:1–27

Second Chronicles 35 is composed of two major stories: the great Passover of Josiah's reign (vv. 1–19) and the story of Josiah's death (vv. 20–27). In each case, the foundation for the story is found in the source narrative of 2 Kings 23: the Passover in 2 Kings 23:21–23 and the death of Josiah in 2 Kings 23:28–30a. But also in each case, the Chronicler has considerably expanded upon his source, providing a much richer narrative that satisfies his theological aims.

1. Observation of the Passover, 35:1–19. Having purified both Temple and country of Baal worship and its influence, the king is now ready to keep the Passover. As with Hezekiah, Josiah's Passover is understood not as a small family-oriented meal but as a nationalistic observance on a grand scale, with its center in Jerusalem. Its purpose is to draw the people together, especially those who live outside the boundaries of Judah in formerly Israelite lands, and to bind them to king and Temple.

Throughout the narrative of Josiah's Passover, the emphasis is on the propriety of the celebration. It is celebrated in Jerusalem, following the precedent set by Hezekiah and in accordance with the requirements of Deuteronomy 16:5–6 that the sacrifice be offered "at the place where the LORD your God will choose as a dwelling for his name" (i.e., Jerusalem). It is done at the proper time in the calendar, the fourteenth day of the first month, in distinction from Hezekiah's celebration but in accord with Exodus 12:18, and in conjunction with the seven-day Festival of Unleavened Bread (Ex. 12:15 and Deut. 16:3–4). Care is taken that the divisions of Levites are reviewed and that all Levites—whether musicians, gatekeepers, or those serving in the sacrificial process—are in their proper places (vv. 4–6).

Josiah's instructions to the Levites are curious. In verse 3, Josiah appears to be telling the Levites to cease carrying the ark and take up other duties of service:

> 35:3 He said to the Levites who taught all Israel and who were holy to the LORD, "Put the holy ark in the house that Solomon son of David, king of Israel, built; you need no longer carry it on your shoulders. Now serve the LORD your God and his people Israel.

Readers of Chronicles will clearly remember that David's instructions to the Levites contemplated this very change in the nature of their work in 1 Chronicles 23:26 and that Moses had instructed the Levites concerning duties other than bearing the ark in Numbers 3:6–9. The Chronicler may be reflecting a tradition that ascribes the redefinition of the Levites' responsibility to Josiah (rather than David, Solomon, or Hezekiah). Alternatively, the words here may reflect the understanding that the Levites are permanently without specific portfolio and therefore broadly available for duties in the Temple. A third, and less likely, possibility is that the imperative "Put" in verse 3 should be changed to the present perfect, "They have put," thereby recognizing a long-existing condition. In the end, there are difficulties with all three approaches, and the phrase stands as a curiosity.

Preparations for the Passover sacrifice include not only the stationing of priests and Levites but also the provision of animals to meet the needs of the massive numbers of pilgrims to the city for the festival (vv. 7–9). The king, his officers, and the leaders of the Levites all contribute to the flocks of lambs and goats available to serve as Passover sacrifices. In addition, these same officials also provide a large quantity of bulls to be offered in burnt offerings. These were not officially part of the Passover ritual but were common in large celebrations at the Temple; the meat was cooked for distribution to the worshipers in a communal meal.

Verses 10–16 describe the sacrificial procedure itself, and again, all is orderly and careful. The Levites take charge of the actual slaughter and skinning of the animals, while the priests administer the roasting of the meat on the altar and the ritual splashing of blood from the animal on the altar. The animals designated for burnt offerings are set aside for later preparation and feeding to the people according to ancestral groups. Verse 13 represents the Chronicler's compromise between conflicting traditions regarding the Passover sacrifice. Exodus 12:8–9 requires that the Passover sacrifice be cooked "roasted over the fire" and that it not be eaten "raw or boiled in water." But Deuteronomy 16:7 requires that the sacrifice be boiled (the Hebrew verb translated "cook" in the NRSV should be rendered "boil"). The Chronicler settles for a bit of both methods, making clear that the lamb was roasted "with fire according to the ordinance," while the "holy offerings"—an undefined term—were boiled in various cooking vessels. The preparations are so careful and thought-out that the Levites can enable the singers, gatekeepers, and priests to share in the meal without having to cease the performance of their duties. In contrast to the often ad hoc nature of Hezekiah's Passover, the observation by Josiah is smoothly administered.

The conclusion of the Passover celebration in verses 17–19 returns to the source narrative of 2 Kings 23:22–23, but once again with the Chronicler's editorial touch showing clearly. The comment of 2 Kings 23:22 that "no Passover like it had been kept in Israel since the days of the judges" is made specific in 2 Chronicles 35:18: Not since Samuel has such a Passover been held. The effect of the change is to make the celebration of Josiah's Passover unique among the history of the monarchy. As we have seen, Hezekiah—and not Josiah—was the first of the kings to centralize the festival in Jerusalem. Thus, the unique quality to which the Chronicler points is not the location of the celebration; rather, its uniqueness lies in the success with which Josiah includes the whole people of God, both Israel and Judah, a goal Hezekiah tried but failed to accomplish. Also important to the Chronicler's appreciation of Josiah's festival is the role of the Levites, who receive special attention throughout this narrative.

2. Josiah's death and regnal summary, 35:20–27. As with Hezekiah in 2 Chronicles 32, so now again with Josiah in 2 Chronicles 35, history presents the Chronicler with a theological problem. The problem in this case is the untimely death of Josiah at the hands of Neco, king of Egypt. Specifically, why should such a king as Josiah, whose entire life since boyhood has been devoted to obeying the will of God, suffer ignominious death at the hands of a foreign power, normally a sign of punishment in Chronicles?

35:20 **After all this, when Josiah had set the temple in order, King Neco of Egypt went up to fight at Carchemish on the Euphrates, and Josiah went out to meet him. 21 But Neco sent envoys to him, saying, "What have I to do with you, king of Judah? I am not coming against you today, but against the house with which I am at war; and God has commanded me to hurry. Cease opposing God, who is with me, so that he will not destroy you." 22 But Josiah would not turn away from him, but disguised himself in order to fight with him. He did not listen to the words of Neco from the mouth of God, but joined battle in the plain of Megiddo. 23 The archers shot King Josiah; and the king said to his servants, "Take me away, for I am badly wounded." 24 So his servants took him out of the chariot and carried him in his second chariot and brought him to Jerusalem. There he died, and was buried in the tombs of his ancestors.**

The historical circumstances surrounding the death of Josiah are well documented from contemporary sources, even if Josiah's participation in them is not. "Neco" is Neco II, third pharaoh of the Twenty-sixth (Saite) Dynasty of Egypt, who came to the Egyptian throne in 610 B.C. and reigned until 595. As Neco ascended to the throne, the Assyrian empire, long the dominant political power of the ancient Near East, was crumbling under pressure from the combined forces of Medes and Babylonians. Egypt had been an ally of the Assyrians since the mid-650s, when Assyria had liberated the Nile Delta from the grip of Ethiopian kings and restored Egyptian rulers to positions of power. Now that Assyria was failing, and had in fact lost its central homeland in the upper Tigris-Euphrates valley, Egyptian forces were on their way to try to prop up their ally against the Babylonian onslaught. Neco and the Egyptian army did in fact arrive on the Euphrates at Harran in 610 but were unable to stop the Babylonian advance. The last Assyrian king was killed and the Assyrian army destroyed, and by late 610, Assyria had disappeared from the map.

Josiah seems to have gone to meet Neco as the latter was on his way north toward the Egyptian staging area around Carchemish, in northern Syria. The account in 2 Kings 23:28–30 is maddeningly brief, stating only that Josiah went to meet Neco and that "when Pharaoh Neco met him at Megiddo, he killed him." Megiddo is a large and ancient city at the northern end of the Jezreel Valley in Israel, situated at the end of a pass through the ridge of Mount Carmel over which north-south traffic along the seacoast must travel. The 2 Kings 23 account is not clear whether Josiah's death was the result of a battle at Megiddo or perhaps execution at the hands of the Egyptians (Josiah may have been in alliance with the Babylonians). The Chronicler clarifies most of these questions in the narrative he creates to explain the death of Josiah. His answer to the question of the manner of the king's death is that it occurred in battle. His answer to the question of Josiah's motive for engaging in that battle is that Josiah chose to ignore the "words of Neco from the mouth of God" (v. 22).

Scholars have long noted that the account of Josiah's death in battle in 2 Chronicles 35:20–25 is remarkably like the account of Ahab's death in 2 Kings 22:29–40 and in 2 Chronicles 18:28–34. Both kings are advised against proceeding with the attack, both disguise themselves for battle, both are shot by archers, and both are withdrawn from battle in their chariots to die as a result of their wounds. The likelihood is that the Chronicler has fashioned an account of Josiah's death on the model of the death of Ahab.

But why? The answer is that the Chronicler must explain the death of Josiah as a punishment for some sin, and the sin must be his own doing. He finds the misdeed in Josiah's prideful refusal to obey the word of God when it is spoken to him, similar to Ahab's refusal to listen to the prophetic voice of Micaiah in 2 Chronicles 18. The twist in the tale here, however, is that the words of God are spoken in the voice of Neco, a foreign king whose army is passing through Judah on its way to assume a larger role on the international stage. The warning to Josiah is that he is becoming embroiled in matters not his own to attend: "I am not coming against you today," declares Neco in verse 21. More powerfully and also probably more confusingly, Neco claims the authority of Josiah's God in his mission; he has been summoned on this campaign, commanded to hurry, and will brook no interference. Indeed, to oppose Neco in this divinely ordained crusade is to oppose God; thus Neco adjures Josiah, "Cease opposing God, who is with me, so that he will not destroy you" (v. 21)! Confusing as this situation must surely have been to Josiah, it is nonetheless the case, in the eyes of the Chronicler, that Josiah is guilty at least of ignoring the command of God and probably also of seeking to become involved in foreign entanglements. In the background, there is also a sense in which Josiah's campaign against Neco violates the Chronicler's notions about war; namely, that it is the province of God and is waged only at divine behest. Since there is no threat posed to God's people by Neco's trek across Israel, there is no divine sanction of Josiah's actions. In the Chronicler's scheme, he is therefore bound to fail. It is the one blemish on Josiah's record in the Chronicler's eyes, but it is serious enough to explain his early death.

Despite Josiah's refusal to heed God's warnings, his death does not undo the good he has done, nor does it lessen his people's appreciation of his achievements. The record of lamentation for Josiah in verses 24–25 is without parallel in Chronicles, and includes reference to a lament composed by Jeremiah. The book of Lamentations is sometimes thought to be that referred to by the Chronicler here, but Lamentations is concerned with the fall of Jerusalem to the Babylonians rather than the death of Josiah. We thus have neither the lament of Jeremiah nor the book of "Laments" mentioned by the Chronicler.

Josiah's death extinguishes the last bright light in the story of Israel and Judah. The kings of the last two decades of Judah's existence reign briefly and are unworthy in the eyes of both the narrator of 2 Kings and the Chronicler. Obedience to the will of God and faithfulness in worship are abandoned, and the nation plunges inexorably into the darkness of defeat and exile. The value of Josiah's reign is largely as a model for the possibilities of obedience, but even that image is colored by the knowledge that the disaster about to unfold is only temporarily delayed. These chapters have therefore a bittersweet, tragic quality about them; they testify to the great righteousness of a faithful king, but they acknowledge that righteousness to be too little too late.

20. The Last Kings of Judah and the Fall of Jerusalem
2 Chronicles 36:1–23

In a very important sense, the whole story of the people of Israel has been leaning ahead throughout the Chronicler's narrative to the moment of the fall of Jerusalem described in 2 Chronicles 36. The destruction of the city and the exile of the people of Israel to Babylon is the great climax of the story of faithfulness and apostasy that has dominated these pages.

Following the fall of the Assyrian empire in 610 B.C. and a subsequent defeat of Egyptian forces by the Babylonians in 605, Babylonian claims to control of Palestine were uncontested except by various local powers. Some of those smaller kingdoms capituled to Nebuchadnezzar, Babylonian king from 605 to 562; others resisted and suffered severely at the hands of the Babylonian army. Judah tried both strategies. There was within Judahite politics of the day a party that counseled cooperation with the Babylonians as a means of survival, as well as a party that championed the notion of resistance and revolt (for a study in the contrast of these positions, see Jeremiah 28–29). The resistance party gained the upper hand in Judah's policy about 599 and again about 590; each time the result was a devastating invasion and conquest by the Babylonians. The city of Jerusalem was captured in March 597 and a portion of the population deported to Babylon in exile. After resistance flared again, the Babylonians besieged the city a second time, and in July 587, they breached the wall, captured the king and his court, plundered the city, and burned the Temple and palaces. A second and larger group of exiles was deported to Babylon in the wake of this campaign, and Judah ceased to exist as an independent nation.

The Babylonian exile lasted from 587 until 538, when Babylon was conquered by Cyrus, king of Persia. The Persians thought of themselves as enlightened rulers, and they reasoned that a conquered people allowed to maintain some autonomy in its own land was less likely to revolt. Thus, after securing Babylonian holdings in his own hands, Cyrus permitted captured peoples to return to their own homelands to reestablish their religious and governmental institutions so long as they paid annual tribute to the Persian court. This period of restoration lasted on through the Chronicler's own day; it saw the rebuilding of the city and the new Temple. Throughout the period, Jews filtered back into their homeland, seeking to build anew the kingdom God had given them.

The Chronicler's version of the last days of Judah is, as one might expect, highly theologized; it is designed to make the point that the destruction of the city was the deserved result of the sinfulness and apostasy of the king and the people. By the same token, the Chronicler also knows that God uses even the destruction of what has been to give birth to what will be; thus, the account ends on a note of hope and promise that far outstrips the guarded optimism of 2 Kings 25:28–30. The final two verses of 2 Chronicles 36 are nearly identical to the opening verses of Ezra (Ezra 1:1–3a); they point the way toward a future the Chronicler knows is there for Israel, a future that is the Chronicler's own era where, it is hoped, the lessons of Israel's past will bear fruit.

The story of the last days of Judah in 2 Chronicles 36 has six sections: the reigns of the last four kings, Jehoahaz (vv. 1–4), Jehoiakim (vv. 5–8), Jehoiachin (vv. 9–10), and Zedekiah (vv. 11–14), the description of the fall of Jerusalem (vv. 15–21), and the edict of Cyrus (vv. 22–23).

1. Jehoahaz, 36:1–4. Josiah's unexpected death in battle summons the "people of the land" into action once again (see 34:1 and commentary) to elect Josiah's successor, just as they had elected Josiah himself. But their choice—Jehoahaz, a younger son of Josiah—is unacceptable to Pharaoh Neco, and he is removed from the throne and imprisoned. Neco names in his place Eliakim, an older son, who takes the throne name Jehoiakim.

Neco's reasons for deposing and replacing Jehoahaz are not stated. Perhaps, as the choice of the "people of the land" like Josiah, Jehoahaz is perceived to oppose Egyptian plans in Palestine and is removed as a potential obstacle. Perhaps he was already known as a Babylonian sympathizer. Perhaps the reason was some personal animus on the part of the Egyptian king. No final answer to the question is available.

The Chronicler provides no religious evaluation of Jehoahaz's reign; in this, Jehoahaz is unique among the kings of Judah. Certainly one was available in the source narrative; 2 Kings 23:22 indicates that Jehoahaz "did what was evil in the sight of the LORD." It may be simply that the phrase was omitted by accident rather than by design.

2. Jehoiakim, 36:5–8. Jehoiakim's eleven-year reign (608–598 B.C.) covers the final decade of Judah's independence. As an ally—or perhaps a puppet—of the Egyptian pharaoh, he would have been a natural target for Babylonian military campaigns in the region as the Babylonians extended and tightened their control over Palestine. Jehoiakim may in fact have vacillated between Babylonian and Egyptian sympathies and finally decided on resistance to the Babylonians. It was a fatal choice. The first Babylonian conquest of Jerusalem took place on 17 March 597. According to 2 Kings 24:6, Jehoiakim died in Jerusalem in the final days of the Babylonian siege, leaving his son Jehoiachin on the Judahite throne. Second Chronicles 36:6 preserves a different tradition; namely, that the Babylonian king Nebuchadnezzar captured the city while Jehoiakim was still alive and took the Judahite king back to Babylon in chains. By making this change in his source, the Chronicler insures that none of the final kings of Judah died in peace in their capital city; instead, all lived out their final days deprived of the institutions of political and religious life that had supported the Judahite monarchy. The point here is surely a theological rather than a historical one: The price for "doing what was evil in the sight of the LORD" is the loss of everything that gave the life of the king meaning and purpose.

As part of the captured plunder from the city, Nebuchadnezzar takes "some of the vessels of the house of the LORD" (v. 7) for installation in the royal trophy room in Babylon. The Chronicler is careful to note that only "some" and not "all" the vessels are taken, not as a result of any largesse on the part of Nebuchadnezzar but in the service of the Chronicler's theology. With each king taken from the Judahite throne into captivity, a portion of the Temple vessels are also taken away (see vv. 10, 18). The effect is one of gradual loss of both of the great institutions that have been the hallmarks of Judah's identity: the Davidic line and the Temple of the Lord. With each new deposition of the monarch, Judah is less and less a nation, and less visibly the place where the worship of God occurs.

3. Jehoiachin, 36:9–10. Verse 9 makes the claim that Jehoiachin was "eight years old when he began to reign." Most scholars would agree that the text is in error here. The age of the young king at his accession should be eighteen rather than eight. It seems hardly fair or reasonable to argue that an eight-year-old has in the scant three months of his reign either maturity or opportunity to do "what was evil in the sight of the LORD," as is claimed of Jehoiachin in 36:9. But whether eight or eighteen, the ascription of evil deeds to Jehoiachin is surely more influenced by the Chronicler's theological agenda than by specific reality. In his view, none of the final kings of Judah can be credited with any righteousness, and all of them deserve the punishment that falls upon them.

According to 2 Kings 24:8–17, Jehoiachin's brief reign witnesses the Babylonian capture of Jerusalem that the Chronicler ascribes to the reign of Jehoiakim. But, as noted above, the Chronicler is working with a tradition that claims all the last kings of Israel died apart from their land. He preserves that tradition by having Nebuchadnezzar "send for" and "bring" the young king of Judah to Babylon, along with a second set of gold vessels from the Temple. In addition, he omits the vaguely hopeful conclusion of 2 Kings 25:27–30, in which Jehoiachin is released from captivity in Babylon and allowed to live as a pensioner at the Babylonian court. As far as the Chronicler is concerned, Jehoiachin's life ends the moment he departs from Jerusalem; what happens to him beyond the boundaries of the land of Israel is inconsequential and not worth reporting.

4. Zedekiah, 36:11–14. A Babylonian puppet, Zedekiah manages to stay on the throne in Judah for eleven years (597–587 B.C.). Throughout the period, the fires of Judahite independence continued to smolder, until late in his reign they burst into open revolt against Babylon. Once again, Nebuchadnezzar was forced to send his army to enforce his will on Judah, but this time the penalties were much harsher. In mid-July 587, Babylonian forces breached the walls of Jerusalem, sacked the city, looted and burned the Temple and royal palace, and deported a large segment of the population to Babylon into exile. Thereafter, no Davidic king would sit on the throne in Jerusalem, and Judah ceased to exist as a political entity.

The Chronicler, as usual, is less interested in the political ramifications than the theological. For Zedekiah only does he provide a detailed list of the sins and offenses of the king and the people against God: He refused to "humble himself before the prophet Jeremiah who spoke from the mouth of the LORD" (v. 12), he rebelled against Nebuchadnezzar, in spite of having taken an oath before God (v. 13a), and he "stiffened his neck and hardened his heart," refusing to see his suffering as an occasion for repentance and "turning to the LORD" (v. 13b). In addition, the people themselves are found guilty of apostasy for "following all the abominations of the nations" and for having "polluted the house of the LORD" (v. 14). This latter charge is particularly grievous in light of the great lengths to which Hezekiah and then Josiah have gone to purify the house "consecrated in Jerusalem" for the worship and service of the Lord. In effect, the people of Judah have rejected their whole history in the eyes of the Chronicler, from the conquest of the land through David's establishment of true worship and Solomon's construction of the Temple to Hezekiah's and Josiah's efforts to restore what had been lost to faithlessness.

5. The fall of Jerusalem, 36:15–21.

36:15 The LORD, the God of their ancestors, sent persistently to them by his messengers, because he had compassion on his people and on his

dwelling place; 16 but they kept mocking the messengers of God, despising his words, and scoffing at his prophets, until the wrath of the LORD against his people became so great that there was no remedy. 17 Therefore he brought up against them the king of the Chaldeans, who killed their youths with the sword in the house of their sanctuary, and had no compassion on young man or young woman, the aged or the feeble; he gave them all into his hand. 18 All the vessels of the house of God, large and small, and the treasures of the house of the LORD, and the treasures of the king and of his officials, all these he brought to Babylon. 19 They burned the house of God, broke down the wall of Jerusalem, burned all its palaces with fire, and destroyed all its precious vessels. 20 He took into exile in Babylon those who had escaped from the sword, and they became servants to him and to his sons until the establishment of the kingdom of Persia, 21 to fulfill the word of the LORD by the mouth of Jeremiah, until the land had made up for its sabbaths. All the days that it lay desolate it kept sabbath, to fulfill seventy years.

In light of the degradation of king and people, it is no small wonder that a cataclysmic response from God awaits them. Yet even at the moment we expect that disaster, it is forestalled once again by a reference to divine forbearance. Remarkably, God sends not catastrophe but "compassion" on his people, in the form of repeated and persistent prophetic warnings (v. 15). God's compassion is not limited to the people but extends to the now-despoiled "dwelling place" (i.e., the Temple), made abominable by the practice of worship of other gods. The Chronicler displays here not a mechanistic concept of reward and punishment but a nuanced notion that mercy belongs always to God, to use at God's discretion. Even in the eleventh hour, God holds out the possibility for repentance and restoration.

Neither king nor people seem inclined to accept the offer, however, and compound the evil already done by "mocking the messengers of God, despising his words, and scoffing at his prophets" (v. 16). The rejection of the final offer of mercy and compassion brings the nation to the limit of divine patience at last, and the "wrath of the LORD" is finally released. In an ominous phrase, the Chronicler intones the judgment: a wrath for which "there was no remedy" (v. 16).

In the Chronicler's theological system, the destruction of Jerusalem is the response of God to the sinfulness of Zedekiah and the generation of Judah that surrounds him; it is for this reason that the Chronicler has been specific about their misdeeds. It has been a principle of his work that individuals are morally responsible for their own behavior and either enjoy the rewards or suffer the consequences for that behavior in the form of divine response. However, it is also true that the whole story of

Israel's disobedience and faithlessness, its wanderings from the "ways of David" and its refusal to heed prophetic warnings—indeed, its outright mistreatment of the prophets themselves—is summarized and encapsulated in the indictment of verses 15–16. In a sense, the sin of all Israel from its beginnings until now is caught up in the figure of Zedekiah and his faithless people, and the dire consequence of the death of monarchy and nation falls on all at once. It is truly a wrath for which "there was no remedy."

The specifics of God's judgment are few. God, acting through the agency of the Babylonian king, shows "no compassion" now (v. 17) in giving over young and old, male and female, aged and feeble as well as strong and able-bodied as fodder for the Babylonian war machine. We are left to imagine the human tragedy of the war. We are given specific information only about the sacking and burning of the twin institutions that have stood almost from the beginning of Israel's life and now fall with it at the end: the palace and the Temple. The treasuries and treasures of both are looted, and the Temple and royal houses burned. The city walls are torn down, so that the great city of David is now indefensible. The Temple vessels that had not been taken are now destroyed.

The Chronicler's view of the exile—that anyone left alive was taken away to Babylon (v. 20)—conflicts with the reality that the land was not left completely uninhabited but continued to sustain a smaller, poorer population throughout the exile. Once again, however, it is theology rather than history that motivates the description. For the Chronicler, the empty land has rest—"sabbath" (v. 21)—a concept the Chronicler draws from Leviticus. In Leviticus 26:33–35, the picture of the consequence for persistent disobedience is described in this way:

> And you I will scatter among the nations, and I will unsheathe the sword against you; your land shall be a desolation, and your cities a waste. Then the land shall enjoy its sabbath years as long as it lies desolate, while you are in the land of your enemies; then the land shall rest and enjoy its sabbath years.

The point is pivotal: What begins as a punishment of disobedience and faithlessness becomes an occasion for transformation and new possibility. While the people suffer the chastening of exile, the land "rests" and recuperates. The implication, of course, is that it rests and recuperates for the day when Israel might return again and try anew to live in obedience and faith as the people of God.

    6. The edict of Cyrus and hope for the future, 36:22–23. The horizons of that day are the final vision the Chronicler holds out before his readers. These two verses are repeated almost verbatim as Ezra 1:1–3a, a fact that leads many scholars to think that 1 and 2 Chronicles and Ezra-Nehemiah are actually one great work by a single author. As suggested in the introduction to this commentary, it is impossible at this stage to know whether or not this is true. What we can say, however, is that the duplication of these verses in Ezra is a clear sign that the Chronicler understood the great narrative of Israel not to end in the exile but to have a new beginning in the Persian era.

Persia, under the leadership of their first great king, Cyrus, captured the city of Babylon in 538 B.C. The Persians, and Cyrus himself, fancied themselves as enlightened rulers; they believed that the policies of conquest and exile followed by their Assyrian and Babylonian predecessors only encouraged unrest and discontent among conquered peoples. The Persian insight was to allow a modicum of autonomy to local states, to permit exiled populations to return home, and to encourage them to take up and revitalize their own religious traditions as a way of cementing national identity. Small wonder that Cyrus is called "the Great" in history, and referred to as God's "anointed" one in Isaiah 45:1.

Characteristically, the Chronicler views the events of 538 and the ensuing years through the lens of his theology. Cyrus's empire-wide proclamation of amnesty is understood as a prophetic speech on behalf of Israel's God and directed specifically at Israel, God's people. Cyrus's military prowess and accomplishments are the gift of "the LORD, the God of heaven," a term larger in scope than the Chronicler's accustomed "God of Israel" or "God of their ancestors." God has now taken control not merely of events in Israel but on the world stage, and manipulates the nations toward his own ends.

Those ends are explicitly defined: "to build [God] a house at Jerusalem, which is in Judah" (v. 23). Now that the land has rested and been cleansed of its pollution, it is ready again to receive the house wherein dwells the presence and name of the Lord. The summons to build a house rings with biblical references: From the construction of the tabernacle in Exodus to the building of the Temple by Solomon to the great vision of the Temple restored in Ezekiel 40—48, the construction of the house of God is perhaps the greatest mythic vision of ancient Judaism. More important to the Chronicler, it is also a present reality. In the postexile years, a new Temple rose from the rubble of the old, and the struggle for generations of postexilic Jews was to reconstitute the worship and faith of their ancestors. It is to that task that the Chronicler has repeatedly summoned his readers in his own era, through the agency of the great narrative of Israel's life. Now, at its end, he summons them once again, this time more directly than ever. The words of Cyrus echo

David's benediction upon Solomon as the latter takes up the task to build the house of God: "The LORD be with you" (1 Chron. 22:16). They are a summons now not to an individual king but to a whole people, who understands itself by faith and obedience to be the people of God. It is this people who this time must play the Solomonic role:

> 36:23 . . . "Whoever is among you of all his people, may the LORD his God be with him! Let him go up."

Bibliography

Commentaries

Allen, L. C. *The First and Second Books of Chronicles.* New Interpreters Bible 3. Nashville: Abingdon Press, 1999.

Braun, R. *1 Chronicles.* Word Bible Commentaries. Waco: Word Books, 1986.

Japhet, S. *I & II Chronicles.* Old Testament Library. Louisville: Westminster/John Knox Press, 1993.

Jones, G. H. *1 & 2 Chronicles.* Old Testament Guides. Sheffield: JSOT Press, 1993.

Myers, J. M. *1 Chronicles* and *2 Chronicles.* Anchor Bible 12 and 13. Garden City, N.Y.: Doubleday, 1965.

Williamson, H. G. M. *1 and 2 Chronicles.* New Century Bible Commentary. Grand Rapids: Eerdmans, 1982.

Other Works

Ackroyd. P. R. "The Chronicler as Exegete." *Journal for the Study of the Old Testament* 2 (1977): 2–32.

Duke, R. K. *The Persuasive Appeal of the Chronicler: A Rhetorical Analysis.* Journal for the Study of the Old Testament: Supplement Series 88. Sheffield: JSOT Press, 1990.

Graham, M. P.; K. G. Hoglund; and S. L. McKenzie, eds. *The Chronicler as Historian.* Journal for the Study of the Old Testament: Supplement Series 283. Sheffield: JSOT Press, 1997.

Hayes, J. H., and P .K. Hooker. *A New Chronology for the Kings of Israel and Judah and Its Implications for Biblical History and Literature.* Atlanta: John Knox Press, 1988.

McKenzie, S. L. *The Chronicler's Use of the Deuteronomistic History.* Harvard Semitic Monographs. Atlanta: Scholars Press, 1984.